Just Interpretations

PHILOSOPHY, SOCIAL THEORY, AND THE RULE OF LAW

General Editors

Andrew Arato, Seyla Benhabib, Ferenc Fehér, William Forbath, Agnes Heller, Arthur Jacobson, and Michel Rosenfeld

Just Interpretations

Law between Ethics and Politics

Michel Rosenfeld

UNIVERSITY OF CALIFORNIA PRESS

Berkeley   Los Angeles   London

University of California Press
Berkeley and Los Angeles, California

University of California Press
London, England

Copyright © 1998 by The Regents of the University of California

Library of Congress Cataloging-in-Publication Data
Rosenfeld, Michel, 1948–
   Just interpretations : law between ethics and politics / Michel
Rosenfeld.
      p.   cm. — (Philosophy, social theory, and the rule of law ;
4)
   Includes bibliographical references and index.
   ISBN 0-520-21097-2 (cloth : alk. paper)
   1. Law—Interpretation and construction.   2. Law and ethics.
3. Law and politics.   4. Law—Philosophy.   I. Title.   II. Series.
K290.R67   1998
340′.112—dc21   97-8384
                                                                CIP
Printed in the United States of America

1 2 3 4 5 6 7 8 9

The paper used in this publication meets the minimum requirements of American
National Standard for Information Sciences—Permanence of Paper for Printed Library
Materials, ANSI Z39.48-1984 ∞

For Susan

CONTENTS

vii

ACKNOWLEDGMENTS

This book is the culmination of several years of reflection on the problem of legal interpretation in the context of the relationship among law, ethics, and politics in pluralistic societies. My work greatly benefited from several conferences in the United States and abroad. These conferences not only afforded special opportunities to focus on the works of most of the leading theorists discussed in the book but also allowed me to engage in numerous fruitful and enriching discussions with many of them. I am particularly grateful to Jürgen Habermas for having generously participated in an open and wide-ranging dialogue on law, ethics, and democracy in connection with the conference devoted to his work held at the Cardozo Law School in New York; and to Jacques Derrida whose works have profoundly influenced my views, provided me with a continuing source of inspiration, and led me to novel and rewarding ways of exploring the nexus between law and ethics.

Several colleagues have read the manuscript, in whole or in part, at one stage or another, and offered much-appreciated helpful and incisive criticisms, comments, and suggestions. They include Andrew Arato, David Carlson, Paolo Comanducci, Thomas Grey, Riccardo Guastini, Marci Hamilton, Arthur Jacobson, Frank Michelman, Chantal Mouffe, Pasquale Pasquino, Richard Posner, William Rehg, Renata Salecel, Scott Shapiro, Paul Shupack, Michel Troper, and Slavoy Zizek. I also wish to thank Edward Dimendberg, philosophy and humanities editor at the University of California Press, for his encouragement and wise counsel. Finally, I am grateful to Theresa Moser, Sydney Smith, and Linda Goebel, my student research assistants at Cardozo, who labored hard and well to help the project along smoothly.

I am extremely fortunate to have benefited in the course of this project from great personal as well as professional support. Susan Thaler, my wife, has been a wonderful companion and partner throughout, and she deserves much credit for helping me maintain a balanced perspective through the inevitable ups and downs that a project of this magnitude entails. My children Maia and Alexis continue to be a steady source of much joy and intellectual stimulation. Moreover, while I fully realize that this is not the place to dwell on their manifold talents and accomplishments, I cannot help mentioning that my son Alexis's growing interest in philosophy has been particularly gratifying and challenging.

Earlier versions of materials contained in chapters I, II, IV, V, and VI were published in various works respectively in the *Cardozo Law Review* and the *Harvard Law Review.* I wish to thank both publications for agreeing to my use of these materials in this book.

Introduction

Interest in a subject increases dramatically when that subject becomes problematic. Legal interpretation is a good case in point. So long as laws must be applied and legal disputes adjudicated, legal interpretation cannot be avoided. More broadly, law itself is an interpretive enterprise inasmuch as good laws and a just legal system depend on fair and faithful interpretations of the legitimate needs, aspirations, and objectives of those who comprise the relevant polity. In cohesive polities sharing a common vision of the good, legal interpretation is not likely to be a major issue. To be sure, legal interpretation may give rise to a number of technical issues in such polities, but it is not likely to figure as a problematic and divisive political issue. In contrast, at times, such as during the last couple of decades in the United States, legal interpretation becomes a primary focus of discussion and controversy.[1] When that happens, moreover, preoccupations relating to interpretation center around the *meaning* of law as an institution (Dworkin 1986, 47) and the role of law in the context of a cogent and legitimate normative universe, rather than around "the traditional set of questions about how a particular word, phrase, or instrument should be given effect in some particular context" (Cover 1983, 7). For the sake of convenience, we may refer to interpretive issues relating to larger controversies about the meaning of law and its place in the normative universe as involving "interpretation in the broad sense" and to traditional technical interpretive issues as pertaining to "interpretation in the narrow sense." Moreover, unless otherwise indicated, "interpretation" should be understood to mean "interpretation in the broad sense."

1. Among the voluminous literature on the subject, two representative symposia deserve singling out: Symposium 1982 and the two-volume Interpretation Symposium 1985.

For justice to be achieved and for a legal system to qualify as legitimate requires just interpretations of applicable laws and, more generally, laws that are themselves the product of just interpretations. These just interpretations, in turn, depend on legal interpretation in both the broad and the narrow sense. In the case of the application of laws, it may be that only interpretation in the narrow sense is involved, or that both the broad and the narrow senses of interpretation are implicated. In the case of lawmaking or of law derivation,[2] on the other hand, interpretation in the broad sense is inevitable, but may only become clearly visible in cases in which its normative presuppositions arc significantly contested. In any event, once these normative presuppositions become a matter of dispute, interpretation in the broad sense is likely to permeate the debate over lawmaking, law derivation, adjudication, and other forms of law application.

From the standpoint of interpretation, the meaning and role of law must be shaped in relation to the normative presuppositions and objectives of the polity. This means, on the one hand, that a suitable division of labor must be established among law, ethics, and politics in order to optimize their respective contributions to the normative project launched by the polity. This also means, on the other hand, that lawmaking must result in just laws, and adjudication in just applications of laws, as measured against the normative commitments of the polity. In homogeneous polities with a broad-based consensus on normative presuppositions and objectives, neither the division of labor among law, ethics, and politics nor the criteria for just laws and just adjudication are likely to be significantly contested, with the consequence that the work of interpretation will tend to be uneventful and hence subject to little notice. Indeed, in such polities, law, ethics, and politics would be mutually reinforcing and complementary, making their interrelationship harmonious and thus minimizing the importance of drawing precise boundaries between their respective domains. Furthermore, in such polities, whereas disagreements over just laws and just adjudications might be inevitable and even frequent, there would be virtually no dispute over the legitimate normative criteria for evaluating laws and adjudications. Under these circumstances, awareness of interpretation in the narrow sense should by far outpace preoccupation with interpretation in the broad sense.

Matters are bound to be quite different in heterogeneous polities with diverging normative presuppositions and objectives. Moreover, these polities may conceivably cover a broad spectrum that extends from nearly homogeneous polities to polities that are so utterly divided along normative

---

2. By "law derivation," I refer to common law adjudication, which I discuss more extensively in chapter I, and to the delimitation of legal norms through application of constitutional constraints on legislative enactments.

lines that there appears to be no common ground whatsoever between the various warring factions. For our purposes, however, it suffices to concentrate on two paradigmatic cases along the above spectrum, for these two cases reveal the most salient features of typical conflicts regarding interpretation within heterogeneous polities.

The first of these cases—which may be labeled the case of the "modern polity"—is that of a polity with a plurality of competing conceptions of the good, but also with a broadly based shared understanding on how to handle this plurality consistent with the common objective of promoting unity and cohesiveness. In such a modern polity, maintaining a balance between plurality and unity would be a predominant concern that could be met through a careful division of labor between law, ethics, and politics and through adhesion to different criteria for purposes of evaluating lawmaking and adjudication. More specifically, plurality would be preserved through allocation of fundamental rights, and unity promoted through democratic self-governance. Within this scheme, the constitution would play a pivotal role as it would both delimit the requisite fundamental rights supposed to remain beyond the reach of ruling majorities and set the structural framework for democratic self-government. Furthermore, in so doing, ideally the constitution would, through protection of fundamental rights, insulate ethics from encroachments by law and politics; and, through structural constraints, demarcate a clear boundary between law and politics. Thus, although both law and politics would be shaped by a majoritarian process, law would embody the will of a past majority as formalized through the legislative process, whereas politics would embody the ongoing struggle to command future majorities.

In the modern polity, conflicts concerning interpretation seem likely to be primarily confined to the realm of constitutional adjudication. Indeed, given the relevant circumstances, achieving a proper balance between plurality and unity hinges on constitutional interpretation that neither underprotects nor overprotects fundamental rights. Underprotection threatens the preservation of diversity among conceptions of the good, whereas overprotection leads to unwarranted infringements on legitimate majoritarian policy making. Also both underprotection and overprotection produce the same risk, namely that one of the competing conceptions of the good will gains the upper hand over its rivals. And if that happens, it would undermine the neutrality among conceptions of the good on which the polity's unity depends. All of this, of course, is compounded by the fact that most constitutions, because of their need for flexibility and for adaptability in the face of evolving circumstances, contain general, open-ended provisions that seem particularly prone to interpretive abuse. To cite but one example, the Fourteenth Amendment to the United States Constitution provides that no state shall deprive any person of life, liberty, or property, without "due process of law," which has variously been invoked to strike down economic regulation affording workers minimum wage or maximum hours protection on laissez-faire property and freedom of contract grounds;[3] to uphold unenumerated privacy rights;[4] and to recognize a fundamental right to abortion.[5]

The principal interpretive dilemma confronting the modern polity concerns *how* and *where* to draw the line between majoritarian and antimajoritarian legal norms so as to strike a fair and workable balance between unity and diversity. Moreover, because of the lack of a stable common reservoir of universally shared ethical values, it may be too ambitious to aim for both the "how" and the "where," consequently splitting the modern polity between those who believe that interpretation should concentrate on the "how" and those who maintain that it should aim at the "where." The debate between representatives of these two interpretive approaches goes back a long way as evidenced by one of the earliest decisions by the United States Supreme Court in *Calder v. Bull.* One of the opinions in that case adopted a social contract–natural rights approach to constitutional interpretation in order to determine where to draw the line between permissible and unconstitutional state legislation.[6] Another opinion, in contrast, rejected any appeal to natural justice and endorsed an interpretive approach relying on legal positivism, whereby constitutional adjudication must be based on a comparison between the challenged statutory text and the constitutional text while remaining mindful of the hierarchical superiority of the latter.[7]

In the modern polity, the tension between naturalism and positivism[8] cannot be satisfactorily resolved and is hence prone to foster instability. Naturalism, even if sufficiently determinate, cannot guarantee impartiality. Positivism, on the other hand, while strictly speaking impartial, cannot avoid being arbitrary. Furthermore, naturalism's lack of impartiality stems from its inability to yield interpretations that remain neutral as between all affected conflicting conceptions of the good. In contrast, positivism, to the

---

3. See *Lochner v. New York* (1905) (striking down maximum hours regulation); but see *West Coast Hotel Co. v. Parrish* (1937) (upholding minimum wage legislation while repudiating interpretation of the Constitution as prohibiting economic limitations on freedom of contract rights).

4. See *Griswold v. Connecticut* (1965).

5. See *Roe v. Wade* (1973).

6. *Calder v. Bull* (1798), at 386 (opinion of Chase, J.).

7. Ibid., at 398 (opinion of Iredell, J.).

8. The jurisprudential conflict between naturalism and positivism emerges, primarily, as an epistemological one. For present purposes, however, I leave epistemological issues aside to concentrate on the respective *hermeneutic* implications of naturalism and positivism.

extent that it yields determinate interpretations,[9] can remain impartial in that it is formally reducible to a procedure that is *inherently* neutral as between conflicting conceptions of the good. For example, if legal positivism were equated with mechanical application of the will of legislative majorities, then it would be ultimately reducible to the decisional procedure that consists in adopting those proposals for which the requisite majority has cast its vote. For all its impartiality, however, positivism cannot escape arbitrariness, for none of the procedures on which it might rely, whether they be democratic procedures, rules of recognition (Hart 1961, 197), or a Kelsenian *Grundnorm* (Kelsen 1961, 115–18), can, in the last analysis, succeed in becoming self-justifying. Indeed, rules of recognition or a *Grundnorm* must ultimately be postulated, and lacking any recourse to metaphysical or religious foundations, such postulation cannot be given any further justification. Democratic procedures, on the other hand, could be purged of vestiges of arbitrariness if they could be convincingly linked to a relevant unanimous consent among all the members of the polity. But that seems virtually impossible in any modern polity with genuine differences among conflicting conceptions of the good.

In light of the unresolvable tension between naturalism and positivism, what holds together the modern polity is a contingent overlap between the interpretive outcomes of these two approaches. Moreover, naturalism and positivism are likely to lead to many of the same interpretive outcomes either because of actual convergence among diverse conceptions of the good or because of widespread agreement on the ways to handle differences in order to promote common interests, or else because of some combination of partial convergence and partial agreement. Consistent with this, the greater the scope of the overlap between the interpretive outcomes of the two aforementioned approaches, the less legal interpretation is likely to seem biased or arbitrary.

More recently, the scope of overlap between naturalist and positivistic interpretive outcomes has been diminishing significantly, not only in the United States, but also in other constitutional democracies, such as France and Germany. This phenomenon is particularly manifest in the realm of constitutional adjudication, where the legitimacy of the interpretations of the constitutional judge has come under sharp attack.[10] As overlapping out-

---

9. Whether positivism always, or only sometimes, leads to determinate results depends on how it is conceived. For example, if an adjudicator were strictly bound by the text of a statute, and without any authority to go beyond the four corners of that text, he or she may lack sufficient exegetic and hermeneutical tools to arrive at any cogent application of the statute before the court to the facts in dispute.

10. In the United States, where this problem—which is referred to as the "countermajoritarian problem"—has received the most attention, there is a very extensive literature on the

comes recede, naturalism looms as increasingly biased and positivism (and the majoritarian process on which it depends) as increasingly arbitrary.[11] Moreover, greater arbitrariness calls for increasing constitutional safeguards against the encroachments of ordinary legislation, but greater bias undermines the legitimacy of imposing constitutional constraints on legislation that commands majority support.[12] In short, as constitutional adjudication becomes ever more ubiquitous, the legitimacy of constitutional interpretation becomes increasingly questioned.

This brings us to the second of the two paradigmatic cases mentioned above, which may be referred to as the case of the "postmodern polity." Like the modern polity, the postmodern one is characterized by the existence of a plurality of conceptions of the good. Unlike its modern counterpart, however, the postmodern polity lacks a broadly based shared understanding of how to promote unity and cohesiveness while at the same time preserving its plurality and dealing fairly with the issues that arise as a consequence of its diversity. From an interpretive standpoint, the transition from the modern polity to the postmodern one is linked to the erosion of the persuasive power of naturalism and positivism. Although this transition may be gradual, the boundary between the modern and the postmodern polity is crossed when naturalism *completely* loses its sway and when positivism becomes regarded as *merely* arbitrary. More specifically, appeal to naturalism seems foreclosed in the postmodern polity, because all interpretation seems inextricably bound to only some among the many competing conceptions of the good, thus belying any pretense to universalism. In other words, there can be no naturalism in the absence of some version of universalism, and in the postmodern polity, no interpretation can be justified under *all* existing conceptions of the good, or above and beyond such conceptions. Accordingly, in the postmodern polity, the justification of interpretation is at best purely local.

On the other hand, another consequence of the apparent complete surrender of the universal to the local is that the procedural trappings of posi-

---

subject. The leading works include Bickel 1962 and Ely 1980. For a French account of the problem, see Rousseau 1994; and for a German view, see Schlink 1994.

11. Looking at matters more closely, as a polity's scope of agreement dwindles naturalism becomes not only more biased but also more arbitrary. But what makes it more arbitrary is perception of its parochialism in light of its pretensions to universality. Similarly, under these circumstances, positivism looms not only as more arbitrary but also as less impartial. Indeed, given its arbitrariness, nothing seems to justify its results, which benefit some more than others.

12. John Ely (1980) has attempted to resolve this latter difficulty, by arguing that the U.S. Constitution is predominantly process based and thus primed to buttress democratic procedures rather than imposing substantive norms. Constitutions—or at least those that like that of the United States afford protection to fundamental rights—however, are not reducible to mere procedural charters. For a persuasive refutation of Ely's thesis, see Tribe 1980.

tivism cease to have any inherent appeal. Inasmuch as the interpretive outcome of positivism is perceived as favoring certain local preferences over others, regardless of its procedural attractions, positivism looms as ultimately no less parochial than its plausible alternatives. Consistent with this, whether the adjudicator faithfully follows the will of the legislator or draws on subjective values to reach a decision, judicial interpretation would appear incapable of transcending parochialism.

With the postmodern collapse of naturalism and positivism, law seemingly loses its connection to ethics and becomes indistinguishable from politics. Moreover, as commonly held norms and values recede nearly completely, and as all institutional means for regulating intersubjective interaction seem inevitably biased in favor of some of the competing conceptions of the good that divide the postmodern polity, all attempts to achieve justice through interpretation appear doomed to failure. In short, in the postmodern polity, all interpretations seem to be just interpretations—that is, mere interpretations or nothing but interpretations.

In this book, I explore whether the crisis in interpretation that confronts the postmodern polity can be overcome and whether it is possible to construct a path leading to just interpretations—in the sense of interpretations comporting with justice—after the demise of naturalism and the inadequacy and loss of legitimacy of positivism. In pursuing this endeavor, I critically examine and draw on recent American and European theories bearing on legal interpretation, law, justice, ethics, and politics, with a view to uncovering plausible avenues of escape from the interpretive predicament linked to the postmodern polity. Moreover, as these theories suggest ways in which the postmodern crisis in interpretation might be overcome, but do not themselves provide fully satisfactory solutions, I elaborate an alternative theory, which, I argue, affords the best possible solution to the problem of interpretation in the postmodern polity.

The book is divided into three parts. Part One, which assesses the theoretical implications of the current crisis in interpretation and which investigates some of the most important conditions that would have to be met to solve this crisis, is made up of three chapters. Chapter I takes a closer look at the crisis in interpretation; focuses on the nexus between deconstruction and this crisis; briefly discusses the shortcomings of certain contemporary theories—most notably Ronald Dworkin's theory of law as integrity with its process-based approach—aimed at solving this crisis; and indicates how Jacques Derrida's brand of deconstruction, with its ontology based on the split between self and other and its ethics of commitment to the other, far from causing or exacerbating the crisis, actually paves the way for its solution. Chapter II evaluates what appears at first a particularly attractive way of leaving behind the crisis in interpretation, namely the return to formalism, or more accurately, the adoption of neoformalism. Based on an examination of Stanley Fish's bare neoformalism and Ernest Weinrib's Aristotelo-Kantian neoformalism, Chapter II concludes that neoformalism is ill suited to lead us past the crisis in interpretation. Finally, Chapter III tackles the crucial question of justice, which lies at the core of the crisis in interpretation experienced by the postmodern polity. Confronted with the paradox of justice, which must be at once universal and singular, and with the violence it inevitably engenders, the analysis in Chapter III leads to the conclusion that the solution to the crisis in interpretation requires pursuing comprehensive justice while realizing that imperfect justice is the most that can be hoped for.

Part Two considers ways of sidestepping the crisis in interpretation by dealing with the gap between justice according to law and justice beyond law in ways that minimize the need for interpretations—or, more precisely, the need for contestable interpretation—thus in a sense putting an end to interpretation. Chapter IV examines Niklas Luhmann's autopoietic theory of law as self-referential, which implies a radical split between law, ethics, and politics. Chapter V provides a critical assessment of Jürgen Habermas's procedural paradigm of law as it emerges in the context of his discourse theory. Whereas Luhmann's theory involves a novel and more sophisticated conception of positivism, Habermas seeks to close the gap between justice according to law and justice beyond law in a dialogical manner that leads to universalism, and thus ultimately bears a certain affinity to naturalism. As neither Luhmann nor Habermas succeeds in putting an end to interpretation, chapter VI turns to pragmatism, and tests whether the latter's shift in focus from ends to means can lead to the end of interpretation. It concentrates on the very different versions of pragmatism espoused respectively by Richard Posner and Richard Rorty and seeks to distill the common elements in them. Chapter VI closes by assessing whether pragmatism can put an end to interpretation through an examination of how pragmatism fares when confronted with the vexing conflict over hate speech. Based on that examination, pragmatism fails the test, and pursuit of the end of interpretation, while attractive, proves to be ultimately unproductive.

Part Three offers an alternative theory for coping with the crisis in interpretation. This theory acknowledges the inevitability of partial interpretations, the constraints of imperfect justice, and the impossibility of surmounting the split between self and other. Relying on an approach driven by counterfactual reconstruction, the proposed alternative theory advances the thesis that the best possible solution to the crisis in interpretation hinges on turning the inescapable pluralism of the postmodern polity into the guiding normative principle. The kind of normative pluralism that proves suitable for the task is "comprehensive pluralism," a substantive version of pluralism capable of harnessing the conflict among competing conceptions of the good in the quest to narrow the gap between self and other and individual and community. By means of counterfactual reconstruction, comprehensive pluralism can enlist partial subjects, imperfect justice and open-ended law to frame just interpretations that may be partial and time-bound but that need not be arbitrary or merely reducible to parochial ethics or politics. Chapter VII generally elaborates the normative framework carved by comprehensive pluralism, focusing on the contrast between pluralism in fact and pluralism as a norm; on the functioning and counterfactual uses of comprehensive pluralism; on the superiority of comprehensive pluralism over its principal postmetaphysical rivals, namely liberalism, republicanism, and communitarianism; and on the implications of comprehensive pluralism for a cogent and defensible division of labor between law, ethics, and politics. Finally, chapter VIII completes the discussion of comprehensive pluralism, by concentrating on salient particulars of its interpretive implications in the quest for determinate and concrete meanings. Special attention is given to the problem of interperspectival comparisons for purposes of better accommodating self and other; the question of internal transformability of self and others as a means to close the gap between them; and on the limits of comprehensive pluralism as gauged in terms of its ability to contribute to the resolution of difficult and divisive issues such as euthanasia and abortion.

PART ONE

The Demand for Just Interpretations

CHAPTER ONE

Deconstruction and Legal Interpretation, or the Uses of Derrida in the Face of an American Crisis

I. DECONSTRUCTION AND THE CRISIS IN LEGAL INTERPRETATION

In America, for a generation the practice of legal interpretation has been mired in a deep and persistent crisis. This crisis extends both to the realm of private law (Abel 1982, 185–200; Dalton 1985; Feinman 1983) and to that of public law (Freeman 1978). Even justices on the United States Supreme Court have increasingly become pitted against one another in fierce and often vituperative debate over questions of legal interpretation.[1]

In the broadest terms, the crisis reflects a loss of faith concerning the availability of objective criteria permitting the ascription of distinct and transparent meanings to legal texts. Moreover, this loss of faith manifests itself in the intensification of conflict among the community of legal actors, the dissolution of any genuine consensus over important values, the seemingly inescapable indeterminacy of legal rules, and the belief that all the dispositions of legal issues are ultimately political and subjective. The roots of the crisis affecting legal interpretation can be traced back to the Legal Realists' critique of legal formalism (Cohen 1935; Pound 1908; Yablon 1987, 615–24), and a comprehensive exposition of multifaceted dimensions of this crisis can be found in writings of scholars associated with the Critical Legal Studies (CLS) movement (Kelman 1981; Kennedy 1979; Unger 1983).

---

1. For examples of recent bitterly divided and acrimonious decisions, see *Garcia v. San Antonio Metropolitan Transit Authority* (1985); *Webster v. Reproductive Health Services* (1989); *Texas v. Johnson* (1989); *City of Richmond v. J. A. Croson Co.* (1989). In Croson, for instance, Justice Marshall's dissent characterized the Court's majority as taking a "disingenuous approach" (ibid., at 746). See also Rosenfeld 1989b.

A. *Deconstruction's Challenge to Legal Interpretation*

Deconstruction appears to buttress the proposition that application of legal rules and legal doctrine is ultimately bound to lead to conflict, contradiction, and indeterminacy. Any attempt at defining deconstruction is hazardous at best as there is disagreement over whether deconstruction is a method, a technique, or a process based on a particular ontological and ethical vision (Norris 1987, 18–27). Nevertheless, leaving these difficulties aside for now, it seems fair to assert that deconstruction postulates that writing precedes speech instead of operating as a mere supplement to speech (ibid., 23–24, 127), stresses that every text refers to other texts (ibid., 25), and emphasizes that discontinuities between the logic and rhetoric of texts create inevitable disparities between what the author of a text *means to say* and what that text is nonetheless *constrained to mean* (ibid., 19). In other words, in the context of deconstruction, all texts (whether oral or written) are writings that refer to other writings. A text is not a pure presence that immediately and transparently reveals a distinct meaning intended by its author. Instead, from the standpoint of deconstruction, every writing embodies a failed attempt at reconciling identity and difference, unity and diversity, and self and other. A writing may give the impression of having achieved the desired reconciliation, but such impression can only be the product of ideological distortion, suppression of difference, or subordination of the other. Consistent with these observations, legal discourse— and particularly modern legal discourse with its universalist aspirations— cannot achieve coherence and reconciliation so long as it produces writings that cannot eliminate from their margins ideological distortions, unaccounted for differences, or the lack of full recognition of any subordinated other.

For those who take the challenge posed by deconstruction seriously, there can be no easy solution to the crisis affecting legal interpretation. Thus, for example, there cannot be a return to the much-vaunted among American constitutionalists narrowly circumscribed and simpler jurisprudence of original intent wherein the meaning of legal texts can be precisely framed by reference to some transparent, self-present intent of the framer of a constitution, a legislator, or a party to a private contract. As Arthur Jacobson (1990) has persuasively argued, even divinely prescribed law involves multiple writings, erasure, and intersubjective collaboration. Accordingly, in light of deconstruction, resort to the jurisprudence of original intent can only lead to a paralyzing idolatry (ibid., 1118–20, 1125–32) that forecloses any genuine intertextual elucidation of legal relationships. In other words, by isolating a particular writing and by elevating it above all other writings in such a way as to sever the intertextual links that constitute an indispensable precondition to the generation of meaning, the jurisprudence of original intent both promotes blind worship of the arbitrary and the unintelligible and blocks discovery of the intertextual connections necessary to endow legal acts with meaning.

Other attempts at overcoming the crisis affecting legal interpretation do not fare significantly better in the face of the challenge posed by deconstruction. For example, the claim that an adequate standard of legal interpretation can be fashioned by reference to the intersubjective perspective of an "interpretive community" (Fiss 1982, 744) can only prevail through the suppression of difference and the subordination of the dissenting other. Indeed, as evinced by the very crisis sought to be overcome, legal interpretation becomes manifestly problematic *because* of conflict and fragmentation *within* the interpretive community. Therefore, unless appeal to the interpretive community comes on the heels of a genuine resolution of the aforementioned conflict and fragmentation, such an appeal would only make sense if it were accompanied by suppression of some of the clashing voices found in the interpretive community.

Attempts at solving the crisis affecting legal interpretation through submission of legal issues to an interpretive framework informed by extralegal values also prove ultimately unsatisfactory. Take, for example, the law and economics approach according to which, in the most general terms, legal rules and legal doctrine should be interpreted in such a way as to promote wealth maximization (Posner 1977). Even assuming that law and economics were capable of yielding determinate outcomes, it would still fail to meet the challenge posed by deconstruction. This is because there is no consensus that the sole purpose of law is to advance the interests of *Homo economicus*. And, to the extent that such consensus is lacking, the canons of legal interpretation derived from the law and economics approach would operate in disregard of the extralegal values of a substantial portion of the community of legal actors.[2] More generally, unless there is a societywide consensus on extralegal values, no canons of legal interpretation based on extralegal values can possibly meet the objections raised from the standpoint of deconstruction.

B. Dworkin's Process-based Law as Integrity Theory and
the Crisis in Legal Interpretation

There is a different kind of approach to the crisis of legal interpretation that may initially seem particularly attractive because it does not apparently

---

2. Whereas law and economics *standing alone* fails to met the challenge of deconstruction, this does not necessariy mean that it would fare the same if subsumed under a more broadly encompassing approach such as pragmatism. Significantly, in his later writings Posner has articulated a pragmatist defense of law and economics. Compare Posner 1995 with 1977. The interpretive case for law and economics as subsumed under pragmatism will be assessed in chapter VI.

rely on a concrete definition of the object of legal interpretation or on contested extralegal values. This kind of approach stresses the *process* of interpretation above the object of interpretation or the substantive values espoused by the interpreter. It is a procedural approach insofar as it suggests that so long as legitimate interpretive procedures are followed, the interpretive outcome will be justified regardless of actual substantive disagreements concerning the object of interpretation or extralegal values held by members of the community of legal actors.

A prime American example of the approach under consideration is provided by Ronald Dworkin's theory of law as integrity developed in his *Law's Empire*. In its broadest outlines, the theory of law as integrity maintains that legal interpretation does not take place in a vacuum but that it is a historically situated practice. An interpreter confronted with the task of determining what the law requires in a particular case must refer to relevant past instances of legal interpretation in order to be in a position to provide the best possible interpretation of the law in the case at hand. Dworkin analogizes the task of legal interpretation with that of writing a chain novel (1986, 228–32). A chain novel, in Dworkin's conception, is a work of collective authorship, with each chapter being written by a different individual author. Each is constrained by the previously written chapters and must ensure that the chapter he or she is about to write "fits" with the preceding chapters and contributes to the preservation of the integrity of the novel. Moreover, each author must endeavor to write the best possible novel consistent with the aesthetic constraints imposed by the need to incorporate already completed chapters. Similarly, in Dworkin's view, a judge confronting a hard case must decide it on the basis of the best possible legal interpretation compatible with establishing a fit between the case at hand and the line of relevant historical judicial precedents in a way that preserves the integrity of law as a practice that evolves over time.

Dworkin's approach is intertextual, and although formal and procedural, it is not purely abstract. The substantive values of the community of legal actors do not directly figure in legal decisions, but they are not simply severed from the process of legal interpretation. Traces of these substantive values are embedded in the legal precedents that confront the legal interpreter and must therefore be implicitly taken into account by the latter in his or her formulation of an interpretation that is compatible with precedent while preserving the integrity of the legal process.

Under closer scrutiny, Dworkin's theory of law as integrity fails to provide an acceptable solution to the crisis affecting legal interpretation. The principal reason for this failure is, as Alan Brudner has perceptively indicated, that the criterion of fit is too indeterminate to endow Dworkin's principle of integrity with a sufficiently concrete meaning (Brudner 1990,

1156–57). Indeed, Dworkin's requirement of fit and integrity is reducible to an appeal to coherence made in an interpretive universe that has been stripped of intelligible criteria of coherence (ibid., 1158). Either the measure of fit and integrity is based on some set of substantive values such as those embedded in certain relevant judicial precedents or it is reducible to a purely formal and abstract notion that cannot be given any nonarbitrary concrete instantiation. If fit and integrity depend on particular substantive values—even if these values have been filtered through the interpretive process involved in the attempted reconciliation of judicial precedents—then Dworkin's theory is ultimately subject to the same criticisms as those theories that select one set of contested substantive extralegal values over others or that posit some such values as dominant and the remainder as subordinate. On the other hand, if fit and integrity are to be understood in purely formal and abstract terms, cut off from all extralegal substantive values, then the coherence they seek is a mere transcendent ideal devoid of any particular concrete purchase (ibid.).

Although Dworkin's principle of integrity fails to deliver the means to overcome the challenge posed by deconstruction, the notion of integrity should not be discarded altogether. Indeed, integrity may play a useful, if more modest role than that reserved for it by Dworkin in the quest for a satisfactory solution to the crisis affecting legal interpretation. That role is a critical one, and it consists in serving as a constant reminder against the acceptability of a conception of law that tolerates the reduction of law to mere politics—that is, politics in the pejorative sense of the unprincipled, shrewd, and often manipulative quest for advantage in the political arena. Even if no concrete embodiment of law as integrity is presently attainable, drawing attention to the absence of integrity may foster resistance against abandoning law to politics. In short, while legal interpreters may lack a positive conception of integrity, integrity can nevertheless still play the important negative role of standing in for the coherence and the principles that law that is reducible to politics lacks.

II. DECONSTRUCTION AND THE RELATIONSHIP BETWEEN LAW AND POLITICS

What has been established thus far is that deconstruction confirms the genuine nature of the crisis affecting legal interpretation and that from the standpoint of deconstruction none of the above-mentioned approaches designed to overcome this crisis is capable of achieving success. An important question, however, has not been addressed yet, namely whether deconstruction lends support to the proposition that law is ultimately reducible to politics. In this section I address this question and conclude that deconstruction, as I understand it, requires rejecting that proposition. This conclusion, moreover, leads to a further question concerning what there is about law—or more precisely, about legal interpretation—that makes legal practice irreducible to the practice of politics (in the sense specified above). This last question will be explored in the next chapter, principally by means of an assessment of the hypothesis that law can overcome the interpretive crisis that besets it and escape the stranglehold of politics through a return to legal formalism—or more precisely, to a new legal formalism that is more sophisticated than its traditional American counterpart.

A. The Meaning of Deconstruction and the Deconstruction of Meaning

To determine properly whether deconstruction supports the proposition that law is reducible to politics, it is necessary first both to further specify what is understood by deconstruction in the context of the present discussion and to articulate the rudimentary outlines of a workable conception of law. So far, I have stressed the following features of deconstruction: the priority of writing over speech, the intertextual nature of all writings, the dichotomy between what a writing is intended to mean and what it is constrained to mean, and the failure of every writing fully to account for difference or for the other. Moreover, the combination of the priority of writing and its intertextual nature causes all meaning to be *deferred*. The meaning of a writing is neither immediately given nor self-present but depends on some future reading (or re-collecting) of that writing's past. And since all reading involves a rewriting (Jacobson 1990), all meaning depends on a future rewriting of past writings as rewritten in the present writing that confronts the interpreter. A present writing is a rewritten past writing and a not yet rewritten future writing. Or put somewhat differently, a present writing is both a completion and an erasure[3] of a past (or no longer present) writing and a text that must face erasure and completion by some future (or not yet present) writing in order to acquire meaning. In a word, from the standpoint of deconstruction, meaning depends on the transformation of what is no longer present by what is not yet present.

To the extent that meaning requires both a constant reinterpretation of the past and a perpetual openness to future reinterpretation, it would appear to dissolve in an infinite regress that travels in both temporal directions. Every past was once a future and then a present, and every future shall become a present and then a past, and accordingly meaning can seem-

---

3. All rewriting presumably seeks both to preserve and to supersede—i.e., to improve, to clarify—the writing it seeks to restate. Hence, rewriting involves both completion and erasure of the text with respect to which it constitutes itself as a rewriting.

ingly never become ascertained. Or more precisely, inasmuch as present writings are opaque, paradoxically, the meaning of a text could possibly be anything except that which it presently appears to be. Consistent with this analysis, moreover, the crisis affecting legal interpretation could never be overcome so long as one shared the perspective of deconstruction. Indeed, if the search for meaning leads to an infinite regress, those with the greatest power or cunning will impose their (arbitrary) meaning, and law will dissolve into politics.[4]

In the conception referred to above, deconstruction is viewed exclusively as an interpretive method or technique. And, taken as a mere interpretive technique disconnected from any larger framework, deconstruction seems only fit to destabilize all meanings by systematically unveiling the contradictions embedded in every writing and by constantly but fruitlessly inverting the binary oppositions (e.g., mind/nature, subject/object, masculine/feminine) that circumscribe every text. In contrast to this latter conception of deconstruction, however, there is another that, while preserving a necessary link between past, present, and future writings, does not inescapably lead to the conclusion that all ascriptions of meaning turn out to be arbitrary.[5] This alternative conception does not cut off the process of deconstruction from the realm of ontology or from that of ethics.[6] Indeed, in this alternative conception, the deconstructive process implies an ontology of the unbridgeable separation of the self from the other (or put in a way that seems less likely to provoke a return to the sterile interplay of binary oppositions, an ontology of infinite postponement of the complete reconciliation of self and other). Moreover, this ontology is supplemented by an ethic of inclusion of and care for the other—an ethic that must always be attempted and renewed but that can never be satisfied because the meaning of "inclusion" and of "care" can never be sufficiently determined to the extent that the self always remains (somewhat) estranged from the other.

4. Derrida rejects the equation of knowledge and power (Norris 1987, 217).

5. No conception of deconstruction can be advanced with confidence, as every such conception is subject to further deconstruction. This, however, is not particularly distressing in the context of the present analysis, as the object is not to find the best conception of deconstruction. Rather, the object is to fasten onto *a* plausible conception of deconstruction that seems particularly well suited to shed light on the important questions raised by the crisis affecting legal interpretation.

6. While any conception of deconstruction presented in the course of this discussion involves, at best, one among many possible readings or rewritings of Derrida's conception of deconstruction, it is noteworthy that Derrida apparently conceives of deconstruction as possessing a definite ethical dimension. See Norris 1987, chap. 8. Moreover, according to Norris, "For Derrida, the realm of ethical discourse is that which exceeds all given conceptual structures, but exceeds them through a patient interrogation of their limits, and not by some leap into an unknown 'beyond' which would give no purchase to critical thought" (ibid., 224).

In short, in this alternative conception of deconstruction, on the ontological plane, difference can never be fully reintegrated within a totality that encompasses self and other, whereas on the ethical plane, difference both incessantly requires and perpetually frustrates the gesture of inclusion and caring extended toward the other.[7]

Within the alternative conception of deconstruction just outlined, meaning, although never permanently fixed, does not thereby become purely arbitrary. Because the requirements of ontology and those of ethics are inscribed in history—that is, because they leave their mark on the succession of concrete historical social formations—at every moment, they constrain the range of possible legitimate meanings without ever imposing a single, fully determinate meaning. Hence, ontology and ethics, which are always projected both toward the past and toward the future, constantly open and close possible paths of interpretation without ever settling on any single, distinct, clearly articulated, and exhaustively circumscribed meaning.

Given that the alternative conception of deconstruction advanced here is thoroughly committed to the intertextual nature of all writings, the escape from the pure arbitrariness of meaning can only be effectuated by engaging texts at a proper level of abstraction. Indeed, at too high a level of abstraction, all meanings appear to be fully interchangeable, as every writing is grasped in its infinite regress along the opposite directions of its endless past and its perpetually incomplete future. At too low a level of abstraction, on the other hand, meanings would remain completely opaque as myopic concentration on the features of individual texts would tend to conceal or obscure the relationships between such texts and other texts.

A proper level of abstraction can be reached, however, by grasping texts in their unfolding as part of the process of historical formation that gives shape to the ontology of postponement of the reconciliation of self and other and to the ethical call to the other renewed by each such postpone-

---

7. In this connection, it is worth mentioning Derrida's predominant preoccupation with the writings of Hegel. See Derrida 1981, 77: "We will never be finished with the reading or rereading of Hegel, and in a certain way, I do nothing other than attempt to explain myself on this point." For others among Derrida's writings dealing with Hegel, see Derrida 1976, 1982, 1986. Turning the tables on Derrida, one could characterize his deconstructive enterprise in Hegelian terms, as an ontological privileging of difference that makes it irreducibly transcendent, thus preventing its sublation (*Aufhebung*) within a totality encompassing both self and other. Because of this ontological privileging of difference, moreover, deconstruction requires the perpetual deferral of the reconciliation between individual morality—i.e., Hegelian *Moralität*—and the ethical life of the community—i.e., Hegelian *Sittlichkeit*. For a particularly illuminating analysis of the relationship between the thought of Derrida and that of Hegel, see Brudner 1990, 1191–98. For a discussion of the conception of meaning within a Hegelian framework, see Rosenfeld 1989a.

ment. In each historical epoch, there are writings that are *meant* to reflect a concrete vision of the desired reconciliation between self and other but that are *constrained* by the very vision they embrace to produce yet another picture of the further postponement of such reconciliation. Moreover, the latter picture serves to expose the limits of the particular vision or reconciliation it reflects. And, as they become manifest, these limits suggest particular forms that the renewed ethical call to the other might have to take under the circumstances. In other words, the very limits of a vision of reconciliation indicate how that vision has failed, and suggest to the about to be renewed ethical call to the other which particular failures should be avoided and which obstacles need to be overcome. Similarly, each emerging vision of reconciliation is informed by the particular failures and contradictions of its historical predecessors as well as by the shortcomings of recent ethical calls to the other.

Conducted at the proper level of abstraction and applied to the historical succession of diverse forms of attempted reconciliation between self and other, intertextual interpretive practice does not culminate in aimless conflict and hopeless indeterminacy. Whereas it cannot avoid conflict, such interpretive practice can reveal particular conflicts that invite a finite range of possible solutions. Similarly, such interpretive practice unavoidably leads to indeterminacy, but not to the kind of indeterminacy that justifies virtually every conceivable meaning. Rather, it is the kind of constrained indeterminacy that results from the interplay between semantic path openings and closings guided by the actual historical succession of intertextual forms of attempted reconciliation between self and other.

It may seem implausible, given the unlimited intertextuality of all writings, that any particular meaning should be able to muster sufficient strength—albeit only for a fleeting moment—to resist being swept away in the ceaseless exchange of semantic markers. Or, put somewhat differently, it may seem inconceivable, in light of the past and future infinite regresses to which the intertextual ascription of meaning is subject, that the temporary emergence of any particular meaning would be the product of anything but an arbitrary purely subjective choice. And if this proved to be the case, then we would all wind up permanently trapped between the poles of an insurmountable binary opposition pitting the subjective against the objective.

Meaning, however, is neither subjective nor objective but intersubjective. Also, acknowledgment of a ceaseless exchange of semantic markers does not compel the conclusion that on a given historical occasion any meaning could be legitimately substituted for any other meaning. These two propositions may not be self-evident, but they are consistent nonetheless with the alternative conception of deconstruction being advanced here.

B. Analogy between Semantic Value in Intertextual Exchanges and Economic Value in Market Exchanges

To shed further light on the plausibility of these two propositions, it might be useful to refer to certain parallels between the production of semantic value through intertextual exchange and the production of economic value through the exchange of commodities in the marketplace.[8] Assuming a fully developed rational market with participants who are utility maximizers, the exchange of commodities depends on such commodities having value.[9] More specifically, exchange depends on commodities having two different kinds of value: use value and exchange value.[10] Unless a commodity had some use value for some ultimate consumer, no one would desire to acquire it, and there would be no point in exchanging it. On the other hand, unless commodities had exchange value, that is, unless they were commensurable, they could not become objects of rational exchange.

In the most rudimentary market imaginable, with two individual participants who possess equality in bargaining power, exchange value and use value appear to be closely linked to one another, and all market values appear to be subjective. In such a market, for example, it would seem as rational for the market participants to exchange two apples for three oranges as it would for them to exchange three apples for two oranges. That is because the choice between these two transactions is heavily dependent on the participants' respective relative subjective preference as between apples and oranges and because the exchange value of apples relative to oranges appears to be a direct function of the relative use value of apples to oranges for each of the two participants.

In a fully developed market economy with huge numbers of market participants, on the other hand, market values seem to be objective, whereas use value and exchange value appear devoid of any palpable connection. Indeed, in a fully developed perfect market, the well-established and well-publicized price of a widely traded commodity does not seem susceptible to change as the result of the efforts of any individual competitor.[11] More-

8. See Herrnstein Smith 1990, 1304: "Value judgments may themselves be considered commodities—useful, appropriable, and thus valuable, in numerous ways. Moreover, some of them are evidently *worth more* than others *in the relevant markets*" (emphasis in original).

9. Indeed, since the exchange of commodities requires some effort and, when such exchange is not simultaneous, some risk, utility-maximizing market participants endowed with rationality of means would not engage in such exchange unless the commodities involved had some value for them.

10. For a more comprehensive discussion of the relation between use value and exchange value and of the relation between subjective and objective values in the context of a developed market economy, see Rosenfeld 1985, 814–17, 832–39.

11. See Samuelson 1976, 455: "A perfect-competitor is too small and unimportant to affect market price."

over, no matter how intense the desire of an individual consumer may be for a particular commodity, such consumer would appear to have no measurable effect on the exchange value of the commodity in question. In a fully developed market, therefore, it would be irrational for anyone to buy a commodity (significantly) above, or to sell it (significantly) below, its market price.

On closer scrutiny, the values of commodities on the rudimentary market are no more purely subjective than they are strictly speaking objective on the fully developed market. In both cases, such values are intersubjective as they are the product of a combination of, or a compromise between, the diverse subjective desires that seek fulfillment through market transactions.[12] Even in a rudimentary market with two participants, the terms of the contract for the exchange of commodities are not the product of the subjective will of either of the two participants but rather the product of their common will, which is intersubjective.[13] On the other hand, in a fully developed market, if the value of a widely traded commodity appears to be objective, it is not because it is determined in relation to some objective criterion that is independent from the subjective desires of the market participants. Indeed, in a fully developed market just as in a rudimentary one, value is the product of an intersubjective compromise involving the subjective input of each market participant. The only difference between these two markets is that in the fully developed market the subjective input of each individual participant becomes so infinitesimal relative to the sum of subjective inputs as to become virtually imperceptible.

As we move from the rudimentary to the fully developed market, the precise relationship between use and exchange value becomes more difficult to grasp. In a fully developed market, most exchanges may be made among traders who are several steps removed from a commodity's ultimate consumer. To the extent that such traders concentrate on trading the commodities in which they deal, they are likely, for the most part, to ignore the use value of those commodities. On the other hand, in a sophisticated, fully developed market, the use value of a commodity may be more the product of an intersubjective compromise between the exchange objectives of traders and the subjective desires of ultimate consumers than merely the product of only the latter.[14] Be that as it may, however, even in the most sophis-

12. For an argument that is similar in many key respects and that concerns value in general, see Herrnstein Smith 1990.

13. See Hegel 1952, ¶40 (contract is the transfer of property from one to another in accordance with a common will).

14. Cf. ibid., ¶191A ("the need for greater comfort does not exactly arise within you directly; it is suggested to you by those who hope to make a profit from its creation"); Galbraith 1976, 127 (consumer wants are to a large extent created by producers).

ticated of modern markets, where money makes all commodities fungible from the standpoint of exchange, the exchange of commodities only makes sense so long as there is some dynamic relationship between use value and exchange value.

Useful parallels can be drawn between the production of semantic value through intertextual exchange and the production of economic value through the exchange of commodities in two principal areas. First, the intersubjectivity of all meaning is produced in a way that is analogous to the generation of intersubjective values in the economic marketplace. Second, the manner in which the interchange of semantic markers is prevented from resulting in a senseless and arbitrary ritual structurally resembles the process by which use values become engrafted on exchange values in order to prevent market transactions from becoming irrational and pointless.

All meaning—or at least all meaning relating to events and transactions in the social and political sphere where the community of legal actors is located—is intersubjective in that it requires some collective consensus or compromise concerning the setting of certain particular intertextual relationships. In other words, all meaning-endowing interpretations in the context of the social and political sphere require a collaborative collective rewriting of historically situated textual material that confronts a group of actors. Moreover, such collaborative rewriting may be the product of a preexisting agreement concerning relevant values among the group of actors involved, or the product of a dialogical compromise bearing a marked resemblance to the process of contract formation in the economic marketplace.[15]

The size of the group of actors that engages in collaborative rewriting can range from a minimum of two to a maximum of all actors confronted with the task of interpreting the same text. Moreover, any actual community of actors is confronted with the task of interpreting a multitude of different texts. Agreement concerning the interpretation of some of these texts may be widespread while at the same time the interpretation of other texts may be highly contested. Also, the nature and scope of particular widespread agreements are bound to affect the kind of interpretive disagreements likely

15. Paradigmatically, contract formation involves a bargained-for intersubjective mediation between initially conflicting subjective desires. Both parties to a prospective contract seek to obtain as much as possible in exchange for as little as possible. A contract is struck when a compromise is reached. Such compromise is likely to provide each party with less than originally hoped for but with enough to make it more advantageous for each of them to enter into a contract than to walk away from it. Similarly, two actors with initially incompatible subjective value-laden approaches to a historically situated text by which they are jointly confronted cannot collaboratively rewrite it unless they first negotiate a mutually acceptable intersubjective standpoint from which they can produce a common interpretation.

to be produced in a given community of actors.[16] In general, consensus, compromises, and conflicts are fluid rather than fixed because the relationship between them is dynamic as any change in one of the three is bound to produce corresponding changes in the other two. Finally, even when an attempt at a particular collaborative rewriting fails completely because not even two actors can agree to take a common standpoint, such failure need not undermine intersubjective values and may in fact serve to reinforce them. Indeed, the search that culminates in the failure to reach agreement with respect to some values may itself have been prompted by agreements concerning other values, and that search may serve to reinforce commitment to those other values. Thus, for example, two would-be contractors, whose efforts fail because they cannot agree on mutually acceptable terms of exchange, may nevertheless by their very efforts reaffirm their joint commitment to the values of market competition and freedom of contract.

Any semantic value generated through a collaborative rewriting is intersubjective regardless of whether it seems subjective (as the product of only a handful of actors) or objective (as the product of virtually an entire community of actors). So far, therefore, the analogy between the intersubjective production of semantic value and the intersubjective production of economic value appears to hold nicely. It may be objected, however, that there is a crucial disanalogy between these two modes of producing values. According to this objection, the very nature of economic exchange makes it impossible for less than two actors to generate economic value in a free market economy. But there is nothing inherent in the nature of interpretive practice that compels the conclusion that a single individual acting alone cannot rewrite texts in a way that generates new semantic values.

If this objection were valid and rewriting were not necessarily collaborative, then meaning could be purely subjective and interpretation an essentially solipsistic activity. At least from the perspective of the alternative conception of deconstruction advanced here, however, this objection misses the mark. Indeed, even if interpretation were not collaborative in the sense

---

16. In other words, a broad consensus concerning certain intersubjective values closes certain paths of legitimate disagreement while opening (or leaving open) other such paths. For example, if an entire community agrees that all human beings are created equal, then feminist claims for greater equality between the sexes cannot be contested legitimately by arguing that God created women to serve men. Such feminist claims could be legitimately contested, however, by an argument to the effect that while men and women are entitled to equal rights, they are not entitled to equal pay to the extent that physical differences between the sexes make women less desirable than men in the marketplace for jobs. But if a widespread consensus developed concerning the proposition that physical differences between the sexes do not justify different treatment in the job marketplace, then neither of the two above-mentioned arguments could legitimately be advanced in opposition to the feminist claims.

of involving a group of actors jointly engaged in the present rewriting of a past writing, it would still have to be collaborative and intersubjective to be meaningful. At the very least, interpretation requires a collaboration over time among a past actor, a present actor, and a future actor. A reading of a past writing can only be conceivable as a rewriting if there is some intersubjective basis on which semantic connections between the past writing and the rewriting can be established. Furthermore, to the extent that the meaning of a rewriting depends on future readings of that rewriting, interpretation also depends on the existence of an intersubjective basis for the establishment of semantic connections between present and future writings. On the other hand, if such intersubjective basis were lacking, the interpretation of a past writing would not involve a rewriting (a reading being impossible unless writer and reader share a common language) but an original writing devoid of any *meaningful* connection to any past or future writing. Hence, a writing is meaningless unless it is the product of an intersubjective collaboration (co-laboration) over time that involves a minimum of three actors.

That interpretation is intersubjective and collaborative may be a guarantee against meaninglessness, but it is no guarantee against the unrestricted interchangeability of all meaning. A rewriting must bear both some semantic connection to and some semantic difference from that of which it is a rewriting.[17] Accordingly, the question becomes whether the degree of such connection and difference is in any way constrained, or whether any degree of connection no matter how tenuous and any degree of difference no matter how extreme are acceptable provided that they are the product of a collaboration among a minimum of three persons. If the answer is the latter, then virtually every semantic marker would seem to be exchangeable for any other such marker, and rewriting would be encumbered by practically no constraints. If the answer is the former, on the other hand, then the question becomes one of knowing which constraints to impose and how those constraints would make it possible to distinguish between acceptable and unacceptable rewritings.

Consistent with the alternative conception of deconstruction advanced here, constraints regarding the process of rewriting are both necessary and provided by the ontology and ethics that underlie deconstruction. As already mentioned, the operative ontological constraint narrows the range of acceptable rewritings to those that recast the concrete historical writing

---

17. It is conceivable in a purely formal sense that a rewriting would do no more than restate in different words the very meaning of that of which it is a rewriting. From the standpoint of deconstruction, however, rewriting involves erasure and projection into the past as well as into the future, and can therefore never be merely a plain restatement of that of which it is a rewriting.

on which they elaborate as a vision of a failed reconciliation between self and other and expose the specific aporias, contradictions, and blind spots that require the further postponement of the desired reconciliation. Moreover, the operative ethical constraint requires that rewritings as writings (a rewriting being a writing for a future rewriter) specify a renewed ethical call to the other from the standpoint of exceeding the specific historically grounded limits of the vision of reconciliation that has just been interpreted as inadequate.

As also already pointed out, the ontological and ethical constraints imposed by deconstruction do not usually dictate a single determinate meaning. Rather, they operate through interconnected path-opening and path-closing mechanisms that legitimate certain meanings and bar others. Moreover, these mechanisms appear to be constraining without necessarily directly imposing or barring any isolated individual meaning in a way that is reminiscent of how use value indirectly constrains the definition of exchange value in a fully developed market. In both cases, an otherwise seemingly unconstrained, unstoppable, and open-ended exchange process is kept within certain bounds through the indirect application of normative markers that endow exchange with meaning through punctuation of its flow.

C. Ontological and Ethical Constraints of Deconstruction and Rejection of Mere Politics

The interconnected path-opening and path-closing mechanisms associated with the ontological and ethical constraints imposed by deconstruction frequently leave considerable leeway for rewriting historical texts. If two interpretive avenues are equally open, only in the future could it become possible to determine whether either of the two would have been better than the other.[18] Because of this, the indeterminacy that inevitably accompanies the interpretive process makes room for potential abuses. By weaving in and out of different open paths of argumentation, an interpreter may skirt his or her ethical obligation and subvert the interpretive process to personal advantage. Indeed, since the complete and definitive reconciliation of self and other is subject to perpetual postponement, every attempted reconciliation pursued along an open path produces a certain configuration of benefits and burdens to be divided between self and other. To the extent that these configurations vary from one form of attempted recon-

---

18. Whereas the ethical call to the other requires overcoming the particular shortcomings of the failed vision of reconciliation that gives such call its renewed impetus, since no definitive form of the reconciliation between self and other is possible, no blueprint for the ethical call to the other is ever available.

ciliation to another, an unscrupulous interpreter may exploit the availability of several genuine avenues of attempted reconciliation, by shifting back and forth from one to the next so as to maximize personal benefits and minimize personal burdens.

To prevent abuses, interpreters should be held to a standard of integrity according to which shifts from one available interpretive avenue to another would only be justifiable if accompanied by a full and sincere assumption of all the burdens associated with the latter interpretive avenue. Consistent with this requirement of integrity, an interpreter may not resort to an available interpretive avenue to press for an advantage on one occasion and then on the next occasion, abandon that interpretive avenue in favor of another in order to avoid a burden. An interpreter, however, may switch from one available interpretive perspective to another if that interpreter sincerely believes that the latter perspective is better suited to promote the attempted reconciliation sought and if he or she is fully prepared to assume all the burdens that might flow from adoption of the new perspective.[19]

Any interpretive practice that operates within the ontological and ethical constraints of deconstruction, including the requirement of integrity, cannot be reducible to politics in the pejorative sense identified above. These constraints, indeed, are clearly incompatible with any unprincipled, shrewd, or manipulative quest for advantage in the arena of intersubjective relationships. Accordingly, deconstruction may point toward a satisfactory solution to the crisis affecting legal interpretation. Whether deconstruction can actually contribute to such a solution, however, depends on whether its ontological and ethical presuppositions are compatible with law and legal interpretation.

Before exploring whether deconstruction (in the alternative version advanced here) may be legitimately applied to law, it is necessary briefly to further consider the universe that lurks beneath the surface of deconstruction. Deconstruction's presupposition of the perpetual postponement of the reconciliation of self and other implies the existence of an intersubjective universe that is inevitably split into self and other. Moreover, deconstruction's postulation of the ethical necessity of the constant renewal of the call to the other makes it imperative to engage in a search for vehicles of social interaction that promise (although they will be eventually proven not to be able to deliver on their promises) the possibility of a form of

---

19. The requirement of integrity in the context of deconstruction is hence much more circumscribed than Dworkin's principle of integrity, mentioned above. Moreover, deconstruction's requirement of integrity is not an additional constraint to be added to existing ontological and ethical constraints. The requirement of integrity is implicitly contained in those constraints but needs to be made explicit to better indicate the actual sweep of the constraints of which it forms a part.

reconciliation between self and other that allows for the concurrent full flourishing of self and other. Finally, the concepts of self and other should not be understood as referring to fixed entities but instead as designating relationships respectively of identity and of difference or alterity. Thus, depending on the particular context, both "self" and "other" may refer to an individual or a group, to an economic class or an ethnic minority, to tribes or nations, and to temporary as well as to permanent groups. Also, two (individual or collective) actors may concurrently be part of the same self for some purpose, while standing vis-à-vis one another in a relation of self to other for some other purpose. For example, white men and women may constitute a single self in the context of racism against blacks—that is, such men and women identify with one another as being white and relate to blacks as "the other"—and self and other in the context of the relationship between the sexes, where difference is defined along gender lines.

D. Modern Law's Possible Embrace of Deconstruction to Overcome Mere Politics

Consistent with the preceding observations, law can embrace deconstruction if it constitutes itself as a practice oriented toward a universe of social actors split into self and other and if it conceives its mission as seeking to bridge the gap between self and other without sacrificing or compromising either of the two.[20] To be sure, not all conceptions of law satisfy these two conditions. Nevertheless, a strong case can be made that the complex legal system of modern Western democracies in general and the American legal system rooted in the common law and a written constitution in particular do in fact satisfy these two conditions.

In their broadest outlines, modern legal systems prevalent in Western democracies are characterized by, among other things, group pluralism (Unger 1976, 66); general rules of law that are universally applicable to all regardless of status or group affiliation (ibid., 69) and that prescribe duties and entitlements to individuals (ibid., 83, 86); and the separation of legislation from adjudication, which is designed to buttress the autonomy of law by sharply separating the function of applying legal norms to particular cases from the political function.

20. A distinction must be drawn between law embracing deconstruction—that is, availing itself of the interpretive process of deconstruction—and law as an object for deconstruction—that is, as a subject matter submissible to the interpretive practices of deconstruction. In the former case, deconstruction becomes internalized within law, whereas in the latter, deconstruction remains external to law. In the former case, moreover, law is irreducible to politics, whereas in the latter, law might well be reducible to politics. Indeed, in the latter case, deconstruction might well reveal the aporias, blind spots, and contradictions of a legal discourse that envisions itself as being severed from politics, and based on these revelations, deconstruction might quite conceivably lead to the conclusion that law is ultimately reducible to politics.

Group pluralism obviously entails social divisions into self and other. General rules of law universally applicable to all actors regardless of their group affiliations, on the other hand, can be viewed as evincing attempts at reconciliation of self and other within an order of duties and entitlements that transcends the divisions arising from the clash of divergent group interests. These attempts at reconciliation, however, are ultimately doomed to fail. This is because whereas they may reconcile antagonistic interests from a formal (and/or procedural) standpoint, even universal laws cannot avoid, from a substantive standpoint, privileging certain antagonistic interests over others.[21] So long as a legal system operates in the context of group pluralism and through the application of general laws that are universally applicable, therefore, law meets the two conditions that entitle it legitimately to embrace deconstruction.

Because of its constitution and common law tradition, the American legal system encompasses a conception of law that seems particularly well suited to incorporate deconstruction. The American Constitution is designed for a pluralistic society with antagonistic interests, and it seeks to reconcile self and other through prescriptions for accommodation designed to allow both of them to flourish. For example, the Constitution embraces federalism to reconcile local interests and national interests through a complex interplay between identity and difference.[22] Another proof of the Constitution's commitment to a pluralistic society and to the attempted reconciliation of self and other is provided by the adoption and judicial elaboration of the Bill of Rights. The Bill of Rights recognizes the split between the individual and the community and seeks to prevent communal suppression of individual difference through the grant of entitle-

---

21. See Unger 1976, 129: "The conditions of liberal society require that the legal order be seen as somehow neutral or capable of accommodating antagonistic interests. . . . Yet every choice among different interpretations of the rules, different laws, or different procedures for lawmaking necessarily sacrifices some interests to others."

22. To the extent that it is accepted as the fundamental social charter by all the citizens of the United States, the Constitution plays a principal role in the formation of a national identity that promotes a nationwide notion of collective selfhood. On the other hand, the Constitution recognizes the split between the states and the nation and proposes a reconciliation designed to preserve the respective identities of the states and of the nation. Because of the open-ended nature of the constitutional text and because the practice of judicial review subjects it to endless rewriting, however, the work of reconciliation seems bound to remain forever incomplete. For a recent example of the difficulties involved in applying constitutional notions of federalism in an attempt to reconcile state and federal concerns, compare *National League of Cities v. Usery* (1976) (federalism bars imposing certain federal labor standards on employees of a state) with *Garcia v. San Antonio Metropolitan Transit Authority* (1985) (federalism permits imposing the same labor standards on employees of a state). For an extended discussion relating to the identity of the constitutional subject, see Rosenfeld 1995.

ments that impose antimajoritarian limits on the democratic process. The long history of litigation under the Bill of Rights indicates, however, that no stable or lasting reconciliation between self and other, identity and difference, or individual and community seems likely under the auspices of the Constitution or as a consequence of the interplay between democratic majoritarianism and constitutional restraints.[23]

The very nature of the common law makes it a prime candidate for the incorporation of deconstruction. The common law involves the fashioning of legal rules and the allocation of duties and entitlements by judges who seek to reconcile precedents. As Arthur Jacobson notes, the common law requires three writings: a past writing, a present writing, and a future writing (1990, 1106). The common law judge is confronted with antagonistic litigants and must extract a rule of law designed to settle the dispute before him or her from a reading (rewriting) of judicial precedents. The judge's decision is a present writing that rewrites the past writings that count as precedents. The present writing that embodies the judicial decision allocates entitlements and duties among the litigants and partakes in the formulation of a rule of law designed to provide a framework for the reconciliation of antagonistic interests such as those possessed by the litigants. The rule of law implicit in the present writing of a deciding judge, however, may well be insufficiently articulated to be grasped before it is "rewritten" in the writing of some future judicial decision. As an illustration, consider the following example involving a legal rule that cannot be grasped until it becomes further elaborated in a future judicial opinion. A landowner brings a lawsuit against his neighbor because the latter's cat has entered on plaintiff's property where it has caused damage for which the plaintiff seeks to be reimbursed. Moreover, the only relevant precedent involves a case holding that the owner of a cow is liable to his neighbor for the damage caused to the latter's property by the cow following its unauthorized entry on the plaintiff's property. Under those circumstances, the judge sitting in the case concerning the cat can infer at least two different rules from the precedent involving the cow. The first rule is that the owner of a large animal is liable for any damage caused by the latter following unauthorized entry on the neighbor's property. The second rule is that an owner is thus liable for any such damage caused by any of his or her domestic animals.

---

23. One notorious example of a recent failure to reconcile self and other or individual and community or identity and difference in the context of the constitutional jurisprudence of the Bill of Rights is furnished by the Supreme Court's series of decisions on the constitutional right to privacy since its landmark decision in *Griswold v. Connecticut* (1965). See, e.g., *Bowers v. Hardwick* (1986); *Roe v. Wade* (1973); *Planned Parenthood of Southeastern Pennsylvania v. Casey* (1992).

Since a cat is a small domestic animal, the plaintiff will lose his case if the judge infers the first rule from the precedent, but he will win if the judge instead infers the second rule.

Now, suppose further that the judge in the case of the cat rules in favor of the plaintiff after concluding that the situation involving the cat is in all relevant respects analogous to that regarding the cow. But the judge leaves unclear the basis for the analogy she draws between the case of the cow and that of the cat. Under those circumstances, it will be left to another judge before whom the next case in the series will be brought at some future date to infer which legal rule might cover all three cases consistent with the results in the respective cases of the cow and the cat. Thus, the judge before whom the third case will be brought may decide, for example, that the rule to be inferred concerns all of an owner's domestic animals or that it instead covers all animals, whether domestic or not, that usually live on the owner's property. The important point, however, is that no matter which of these two alternative legal rules is eventually chosen, the legal rule that accounts for the result in the case of the cat cannot become explicit until its articulation in the course of the judicial resolution of some subsequent case. More generally, the final formulation of the rules of law that account for the attempted judicial reconciliation of self and other in the hands of common law judges must always be postponed until the dusk will have settled on the last of the future adjudications.

In sum, some conceptions of law—and, in particular, the American legal system with its Constitution and its common law tradition—seem well suited to incorporate deconstruction as an internal process designed to map a realm of legitimate legal relationships. Accordingly, deconstruction is in principle capable of contributing to the resolution of the crisis affecting legal interpretation. It remains to be determined, though, *how* deconstruction might inform the practice of legal interpretation so as to successfully repel the threat of absorption into the universe of mere politics. One tempting hypothesis, which will be critically examined in the next chapter, is that law can escape from mere politics by embracing some recently conceived revamped versions of legal formalism.

CHAPTER TWO

The Temptations of the New Legal Formalism

From the Bare Formalism of Fish to the Aristotelo-Kantian Formalism of Weinrib

In the context of American legal theory, two significantly different conceptions of legal formalism have emerged, which may be referred to respectively as the "old formalism" and the "new legal formalism." The old formalism, which was the target of attacks by the Legal Realists and CLS, holds that application of a legal rule leads to determinate results due to the constraints imposed by the language of the rule.[1] In contrast, the new legal formalism envisions law as an internally unfolding dynamic practice that carves for itself a domain of social interaction that remains distinct from the sphere of politics.[2] Mindful of CLS critiques of its predecessor, the new legal formalism depends neither on the belief in the transparency of language nor on the requirement that legal doctrine or legal rules lead to determinate outcomes.[3] Nevertheless, the new legal formalism is properly considered to be a type of formalism to the extent that it maintains that something internal to law rather than some extralegal norms or processes determines juridical relationships and serves to separate the latter from nonjuridical social relationships, including political ones.

1. See Schauer 1988, 510; see also Unger 1983, 564 (legal formalism is usually understood to describe the "belief in the availability of a deductive or quasi-deductive method capable of giving determinate solutions to particular problems of legal choice").

2. If "origins" for this new legal formalism need be sought, one place where they may be found is in the vigorously antiformalist writings of Roberto Unger. See Unger 1983, 564 (legal formalism evinces "a commitment to, and therefore also a belief in the possibility of, a method of legal justification that can be clearly contrasted to open-ended disputes about the basic terms of social life, disputes that people call ideological, philosophical or visionary"). For evidence of reliance by a proponent of the new legal formalism on Unger's formulations, see Weinrib 1988, 953.

3. See, e.g., Weinrib 1988, 1008: "Nothing about formalism precludes indeterminacy. . . . For formalism the possibility of indeterminacy neither can, nor need be, avoided."

As will become obvious soon, the two different versions of the new legal formalism—respectively formulated by Stanley Fish (1994, chap. 11) and by Ernest Weinrib (1988)—that will be discussed here differ vastly from each other in several key respects. They do share certain important features in common, however, which make them both attractive candidates to carry out the interpretive tasks confronting law conceived as having internalized deconstruction.[4] Fish's central point is that legal formalism is not something given but something that must be constantly made and remade (1994, 156). In the dynamic process of making itself formal, moreover, law internalizes values from the ethical and political world and transforms them into legal values (ibid., 157–59). For Weinrib, on the other hand, what endows juridical relationships with a separate identity are the forms of justice, namely corrective and distributive justice. But to establish the meaning and separate identity of juridical relationships, it is not sufficient to contemplate the forms of justice like Platonic forms or the forms of geometry (1988, 1002–03). The nexus between the forms of justice and particular juridical relationships is immanent, and it can only be made explicit by unearthing the links that connect particular socially and historically situated juridical relationships to the more abstract forms of justice that endow such juridical relationships with meaning (ibid., 1003).

The principal similarity between these two approaches to legal formalism lies in their reliance on a dynamic process that leads to the immanent unfolding of the connections pointing toward the unity of law's content and its form. With this in mind, let us now look more closely at these two versions of the new legal formalism to determine whether, and how, they might be used to solve the crisis affecting legal interpretation in the context of law conceived as having internalized deconstruction.

I. THE BARE FORMALISM OF FISH

The making of law's formal existence, according to Fish, involves a double gesture. Law must absorb and internalize that which threatens it from the

4. It should be pointed out from the outset that neither Fish's nor Weinrib's version of legal formalism taken as a whole is likely to satisfy the requirements of the alternative conception of deconstruction advanced in chapter I. Indeed, Fish's legal formalism is based heavily on an identification of law with rhetoric that is more in tune with the conception of deconstruction as an interpretive technique or method than with the alternative conception embraced here. Weinrib's legal formalism, on the other hand, places substantial reliance on the rationality of law and is thus vulnerable to a Derridean charge of undue "logocentrism." Accordingly, in assessing the suitability of Fish's and Weinrib's theories for purposes of elaborating an interpretive practice consistent with a conception of law as embracing deconstruction, emphasis will be placed on those features of the respective theories which seem most compatible with the alternative conception of deconstruction adopted here.

outside, and in particular ethical and political values (Fish 1994, 156). But, at the same time, law must deny that it is appropriating extralegal values (ibid., 141). In other words, the law cannot simply carve for itself a path that remains beyond ethics and politics. Yet the law cannot admit dependence on the ethical and the political, for that would threaten to deprive law of any distinct identity. To resolve this dilemma, the law simultaneously incorporates ethical and political values and denies that it is doing so. This incorporation, however, is not all-encompassing. In the process of making itself formal, the law only incorporates certain ethical and political values while repelling others.

Law's efforts to achieve a formal existence must be ceaseless and energetic, according to Fish, because the law must constantly overcome formidable obstacles to carve out and sustain an identity of its own (ibid., 141). Economic, ethical, and political pressures have been poised throughout history to overwhelm law, but legal doctrine, argues Fish, against all odds, has managed to survive. And it is this sheer survival that sustains law's identity (ibid., 156).

Fish believes that, through numerous stratagems, legal doctrine can defuse not only ethical and political controversy but also conflicts regarding interpretation (ibid., 142–43). Because he is thoroughly committed to the proposition that all meaning is contextual, Fish cannot endorse the old legal formalists' belief that the plain meaning of legal language enables the application of legal doctrine to produce determinate results. Fish's new legal formalism postulates instead that plain meaning is "made"—that is, that it is fashioned or contrived—through the force of rhetoric (ibid., 152–53, 156).

The "making" of (plain) meaning also involves a dynamic process of incorporation and rejection that remains largely concealed through the force of rhetoric. But to preserve itself from a complete surrender of law to rhetoric, legal interpretation must be able to give the impression that something internal to law operates to constrain the unlimited exchange of semantic markers. According to Fish, it is legal doctrine that provides (or gives the impression of providing, depending on how one rewrites Fish's text) the means to constrain the free flow of legal meaning and that thus sustains the autonomy of law as a practice (ibid., 151–52). Moreover, legal doctrine, according to Fish, fulfills its constraining function by requiring that legal arguments travel along those paths that make possible the avoidance of a head-on collision with legal doctrine (ibid., 143).

In the last analysis, the constraints that legal doctrine imposes in the context of Fish's theory of legal interpretation are purely formal. Legal doctrine, for example, does not bar the importation of ethically based arguments into legal discourse. But because it has incorporated selected ethical values that it privileges while concealing that it has done so, legal doctrine both skews the ethical landscape it traverses and forces the submersion of the ethical values that inform legal arguments. Moreover, legal doctrine does not foreclose any legal interpretation, even one that directly contradicts that doctrine's traditionally accepted meaning, provided only that the interpretation in question follow a path that permits the avoidance of the appearance of contradiction. Thus, Fish believes that legal interpretation can succeed in totally contradicting the (accepted) meaning of a legal doctrine, provided that it present the new meaning as expanding and supplementing what is encompassed by the legal doctrine rather than as promoting a contrary legal doctrine.

To be in a better position to assess Fish's new legal formalism, it is useful to examine one of the specific examples he discusses—namely that relating to the legal doctrine of consideration in American contract law. "Consideration," a term of art, refers to the requirement of a quid pro quo that makes an agreement enforceable.[5] According to modern contract law, only agreements that satisfy the requirement of consideration—that is, agreements that embody a mutuality of bargained-for exchange—are legally binding (ibid., 157). Consideration thus serves to distinguish between promises or agreements that are *legally* binding and those that are only *morally* binding.

Consistent with Fish's view of it, the requirement of consideration is purely formal in at least two senses. First, consideration operates to distinguish enforceable exchanges from all other events in the flow of history (ibid.). In other words, the doctrine of consideration is used to impose a given abstract form on certain transactions in order to lift the latter out of their concrete spatiotemporal context. Second, consideration is purely formal in the sense of requiring compliance with certain formalities—that is, each party to an agreement must exchange something for something else at the time of making the agreement[6]—without permitting any inquiry into the substantive terms of the exchange—that is, the relative values of the things exchanged (ibid., 157).

On this view, consideration not only exemplifies the dichotomy between legal and moral obligation, it also appears to play an active role in establishing it and maintaining (reestablishing) it. Indeed, consideration iterates (and reiterates) the difference between legal and moral obligation each time it requires enforcing a contractual obligation that appears to be unfair (or not enforcing a morally compelling promise). Furthermore, considera-

---

5. Restatement (Second) of Contracts §71 cmt. a (1979). Consideration has also been described as the "element of exchange required for a contract to be enforceable as a bargain" (ibid.).

6. Typically, the parties exchange promises of future performance or make such a promise in exchange for a present performance.

tion serves to abstract legal relationships from the general historical flow of intersubjective relationships. Under modern contract law, consideration brackets the moment of agreement and disconnects it from both its past and its future.[7] Thus, the operation of the doctrine of consideration seems to demonstrate how law strives to carve out an independent existence for itself, by ascending to a level of abstract formalism from which it can negate (or differentiate itself from) both history and morality.

Fish emphasizes, however, that for all that the doctrine of consideration marks a clear boundary between law and morality, it fails to keep morality from permeating contractual exchanges. The binary distinction of law/morality actively promoted by the doctrine of consideration masks another binary opposition that *actually* shapes the realm of modern contractual transactions. That latter binary opposition involves two different moralities: the morality of the marketplace, which is the morality of abstract and ahistorical agents engaged in arm's-length dealings (ibid., 159), and a morality concerned with fairness, justice, sympathy, and compassion. As envisaged by Fish, therefore, the doctrine of consideration proclaims a dichotomy between law and morals but operates according to the canons of market morality.

It may appear, based on the preceding remarks, that the purpose of the doctrine of consideration is to imbue contract relationships with the morals of the market and to foreclose further moral debate concerning contracts by presenting law as being beyond morals. Fish, however, accords the doctrine of consideration a much more modest role. Indeed, as he sees it, consideration privileges the morality of the market but does not exclude other moralities from silently penetrating into the realm of contractual transactions (ibid., 162–64). All that the requirement of consideration demands is that the other moralities be filtered through paths of argumentation that do not lead to head-on collisions with the official narrative designed to keep consideration in place. Accordingly, these other moralities can inform contract doctrines that are inconsistent with the doctrine of consideration, provided that the former doctrines do not appear to contradict the requirement of consideration.

As an example of a modern contract doctrine that is supposed to supplement the doctrine of consideration but that is clearly inconsistent with it, Fish cites the doctrine of contract implied in law (ibid., 159–60). Unlike

7. Under modern contract law, the mutuality of bargained-for exchange must occur in the present tense of the entering into the agreement. Under premodern contract law, in contrast, a past benefit conferred on a promisor was deemed adequate consideration for his or her subsequent promise to become legally binding. See Rosenfeld 1985, 829. As a matter of fact, "the old doctrine of consideration was presumably an attempt to confine legitimate contractual transactions within some broad parameters of fairness" (ibid.).

a contract implied in fact, which is based on the the parties' intent,[8] a contract implied in law allows a judge to disregard the intention of the parties and impose terms based on justice and equity.[9] Thus, we seem to have come full circle. What the requirement of consideration bars makes a full-fledged reentry into the precincts of modern contract law through the deployment of the doctrine of contract implied in law. Fish's treatment of the example of consideration clearly indicates that the constraints derived from lawmaking, itself formal, are purely procedural and not substantive. The path-closing mechanisms associated with legal doctrine amount to no more than the imposition of a rhetorical etiquette on the practice of legal argumentation. For all practical purposes, under Fish's theory, the meanings generated through legal interpretation are the exclusive product of rhetorical force.

Fish's equating of law with the rhetoric of the empowered appears to place him squarely in the camp of those members of CLS who claim that law is ultimately reducible to politics. Fish insists, however, that his position differs significantly from that of CLS. While he acknowledges that his conception of the development of legal doctrine as being ad hoc and contradictory is the same as theirs, Fish maintains that the conclusions he draws from this differ significantly from CLS conclusions (ibid., 168). Whereas CLS laments the use of the inherent indeterminacy of legal doctrine as a means to advance the political agenda of the powerful under the guise of a politically neutral rationality, Fish unabashedly celebrates such use (ibid., 168–70). Moreover, Fish contends that it is a mistake to insist that judicial precedents be reconciled (ibid., 169). Indeed, Fish goes on to argue, it is only in the particular circumstances of an individual controversy that given legal arguments actually succeed or fail. That cases are *decided* is law's triumph. Doctrinal inconsistencies spreading over numerous cases may be troubling from the standpoint of philosophy but not from the internal perspective of legal practice.

In the last analysis, far from providing a solution to the crisis affecting legal interpretation, Fish's new legal formalism compels the conclusion that the only way to punctuate the ceaseless flow of exchange of semantic values produced by law as an interpretive practice is through ad hoc exercises in power. Thus, legal practice may feign to transcend but is in fact animated by politics. Also, the dynamism of Fish's legal formalism is ultimately deceiving, because it is the dynamism of someone who runs in place rather than the dynamism of those on the move toward a new destination.

8. For example, when a person enters a restaurant and orders food, it can be reasonably inferred that the intention of both the patron and the restaurant owner is to exchange the ordered meal for the price of that meal calculated by reference to the menu that the patron consulted before ordering.

9. See, e.g., *Continental Forest Products, Inc. v. Chandler Supply Co.* (1974), at 743.

Because it locates justification in the purely present act of the decision maker,[10] Fish's new legal formalism leads to a perpetual celebration of the status quo (of each decision regardless of its content). Accordingly, Fish's formalism lacks the means to launch any real attempted reconciliation of self and other. Due to the constraints imposed by its abstracting and atomizing features, Fish's formalism can only offer a temporary palliative for the fissure of the body politic into self and other. Yet for all the shortcomings of his theory, Fish's analysis does yield some salient insights into the crisis affecting legal interpretation. Chief among these insights are the need for law constantly to carve out an identity for itself; the need for law to incorporate and rework extralegal value-laden materials from the realms of ethics and politics; and the need for law as a practice not to be ultimately reducible to any other practice, such as politics or philosophy.

All three of these insights relate to the dialectic between law and the universe of extralegal norms, practices, and values. Fish is correct in insisting that law must simultaneously plunge into and differentiate itself from the realm of the extralegal, and that to accomplish this law must remain constantly on the move. As we shall see, Fish's analysis becomes problematic, however, when it comes to assessing the law's incorporation and reworking of extralegal materials and the relationship between law as a practice and other practices.

What is most important about law's constant dynamic striving to carve out an identity for itself is the process of differentiation itself. *What* law is different from and *how* law is different from it may be subject to change (within certain limits beyond which juridical relationships would be altogether impossible). Thus, it seems futile to search for a universal form of mediation between legal and nonlegal relationships. Instead, the task for law is, as Fish aptly indicates, to "make" a formal existence for itself, that is, to emerge and distinguish itself from the particular sociohistorical context in which it is located. In other words, although there is no universal form by which law becomes law, at each moment of its existence law must find *a* form (or several forms) through which it can express its difference from the particular extralegal materials on which it presently depends. Fish's analysis becomes unpersuasive, however, in its reduction of law into arbitrary rhetorical gamesmanship. While law and legal doctrine mediate the ethical material with which they deal, they do not necessarily dissimulate it. Moreover, while the meaning of a legal doctrine may not be simply or directly inferable from the moral vision it incorporates, such moral vision places *substantive,* not merely formal or procedural, constraints on the le-

---

10. This act is "purely present" in that it is lifted out of the flow of historical events and has no past or future. Indeed, the decision maker's decision is legitimated because of the decision maker's present authority rather than because of any links to past or future writings.

gitimate use of that legal doctrine. In general, the extralegal values that inform legal doctrine do not make its meaning transparent. Nevertheless, those values serve to open and close certain possible (substantive) semantic paths for legal interpretation.

These points can be profitably illustrated by a return to the modern contract doctrine of consideration. Fish is correct in stressing that this doctrine incorporates the morals of the market to the exclusion of other moral visions. The remainder of his account of consideration, however, is much more questionable. This becomes apparent, moreover, if one takes a closer look at the morals of the market.

One of Adam Smith's well-known insights is that a market economy better serves the common good if every individual who trades in the market pursues his or her self-interest rather than that of society.[11] It does not follow, however, that because market participants ought to pursue self-interest rather than altruism, morals are altogether expelled from the economic sphere. If it made no difference whether market actors pursued their self-interest or acted out of altruistic motives, then arguably market relations would by and large escape the fetters of morality. But it does make a difference because altruism would not promote society's good as well as self-interest, and therefore it seems quite proper—if counterintuitive—to claim that individuals who participate in the market have a moral obligation to pursue self-interest.[12] Accordingly, consistent with Smith's theory, the individual is always subject to moral constraints, but these constraints differ depending on whether the individual is acting in the economic sphere or any other sphere of intersubjective interaction.[13]

Bearing in mind that "a regime of contract is just another legal name for a market" (Unger 1983, 625), let us now subject consideration to a Smithian conception of the morals of the market. The modern doctrine of consideration wholly incorporates, and is justifiable in terms of, the morals

---

11. See Smith 1976a, 477–78. For a more extended discussion of Adam Smith's views and of the morals of the market, see Rosenfeld 1985, 873–77.

12. To the extent that individuals are naturally inclined to pursue their self-interest, it may sound odd to speak of an "obligation" to act out of self-interest. Nevertheless, if one is willing to admit that it is possible for individuals to choose to act out of motivations other than self-interest, then it is not inconsistent to claim that the individual has a moral obligation to act out of self-interest even though he or she might be naturally inclined to do so in most cases. See Dumont 1977, 61: "Economics escapes the fetters of general morality only at the price of assuming a normative character of its own."

13. According to Smith's theory, while in the economic sphere the individual must act out of self-interest, in other spheres he or she must act out of sympathy. See Smith 1976b. Notwithstanding these differences, however, Smith derives both the morals of the market and the morals of sympathy from a single moral vision predicated on utilitarian values.

of the market.[14] Indeed, consideration requires the kind of quid pro quo that should be expected of agents who bargain to advance their self-interests.[15] Furthermore, consideration does not have to be interpreted as dissimulating its incorporation of the morals of the market by stressing the distinction between legal and moral obligation. Strictly speaking, the distinction that consideration highlights is that between the morals of the market and the morals of other spheres. Thus, it seems fair to interpret consideration both as not attempting to hide that it incorporates moral values and as incorporating moral values derived from a single moral vision.

This leaves the more difficult question of how to reconcile the coexistence of consideration and contracts implied in law. The difficulty here is not the one raised by Fish but rather one stemming from the fact that different hypotheses may provide equally persuasive accounts for the juxtaposition of consideration and contract implied in law. For example, such juxtaposition may be equally legitimate under the morals of the market[16] or under a clash of conflicting moral visions concerning the market and the law of contract.[17] Moreover, in both these cases legal doctrine and legal interpretation would be substantively constrained by the moral vision or moral visions they incorporated. The nature and scope of the doctrine of consideration would vary depending on the particular moral vision that is

14. For a more comprehensive discussion of this point, see Rosenfeld 1985, 827–32.

15. Promises to make a gift that are unenforceable as lacking consideration, on the other hand, are generally motivated by altruistic rather than self-interested concerns. Accordingly, consistent with Smith's analysis, such promises are less likely to promote the economic common good than promises purely motivated by self-interest.

16. Under this hypothesis, the proper function of contract law is to enforce exchange agreements motivated by self-interest. Consideration is a principal means to assure that contract fulfills its proper function, particularly in less developed markets where the subjective expression of self-interest by an agent is likely to be the best available evidence of that agent's self-interest. In fully developed markets where no single individual has a perceptible influence on the exchange value of commodities, however, an agent to a transaction may not always be the best judge of his or her own self-interest with respect to a given exchange transaction. Accordingly, contracts implied in law may be justified as a means to secure the promotion of an individual's self-interest where that individual is not in the position to be the best judge of his or her own self-interest.

17. Unger, for example, has argued that modern contract doctrine has been defined by vision and countervision, involving on the one hand freedom of contract and market values and on the other, communitarian values and fairness (1983, 616–33). Moreover, in the context of a conflict between moral visions, law may well be more indeterminate and more incoherent than when it is firmly anchored in a single moral vision. Thus, it may be that consideration and contracts implied in law respectively embody conflicting moral visions and that no valid internal connections could be drawn between these two legal doctrines. But in that case the failure is not with legal doctrine or legal interpretation but with the lack of a unified moral perspective.

deemed to be operative. But regardless of which plausible moral vision is adopted, *some* substantive constraints are bound to be imposed on what should count as legitimate interpretations of the doctrine of consideration.[18]

The last of Fish's insights that requires brief consideration is that law as a practice is not ultimately reducible to any other practice, such as politics or philosophy. The principal lesson taught by this insight is that law carves out an independent existence for itself, not because of the material it incorporates, but because of the way in which it deals with such material. Philosophy and law, for example, may be concerned with the same ethical values, but whereas philosophy may consider how these values might fit within certain theoretical frameworks, law is likely to rework them and to give them expression (or to reinscribe them) in legal doctrine. Because of this, moreover, it would be just as inappropriate to engage in abstract philosophical debate concerning a moral value that happens to be embedded in legal doctrine before a court of law as to cite judicial opinions as dispositive on controversies concerning moral values to an assembly of professional philosophers.

Not only does Fish assert that law is not reducible to any other practice, he asserts that law as a practice is self-contained, so that there is no overlap between law and other practices. Fish acknowledges that law may be assessed from the standpoint of other practices, such as philosophy. But a philosophical assessment of law, he would insist, cannot form part of the practice of law. More generally, for Fish, any theory of law would involve the practice of theory but could not belong to the practice of law.[19] There is a sense in which Fish's conception of law as a self-contained practice is unexceptionable. Indeed, to the extent that law is given structure by, and functions in accordance with, a particular combination of certain rules, norms, standards, and conventions, it seems clear that it is a unique and self-contained practice. In this sense, law is a self-contained practice just as is a game like chess or checkers. Thus, although the same board can be used for both chess and checkers, it would be obviously inappropriate to

18. Another plausible hypothesis is that the moral vision that encompasses the morals of the market has become so eroded that contract law as a distinct and independent body of mutually consistent legal doctrines has disintegrated. This hypothesis is endorsed by the proponents of the death of contract thesis. See, e.g., Atiyah 1979; Gilmore 1974. Under this hypothesis the doctrine of consideration may seem incoherent, but that would be because of the collapse of its moral foundation rather than because of any inherent problem with legal doctrine as such.

19. Thus, consistent with Fish's vision, there is a parallel between the appropriation by law as a practice (through incorporation and transformation) of materials from other practices such as morals and politics and the appropriation by the practice of theory of legal materials such as legal doctrines as subject matters for evaluation.

claim that there is an "overlap" between the practice of chess and that of checkers. Moreover, on any given occasion, one would determine whether the board in question was a chessboard or a checkers board, not by reference to the nature of the board, but to the dynamic relation between the board and the rules and conventions of the game being played on it. When two people are moving chess pieces on the board according to the rules of chess, then the board is a chessboard, and the practice involved—which incorporates the board as an element within it—is the practice of chess. Similarly, in the sense in which law is properly viewed as a self-contained practice, the same argument—for example, that equality requires equal treatment of those who are in the same essential category[20]—would belong to the practice of law, when made by a litigating attorney to a judge in court, and to the practice of philosophy, when made by a university professor conducting a philosophy class.

Because law as a practice is not simply a game like chess or checkers, however, there is an important sense—which Fish altogether fails to capture—in which law is a practice that is open to and that overlaps in part with other practices. Unlike a game such as chess or checkers, which is a self-contained practice, law is a highly complex and dynamic practice that can incorporate not only decontextualized materials from another practice but also—albeit to a limited extent—the very processes by which the latter practice generates its materials. Thus, there are cases in which lawyers not only refer to ethical values but also make philosophical or ethical arguments that are subject to the same processes of generation, validation, and refutation as if they had been made in the course of a serious philosophical discussion. For example, there are cases in American constitutional law where neither the constitutional text, nor the intent of the framers, nor precedent can offer sufficient guidance to settle an actual controversy.[21] In such cases, ethical or philosophical arguments concerning such values as freedom, equality, or privacy may be legitimately invoked and may well determine the judicial outcome.

As a specific illustration, consider the Constitution's equal protection clause, which constitutionalizes the conception of equality (Fallon 1987, 1205). In several equal protection cases, the crucial question for the court

20. Compare Perelman 1963, 16 (according to the principle of formal justice "beings of one and the same category must be treated the same way") with *Trimble v. Gordon* (1980), at 780 (Rehnquist, J., dissenting) (the equal protection clause of the Fourteenth Amendment does not require "that all persons must be treated alike. Rather, its general principle is that persons similarly situated should be treated similarly").

21. See Fallon 1987, 1189–90 (the practice of constitutional interpretation recognizes the relevance of at least five types of arguments, including "value arguments" making claims about justice, morality, or social policy).

to resolve is whether constitutional equality requires equal treatment or equality of result.[22] Frequently, this question cannot be answered by reference to the kinds of arguments that might be preferred by those who regularly engage in the practice of constitutional interpretation—namely arguments from the text of the Constitution, or the framers' intent, or judicial precedent. Accordingly, the requisite decision must ultimately rely on the kinds of arguments and evaluations that are customary within the practice of moral and political philosophy (Fallon 1987, 1205–06). In short, in those cases where only philosophical arguments can suggest whether one of two possible legal outcomes is preferable to the other, the practice of constitutional interpretation overlaps with that of philosophy. In other cases, philosophical arguments may be relevant but subordinate to other arguments, or may be altogether trumped by other arguments. Thus, there are overlaps between the practices of law and philosophy, although these overlaps are limited in nature.[23]

It should not be surprising that law as a practice should be open to and overlap with other practices. Indeed, games such as chess, checkers, or even baseball or basketball can be seen as self-contained ends in themselves in a way that law cannot. These games bear no connection to one another as practices, and suggesting that the rules or conventions of one of them should be made applicable to another would be ludicrous. Law, however, is not an isolated practice but rather one of a cluster of interrelated practices that need not be viewed exclusively as ends in themselves. These interrelated practices, which include ethics and politics as well as law, are linked, at some level, by a common pursuit of the reconciliation of self and other within the sphere of social interaction. To be sure, each of these practices undertakes this common pursuit in its own way, and sometimes they may each diverge significantly from the other. But at other times they converge and overlap, thus belying Fish's unduly reductionist thesis.

In the last analysis, Fish's atomistic tendencies and his underestimation of the richness and complexity of law as a practice lead him to the unwarranted conclusion that law is *in all relevant senses* a self-contained practice. Fish is right that law is a distinct practice that is capable of incorporating and transforming materials from other practices. To the extent that ethical, political, and philosophical arguments have a genuine place *within* the practice of law, however, that practice is not self-contained. But if law as practice is distinct but not self-contained, the question arises anew as to whether

22. This question has been at the heart of the affirmative action cases decided by the Supreme Court. See Rosenfeld 1991a, chap. 7; 1989b.

23. For a more extensive analysis of the relationship between the practice of philosophy and that of constitutional interpretation in the context of the equal protection clause, see Rosenfeld 1991a, chap. 6.

there is something internal to law (other than Fish's purely procedural and purely tautological conception of law as a self-contained practice) that makes it in essence different from the interrelated practices with which it overlaps. Ernest Weinrib's new legal formalism suggests an affirmative answer to this question. Accordingly, I shall briefly turn to Weinrib's theory to determine how it might contribute to the solution of the crisis affecting legal interpretation.

II. THE ARISTOTELO-KANTIAN FORMALISM OF WEINRIB

Reduced to its bare essentials, Weinrib's new legal formalism postulates that law remains distinct from politics to the extent that law's structure is intelligible as an internally coherent practice (Weinrib 1988, 951). Moreover, the internal coherence of law can be grasped, according to Weinrib, through interpretation (ibid., 1014). As Weinrib specifies, "from a perspective internal to the law's content, formalism draws out the implications of a sophisticated legal system's tendency to coherence by making explicit the justificatory patterns to which the content of such a system must conform" (ibid.). In other words, in a mature legal system, interpretation—and Weinrib has in mind principally judicial interpretation (ibid., 1004–5)—reveals law's tendency toward internal coherence through the articulation of immanent links between the form and the content of particular juridical relationships. At the most abstract level, the forms of juridical relationship envisaged by Weinrib are universal and ahistorical (ibid., 1011), but the process of judicial interpretation nevertheless remains dynamic. This is because the concrete juridical relationships to which such forms must be immanently linked are embedded in particular social and historical contexts and because judicial decisions must employ the public meanings developed in and applicable to such contexts (ibid.).

As already mentioned, the abstract forms that endow juridical relationships with meaning, according to Weinrib, are the forms of justice, namely corrective and distributive justice. Weinrib further indicates that these two forms of justice are irreducible and that accordingly particular juridical relationships come either within the sweep of corrective justice or within that of distributive justice, but never within that of both (Weinrib 1988, 980, 984). Moreover, drawing on Aristotle's insight, Weinrib emphasizes that, paradigmatically, the juridical relationships that embody the forms of justice are those "that obtain between parties regarded as external to each other, each with separate interests of mine and thine" (ibid., 977). In other words, juridical relationships involve agents who are connected through external links as opposed to such internal interpersonal links as those forged through love or virtue (ibid.).

Thus far, Weinrib's brand of new legal formalism seems to mesh well with law conceived as having internalized deconstruction. Indeed, the universe in which Weinrib locates juridical relationships is one in which there is a clear split between self and other. Juridical relationships understood in terms of the forms of justice, on the other hand, appear to provide a path toward the reconciliation of self and other, all the while permitting self and other to remain external to one another. But before any further assessment of the apparent virtues of Weinrib's new legal formalism is possible, it is necessary to take a somewhat closer look at the forms of justice he invokes and at the way in which they are supposed to endow juridical relationships with distinct meaning consistent with his conception of law as being irreducible to politics.

As understood by Weinrib, corrective justice involves the award of damages that simultaneously quantifies the wrongdoing of one party and the suffering of the other party in a bipolar (voluntary or involuntary) private transaction (ibid., 978). Moreover, under this view, all bilateral relationships characteristic of the private law of torts and contracts are ultimately intelligible in terms of the structure of corrective justice (ibid.). In other words, the legal universe carved out by juridical relationships intelligible in terms of corrective justice is one in which formally equal individual legal actors are initially placed side by side owing each other nothing but reciprocal negative duties (of noninterference) (ibid., 999). The initial equilibrium maintained by a network of reciprocal negative duties that makes for purely external relationships among legal actors, however, is bound to become upset as individuals either seek the cooperation of others in the pursuit of self-interest (contract) or voluntarily or involuntarily interfere with others in the course of such pursuit (tort). Corrective justice, through the award of damages, undoes (erases) the positive entanglements of (unfulfilled) contracts and the interferences of torts, and thus purports to reestablish (reinscribe) the initial equilibrium between purely externally linked equals.

Corrective justice, argues Weinrib, deals with the immediate relationship of person to person (ibid., 988) and is completely removed from politics (ibid., 994), as it merely seeks to restore the initial equilibrium between a doer and a sufferer regardless of the actual wealth, merit, or virtue of the interacting legal actors (ibid., 997). Thus, it apparently makes no difference whether one is politically inclined to advance the interests of the wealthy or the poor, as there is only one legitimate way to resolve legal disputes arising under private law: that is, by commanding payment of the quantity of damages that corrective justice requires to restore the initial equality between doer and sufferer. Accordingly, as Weinrib sees it, the judicial task in the context of dispensing the quantitative equality mandated by corrective justice is limited to the specification of the actual damages required in the particular case to be adjudicated (ibid., 993).

In contrast to the quantitative equality of corrective justice, distributive justice requires the implementation of proportional equality. Whereas corrective justice is concerned with the recovery of a status quo ante, distributive justice requires the allocation of the benefits and burdens of social cooperation in the proportions set by an applicable criterion of distribution (ibid., 988). Also, consistent with Weinrib's analysis, unlike corrective justice, distributive justice cannot be completely severed from politics. Indeed, settling on any given criterion of distribution for purposes of achieving proportional equality involves a political decision (ibid., 989). Thus, for example, whether certain benefits ought to be distributed equally in proportion to need or in proportion to merit depends not on anything inherent to law or to juridical relationships but instead on some collective decision that remains extrinsic to law and that must draw, at least in part, on political considerations.

Although distributive justice cannot avoid politics, Weinrib maintains that the former is not thereby reducible to the latter (ibid., 990). Once a particular criterion of distribution has been selected, distributive justice requires that juridical relationships conform to the proportional equality mandated by that criterion (ibid., 991–92). Moreover, Weinrib also believes that inherent in the very notion of distributive justice there is a conception of personhood and of equality that constrains all legitimate juridical relationships falling within the scope of that form of justice (ibid.). The concept of personhood thus requires judges to make sure that people engaged in the relevant juridical relationships are not treated as things; the concept of equality, that each person be treated as an equal consistent with the dictates of the prevailing criterion of distribution (ibid.).

Distributive justice, particularly through its conception of personhood and equality, is supposed to preside, in Weinrib's formalist vision, over the domain of public law. On the one hand, Weinrib maintains that the notions of personhood and equality impose nonpolitical constraints on the legislative and administrative processes (ibid., 991). On the other hand, Weinrib argues, "the positive law may give effect to the fundamental values of personhood and equality in a variety of ways: by incorporating them into the techniques for construing statutes, by elaborating notions of natural justice or fairness for administrative procedures or by enshrining specifications of personhood and equality into constitutional documents" (ibid.).

Corrective and distributive justice, as conceived by Weinrib, may be viewed as offering two distinct (and irreducible to politics) paths toward the reconciliation of self and other as persons capable of engaging in mutually external relationships. Corrective justice promotes the minimal harmony of mutual noninterference through the spread of a quantitative equality that ritualistically effaces the encroachment of a wrongdoing self on a suffering other. Moreover, since the self's devotion to its own interests is bound to cause interference with the negative rights of others, the completion of the mission of corrective justice must be deferred until such time as the self becomes completely self-sufficient—an impossibility in terms of deconstructionist ontology.

Distributive justice, on the other hand, also aspires to promote mutual noninterference by defusing the conflict between self and other over the allocation of collectively generated benefits and burdens. By instituting proportional equality, distributive justice circumscribes an order within which each person can see himself or herself as a moral equal who is treated as an end rather than merely as a means by being given his or her due. Because each individual self is ascribed a dignified place within the order carved out by the proportional equality of distributive justice, moreover, the self can presumably renounce confrontation with the other as a means to secure the socially generated goods that self-respect and dignity require. Thus, distributive justice, much like corrective justice, tends toward a harmony of purely external relationships of noninterference between a self and an other who have competing claims on the products of social cooperation.

Finally, the task of distributive justice, like that of corrective justice, can never be completed, both because presumably there will always be new goods to be distributed according to proportional equality and because the particular criterion of distributive justice to be applied in given social and historical circumstances is likely to be a subject of political controversy so long as society remains divided into self and other.

Not only do corrective and distributive justice as the forms of justice seem highly compatible with law conceived as having internalized deconstruction but they also allow for indeterminacy in the course of discharging their meaning-endowing function. Indeed, in Weinrib's assessment, indeterminacy is inevitable in the course of applying abstract forms to particular juridical relationships that necessarily comprise an element of contingency (ibid., 1009). Indeterminacy, however, is only objectionable if it allows juridical relationships to be ultimately swept into the whirlwind of politics. The indeterminacy created by the application of Weinrib's forms of justice does not. As Weinrib states, "The forms of justice determine juridical relationships by representing the justificatory structures through which those relationships can be understood as the sorts of thing that they are and to which they must conform if they are to be intelligible. The forms of justice are thus determinative as the distinctive—not the exhaustive—modes for the understanding of law" (ibid., 1009–10). In other words, although the forms of justice may not determine the outcome of every case, only those outcomes that are consistent with the forms of justice (and hence not merely reducible to politics) may be legitimately defended. Thus, even when not completely determinative, the forms of justice operating in the context of Weinrib's formalism are supposed to perform a path-closing function capable of preventing the slippage of the legal into the political. If Weinrib's conception of the two forms of justice and of their potential for making juridical relationships immanently intelligible were acceptable, then his new legal formalism would provide a genuine solution to the crisis affecting legal interpretation. Unfortunately, as convincingly demonstrated by Alan Brudner, Weinrib's new legal formalism is ultimately unacceptable to the extent that it rests on certain arbitrary and unwarranted premises (1990, 1168–81). In the remainder of this section, I briefly focus on these premises with a view to determining whether, and to what extent, Weinrib's insights might still be incorporated in a satisfactory resolution of the crisis affecting legal interpretation.

From the standpoint of our own concerns, there are two basic flaws with the premises underlying Weinrib's formalist thesis: the first relates to his conception of the forms of justice; the second, to his appraisal of the relationship between corrective and distributive justice. More specifically, the first flaw, as noted by Brudner, derives from Weinrib's elevation of one (among many possible) historically grounded and ideologically determined version of what is entailed by corrective and distributive justice as the universal and ahistorical essence of those forms of justice (ibid., 1173). Moreover, the reason this flaw is particularly troublesome is because it reveals that Weinrib's apparent depoliticization of the forms of justice is achieved through the privileging and enshrining of a particular ideological vision that is certainly subject to political debate. The second flaw stems from Weinrib's insistence on the existence of an unbridgeable gap between corrective and distributive justice and from his assertion that corrective justice is concerned with immediate relationships among persons. At least under some conceptions of the forms of justice, there need be no insurmountable gap between corrective and distributive justice. Also, when all the relevant considerations are taken into proper account, it becomes clear that the relationships that come within the sweep of corrective justice must be mediated ones. Furthermore, to the extent that there is no gap between the two forms of justice and that all relationships encompassed by either of the two must be mediated ones, these cannot be, contrary to Weinrib's claim, a total separation between politics and corrective justice.

Two of the principal unwarranted assumptions made by Weinrib are that the domain of corrective justice must preside over a regime of purely negative rights and that distributive justice necessarily involves respect for Kantian notions of equality and personhood. Corrective justice can operate in the context of purely negative rights under certain particular historical and ideological circumstances, namely those associated with a free market economy (ibid., 1178–81). Thus, private law shaped so as to afford the greatest possible legal protection to free market transactions would undoubtedly be primarily oriented toward the protection of the negative rights and freedoms best suited to promote the orderly proliferation of market exchanges. And, under those circumstances, corrective justice would be quite properly confined to "undoing" the entanglements having resulted in infringements on negative rights and freedoms. Nothing in corrective justice as a form of justice taken at the highest level of abstraction, however, precludes extending corrective justice to cover a regime of positive rights, or, in other words, a legal system in which private legal actors are charged with positive duties toward one another. Corrective justice is necessarily backward looking, in that it must pick some point in the past and set it as a baseline. After selecting its baseline, corrective justice must compare the set of intersubjective relationships existing at the baseline and that which is the force at the subsequent time at which a claim for compensation arises. Corrective justice must also introduce a concept of "disruption" pursuant to which it can distinguish between compensable and noncompensable deviations from the baseline. Weinrib seems to assume that if we seek to establish the baseline logically, by carrying corrective justice to its highest level of abstraction, we will all be led by reason to the same point: a static universe of purely abstract egos who remain entirely independent from each other and who scrupulously refrain from interfering with one another as a consequence of their strict adherence to a regime of purely negative rights and duties. Moreover, for those who accept this point as providing a purely logically compelled—and hence completely apolitical—baseline, the definition of what should count as a compensable disruption is self-evident: any deviation from the status quo of the baseline that involves a violation of a negative right.

Logic alone, however, does not compel acceptance of the atomistic universe that Weinrib projects at the highest level of abstraction. Indeed, it hardly seems contradictory to contend that at the highest level of abstraction, persons are cleansed of their selfish individualistic concerns and that they are mutually dedicated to the maintenance of social harmony and welfare within their community through the deployment of care, concern, and an elaborate network of positive rights and duties. Within this communitarian vision, moreover, the baseline would be one of solidarity and mutual assistance, and any deviation involving a violation of a positive duty would quite naturally qualify as a compensable disruption.

Neither Weinrib's atomistic vision nor its communitarian counterpart is in any sense logically compelled. Each of them figures as an originary myth suited to buttress a particular ethical and political ideology. More generally, setting a baseline for corrective justice involves an irreducibly arbitrary—

that is, political and ideological—element. And because of this, corrective justice no more requires the imposition of purely negative rights than a regime heavily composed of positive rights. Thus, for example, it seems entirely legitimate for tort law to impose, at least under certain conditions, on individual actors a positive duty to rescue fellow human beings who are in danger. Corrective justice in the latter case would have to extend to nonfeasance and not merely to misfeasance as Weinrib would have it, but that would simply reflect one possible legitimate choice among several plausible alternative ethical and political visions.[24] In short, it is only by suppressing alternative political visions of the proper role of corrective justice that Weinrib succeeds in conveying the impression that corrective justice is apolitical.

As we have seen, Weinrib does concede that distributive justice has a political component, but he insists that it nevertheless transcends politics to the extent that it imposes a duty to abide by Kantian notions of personhood and equality. Unless one incorporates these Kantian notions tautologically in the very definition of distributive justice, however, there is no reason to assume that all plausible conceptions of distributive justice need include such Kantian notions. For example, there seems to be nothing contradictory about a feudalist conception of distributive justice, according to which persons are inherently unequal depending on the social class into which they are born, according to which much greater dignity attaches to those born into aristocratic families than to commoners, and according to which distributions should be made unequally, with a disproportionate share of society's goods going to the members of the aristocracy.[25] Once again Weinrib has taken one possible conception—or in this case, more precisely, a class of possible conceptions—of a form of justice and presented it as universally valid. But to the extent that distributive justice at the highest level of abstraction does not imply Kantian notions of personhood and equality, judicial protection of the latter is not likely to be apolitical in the sense that Weinrib intends.

Turning to the second principal flaw underlying Weinrib's premises, the unbridgeable gap that he perceives between corrective and distributive justice does not extend to all plausible conceptions of the relation between

24. Just as in the context of a Smithian market economy in which morals are not expelled from the marketplace, a vision of corrective justice as applying exclusively to a regime of negative rights is not apolitical. Instead it is informed by the particular morals and politics that underlie the free market economy.

25. It may be objected that in a feudal society distributions of benefits and burdens would not be conceived in terms of distributive justice. Even conceding this point, the fact remains that there is no *logical* impediment against a feudal conception of distributive justice such as the one outlined here.

the two forms of justice. To be sure, there is one sense in which there is an irreducible difference between corrective and distributive justice: the former is backward looking whereas the latter is essentially forward looking.[26] In another sense—which is more important in terms of the relationship between law and politics—however, corrective and distributive justice may be harmonized (at least under certain conceptions) under a unified all-encompassing system of justice. Such a unified system may comprise several components such as distributive, corrective, and procedural justice but is above all characterized by its possession of an internal congruence and harmony that binds all its component parts together in a single whole that is greater than the sum of its parts. Such a unified system of justice may rely, for example, on an overriding criterion of justice to be applied to all distributions. Distributions, however, may be tampered with, through interference either with the process of distribution or with the products of such distribution. And, at least in the latter case, corrective justice, subsumed under the relevant overriding criterion of justice, may be called for as a means to preserve the integrity of the then-operative all-encompassing system of justice.[27]

To the extent that the *measure* of compensation under corrective justice depends on a criterion of justice that is applicable across the board to all

26. It may be objected that from the standpoint of adjudication, both forms of justice must be viewed as backward looking given the very structure of adjudication. On reflection, however, this objection misses the mark. Corrective justice seeks to recapture the past whereas distributive justice—whether oriented toward a past, present, or future moment—construes all points in time on which it focuses as presents looking into the future. As an illustration, consider the following. A municipality has as a distributive rule that each of its adult members is entitled to be provided by government with housing having a market value of $50,000, and a corrective rule that a victim of intentional wrongdoing is entitled to full compensation in kind or in the market value equivalent of his or her loss by the wrongdoer. Suppose now that A collected her $50,000 government subsidy and invested $50,000 of her own money to have a $100,000 house built. After A has moved into her new house, B, an arsonist, burns it to the ground. A could sue B and obtain $100,000 in damages under corrective justice. In that case, the judicial objective would be to re-create as nearly as possible the moment preceding the wrongdoing in a ritualized attempt to erase that act of wrongdoing. On the other hand (assuming that B is destitute), A could bring an action to establish that she is (distributively) entitled to a $50,000 housing subsidy (even though she has already received such a subsidy in the past). In this latter case, applying legal norms derived from distributive justice, the judge would have to focus on two past moments: that of the destruction of A's house by arson and the earlier moment in which she received her original housing subsidy. But such judicial focus on the past would not be for purposes of reinstating the past (as the judge in this action does not seek to put A in the position to have a new $100,000 house similar to the one she owned prior to the arson). Instead, it would be for purposes of determining whether these judicially framed past events give rise to a present entitlement to a future distribution.

27. For a discussion of the argument that the implementation of corrective or compensatory justice is necessary to buttress the achievements of distributive justice in the face of violations of distributive entitlements, see Rosenfeld 1991a, chap. 1.

intersubjective dealings coming within the sweep of an all-encompassing system of justice, corrective justice cannot be completely apolitical. Indeed, selection of one among several available criteria of justice inevitably involves the making of a political choice, and that choice bears some imprint on the articulation of the dictates of corrective justice. Also, because of this, the intersubjective transactions that come within the purview of corrective justice necessarily involve mediated relationships between legal actors.[28]

Notwithstanding the failure of Weinrib's legal formalism persuasively to detach law from politics, some of his insights might be profitably incorporated in the search for a solution to the crisis affecting legal interpretation. Specifically, whereas corrective justice cannot rid law of politics, it structures the relationships between self and other to which it applies in a distinctive manner that makes them distinguishable from political and ethical relationships. In other words, while not excluding the ethical or the political, corrective justice rearranges them in a way that gives a distinctive legal contour to the relationships that come within its scope. Furthermore, whereas Weinrib's conception of distributive justice is both time bound and ideo-

---

28. To illustrate these points, let us consider the example of a breach of contract. Suppose that the buyer in a contract for the sale of goods refuses to pay the seller after receipt of the goods in accordance with the terms of the contract. While it seems obvious that corrective justice requires that the buyer compensate the seller for the buyer's breach of contract, it is not self-evident what the measure of damages should be. Should it be the contract price? The market price of the goods? Or the "just" or "fair" price for such goods? Moreover, stipulation that the objective of corrective justice is the simultaneous wiping out of the wrongdoing of the defendant and of the suffering of the plaintiff through an award of damages does not suffice to establish the proper measure of damages. It might be interjected that it is obvious that the contract price is the proper measure of damages, since payment of the contract price as damages would put buyer and seller in the position in which they would have been absent any breach. On careful consideration, however, it should become apparent that the contract price only affords the proper measure of damages if it is (distributively) just (or at least not unjust). Thus, if under the applicable overall principle of justice, the market price of goods is deemed just, then if the contract price in question happens greatly to exceed the market price it would be unjust and could not provide the proper measure of damages in the breach of contract case. Strictly speaking, in the latter case the collection of that portion of the contract price which is in excess of the market price would itself constitute wrongdoing calling for compensation. And in view of the two wrongdoings involved—namely the buyer's failure to pay for the goods and the seller's attempt to collect that portion of the contract price which is in excess of the market price—corrective justice would require (as the simultaneous erasure of both wrongs) that the buyer defendant pay the market price of the goods as damages to the seller plaintiff. In short, since the measure of damages depends on what counts as a wrongdoing under a particular criterion of (overall) justice, the relationships that come within the scope of corrective justice are clearly mediated, and the content of corrective justice is itself derived from substantive principles of justice inevitably grounded in politics. For an extensive discussion of the relationship between contract and justice, including the relationship between corrective or compensatory and distributive justice in the context of contract, see Rosenfeld 1985.

logically conditioned, the Kantian constraints it imposes nevertheless arguably provide a legitimate way to distinguish legal from purely political relationships in the context of those legal systems that share its ideological assumptions. Significantly, the contemporary American legal system with its constitutional rights to due process and equality and with its numerous private law doctrines grounded on premises of individual autonomy and equality clearly seems congruent with the ideological assumptions embodied in Weinrib's conception of distributive justice. Finally, Weinrib's insight that law is concerned with external relationships between persons furnishes apparently cogent means of demarcation between legal relationships and purely ethical ones.

Consistent with the preceding assessment of the new legal formalism, resolution of the crisis in legal interpretation to clear the path toward just interpretations requires recourse to both justice and the distinction between law, ethics, and politics. But since formal justice has proven inadequate, we must look to substantive justice. Substantive justice, however, is problematic to the extent that it is difficult to disentangle from contested conceptions of the good. In the absence of neutral Kantian constraints, the ideal of legal justice must fall between the rigorous demands of ethical justice and the lax controls of political justice. To compound the problem, as we shall see in the next chapter, justice rests on a paradox and proves inextricably linked to violence. This does not mean that there is no path toward just interpretations, but only that to get to that path, we must first overcome several daunting obstacles.

CHAPTER THREE

Just Interpretations?

Law, Violence, and the Paradox of Justice

To overcome the crisis in legal interpretation, it is imperative to establish meanings that comport with justice—that is, meanings that make for a fair equilibrium between the respective needs, interests, and aspirations of the self and those of the other. Moreover, to the extent that law as a practice is not coextensive with ethics or politics, just (legal) interpretations cannot be ultimately reducible to ethical or political justice. On the other hand, since, as discussed in Chapter II, law is not self-contained but partially overlaps with ethics and politics, justice in the context of law cannot be legitimately confined to justice according to law—the latter consisting in treating each person in conformity with his or her legal entitlement (Perelman 1963, 9–10). Indeed, in any contemporary constitutional democracy, establishing a person's legal entitlements is rarely, if ever, merely a matter of mechanical application of transparent legal rules to easily circumscribed facts. And even if it were, that still would not assure a just apportionment of legal entitlements, or preclude that implementing alternative interpretive strategies would lead to greater justice in at least some of the relevant cases.[1] Also, as we shall see, to compound the problem, justice itself rests on a seemingly insurmountable paradox that inextricably links it to violence.

The possibility of just interpretations thus seems to be tied to the fate of justice. With this in mind, section I below explores how the paradox on

---

1. Even assuming consensus on the literal meaning of a statutory or constitutional provision, it is still defensible to press for an alternative interpretation to avoid injustice. It is at least arguable that, absent clear and convincing evidence to the contrary, one ought not impute to constitutional framers or to legislators the rigid intent to stick to the literal meaning of the legal texts for which they are responsible even at the cost of perpetrating significant manifest injustices.

which it depends constrains justice and how the constraints in question bind justice to violence. Section II reassesses the relationship between different forms of justice—such as distributive, corrective, and procedural justice—and between different domains of justice, namely ethical, legal, and political justice. Finally, section III indicates how the conclusions reached in sections I and II reinforce the call for just interpretations while at the same time cautioning against the hope for any comprehensive or definitive solutions.

I. THE PARADOX OF JUSTICE AND THE INEVITABILITY OF VIOLENCE

As the means to strike a fair equilibrium between self and other, justice confronts the paradox of having to be at once both universal and singular. To be fair to the other, justice must consider him or her in all his or her singularity; but to strike an equilibrium between self and other, justice must avoid speaking in the voice of either one of them and is thus compelled to embrace a universal language that transcends the peculiarities of all the selves that come within its sweep. Jacques Derrida succinctly captures this paradox of justice when he writes, "To address oneself to the other in the language of the other is, it seems, the condition of all possible justice, but apparently, in all rigor, it is not only impossible . . . but even excluded by justice as law [*droit*], inasmuch as justice as right seems to imply an element of universality, the appeal to a third party who suspends the unilaterality or singularity of the idioms" (1992, 17). In other words, there is an insurmountable gap between justice as law, which must remain forever universal, and justice as giving to each what is his or her due, which necessarily involves an element of irreducible singularity.

Derrida's dichotomy between justice as law and justice as each person's due is reminiscent of Aristotle's distinction between justice as equality and justice as equity (Aristotle 1980, bk. 5). In Aristotle's view, justice according to law must speak in universal terms that are susceptible, in some cases, of producing inequities. To remedy this problem, recourse to equity is necessary as "a correction of law where it is defective owing to its universality" (ibid., 1137b, lines 27–28). In other words, to be universal in its scope, law must abstract from (at least some of) the singularities of the persons made subject to its dictates. For example, to foster justice in market exchanges, contract law must disregard many singularities such as the personal well-being, family status, or religious commitments of would-be contractors.[2] Indeed, if exchanges projected into the future among strangers eager to seize

2. For a more extended discussion of the role of abstraction in contractual relations, see Rosenfeld 1985, 807–20.

the opportunities offered by the marketplace promote distributive justice, then consideration of singularities invoked to frustrate otherwise valid contractual agreements would be unwarranted.

In some exceptional cases, however, disregard of certain singularities would clearly lead to unwarranted inequities. For example, let us assume that justice in contract is well served by a general rule providing that, absent explicit terms to the contrary, payment under a contract for services shall only become due on full completion of such services. Let us assume further that *A* has contracted with *B* to paint *A*'s house and that after having completed 98 percent of the job, *B* becomes permanently paralyzed and is then unable to complete his contractual undertaking. Even if *A* is fully satisfied with the quality of *B*'s work, straightforward application of the general rule would legally entitle him not to pay anything to *B*. In strict Aristotelian terms, that result might not be unjust, but it would nonetheless be grossly inequitable. Under such exceptional circumstances, the harshness of the applicable contractual rule could be mitigated through use of an equitable remedy, such as that provided by the Anglo-American doctrine of *quantum meruit*,[3] which would require *A* to pay *B* for the actual value of the painting services performed by *B* for the benefit of *A*.

In spite of the similarities between their respective views, there is a crucial difference between Aristotle's and Derrida's conceptions of justice. Whereas for Aristotle justice as equity is meant to supplement justice as equality, for Derrida justice as each person's due is not only impossible but also completely frustrates the achievement of justice as law. In the Aristotelian universe, justice as equality is the rule and justice as equity is introduced to deal with the exception. For Derrida, in contrast, every case appears to be an exception, or more accurately—in view of the respective demands of equality and of the irreducible singularity of the other—every case should (but is inevitably bound to fail to) satisfy both the rule and the exception.[4]

The disjunction between justice as equality and justice as equity is linked—in the Derridean vision—to a series of insurmountable oppositions that include the clash between self and other, the singular and the universal, the concrete and the abstract, and the rule and its exceptions.

---

3. *Quantum meruit* means "as much as deserved" and measures recovery under an implied contract to pay compensation as the reasonable value of services rendered. It is an equitabe doctrine, based on the principle that no one who benefits by the labor and materials of another should be unjustly enriched thereby (Black 1990, 1243).

4. Strictly speaking, the exception is defined in terms of the rule from which it deviates, and is thus in some sense subordinate to the latter. In the context of a Derridean vision, however, the subordination of the exception to the rule would unduly privilege the latter over the former. Accordingly, I use rule here primarily to denote the universal side of justice and exception to refer to its singular pole.

Moreover, the Derridean account of justice is particularly compelling inasmuch as the ultimate realization of justice depends on *full consideration* of *all* similarities and *all* differences that come into play in the course of intersubjective dealings between self and other. Without similarities, there could be no equality, and hence no justice, as no two persons could ever be deemed to be in any meaningful sense alike. Without differences, on the other hand, the very distinction between self and other would vanish and the very concept of justice would become superfluous, if not altogether meaningless.

To establish the requisite similarities called for by justice, it is necessary to move away from the thoroughly concrete position according to which each person is radically singular as the embodiment of a unique set of spatiotemporal coordinates. This must be done to reach a more abstract level where certain relevant similarities can be established above and beyond— or in spite of—certain differences. For example, attempts to justify unequal treatment of the sexes often point to concrete differences, such as the fact that only women can get pregnant.[5] Conversely, calls for gender equality are likely to involve ascending to a level of abstraction from which certain differences become unimportant or nearly imperceptible. Thus, arguments for equal treatment of men and women at the workplace are likely to be bolstered by downplaying differences between the sexes, either by depicting men and women as if they possessed no sexual identity or by portraying women at the workplace as fully able, for all relevant purposes, to behave like men. In short, confronted with a discriminatory workplace, women may have to sacrifice some of their singularity to strive for as much justice as could be obtained from establishing parity with men.[6]

The inescapable and insoluble clash between the singular and the universal and the concrete and the abstract is actually much more pronounced than might appear from the previous example regarding gender relations. Indeed, gender-based differences are construed at a fairly abstract level through the opposition between the similarities that link every man to his fellow men and the similarities that group together every woman and her fellow women. In contrast, there are differences between one individual

5. See, e.g., *Michael M. v. Sonoma County Superior Court* (1981) (constitutional equality does not bar criminalizing consensual sex with underage female while not criminalizing same with underage male, on the grounds that only females can get pregnant).

6. There is, of course, another way of pursuing gender-based justice, namely by taking genuine gender-based differences into account without exploiting them for purposes of fostering inequality. Even a move in that direction, however, could not eliminate the gap between the singular and the universal. It may make more room for the singular and loosen the grip of the universal, but neither could ultimately yield to or blend into the other without the elimination of all possibility of justice.

and another that are accounted for by the fact that no two persons are exactly alike. These latter differences seem much more singular than gender-based differences, and much less susceptible of figuring in a coherent scheme of integration of the singular and the universal.

A person's individual pain threshold marks the kind of difference that sets every individual apart from every other individual and well illustrates the scope of the insurmountable gap that lies between the singular and the universal. Thus, uniform application of a law that prescribes a set physical punishment for a particular offense may well lead to barely noticeable pain in some cases and almost intolerable pain in others. Simply adjusting the punishment in accordance with a recipient's pain threshold would not solve the problem, however, as it would result in dispensing unequal punishment for the same offense.[7] To be sure, if all conceivable similarities and differences among human beings could be fully grasped, comprehensive justice capable of integrating the singular and the universal would be, at least in theory, possible. Inasmuch as the self cannot fully capture the irreducible singularity of the other, however, the singular and the universal are bound to continue pulling in opposite directions, and comprehensive justice remains impossible.

The impossibility of accounting for *all* similarities and differences enhances the attractiveness of interpreting justice as revolving around *relevant* similarities and differences. For example, notwithstanding that comprehensive justice may be impossible, racial discrimination in employment may still be cogently interpreted as unjust on the grounds that racial differences ought to be irrelevant in the context of employment. In a pluralist society with competing conceptions of the good, however, there are bound to be disagreements over which similarities and which differences ought to be considered relevant. Thus, for instance, a libertarian would consider differences in wealth to be irrelevant and conceive justice as only requiring formal equality under law. An egalitarian, on the other hand, would argue that such differences are clearly relevant and that justice calls for redistributions designed to narrow the gap between rich and poor. In short, not only does the insurmountable barrier between self and other make comprehensive justice impossible, but the competing conceptions of the good, which divide self from other in pluralist societies, appear to relegate any criterion of justice—that is, any criterion for distinguishing relevant similarities and differences from irrelevant ones—to contingency. Accordingly, consistent

---

7. This problem is compounded if physical punishment is prescribed as retribution for having physically injured a victim. If the intensity of the punishment is adjusted depending on the pain threshold of the wrongdoer who is slated for punishment, should it also be adjusted to account for the pain threshold of the victim?

with Derridean logic, justice looms as both perpetually incomplete and incapable of carving out a position that is impartial as between competing conceptions of the good.

Because it is caught in the insurmountable oppositions between the singular and the universal and between the concrete and the abstract, justice cannot avoid producing violence. When the self presses its claims in the name of justice, it is bound to do violence to the other. But, by the same token, when the self restrains the pursuit of its own claims to do justice to the other, it does violence to itself. More particularly, when justice according to law derives from the self's conception of the good, it does violence to the other in at least two different ways. First, implantation of norms of justice that contravene the other's conception of the good amounts to violence against the other's integrity and an assault against the latter's freedom inasmuch as it denigrates the other's innermost normative convictions in the name of justice. Second, even assuming consensus on a particular conception of the good, justice according to law requires legal interpretation, which, unlike other kinds of interpretation such as literary interpretation, is inevitably linked to violence. As Robert Cover has aptly noted,

> Legal interpretive acts signal and occasion the imposition of violence upon others: A judge articulates her understanding of a text, and as a result, somebody loses his freedom, his property, his children, even his life. Interpretations in law also constitute justifications for violence which has already occurred or which is about to occur. When interpreters have finished their work, they frequently leave behind victims whose lives have been torn apart by these organized, social practices of violence. Neither legal interpretation nor the violence it occasions may be properly understood apart from one another. (1995, 203)

Consistent with this, moreover, even in the imaginary realm of perfect justice where comprehensive justice becomes possible, justice would still be linked to violence, albeit justified violence. In our own world, however, given the impossibility of accounting for the irreducible singularity of each human being, not even consensus over a universally shared conception of the good could rid justice of all unjustified violence.

It would be not only dangerous but also plainly erroneous to infer that it necessarily follows from belief in the impossibility of achieving justice, and in the inevitability of the link between violence and the pursuit of justice, that the quest for justice is meaningless, or that all plausible dispositions of the conflicting claims of self and other are likely to be normatively equivalent. Indeed, at least in the context of commitment to the ontology of infinite postponement of the complete reconciliation of self and other and to the ethics of inclusion and care discussed in chapter I, the quest for justice is a permanent ethical imperative. Moreover, notwithstanding that comprehensive justice is impossible, some injustices seem far more objectionable than others. As already hinted above, a law bent on ruthlessly denigrating the other's conception of the good would clearly be much more reprehensible than a law genuinely intended to accommodate the other's concerns but which nonetheless falls short because of its unavoidable failure to fully account for the other's singularity. Accordingly, a law that institutionalized religious intolerance would clearly be vastly more unjust than a law that intended to provide equal accommodation to all religions but that fell short because some of the objectives of certain religions happen to be in direct conflict with those of others.

Similarly, just as not all injustices stand on the same footing, not all violence necessarily linked to justice is equally reprehensible. Thus, the violence emanating from implementation of a law squarely bent on assaulting the other's conception of the good clearly ranks as more despicable than the violence associated with application of a criminal law against someone who can be fairly deemed to have freely consented to its enactment. Moreover, even if justice according to law prescribes the *same* violence in two different types of cases, one of these may be much more objectionable than the other. For example, imposing the same long prison sentence for failure to convert to the state's official religion and for treason by a naturalized citizen who freely chose to apply for citizenship, seems much more objectionable in the first case than in the second. And this remains true regardless of whether one deems the punishment in the second case to be fair or disproportionate. Assuming one acknowledges that punishing treason is legitimate, at most the long prison case meted out in the second case is disproportionate. In contrast, the punishment in the first case is altogether reprehensible and the violence it involves wholly unjustifiable.[8]

Consistent with the preceding observations, neither the impossibility of justice nor its inextricable link to violence detracts from the imperative necessity of its pursuit. The key question, however, is whether such pursuit can be made meaningful in light of the seeming impossibility of overcoming the oppositions between the universal and the singular, the abstract and the concrete, and the legal rule and its exception. In other words, admitting that some injustices seem patently more offensive than others and that not all violence emanating from law strikes us as equally reprehensible, how can we expect to discover any principled way to rank laws and to endorse

8. It is logically plausible to take the position that no institutionalized violence toward any other is ever even partly justifiable. Such a position, however, would equally delegitimize all law and render just interpretations completely superfluous. In addition, any principled proponent of this view would be forced to admit that a law commanding the punishment of those responsible for a genocide could not be justified any more than a law commanding that a genocide be carried out. For this reason, simply refusing to legitimize any law due to its inextricable link to violence would lead to most unfortunate consequences.

legal interpretations according to their relative justice—or, relative degree of injustice—while, at the same time, continuing to maintain that justice itself is impossible? As we shall see below, the impossibility of justice emerging as the culmination of the deconstruction of the concept of justice according to law can be harnessed to provide a critical vantage point for a reconstruction allowing for cogent evaluation of conflicting claims to partial justice notwithstanding the ultimate impossibility of justice.

II. RECONSTRUCTING THE LINKS BETWEEN THE FORMS AND DOMAINS OF JUSTICE IN LIGHT OF ITS IMPOSSIBILITY

Set against the impossibility of justice, reconstruction becomes necessary to carve out a path toward just interpretations consistent with a genuine commitment to the pursuit of justice. Moreover, the best that one can hope for under these circumstances is that reconstruction point to meaningful alternatives in light of the ongoing, and ultimately impossible to overcome, clash between the demands of comprehensive justice and the inevitability of incomplete and hence imperfect justice. The objective of reconstruction is to identify ways in which the gap between comprehensive justice and incomplete justice might be narrowed. Paradoxically, however, meaningful reconstruction requires both accentuating the comprehensive potential of justice—by linking together the different *forms* of justice—and stressing its inherent incompleteness—by separating the various *domains* of justice from one another as much as possible.

A. Linking the Forms of Justice:
On the Nexus between Distributive, Corrective, and Procedural Justice

As pointed out in chapter II, in the course of the discussion of Ernest Weinrib's formalism, the forms of justice, and in particular distributive and corrective justice, cannot be successfully severed altogether from one another. Consistent with that conclusion, and with the realization that justice is impossible but that some injustices are far more objectionable than others, I argue in this section that optimal reconstruction requires that the various forms of justice be linked together and be made as consistent with one another as possible. Approaching questions of justice from the standpoint of comprehensive justice offers several advantages over the alternative based on treating the different forms of justice as if they were essentially detached from one another. First, from the standpoint of comprehensive justice it becomes much easier to realize that conflicts between conceptions of justice are much more likely to stem from clashes between underlying conceptions of the good than from discontinuities among the various forms of justice. In other words, by embracing the viewpoint of comprehensive justice, it becomes much less likely that substantive differences, clashing value preferences, and ideological biases will become concealed behind the purely formal battles for divisions of territory among distinct forms of justice.[9]

Second, rigid separation between the various forms of justice needlessly causes many situations to fall between the cracks, thus arbitrarily restricting the range of principled dispositions of claims to justice. For example, in the paradigmatic case of corrective justice, the wrongdoer's gain is equivalent to the victim's loss, with the consequence that justice can be achieved through transfer of the wrongdoer's gain to the victim. But what if the wrongdoer's gain exceeds the victim's loss? Or if the latter's loss exceeds the wrongdoer's gain? In the context of strict separation between the forms of justice, implementation of corrective justice would leave a wrongdoer with any gain in excess of his victim's loss and saddle a victim with absorption of any loss that exceeds her victimizer's gain. From the standpoint of comprehensive justice, in contrast, those undeserved excesses could be avoided. For example, a wrongdoer's excess gain could be recovered consistent with prevailing standards of retributive justice, and a victim's excess loss could be wiped out through application of relevant norms of distributive justice. In short, greater justice could be achieved through reliance on the convergence between distributive, corrective, and retributive justice than through erection of formalistic boundaries between them.

Third, comprehensive justice is much better suited than the forms of justice taken separately to deal with the fact that—even leaving aside that it will always remain imperfect and incomplete—justice can only be achieved in a piecemeal way. This is perhaps best exemplified by reference to the case-by-case approach typical of the common law, which was discussed in chapter I. As will be remembered from the cases involving respectively a landowner's cow and a landowner's cat causing harm to a neighbor's land, under the common law, the justice of any present adjudication is dependent on future adjudications, and the ultimate justification of any adjudication must await the advent of the last adjudication for all time. Against this background, comprehensive justice can serve both as a reminder of the piecemeal nature of every adjudication and as a counterfactual suited for use as a critical tool of reconstruction.[10] Indeed, counterfactuals placed within the broader sweep of comprehensive justice can afford a useful critical perspective on instances of adjudication and convey a sense of the direction that

---

9. With respect to formalism's predisposition to conceal ideological biases, see the discussion of Weinrib's conception of corrective justice, chapter II, above.

10. Reconstructive theory establishes analytically useful models through supplementation of empirical data with counterfactuals. For a more extensive discussion of counterfactuals, see chapter V, below.

piecemeal adjudication ought to take to generate *relatively* greater justice or lesser injustice.

Although it may be easier to grasp in the case of the common law, the piecemeal nature of adjudications pursuant to justice according to law extends to other systems of adjudication prevalent in contemporary constitutional democracies. This follows from the fact that the pursuit of justice in any complex pluralistic setting can only focus, at any given time, in limited ways on a handful among the vast array of similarities and differences coming into play in the course of interaction between self and other. For example, in a polity where differences between the sexes have been exploited to relegate women to an inferior status, the pursuit of gender-based equality would have to focus on identity at the expense of difference and on abstract equality rather than on a more complex equality suited to take differences into account without transforming them into badges of inferiority. In other words, where gender-based differences have been pervasively implanted as marks for casting women as inferiors, difference must be uncoupled from inferiority to pave the way to the kind of equality that properly accounts for relevant differences. Such uncoupling, however, is unlikely to take place unless the image of women-as-different-and-hence-inferior is first neutralized through promotion of the counterimage of women-as-similar-and-hence-equal. Thus, abstract equality-as-identity—albeit partial and incomplete—looms as a necessary first state in the progression toward a more nuanced and more encompassing equality-as (accounting fairly for)-difference.[11]

As already pointed out in chapter II, a unified system of justice is better suited than a fragmented one to promote justice with integrity. Accordingly, not only logics but also normative concerns call for binding distributive, corrective, and procedural justice together under the aegis of comprehensive justice. This does not mean, of course, that in actual practice corrective and distributive justice cannot be kept to a large extent separate. Indeed, even conceding that both corrective and distributive justice require commitment to contestable substantive norms, one may still opt to appeal to mutually inconsistent norms depending on whether one is dealing with corrective or distributive issues. For example, it is possible to embrace a utilitarian criterion of distributive justice and at the same time maintain that theft is a compensable wrong regardless of the utilitarian consequences of such compensations. In that case a libertarian conception of the good informs corrective justice while a utilitarian conception is reserved for dis-

---

11. The conflict between equality-as-identity and equality-as-difference and its interpretative ramifications is well illustrated by the debate over affirmative action. See, e.g., art. 3 of the German Basic Law and its 1994 amendment.

tributive justice. As against such actual practices, however, comprehensive justice subsumes all the forms of justice under a single conception of the good, for example, utilitarian or libertarian, thus yielding a counterfactual. This counterfactual, in turn, affords a coherent critical standpoint making for a principled determination of the shortcomings of any actual attempt to achieve justice while, at the same time, pointing to available paths toward greater—if ever imperfect—justice.

Recourse to comprehensive justice also serves to underscore the limits to the permeability of the various forms of justice. This can be illustrated by focusing on the conflict between corrective and distributive justice in cases in which they are both encompassed within the same conception of the good. For example, suppose that distributive justice requires allocating scarce jobs to the most qualified candidates. Consistent with this distributive principle, corrective justice requires compensating someone who was refused a job for which he or she had proved to be the most qualified candidate. Suppose further that the adequate measure of compensation, under these circumstances, is to provide the victim with the wrongfully denied job or some equivalent job. And, finally, assume that in the overwhelming majority of cases, the most qualified candidates who secure highly competitive jobs are not terminated by their employers for lack of adequate performance on the job.

With this in mind, consider the following scenario. A proves to be the most qualified candidate for job J in year one, but the employer awards J to B, who is clearly less qualified than A. B quits after a year on the job, so that a new competition is held for J in year two. A competes again in year two but loses out to C. Now C is clearly entitled, under the applicable principle of distributive justice, to J in year two, but A is equally entitled to J at that time, under the applicable principle of corrective justice. Since only one person can be awarded J, then (assuming that the employer in question has no other job equivalent to J to offer) either corrective or distributive justice may be satisfied but not both. Furthermore, this example clearly indicates that compensations have distributive effects.

Whether A or C should get J in year two cannot be decided within the ambit of either distributive or corrective justice. This could be decided, however, within the broader perspective of comprehensive justice. For instance, Alan Goldman has argued that in cases similar to the one discussed above, compensation should be given priority over conflicting distributive imperatives, for otherwise valid distributive norms could be consistently violated with impunity (1979, 65–67). Even if all such conflicts between corrective and distributive justice could be satisfactorily resolved under the aegis of comprehensive justice, however, complete justice would still be impossible to achieve. Also, no matter how much more flexible the boundaries between them may become when gauged from the broad perspective of comprehensive justice, corrective and distributive justice would still at bottom remain two distinct and irreducible forms of justice.

Although, as discussed in chapter II, corrective justice is essentially backward looking and distributive justice forward looking, neither is exclusively oriented in one direction. Corrective justice must not only be projected into the past, from the time of compensation to the time of the wrong, but must also complete the same journey in the opposite direction. Indeed, corrective justice must travel from the date of the wrong in the direction of the future, to construct what might have been but for the wrong—an operation that is crucial for purposes of establishing the proper measure of compensation. Whereas, strictly speaking, the work of corrective justice ends at the time of actual compensation, the consequences of its construction of what might have been may well extend further into the future. Thus, in constructing the counterfactual establishing the measure of compensation, corrective justice must avoid the excesses of undercompensation and overcompensation, to prevent adverse retributive or distributive consequences subsequent to compensation.

On the other hand, while distributive justice focuses on future distributions, it must sometimes account for past distributions, or look backward into the past in the course of fashioning apt vehicles for just distributions. For example, John Rawls argues for fair equality of opportunity in the context of the principles of distributive justice that he advocates (1971, 83–89). According to Rawls, fair equality of opportunity requires that "those with similar abilities and skills should have similar life chances . . . irrespective of the income class to which they are born" (ibid., 73). Consistent with this, implementing fair equality of opportunity requires looking to past income discrepancies, so as to be able to devise measures—such as remedial education—designed to eradicate those advantages in the competition for scarce employment positions that are attributable to past disparities in wealth. In other words, discrepancies in income are not "wrongs," but their effect on the competition for scarce benefits must be counted much as the consequences of wrongs under corrective justice. Thus, although for different reasons, distributive justice must on occasion look to the past just as corrective justice is bound to do.

The complex web that intertwines corrective and distributive justice while leaving each of them irreducible at its core also extends to other forms of justice, such as restitutive, retributive, and procedural justice. These latter forms can also complement and mutually reinforce one another, as well as corrective and distributive justice, and yet each of them is bound to remain irreducible at its core. For example, restitutive justice may overlap significantly with corrective justice and with distributive justice as evinced by cases in which restitution achieves the proper measure of compensation while leading to greater efficiency. In other cases, however, restitution may fall short of full compensation and foster distributively undesirable consequences. Thus, returning a factory after a long period to the victim of a wrongful expropriation may be inadequate compensation for the latter's total loss as a consequence of the wrong, and may at the same time be distributively unwarranted if the victim is no longer in a position to run the factory profitably.[12]

Procedural justice is an indispensable component of justice—and of justice according to law in particular—for justice cannot be achieved in the absence of just procedures. For instance, assuming a consensus that theft ought to be punished under retributive justice, if criminal trials for theft resulted more often than not in conviction of the innocent, such trials would clearly promote injustice rather than advance the cause of comprehensive justice. Following Rawls, one can divide procedural justice into two basic types. The first type requires both an independent criterion of distributive, corrective, restitutive, or retributive justice to determine what would count as a just outcome and a procedure designed to lead to such a just outcome. The second type, on the other hand, which leads to what Rawls calls "pure procedural justice," does not require for its operation any reference to an independent criterion of substantive justice. Instead, as Rawls sees it, in the context of pure procedural justice, any outcome is just, provided only that a fair procedure was followed (ibid., 85–87).

Rawls draws a further distinction within the first type of procedural justice between "perfect" and "imperfect" procedural justice (ibid., 85). If the procedure adopted to pursue the outcome prescribed by the relevant criterion of substantive justice assures that outcome, then we have perfect procedural justice; if it does not, then we have imperfect procedural justice. Moreover, justice according to law almost inevitably goes hand in hand with imperfect procedural justice. Indeed, both the civil and the criminal trial, indispensable tools of any modern scheme based on justice according to law, are prime examples of imperfect procedural justice.[13]

Two important consequences follow from the inevitable dependence of justice according to law on imperfect procedural justice. First, even if justice according to law were in perfect harmony with universally embraced norms of justice beyond law, it could not guarantee just outcomes. In other words, the need to rely on imperfect procedural justice is sufficient to make complete justice impossible. Second, the very concept of imperfect procedural

---

12. For a more extended discussion of retribution and restitution in the context of recent transitions in East Central Europe, see Rosenfeld 1996.

13. Significantly, Rawls chooses the criminal trial under the adversary system of justice prevalent in the United States to exemplify what he means by imperfect procedural justice. See Rawls 1971, 85.

justice runs counter to any notion that justice may boil down to an all or nothing proposition. Accordingly, so long as justice according to law cannot rely on pure procedural justice,[14] it cannot avoid depending on a ranking of various procedures according to their relative degree of imperfection.

In sum, linking the various forms of justice within a comprehensive perspective underscores the ways in which justice is impossible and yet necessary to pursue. It also facilitates the kind of counterfactual reconstruction that is needed to shed light on possible paths toward greater perfection while keeping firmly in mind that justice—or at least justice according to law—is condemned to remain forever imperfect.

B. Uncoupling the Domains of Justice:
On the Differences Between Ethical, Legal, and Political Justice

Comprehensive justice may appear to go hand in hand with unifying the various domains of justice. Moreover, the case for unification may seem all the more compelling in light of the rejection in chapter II of the new formalists' claim that law can be severed from ethics and politics. Nevertheless, in the context of a pluralist polity, separating the domains of justice becomes a necessary step in the reconstruction of justice consistent with the imperatives of comprehensive justice. To be sure, since ethics and politics spill over into law, separating the domains of justice cannot consist in purging each of them from all influence coming from any of the other domains. Instead, the aim sought in separating the various domains of justice is to account for all the relevant material but to recast such material in terms of the unique perspective projected from within the particular domain of justice sought to be differentiated from the others. Thus, whereas ethics and politics figure in shaping law, differentiation through projection of a distinct legal perspective would make it possible to cast a different light on materials from ethics and politics which contribute to shaping the law.

In a polity characterized by consensus on a single conception of the good, justice according to law and justice beyond law should combine into a unified continuum largely devoid of conflict or tension. Even in such a setting, the various domains of justice would have to remain somewhat differentiated, but there would be no need to conceive these domains as separate. Indeed, even in the face of a unanimously endorsed conception of the good, considerations of procedural justice would counsel against transforming every ethical duty into a legal obligation. Beyond that, however, there would be little point in insisting on separating the various domains of jus-

14. The question of whether pure procedural justice may offer a workable solution to the problems raised by justice beyond law in a pluralistic contemporary constitutional democracy will be addressed in chapter V, below.

tice as ethical, legal, and political objectives would presumably be mutually consistent and mutually reinforcing.

A pluralist society, in contrast, stands to benefit from separation of the domains of justice. Inasmuch as justice according to law and justice beyond law clash, it seems clearly advantageous to separate law from ethics and politics. Under such circumstances, adoption of a distinctly legal perspective would ideally serve to legitimate law consistent with—or at least in spite of—prevailing clashes among competing conceptions of the good. In other words, in the best of cases, adoption of an appropriate legal perspective would neutralize or minimize conflicts embedded respectively within the domains of ethics and politics. And as a consequence, justice according to law could lead to sufficient cohesiveness to ensure a fair and productive common existence notwithstanding ongoing conflicts in the realms of ethics and politics. With that in mind, and to be in a better position to propose a cogent reconstruction from a distinct perspective circumscribed by justice according to law, it is first necessary to briefly sketch some salient differences between law and ethics, on the one hand, and law and politics, on the other.

i) Differentiating Law from Ethics.   Although a thorough account of the relationship between law and ethics is beyond the scope of this book, it suffices, for present purposes, to address a few key aspects of that relationship from the standpoint of the pursuit of means oriented toward bridging the gap between the self and the other. Consistent with the preceding discussion, both law and ethics should be understood as sharing the common purpose of bridging the gap between self and other, by establishing mutually fair and mutually acceptable links between them. From this perspective, moreover, the principal difference between law and ethics is that ethics seeks to frame and promote *internal* links between self and other, whereas law concentrates on *external* links between them.

Broadly speaking, internal links are those forged through self-constraint, whereas external links are those that are ultimately guaranteed by the threat of sanctions. To be sure, ethical duties and legal ones may overlap, and the threat of sanctions would not preclude adherence to law out of self-constraint rather than out of fear of sanctions.[15] Nonetheless, the distinction between self-constraint and external constraints provides a convenient means to differentiate the realm of ethics from that of law without taking a position on the substantive issues bound to arise in any attempt to map out a legitimate division of labor between ethics and law for any particular society.

The other's irreducible singularity makes it impossible to erase the

15. For a similar view, see Hart 1961, 197.

boundary between self and other, thus ensuring that the other will in some sense always remain "external" to the self. Because of this, the internal links fostered by ethics should be understood, strictly speaking, as attempts to overcome the divide between self and other by projecting plausible yet impossible images of reconciliation. Viewed as an ongoing dialectical process not susceptible of final resolution, ethics demands that the self reach out to the other as if the other were *within* the self while, at the same time, making a creative effort to imagine the *self* within the other. On the other hand, in a constitutional democracy established on the principle that all persons are inherently equal, law requires that each self recognize and treat every other as also being a self. But, in contrast to ethics, law does not call for the self to reach out and attempt to internalize the other. In other words, law demands that the self recognize that the other is a self with a point of view but does not command that the self make efforts to imagine how he or she could be transformed on adopting the other's point of view.[16] Accordingly, legal relationships seek to forge external links in the sense of prescribing that the other should be treated *as if he or she were a self* without imposing any duty to reach to the *actual self within the other.*[17]

The contrast between the internal cohesion of a community unified through the shared values emanating from the same conception of the good and the merely external dealings of strangers whose only common purpose is to preserve the integrity of the market where they come to trade with one another provides an apt metaphor for the divide between law and ethics. Furthermore, if disputes between strangers could be legitimately resolved without resorting to communal values endorsed by only some of those involved, justice according to law could achieve normative validity without reference to justice according to ethics. In pluralist societies replete with clashes among competing communal values, however, it is unlikely that resolutions of conflicts between strangers could rise above the contest between conceptions of the good. Under such circumstances, justice according to law would undoubtedly loom as unjust when viewed from the wider expanse spreading across the various domains of justice. Moreover, this

---

16. I shall further explore this distinction in Part Three, below. For an extended discussion of the differences between recognition of the other as a self or "mere reciprocity" and empathy for the other's point of view or "reversible reciprocity," see Rosenfeld 1991a, 247–49.

17. It may be objected that, at least in some cases, such as where the insanity defense is properly raised in a murder trial, law evinces a concern for the actual self within the other. Strictly speaking, however, and to the extent that the perspective of law as a practice can be differentiated from that of ethics, the insanity defense should be construed as raising the question of whether the accused possessed the requisite capacities to be treated as a responsible self rather than as inviting an inquiry into the beliefs, values, and objectives of the accused in order to shed light on the latter's point of view.

would lead to an impasse unless it were possible to reconstruct the requisite internal links between self and other somewhere beyond the clash among conceptions of the good, or unless the communal norms relied on to reach justice according to law could be effectively severed from their roots in the domain of ethics.

Resort to Kantian morals affords a means to reconstruct internal links between self and other beyond the clashes among competing conceptions of the good. Following the distinction between morality *(Moralität)* and ethics *(Sittlichkeit)* steeped in Kantian and Hegelian philosophy, one may envision "morals" as encompassing universally applicable norms of justice and universally valid rights and duties that transcend all different conceptions of the good. "Ethics," on the other hand, refers, under this conception, to the mores, prudential maxims, and normative standards of a historically grounded community with its own conception of the good.[18] Consistent with this distinction, moreover, since morals offers a universal perspective rising above all parochial clashes, a moral justification of law would pave a way for the reconciliation between justice according to law and justice beyond law in a pluralist society.

As observed in the course of the discussion of Weinrib's neoformalism, however, prospects for neutral Kantian constraints in a pluralist polity seem rather dim.[19] Indeed, whereas the bonds forged through internalization of the same communal mores may be both substantive and strong, the internal links deriving from Kantian morals are likely to be purely formal.[20] In other words, unlike ethics, which supplies the common currency for reciprocal internalization between self and other, Kantian morals must approach the other at such a high level of abstraction (to rise above ethical parochialism) that it largely obliterates all the differences that set the self apart from the other. Accordingly, in the rarified atmosphere of Kantian morals, the self internalizes an other who has lost all traces of individuality. Or, in what amounts to the same thing, the Kantian self must shed his or her own individuality to become linked internally with others similarly purged of individuality in a realm of ends ruled by universal duties. To the extent that Kantian morals reduces self and other to equivalent, and hence interchangeable, abstract egos, it ultimately promotes solipsistic self-constraint.

Strict adherence to Kantian morals, far from normatively buttressing jus-

---

18. Although these respective definitions run somewhat counter to the common understanding of "morals" and "ethics" in English, I adopt them for the sake of clarity as they are consistent with the views of theorists discussed in this book, and in particular with those of Jürgen Habermas, which are examined in chapter V, below. See McCarthy 1990, vii.

19. See chapter II, above.

20. See Hegel's criticism of Kantian morals as formal and empty (Hegel 1952, ¶¶135, 135A).

tice according to law, actually tends to delegitimize it,[21] as the pursuit of external links contradicts rather than complements principled deployment of the categorical imperative. In short, Kantian morals are ultimately so formal and so rigid as to appear otherworldly, and hence largely empty.

Rejection of Kantian morals as ill-suited to the needs of contemporary pluralist society, however, does not necessarily require abandoning all hope of establishing harmony between law and any plausible conception of universalistic morality. Indeed, contemporary theorists, such as Rawls (1971) and Habermas, have set out to recast the Kantian project in terms that are better suited to contemporary concerns. Habermas, in particular, has transformed the Kantian project by replacing Kant's solipsistic monological approach with an intersubjective and dialogical one based on discourse theory.[22] Accordingly, it is conceivable that justice according to law and justice beyond law may be reconciled through morals. Discussion of this possibility, however, is best postponed and addressed in connection with the evaluation of Habermas's discourse theory of law in chapter V.

Leaving morals aside, as already suggested, in a pluralist society, justice according to law could overcome the clash among competing conceptions of the good by neutralizing contested communal norms embedded in law. This might be accomplished by reconstructing the relevant normative universe as comprising a sharp divide differentiating law from ethics. This sharp divide, moreover, would not operate through a splitting of norms according to content. Instead, it would distinguish norms according to the level of commitment and internalization that they call for. Thus, legal norms would require no internalization comparable to that demanded by ethical norms, and no commitment to the communal values embedded in law comparable to that required toward the very same values assuming they inhered in accepted ethical norms.

To illustrate how law might be used to neutralize the grip of contested communal norms, imagine a polity composed of two distinct religious communities. Imagine further that the first of the two religions involved adheres to the belief that Wednesday has been divinely selected as a day of mandatory rest from work. The second religion prescribes rest on Thursday and forbids adopting the mores of other religions, such that if an adherent to the second religion chooses to treat Wednesday as a day of rest, he or she would be betraying a firmly entrenched religious obligation. Now, inasmuch as the second religion's prohibition is against *voluntarily* embracing a religious command issued from another religion, a secular law decreeing

---

21. It is noteworthy in this connection that Kant himself places pragmatism ahead of morals when it comes to evaluating law (Kant 1970, 118–19).

22. For a succinct discussion of the main differences between the respective approaches to morals of Kant and Habermas, see Habermas 1990, 195, 203–4.

Wednesday as the state's official day of rest, based solely on the fact that a majority within the polity prefers Wednesday as the legally prescribed day of rest, may well be acceptable to the followers of the second religion. Indeed the relevant prohibition being against *embracing* and *internalizing* the prescriptions of another religion, making Wednesday a day of rest in order to avoid facing legal sanctions should not compromise any religious belief or obligation. In this case, therefore, making rest on Wednesday an *externally* imposed legal obligation rather than an *internally* self-imposed religious or ethical obligation can make the difference between a religiously acceptable and a religiously forbidden course of conduct.[23]

Even under the best of circumstances, recasting law so as to accentuate its contrasts to ethics will not always result in a successful neutralization of objectionable common norms. For example, in a country where the precepts of fundamentalist religion have been enacted into law, it would be little consolation to an opponent of such religion that it is not necessary to embrace objectionable religious precepts within one's heart to comply with one's legal obligations. In the latter case, the distance between internal acquiescence and external submission remains too close for comfort. In short, in some cases, the distance between law and ethics might be pushed far enough to allow for sufficient neutralization of the thrust of ethics to emerge from under the clash between competing communal norms. The crucial question, therefore, is whether the number of cases in which an adequate distance between law and ethics can be successfully achieved is large enough to meet the needs of a pluralist constitutional democracy. For the moment, however, this question must remain open, as much of the discussion in Part Two of the book bears on it. I shall return to it in Part Three.

As already mentioned, even in a homogeneous society with a commonly shared conception of the good, procedural considerations would preclude a complete overlap between ethics and law. For example, suppose there is a consensus that distributive justice requires allocation of socially produced goods in proportion to each person's subjectively felt needs. This would justify adherence to an ethical duty against staking a claim to scarce goods one does not feel a genuine need for. However, this would not similarly justify imposing the same duty as a legal obligation, as securing compliance would be difficult or unpalatable—for example, the use of a lie detector test might afford the only available reliable means to weed out illegitimate claims. Conversely, compliance with legal norms for ethical reasons does not obliterate the boundary between ethics and law. Thus, the fact that a

---

23. This would not follow, of course, if the second religion commanded that Wednesday be a day of work, or if its adherents believed that resting on Wednesday would be tantamount to capitulating to the prescriptions of the first religion.

person observes a law against murder out of an ethical conviction that murder is wrong does not imply that the legal obligation collapses into the ethical duty. Indeed, the fact that from the perspective of law, all intersubjective relationships are recast as external ones does not preclude the concurrent deployment of internal relationships or motivations. Finally, whereas some laws, such as laws against murder, display an inherent ethical content, others, such as those that prescribe driving on the right side of the road, do not. In spite of this fact, however, from the perspective of ethics, both kinds of law can be construed as rooted in ethical considerations. Thus, since consistent adherence to uniform traffic regulations saves lives, it goes hand in hand, from the standpoint of ethics, with internalization of prescriptions against murder in advancing the ethical objective of valuing and preserving human life.

In sum, focus on the differences between ethical and legal perspectives opens up the promising possibility that justice according to law may be sufficiently severable from justice according to ethics to allow for just interpretations notwithstanding the ongoing conflict between competing conceptions of the good. It remains to be seen, however, whether, and in what ways, this promise may be fulfilled.

ii) Differentiating Law from Politics. It is more difficult to set law apart from politics than from ethics, because politics like law presides over external relationships among intersubjectively engaged actors in pursuit of self-interest. As a matter of fact, democratic lawmaking falls squarely within the domain of politics. Consistent with this, moreover, politics frequently achieves its optimal expression in laws, and conversely laws—or at least legislatively generated laws—owe both their existence and formulation to politics.[24] In short, politics engenders law, which means that for law to achieve any independence from politics, it must succeed in escaping from the fetters of the lawmaker.

Just as it was the case in relation to ethics, the difference between law

---

24. To the extent that lawmaking under the common law is a function of the adjudicative process, arguably it is less fettered by politics than its legislatively generated counterpart. On closer scrutiny, however, common law adjudication involves both a backward-oriented adjudicatory moment and a forward-looking lawmaking one. The adjudicative moment is circumscribed by the judge's backward glance toward the past events that gave rise to the dispute that brought the parties presently before the judge. The lawmaking moment, on the other hand, occurs when the common law judge picks among plausible alternative resolutions of the dispute before the court in terms of projected future consequences, or, in other words, when the judge's present decision is affected by a consideration of its likely future precedential influence. Accordingly, inasmuch as future-looking considerations bear on common law adjudication, the latter can be viewed as a product of politics in the same way that legislatively generated law can.

and politics is not likely to be one of content but rather one of perspective. This may be more difficult to appreciate in the case of politics than in that of ethics, because politics permeates not only lawmaking but often also the subsequent uses and applications of law. For example, in some sense prosecutorial discretion inevitably carries with it a political component. Indeed, in face of the impossibility of prosecuting all those who are believed to have violated a criminal law, a prosecutor must decide which cases to pursue, and that inevitably calls for the exercise of political judgment.[25] However, not all uses of politics associated with the exercise of prosecutorial discretion stand on the same footing. Thus, selective prosecution of users of illegal drugs in the face of massive consumption with a view to maximize the law's deterrent effects clearly involves politics of a different kind than selective prosecution confined to the political enemies of those who are currently in power. Although both cases involve politics, in the first case, politics appears to play but a subordinate role, whereas, in the second case, law is seemingly reduced to a mere tool of politics.

To better grasp how the perspective of law might differ from that of politics and how the political elements within law might be recast from within the domain of justice according to law, it is first necessary to take a somewhat closer look at the domain of politics. Because the term "politics" is an essentially contested one (Connolly 1983, 20), any attempt at a comprehensive definition is at best hazardous. For present purposes, however, suffice it to take a broad view of politics as encompassing setting objectives for the polity and devising means designed to further such objectives. Moreover, to distinguish politics from ethics, it must be added that from the perspective of politics, the polity appears as the locus of external intersubjective dealings between citizens rather than as the locus of expression for the internally appropriated intersubjectively shared common norms of an ethical community.

Although politics always revolves around setting objectives for the polity and fashioning means to attain them, a distinction must be drawn between the *integrated* politics of a normatively cohesive community and the *fragmented* politics of a deeply divided society. In line with that distinction, polities can be ranked according to their relative degree of political integration, along a spectrum that extends from the ideal of total integration to the danger of complete fragmentation. In the optimal case of fully integrated politics, law, ethics, and politics are fully harmonized under the aegis of a

25. Even a seemingly neutral device, such as picking cases for prosecution on the basis of a lottery, involves a political decision. If this is not immediately apparent, consider the choice of the lottery in terms of criticisms to the effect that selection on the basis of the seriousness of the offense or of the notoriety of the offender would constitute a much better use of limited prosecutorial resources.

single conception of the good unanimously embraced throughout the polity. In that case, moreover, politics is shaped through the concerted efforts of a united citizenry committed to fulfilling the best interests of the republic. Accordingly, politics and law combine to provide an external dimension to the very communal norms internalized through ethics. In this setting, ethical, political, and legal justice cohere into a continuous and harmonious whole. Finally, since law and politics complement one another in the commonly shared task of delimiting external relationships in accordance with a single uncontested conception of the good, the division of labor among them amounts essentially to a matter of convenience.

In contrast, at the other end of the spectrum is the nightmare of complete fragmentation, where every individual is pitted against every other individual in a war of all against all. In that scenario, the exclusive aim of politics is survival by any available means, including lawless violence, deceit, and betrayal. Moreover, since, in the context of complete fragmentation, there is no reason for engaging in intersubjective relationships other than to better position oneself to secure individual survival, politics is purely instrumental and hence stands for the opposite of ethics rather than as the other side of the same coin. Finally, in the face of complete fragmentation, there can be no genuine place for law. Indeed, complete fragmentation implies that every individual is a law unto himself or herself, and hence any semblance of law would be but a mask designed to conceal the relentless political struggle for power. Under such conditions, therefore, all law would be completely subservient to politics.

A functioning pluralist constitutional democracy would have to fall somewhere between the above described extremes. Its politics would be neither those of total communal harmony nor those of mere survival. Instead, its politics would consist of a mix of survival and coexistence, of pursuing self-interest against the interests of others, and of harmonizing self-interest with intersubjectively shared common interests. Moreover, whereas in a fully integrated polity, justice would fully emanate from communal norms, and, in a completely fragmented society, there would be altogether no room for institutionalized justice, in a pluralist constitutional democracy politics and law could potentially play a key role in shaping and institutionalizing justice. In particular, in such a democracy, politics and law could promote fairness in the ongoing competition among self-interested actors and work toward a fair reconciliation of self-interest with common interests.

The actual division of labor between politics and law in a partially integrated and partially fragmented pluralist constitutional democracy may be grounded in either of two distinct approaches. Each of these approaches seeks to negotiate the difficult task of promoting the best possible mix of integration and fragmentation for the particular pluralist polity involved. The first of these approaches seeks to constrain fragmentation deriving from conflict and competition, by delimiting a legitimate field of competition and by restricting the means of competition through the deployment of rules of engagement. In other words, the first approach seeks to promote an adequate equilibrium between integration and fragmentation, by channeling competition within the confines of a suitably defined game and by leaving it to law to establish and monitor the requisite rules of the game.

The second approach, on the other hand, relies on thematic rather than structural distinctions. At any given point in the history of a partially integrated polity certain matters are likely to be more settled, or less up for grabs, than others. Consistent with this, it seems reasonable to buttress integration by subjecting relatively settled matters to legal regulation while leaving potentially more divisive or more volatile matters to the day-to-day give-and-take of politics. Conversely, to prevent further undue fragmentation, it may make sense to take certain particularly explosive issues temporarily off the table, by subjecting them to legal regulation. Such regulation may please no one but may nonetheless succeed in partially and temporarily depoliticizing certain inherently divisive issues as all sides to the relevant issue feel they have more to lose than to gain from repeal of existing legal regulation.[26] In short, as no polity can afford constant relentless controversy on all potentially divisive issues, it seems wise to keep a temporary lid on certain issues, and the division of labor between politics and law can be productively garnered for that purpose.[27]

Even if one is prepared to accept the above division of labor between politics and law in principle, one may wonder whether it is possible to find a cogent and principled way to separate law from politics in practice. Indeed, not only do law and politics both deal with external relationships, as already indicated, law cannot be purged of all political influence. Moreover, the intertwining of law and politics cannot be avoided by confining law to defining and regulating the relevant "games." In some sense, the uses of law for game-constitutive and game-regulative purposes lie beyond politics.

26. See Holmes 1988, 19–58 (discussing advantages of avoiding debate on certain divisive issues for purposes of consolidating constitutional democracy).

27. To the extent that the desirable aim is to *postpone* intense conflict on an issue, the choice between law and politics ultimately depends on the current status of the issue. Thus, in a case of fragmentation along communal lines without much intercommunal discussion, a transition from politics to law would intensify rather than temper debate. For example, by constitutionalizing abortion rights in its 1973 decision in *Roe v. Wade* (1973), the Supreme Court succeeded in shifting the debate on abortion away from the everyday politics surrounding the fifty state legislatures toward the seemingly more stable arena of constitutional jurisprudence. Nevertheless, far from cooling the debate on abortion, constitutionalization actually greatly intensified it, hardened antagonistic positions, and significantly deepened fragmentation. See Holmes 1988, 50–52. This notwithstanding, the fact remains that proper negotiation of the divide between law and politics can lead toward a workable balance between fragmentation and integration.

The rules of chess are thus neutral as between all those who play chess. These rules, however, are not neutral in relation to the respective talents of various chess players. Those who have greater talent for chess are accordingly favored in relation to their less talented counterparts, and if the sole purpose for participation in any game were to satisfy a desire to win, then it would be in each person's interest to choose the game in which he or she is most talented. Similarly, so long as different "games" depending on law for their definition and regulation respectively tend to favor different sets of likely "players," game-constitutive and game-regulative laws could not genuinely escape from the fetters of politics.

Even if law is condemned to remain (in the above sense) political, it can nonetheless sustain a sufficiently distinct perspective to—at least temporarily—fend off the sway of raw unmediated politics. In a nutshell, the difference in perspective between law and politics can be grasped through contextualized reconstruction, and it emerges most clearly through the contrast between justice according to law and political justice. Boiled down to its essentials justice according to law can be genuinely linked through reconstruction to appropriate *legal* norms already in place prior to, and effective at the time of, the occurrence of those events that give rise to the relevant claims for legal relief; political justice, on the other hand, is characterized by its inability to establish sufficient links with such preexisting legal norms.

It may be objected that this difference, though intelligible in theory, is bound to remain quite murky in practice. This seems particularly true, moreover, in the case of the common law with its incremental judicial elaboration of legal norms.[28] Furthermore, in some cases the distinction between justice according to law and political justice may seem altogether untenable, such as, for instance, in the case of retroactive laws, which are permissible in the United States, though confined to civil as opposed to criminal law.[29]

Notwithstanding these difficulties, the above-mentioned distinction between legal and political justice can be cogently maintained, provided it is treated as a contextual rather than a formal distinction. Moreover, the distinction in question seems most sharply drawn in the context of corrective justice. Consistent with rejection of Weinrib's conception of corrective justice as unmediated and hence independent from politics,[30] there is no palpable difference between legal and political corrective justice on a formal or structural plane. They both equally require projection toward the past

28. See the discussion of the process of common law adjudication in footnote 25, above.

29. Art. I, § 9, of the Constitution prohibits retroactive criminal laws. This ban, however, does not extend to civil laws. See, e.g., *Calder v. Bull* (1798).

30. See chapter II, above.

to locate a baseline against which the events giving rise to a claim for compensation must be assessed in order to determine whether they can be legitimately interpreted as adding up to a compensable disruption. Although both setting the baseline and defining the disruption cannot escape depending on politics, one may be tempted to distinguish legal from political corrective justice as follows: Legal justice seems confined to those situations in which the baseline has been set and the relevant class of disruptions identified prior to the time that the actual events prompting a claim for compensation took place. In the case of political justice, on the other hand, either setting the baseline or determining what ought to count as a disruption occurs ex post facto.

On closer inspection, however, the above distinction is unsatisfactory, if for no other reason than that it would relegate most common law incremental adjudication to the realm of political justice. Indeed, consistent with the evolving standards of the common law, both the setting of appropriate baselines and the definition of relevant classes of disruptions are ongoing processes linking together past, present, and future adjudications. Pursuant to that process, the common law judge must reread and rewrite the partial descriptions of baselines and disruptions embedded in precedents, with an eye toward striking a just compensation in the case presently before the court—a task that requires projecting the decision about-to-be-made as an integral part of the chain of precedents linking like past adjudications to future ones, hence obligating the judge to reread past inscriptions concerning baselines and disruptions with an eye to the future. In short, although common law adjudication requires a backward look in search of legitimate baselines and appropriate disruptions, it cannot successfully carry out its task without at least partially determining baselines and disruptions subsequent to the events giving rise to the relevant claim for compensation. Moreover, inasmuch as adjudication of claims based on statutory law involves more than mechanical application of transparent rules, statutory interpretation can be likened to common law adjudication in relation to establishing baselines and disruptions.

In the last analysis, the difference between legal and political justice emerges in the context of reconstruction from the standpoint of comprehensive justice. If such reconstruction can locate legal principles, standards, or rules, which can be interpreted legitimately and cogently as operative at the time of events giving rise to a subsequent demand for relief, and which would support *ex ante* a reasonable expectation concerning the actual disposition of that demand for relief, then we have a case of legal justice. Otherwise, only political justice remains possible. In other words, legal justice depends on the possibility of binding together legal norms and historical events in a principled and coherent narrative web in which relevant pasts, presents, and futures are properly aligned and infused with consistent and intelligible meanings through uninhibited circulation within open semantic paths.[31]

The reasonable expectation capable of being projected onto a past that antedates the event giving rise to a claim for compensation thus emerges as the key element in the distinction between legal and political justice. Such reasonable expectation, however, need not necessarily be gauged in terms of the ultimate outcome of any particular claim but may instead be justified in terms of an identifiable process compatible with such ultimate outcome. For example, particular outcomes may not be predictable in the context of common law adjudication, but knowledge of existing precedents and awareness of the processes and legal culture of a common law jurisdiction may suffice to reasonably anticipate a limited range of plausible outcomes. Similarly, familiarity with the process may even bring, under appropriate circumstances, limited use of retroactive laws within the scope of reasonable expectations of typical legal actors. Finally, from the standpoint of contextual reconstruction and consistent with observations made in the course of the preceding discussion of deconstruction,[32] the distinction between written laws and unwritten legal norms is by no means crucial. Indeed, in terms of shaping reasonable expectations, a well-known unwritten legal standard deeply embedded in the legal culture would certainly loom as a more powerful tool than an obscure written legal rule buried in the midst of a long and complex statutory text. In sum, therefore, from the vantage point of contextual reconstruction, political justice can be distinguished from legal justice as follows. In the case of political justice, it is not possible consistently to channel an unbroken chain of reasonable expectations within the spatiotemporal bounds delimited by appropriate legal norms consistent with comprehensive justice through the use of suitable semantic paths.

To illustrate this last point, it suffices to consider the case of a request for corrective justice in the context of a change in the applicable criterion of distributive justice, as a consequence of a political revolution. Suppose, accordingly, that all preexisting rights to private property were abolished in the aftermath of a socialist revolution but were fully reestablished after the eventual repudiation of socialism. Suppose further that under those circumstances, a private property owner who acquired his rights prior to the socialist revolution, and who had his property confiscated by the state pursuant to law during the socialist era, brings suit in a postsocialist court to obtain compensation for the confiscation of his property. Now, assuming

---

31. On the opening and closing of semantic paths for purposes of punctuation of the free flow of meaning, see the discussion in chapter I, above.

32. See chapter I, above.

that the legally sanctioned private property expropriations under socialism were defensible under the socialist conception of distributive justice informing law at that time, it is difficult to imagine a legitimate argument in support of the claim that the confiscation in question amounted to a legally recognizable "disruption." Similarly, in that situation, it is hard to envision a persuasive legal argument concerning the establishment of a plausible "baseline" in connection with the asserted claim for legal compensation. Indeed, at the time of its occurrence, the relevant confiscation was no more a "disruption" than a loss of business owing to competition would be under the legal regime of a capitalist society. Of course, had the confiscation taken place either prior to or subsequent to the socialist era, it would have qualified as a "disruption." But the actual confiscation cannot be effectively projected back to the presocialist era, or forward to the postsocialist era, due to the revolutionary ruptures that severed relevant legal links that might have otherwise bridged the three distinct eras involved. Moreover, it is also because of the two revolutionary ruptures within the relevant time frame associated with the claim for compensation that no cogent legally defensible "baseline" can be set. On the one hand, no plausible "baseline" can be found within the time frame encompassed by the socialist legal regime. On the other hand, both the presocialist and the postsocialist eras constitute fertile soil for legitimate baselines, but neither of them can offer a suitable "baseline" for the purpose at hand. The presocialist era *did* furnish a "baseline" that was entirely suitable at its inception, but that, at least for present purposes, was "erased" as a consequence of the socialist revolution. The postsocialist era, in contrast, furnishes a perfectly viable "baseline" with no forseeable danger of erasure, but it remains useless for present purposes, as the revolutionary rupture that marked the end of socialism prevents its projection into a past distant enough to encompass the actual act of confiscation on which the demand for corrective justice is predicated.

A particularly good actual example of a conflict between legal and political justice is provided by two publicized decisions handed down by the Hungarian Constitutional Court in 1992 and 1993.[33] These decisions, which deal with a clash between the demands of retributive justice and those of procedural justice in the context of a retroactive law, well illustrate how cogent the distinction between legal and political justice advocated here becomes when approached from the vantage point of comprehensive justice. At stake in those decisions was the constitutionality of the postsocialist Hungarian Parliament's retroactivity law designed to lift statute of limitations bars to the prosecution of those guilty of murder and torture in the aftermath of the 1956 revolution. These acts were clearly crimes

33. For an account of these cases, see Constitution Watch 1993–94; Morvai 1993–94; Special report 1992.

under existing laws at the time of their commission, but those who perpetrated them were not then prosecuted for political reasons. With the relevant statutes of limitations having expired by the time of Hungary's transition from socialism to democracy, and in the face of strong political demands for retribution, the Hungarian Parliament retroactively extended the appropriate statutes of limitations to make it possible for future legal prosecutions to take place.

Stressing the paramount importance of the postcommunist Hungarian Constitution's commitment to the rule of law, the Constitutional Court rejected the validity of the Parliament's blanket retroactive lifting of statute of limitations barriers to prosecution. Nevertheless, the court sanctioned prosecution for those crimes that qualified as war crimes or as crimes against humanity, as being consistent with adherence to the rule of law, in view of legal obligations undertaken by the communist government in Hungary on becoming a signatory to certain international conventions prior to the expiration of the relevant domestic statutes of limitations (Constitution Watch 1993–94, 10).

Reconstruction along the lines advocated above demonstrates that the Hungarian Constitutional Court's decisions on retroactivity could not have been more on target. Keeping in mind that considerations of procedural justice militate against reasonable expectation of prosecution past expiration of the relevant statutes of limitations, no good faith coherent legal narrative seems available adequately to link together the 1956 murders and acts of torture (falling short of war crimes or of crimes against humanity) with legitimate current concerns regarding legal retribution which emerged after expiration of the relevant statutes of limitations. Such a coherent legal narrative can be constructed, however, with respect to war crimes and crimes against humanity. Indeed, in the latter case there is no unbridgeable rupture. This is because Hungary's new obligations under international law, which became effective prior to the expiration of any of the relevant statutes of limitations, can be fairly interpreted as tolling such statutes all the way to the present. Accordingly, reconstruction points to the logic of a continuous reasonable expectation of possible prosecution for war crimes and crimes against humanity which spans the entire period from 1956 to the present. Current prosecutions of those who perpetrated these crimes in the aftermath of the 1956 revolution, therefore, fall squarely within the scope of justice according to law.

At bottom, the distinction between law and politics, as it emerges from the preceding discussion, reflects above all a difference in perspective. From law's perspective, legal argument and legal discourse occupy the foreground, with political arguments and values receding to the background. Consistent with this, insurmountable ruptures in legal discourse and irreparable breakdowns in legal argumentation signal a failure to come within the ambit of justice according to law. From the perspective of politics, on the other hand, political preoccupation and values come to the foreground and law is relegated to the background. Moreover, from this latter perspective, law emerges primarily as a vehicle for political action and as an embodiment of political values. Accordingly, politics may sometimes use the form of law, but in such cases law serves as a mask designed to conceal what remains in substance a political struggle. In any event, what is most important is that reconstruction stretched beyond the trappings of mere forms can institute a workable divide between politics and law. That divide, moreover, opens up the possibility that justice according to law could be *set against* political justice to constrain politics in ways that might minimize the danger of undue fragmentation.

III. JUSTICE, VIOLENCE, AND THE NECESSITY OF JUST INTERPRETATIONS

The conclusions that justice is impossible and violence inevitable, that law cannot ever completely rise above politics or break loose from ethics, and that the self cannot overcome alienation from the other might lead to despair or complacency. That would be unfortunate, dangerous, and, above all, unnecessary. As we have seen, some injustices are far worse than others, and not all violence associated with justice according to law is equally reprehensible. Consequently, pursuit of greater justice or lesser injustice, and of eradication of all unnecessary or excessive violence, emerges as a constant imperative for every self concerned with reaching toward the other. In short, imperfect justice calls for efforts toward greater perfection. Moreover, through reliance on counterfactual reconstruction based on the ideal of comprehensive justice, it becomes possible to understand the ways in which prevailing standards of justice are wanting and to devise plausible alternatives suited to lead to greater justice. Counterfactual reconstruction cannot lead to overcoming the opposition between the universal and the singular, the rule and the exception, or the abstract and the concrete, but it can point to the optimal compromises available given existing tensions and plausible avenues of relief as delimited by a reasonably drawn horizon of possibilities.

Counterfactual reconstruction depends on just interpretations. It depends on persuasive readings of current tensions, conflicts, and inequities, and on convincing assessments of plausible ways to improve matters in more equitable ways. Moreover, through critical focus on actual problems and plausible solutions, counterfactual reconstruction allows for settling on the level of abstraction best suited to deal with the most pressing presently unmet claims for justice. Consistent with this, just interpretations should be able to secure temporary solutions and promote relative progress, but it remains an open question, at this point, whether they might also contribute to incremental progress and thus gradually foster permanent gains against injustice. In any event, it is clear that attacks on injustice through just interpretations are bound to be piecemeal rather than exhaustive.

Counterfactual reconstruction relies on drawing together the various forms of justice as much as possible. On the other hand, counterfactual reconstruction may not require separating the domains of justice, but it is certainly compatible with it. Moreover, by uncoupling the domains of justice one apparently maximizes the opportunities for reconciling conflicting claims to justice within the confines of justice according to law. Separation of the domains of justice thus casts justice according to law as the optimal means to bind together a polity torn between the centripetal pull of ethical norms that are not universally shared and the centrifugal pulse of fractionalized politics edging ever closer to unbearable fragmentation. In other words, law would keep at bay the oppressive intrusions of alien ethics and would blunt and slow down political fragmentation to avert social disintegration. Consistent with this, the key interpretive task would be to nourish and sustain the image of law as clearly distinct from ethics and politics. If this could be successfully achieved, then just interpretations would become unproblematic and reducible to straightforward applications of clearly defined precepts embedded in justice according to law. Furthermore, as this process evolved and ethics and politics became relegated to an ever more distant background, justice according to law would presumably depend less and less on contestable (just) interpretations, thus suggesting an eventual convergence between justice and the end of interpretation.

Even if the above scenario proved to be highly unlikely and the separation between the domains of justice unwarranted, law could still provide the focal point for alternative means toward the convergence between justice and the end of interpretation. One possibility would be a return to morals, shorn of its Kantian solipsistic shortcomings, in search of a unifying thread capable of rising above the contest among conflicting conceptions of the good and of stemming the tide of political fragmentation. Assuming the feasibility of such a return to morals, law would not be separable from ethics or politics but could serve as a midpoint between them. Accordingly, law would furnish an institutional locus for mediation between competing ethical and political outlooks pursuant to universally applicable morally derived criteria of right and wrong. Moreover, inasmuch as legal interpretation would be informed by universal moral norms, justice would no longer depend on contestable interpretations, thus again signaling a convergence between justice and the end of interpretation.

The preceding observations suggest that it might be advantageous to combine the pursuit of justice with that of the end of interpretation. I explore this possibility in Part Two. I begin by examining Niklas Luhmann's theory of law as an autopoietic system, according to which law looms as independent from ethics or politics in ways that seem more promising than those advanced by the neoformalists. Next, I take a close look at Jürgen Habermas's discourse theory of law, which purports to adapt Kantian morals to contemporary needs, by ridding it of its solipsistic constraints in order to recast it in a dialogical mold. Finally, I evaluate the potential of pragmatism for lowering our sights and for setting ourselves sufficiently free from ethical conflicts to discover practical ways to improve justice while demystifying interpretation. If the promise of pragmatism proves true, then by renouncing the hope for comprehensive solutions and by narrowing our perspective so as to assure that we do not lose sight of what remains practical, we may perhaps achieve as much justice as is within our reach while at the same time making measurable strides toward the end of (contestable) interpretation.

PART TWO

Justice and the End of Interpretation

CHAPTER FOUR

Justice Confined

Luhmann's Turn to Autopoiesis and Self-Referential Legal Interpretation

I. JUSTICE ACCORDING TO LAW, JUSTICE AGAINST LAW, AND AUTOPOIESIS

The distinction between justice according to law and justice beyond law may connote that justice according to law is somehow incomplete, that it represents but one side of a multifaceted concept of justice. Consistent with that impression, moreover, it may seem that we could advance the cause of justice by lowering our sights and focusing exclusively on legal justice, thus avoiding the vexing conflicts that are bound to surround ethical and political justice in pluralist societies. Another possibility, however, is that on the other side of justice according to law lurks not merely justice beyond law but justice *against* law. In the latter case, justice according to law would be contrary to justice beyond law and its precepts would be antagonistic to communally rooted extralegal norms. Furthermore, in the context of a confrontation between justice according to law and justice against law, the quest for just interpretations looms as more difficult and more elusive.

The notion of a clash between justice according to law and justice against law dates back at least to ancient Greece. In Sophocles' *Antigone,* as will be remembered, Creon, the king of Thebes, had decreed that the traitor Polynices, who had been killed in the field, be left unburied, his body exposed to the dogs and the vultures. Convinced that leaving a human body without burial was an offense against the gods, Antigone rebelled against her uncle Creon's decree and proceeded to bury her brother Polynices. On her subsequent arrest, Antigone admitted to having violated the king's decree but remained unshaken in her belief that her action had been just. Speaking to Creon about his decree, Antigone declared,

That order did not come from God. Justice,
That dwells with the gods below, knows no such law.
I do not think your edicts strong enough
To overrule the unwritten unalterable laws
Of God and heaven, you being only a man.
                        (Sophocles 1985, 138)

While the clash between divine law and human law is a major theme in
Antigone, what makes Sophocles' tragedy so poignant is more than the na-
ked confrontation between divine right and human might. Indeed, notwithstanding her firm conviction that human law must yield to divine justice,
Antigone is prepared to face the consequences of having violated her duties
under human law and thus accepts that she must die for her transgression
against Creon's decree (ibid.). Furthermore, although Creon's insistence
on being obeyed and having his decree enforced at all costs may betray an
undue obsession with law and order, his close family ties to Antigone—who
besides being his niece is also the intended wife of his son—make it impossible for him to refrain from enforcing his decree without appearing to
commit an injustice. For how can a king's decree be just in the eyes of his
subjects if the king's family can violate that decree with impunity?[1]

The tensions produced by the clash between human and divine law may
be alleviated by means of a principled and systematic subordination of the
positive law promulgated by human rulers to the natural law derived from
God or reason. Moreover, the integration of positive and natural law results
in the grounding of legal norms on extralegal values rooted in ethics or
religion. Finally, the viability and legitimacy of a system that integrates positive and natural law depends on the widespread acceptance of a set of ethical or religious values capable of furnishing a workable criterion of justice.

Contemporary pluralist democracies, with their deep divisions concerning fundamental ethical and religious values, however, do not provide fertile grounds for the successful integration of positive and natural law. This
explains the ascendance of legal positivism with its emphasis on the futility
of looking to morality or religion as capable of furnishing a genuine basis
for the legitimacy of law. Furthermore, by negating the possibility of divine
law, legal positivism aspires to defuse the tension between justice according

---

1. See Sophocles 1985, 144, where Creon says of Antigone,

> So she must die. Well may she pray to Zeus,
> The God of Family Love. How, if I tolerate
> A traitor at home, shall I rule those abroad?
> He that is a righteous master of his house
> Will be a righteous statesman. To transgress
> Or twist the law to one's own pleasure, presume
> To order where one should obey, is sinful,
> And I will have none of it.

to law and justice against law. Indeed, legal positivism invites us to abandon the vain hope of finding any universally valid measure of justice beyond law. Instead, legal positivism offers us the more modest relative justice of life under the rule of law.

As already indicated in the introduction, on closer examination, legal positivism is likely to seem arbitrary. Indeed, legal positivism is vulnerable to the charge that it can only resolve the clash between justice according to law and justice against law by making it possible for law to escape completely from the grasp of justice. Operating in societies that are significantly divided regarding fundamental ethical and religious norms, legal positivism ties the legitimacy of law to its pedigree—a pedigree that seems to lead inevitably to the subjective values embodied in the will of a duly recognized sovereign. Whether the legitimate lawmaking sovereign be an absolute monarch or a democratically elected legislature, the values injected into law through the expression of the sovereign's legislative will are bound to remain merely subjective and legitimately contestable so long as some of the monarch's subjects or electoral or legislative minorities adhere to conflicting values. In other words, to the extent that no subjectively held value can be proven inherently superior to any other and that legal positivism sanctions the infusion of the subjective values of the sovereign into law, legal positivism tends to reduce justice according to law to a virtually meaningless formality. If law must privilege certain subjective values over others, it is inherently unjust, and its equal application cannot make up for its arbitrarily unequal impact. In short, insofar as it relies on the subjective preferences of the sovereign, legal positivism not only neutralizes justice against law but also trivializes justice according to law.[2]

Niklas Luhmann's conception of law as an autopoietic system[3] shares

2. Although in the course of the preceding observations I have referred to a crude version of legal positivism that reduces legitimate lawmaking to the explicit expression of the will of the sovereign, the validity of these observations and of the conclusions to which they lead are in no way confined to that particular version of positivism. Thus, for instance, the more sophisticated legal positivism of H. L. A. Hart seems no more immune to the charge of having to rely on arbitrary subjective values than its more primitive counterpart. According to Hart, the primary rules, or first-order rules, govern behavior but are dependent on second-order rules—the "rules of recognition"—for their validity (1961, 97–98). In the absence of objective values, either the second-order rules are infused with subjective values or, if they are "purely" formal, the establishment of the requisite links between first-order and second-order rules through judicial lawmaking necessarily introduces subjective values into the process of legal validation. Thus, in Hart's sophisticated legal positivism the introduction of subjective values may be displaced, but it is by no means eliminated.

3. Autopoietic systems "are systems that are defined as unities as network of productions of components that recursively, through their interactions, generate and realize the network that produces them and constitute, in the space in which they exist, the boundaries of the network as components that participate in the realization of the network" (Maturana 1981, 21).

with legal positivism the belief that the validity of legal norms is not dependent on extralegal norms. In contrast to legal positivism, however, Luhmann's conception seemingly successfully avoids reliance on the injection of subjective values as an indispensable component in the articulation of legitimate legal norms. Law conceived as an autopoietic system is self-referential and produces and structures its component elements.[4] Moreover, as a subsystem of the social system, law's elements and mode of reproduction consist of communications (Luhmann 1990, 3). In other words, autopoietic law for Luhmann must be understood as a network of communications that recursively produce and reproduce communications (ibid.); that is, as a system that marks identities and differences as a function of communications abstracted from other levels of reality, including the one that comprises the formation and projection of subjective value preferences.[5] Accordingly, legal autopoiesis, as conceived by Luhmann, makes it apparently possible for the legal system to remain operationally severed both from extralegal norms and from the imprint of arbitrary subjectivity by relying on self-referential circularity as the foundation of law.[6] Consistent with this theory, Luhmann's legal autopoiesis may furnish the means to safeguard the integrity of justice according to law while at the same time making it safe to abandon an ultimately doomed search for justice beyond law.

It is Luhmann's conception of legal autonomy that renders his theory of autopoietic law particularly attractive from the standpoint of establishing a firm contemporary foundation for justice according to law. Luhmann's claim concerning legal autonomy, however, is highly controversial (Teubner 1987a, 6). According to Luhmann, the legal system is one of a series of autonomous autopoietic subsystems that make up the social system (Luhmann 1987b, 335–48). Moreover, as societies become more complex, the

4. Luhmann states, "Autopoietic systems . . . not only produce and eventually change their own *structures;* their self-reference applies to the production of other *components* as well. This is the decisive conceptual innovation. It adds a turbocharger to the already powerful engine of self-referential machines. . . . [E]verything that is used as a unit by the system is produced as a unit by the system itself. This applies to elements, processes, boundaries, and other structures and, last but not least, to the unity of the system itself" (1990, 3).

5. According to Luhmann, "Autopoietic systems . . . are sovereign with respect to the constitution of identities and differences. They, of course, do not create a material world of their own. They presuppose other levels of reality, as for example human life presupposes the small span of temperature in which water is liquid. But whatever they use as identities and differences is of their own making" (ibid.).

6. See Jacobson 1989a, 1675: "Luhmann's theory of society as communication tolerates neither values nor individuals. Values for him are what the individual *desires,* rather than what is *desirable.* Individuals are the *desiring* creatures of Hobbes' utilitarian calculus, rather than moral beings wresting values into action through norms" (citations omitted).

number of these autopoietic subsystems increases to meet developing needs
for greater functional differentiation (ibid.). Although each of these subsystems is considered to be autonomous, it maintains links to the remaining
social subsystems. Thus, law as an autonomous self-referential subsystem
relates to the other social subsystems as a system relates to its environment.
Or, in other words, from the standpoint of its functional operations, law is
an autonomous system that has other social subsystems, such as the political
and the economic subsystems, as its environment (Luhmann 1990, 176–
78). Consistent with this, the legal system is not severed from contact with
the realms of politics or economics. Nonetheless—and this is crucial—political or economic factors cannot partake in the production and application of legal norms, because, in Luhmann's conception, the legal system
is normatively closed while remaining cognitively open (ibid., 229). Luhmann's insistence on normative closure is difficult to accept, however, given
the widespread belief that political and economic values play a significant
role in shaping legal norms. Similarly, even conceding that society's increasing complexity fuels a need for greater functional differentiation that can
best be satisfied through the proliferation of self-referential autopoietic subsystems, it is hard to imagine that the shaping and application of legal
norms remains closed to the normative input of individual actors engaged
on the legal scene.

    While the issue of the autonomy of autopoietic law is crucial from the
standpoint of assessing the potential contribution of autopoiesis to justice
according to law, this issue is not easily settled. Luhmann's theory of legal
autopoiesis has been the subject of numerous criticisms (Jacobson 1989a;
Lempert 1987; Rottleuthner 1987) but Luhmann has proven to be a very
elusive target.[7] Part of the difficulty with the issue of legal autonomy stems
from the fact that the boundaries of law as a distinct practice may plausibly
be drawn along a wide spectrum ranging from the very narrow to the very
broad. Also, because of his special focus on functional differentiation, Luhmann may systematically privilege law's potential for marking differences
over any capacity it may have to mobilize and integrate wide-ranging normative concerns. Finally, Luhmann's theory tackles law at such a high level
of abstraction that it is hard to get a firm grasp of the empirical implications
of his claim concerning legal autonomy.[8]

    While these difficulties cannot be eliminated, they can be largely circum-
vented by confining the inquiry to the possible connection between the
kind of autonomy generated by legal autopoiesis and the relationship be-

---

    7. Luhmann's excellent article (1992) is typical of the great skill with which he has con-
fronted his critics.
    8. This point is emphasized by Lempert (1987, 187–88).

tween justice and law. The important question is not how narrow or broad the realm of law is as a practice but rather whether there is any plausible sense of legal autonomy consistent with Luhmann's legal autopoiesis which would provide genuine support for justice according to law in the absence of any normative consensus on justice beyond law. Moreover, once the inquiry is properly focused on the latter question, it should become apparent that the key to a satisfactory answer revolves around Luhmann's notion that law's self-referentiality allows for a circular justification of legal norms and operations. Indeed, if legal norms ultimately depend on their own circularity for their justification, then justice according to law would be completely independent from justice beyond law while remaining immune to manipulation based on the pursuit of purely subjective values by individual actors.

Based on the following analysis of the relationship between law and justice and of the possible nexus between law, justice, and legal autopoiesis, I conclude that law cannot achieve the kind of full circularity required to sustain Luhmann's conception of legal autopoiesis. Nevertheless, Luhmann's analysis should not be quickly discounted, for it captures a particularly important aspect of contemporary legal relationships. As I shall argue below, Luhmann perceptively and convincingly analyzes what is a fundamental tendency of modern legal systems toward autonomy and self-referentiality. Because of his reductionist vision, however, Luhmann ends up mistaking the part for the whole. Properly construed, contemporary legal systems should be understood in terms of a dynamic ongoing struggle between a never achieved justice against law and a constantly disrupted justice according to law unsuccessfully vying for separation and autonomy. Accordingly, neither natural law, nor positivism, nor Luhmann's richer and more sophisticated positivistic autopoietic theory can do justice to the dynamic processes characteristic of contemporary legal relationships. The age-old struggle between justice according to law and justice against law dramatized in *Antigone* rages on, without end in sight. But more recently, the form of this struggle has been altered almost beyond recognition, as the unity of justice beyond law has itself given way to division and struggle and as justice according to law has—as Luhmann's theory vividly illustrates—fought hard in the hope of gaining independence from both God and humans.

To buttress these conclusions, I attempt a phenomenological retracing, first, of the breakdown of the unity of justice beyond law in relation to the realm of legal relationships, and then of law's journey toward increasing self-referentiality and autonomy. I then focus on the plausible scope and limitation of the role of legal autopoiesis in the context of *both* the reaction against the breakdown of unity of justice against law and the legal system's efforts at greater self-referentiality and circularity, viewed as two complementary aspects of the same overall process. Finally, I sketch a picture of the possible place of the tendency toward legal autopoiesis in the context of the current struggle between justice against law and justice according to law.

II. LAW AND THE BREAKDOWN OF THE UNITY
OF JUSTICE BEYOND LAW

The concept of justice can be said to revolve around two distinct unities: the unity among the subjects who may claim entitlement to justice—which we may refer to as "horizontal unity"—and the unity among the different normative levels at which justice may be prescribed, including the religious, moral, political, and legal levels—which we may refer to as "vertical unity." One may further postulate that perfect justice occurs where there is both full horizontal and vertical unity. Moreover, in a state of perfect justice, justice is not likely to be an issue on anyone's mind, as there would be no interpersonal disputes or discrepancies among different normative levels.

The question of justice and the call for justice only arise in the face of some breakdown at least in horizontal unity. Indeed, even if vertical unity remains intact, one person could shatter horizontal unity by infringing on another's entitlement. So long as only horizontal unity is breached, infringements of entitlement will give rise to calls for corrective justice. On the other hand, if vertical unity is also broken—either because conflicting criteria of justice are suggested for different normative levels or because such clashing criteria are sought to be applied to the same normative level—then questions of distributive justice as well as of corrective justice are likely to be raised. Questions of distributive justice are most obviously implicated when a breakdown of vertical unity is reflected at a single normative level. In that case, members of society clash over which among competing criteria of distribution ought to be used for purposes of allocating that society's benefits and burdens. Moreover, although perhaps less obvious, questions of distributive justice can also arise when the split in vertical unity cuts across different normative levels. Thus, for instance, distributive justice is at issue when acting in accordance with moral norms would lead to a different allocation of benefits and burdens than that which would result from the application of legal norms.[9]

9. In some cases, a break in vertical unity may be viewed either as raising questions of distribution or questions of compensation, depending on the perspective from which the relevant break in vertical unity is apprehended. Returning to *Antigone* for purposes of illustration, the confrontation that pits Creon against Antigone is essentially one between the dictates of religious or ethical norms and those of legal norms. From the standpoint of Antigone, the confrontation concerns the allocation of benefits and burdens—or more precisely of entitle-

The advent of the market, which, as Max Weber has stated, is "a relationship which transcends the boundaries of neighborhood, kinship group, or tribe" (1968, 637), provides the key turning point toward the greater differentiation characteristic of modern legal systems. As recounted by Weber, economic scarcity prompted individuals to leave their own communities in order to exchange goods with strangers at market. In dealing with such strangers, however, individuals could not rely on the kinship rules that governed relationships within their own community and therefore had to look to universally applicable laws capable of transcending the local biases of intracommunal norms.[10] In other words, interactions in noncommunal spheres between strangers with different ethical and religious values require clearly differentiated laws that scrupulously avoid taking sides with respect to parochial issues or intruding on intracommunal matters. This is paramount for alleviating the misgivings and reducing the uncertainties confronting those who must leave home and deal with strangers willing to trade on the market.

Given the twin aims of avoiding favoritism toward any particular parochial values and fostering regularity and settled expectations regarding dealings in noncommunal spheres, procedural rules loom as an especially apt vehicle for the institution of a highly differentiated set of laws designed to mediate interactions among strangers. Moreover, at least in the case of the laissez-faire economic market, reliance on process-oriented formal or procedural laws not only promotes greater certainty in noncommunal dealings without trampling on substantive communal values but also makes it possible directly to serve the aims of the market by codifying the rules of market competition. To the extent that lawful competition ensures that market transactions collectively will promote the common good, the procedural laws that carve out the nature and scope of such competition at once foster substantive values in the noncommunal spheres while leaving intact preexisting substantive values operative in particular communal spheres.[11]

---

ments and obligations—regarding the disposition of Polynices' mortal remains. From Creon's standpoint, however, the confrontation centers around Antigone's violation of legitimate legal norms, thus primarily raising questions of corrective justice—in the sense of symbolically erasing Antigone's encroachment on the body politic.

10. See Weber 1968; see also Münch 1990, 448–49: The "emergence of interactions with strangers outside the community . . . leads to the differentiation of spheres of non-communal interaction from communal interaction" and requires "new forms of interactions that are not covered by the internal regulation of the community."

11. Consistent with the economic views of Adam Smith, the morals of the market contrast with the morals of other spheres. In the market, individuals are obligated to act out of self-love rather than altruism, as the invisible hand of the process of competition automatically leads those who act out of self-love (but not necessarily those who act out of altruism) to contribute to the common good. See Smith 1976a, 477–78. For a more extended discussion of the rela-

It is important for laws designed to provide procedures for noncommunal relationships to be differentiated from, and to avoid the appearance of depending on, communal norms. Accordingly, the formal, process-oriented and heavily procedural laws designed to facilitate noncommunal exchanges must project an image of detachment from ethical and religious values—an image that can be promoted through spreading of the belief that law itself can become completely independent from religion and ethics. Moreover, accompanying and reinforcing this image and the belief that sustains it, is, of course, the perception—buttressed by the sharp contrast between communal and noncommunal dealings—of a breakdown of vertical unity in the realm of justice, with justice according to law bearing little or no connection to justice beyond law. Thus, as communal dealings increasingly give way to noncommunal dealings among strangers, from the standpoint of justice, both horizontal and vertical unity enter into a process of dissolution that seems headed toward a complete breakdown.

As it appears to become increasingly independent from other levels of justice, legal justice, while retaining compensatory and distributive components, tends to be concerned primarily with procedural matters. Even in the face of complete harmony regarding applicable criteria of corrective and distributive justice, a call to justice may concentrate exclusively on procedural justice. Thus, for instance, a dispute could arise on the subject of the best available procedure needed to implement an agreed upon criterion of corrective justice. What is markedly different about contemporary legal justice, however, is the tendency to concentrate exclusively on procedural justice to the exclusion of the other forms of justice.

Modern law's greater concern with questions of procedure is most probably, in part, due to the fact that strangers tend to be suspicious of one another. As noncommunal dealings occur in settings without established customs and traditions governing interactions, matters of procedure seem bound to leap to the forefront. More important, however, the independent law applicable to noncommunal spheres, which is cut off from the ethical and religious norms operative in communal spheres, seems left with no more desirable path to justice than that of pure procedural justice.[12] Indeed, where the adoption of any substantive criterion of justice would smack of parochialism, the pursuit of pure procedural justice looms as the best possible alternative.

To the extent that free market competition guarantees achievement of the common good, implementation of the laws needed to sustain the free market would produce pure procedural justice. Moreover, among the most

---

tionship between the morals of the market and the morals of other spheres, see Rosenfeld 1985, 875-77.
12. For a definition of "pure procedural justice," see chapter III, above.

important of these laws would be laws regarding contract formation designed to maximize freedom of contract.[13] Thus, assuming the existence of such laws, justice would require the enforcement of freely entered into contracts, not because of the nature of the contractual terms involved, but because of the *fact* that the contractors had freely availed themselves of the rules of contract formation and freely agreed upon the terms of their mutual contractual obligations.[14]

In sum, under optimal conditions and in the presence of a free market model of noncommunal relationships, law acquires independence from other normative spheres, and its implementation is capable of producing pure procedural justice. Under these circumstances, moreover, justice beyond law has most likely become fragmented and largely cast away to a distant horizon. Justice according to law can then claim both independence and self-sufficiency inasmuch as it generates pure procedural justice.

As the market tends to become all-encompassing and local communities recede toward the vanishing point, justice according to law tends to dwarf justice against law and pure procedural justice becomes increasingly sweeping. At the logical culmination of this process, it would appear that law would achieve complete independence and that justice according to law relying on pure procedural justice would occupy the entire domain of justice, rendering justice beyond law completely superfluous. In reality, however, this state of affairs is impossible to realize for at least two principal reasons. First, the expulsion of ethical and religious values from the market is only possible so long as these values can find an outlet for expression in local communities that remain beyond the reach of the market. Thus, while economic exchanges take place among strangers, religious and ethical activities can remain largely confined to local communities among one's family and kinship groups. Relationships among strangers can be sustained to the extent that they are complemented by strong communal bonds. If local communities were to give complete way to market relationships, however, then all intersubjective relationships would be among strangers, and individuals would risk losing all sense of identity unless they could find a way to forge ethical or religious bonds with the strangers they encounter on the market. In short, either ethical and religious concerns are confined to communal spheres that remain beyond the market or they are bound to irrupt on the market for the lack of any other available outlet.[15]

13. Cf. Unger 1983, 625: "A regime of contract is just another legal name for a market."

14. For a more extended discussion of the possible relation between freedom of contract and pure procedural justice, see Rosenfeld 1985, 792–93, 804–5.

15. See Hegel 1952, 148: "Civil society tears the individual from his family ties, estranges the members of the family from one another, and recognizes them as self-subsistent persons. . . . Thus the individual becomes a son of civil society which has as many claims upon him as he has rights against it."

The second principal reason why justice according to law can never come to occupy the entire domain of justice is that market competition is never perfect, and, even if perfect competition could be achieved in the economic sense, the market would still fail automatically to promote a universally acceptable conception of the common good. Moreover, to the extent that unfettered economic competition must be curbed for the common good or public welfare, one must look beyond the market and justice according to law to find legal norms that will prove just and efficacious. So long as the public welfare is perceived as requiring that market relationships be curbed rather than eliminated, justice according to law and pure procedural justice are certain to retain legitimacy within a part of the domain encompassed by justice. The remainder of that domain, however, will call for justice beyond law (and laws embodying norms derived from the latter kind of justice). For example, let us assume that unlimited freedom of contract is deemed unjust insofar as it fosters exploitation of the weak by the powerful, but that the limitation of freedom of contract through the implementation of minimum wage and maximum work hours legislation would suffice to prevent exploitation in labor relations. Under these circumstances, a labor contract would be just, in part because its terms satisfied the minimum wage, maximum hours laws, and beyond that, because of the fact that the contractors freely mutually agreed to enter into it. Furthermore, the minimum wage, maximum hours laws would not be just in themselves but only in reference to some expression of justice beyond law that would itself have to be legitimated in terms of adherence to certain extralegal norms; for example, it is unethical or contrary to religious dogma to exploit human beings. Inasmuch as the labor contract is just because of the fact of agreement, there is room left for pure procedural justice. But since the determination on *how much* room ought to be left for pure procedural justice requires recourse to justice beyond law, in the last analysis, the legitimacy of pure procedural justice also depends on extralegal norms.

There is no fixed point at which communal concerns spill over into an expanding market sphere, nor is there a clear line dividing what ought to be left to the free market from what should be placed beyond its reach. There is also no set prescription concerning how the emerging community of strangers might find a suitable equilibrium between seeking to transform market relationships from within and attempting to circumscribe them through confrontation with nonmarket norms. All those issues are the subject of an ongoing, dynamic process that involves confrontation as well as accommodation and that is therefore likely to produce numerous boundary shifts. One thing, however, does remain constant throughout the unfolding of this process: the presence of justice beyond law. Although it has become prey to fragmentation and to seemingly irresolvable internal clashes, justice beyond law is either present implicitly or it is present as the antagonist from whom justice according to law seeks, but ultimately fails, to wrest an independent existence.

III. LEGAL AUTOPOIESIS, THE BREAKDOWN OF JUSTICE BEYOND LAW, AND THE TURN TOWARD SELF-REFERENTIAL CLOSURE

As already briefly noted, the cornerstones of legal autopoiesis are a conception of law in particular and society in general as networks of communication; the existence of a degree of social complexity that calls for a high level of functional differentiation; the generation of conflict as a means to the creation and application of legal norms; self-referentiality and circularity; the legal (sub)system's normative closure combined with its cognitive openness toward other spheres of social interaction construed as the legal system's environment; and the independence of the legal system as a self-referential network of (legal) communications from the intentions of the persons who engage in legal discourse.

As Gunther Teubner emphasizes, legal systems are not born autopoietic; they can evolve toward greater self-referentiality and thus become autopoietic (1987b, 217–41). Moreover, the crucial moment in the evolution from an allopoietic to an autopoietic legal system is the "central shift from 'external' societal mechanisms of evolution to 'internal' legal mechanisms . . . in the sense that *external mechanisms can only have a 'modulating' effect on legal developments while the evolutionary primacy passes over to internal structural determination*" (ibid., 232; emphasis in original). On the other hand, as Luhmann makes clear, the principal task of law is to stabilize expectations (1987a, 27). Now, in the context of a fully normatively integrated community where the vertical unity of justice remains intact, the stability of expectations would seem clearly better served by an allopoietic legal system firmly anchored on a well-established and largely uncontroverted set of extralegal norms. In the face of a breakdown of justice beyond law, however, the contest among extralegal norms is bound to have a destabilizing effect, and accordingly law may be better poised to buttress settled expectations by turning "inward" and drawing on its own processes and elements.

The combination of the dissolution of the vertical unity of justice and the increasing need to deal with strangers in noncommunal settings creates a strong need for an autonomous legal system. On the one hand, the lack of vertical unity of justice makes it impossible convincingly or authoritatively to reconcile law with any available extralegal norms. On the other hand, because interacting strangers lack commonly shared extralegal norms, it is imperative that they adopt some means of regulation that can stand independently from existing extralegal norms. Moreover, this means of regulation must generate, in the context of noncommunal relationships, the kind of stability of expectations that is customary in normatively integrated communities.

Even if the sphere of noncommunal interaction cannot be stabilized through recourse to ethical or religious norms, it does not logically follow that an autonomous legal system offers the only plausible avenue to the stabilization of expectations. Arguably, the sphere of noncommunal interaction could also be stabilized through a process of political accommodation that avoided reliance on contested ethical or religious norms. Both autonomous legal and political systems would bring increased stability to noncommunal spheres through the deployment of a communicative process. The political system, as understood here, would involve the accommodation of conflicting interests through series of ad hoc compromises among contending groups vying for power and influence in order to be in a better position to promote their own interests. Moreover, although political compromises would themselves be ad hoc, the political process in which they would be embedded could well unfold within a stable political structure—such as, for example, a parliamentary democracy—capable of lending firm support to important normative expectations.

Following the discussion in chapter III, the principal difference between a legal and a political resolution of a conflict lies in that legal resolutions do not consist of ad hoc compromises but rather of determinations involving the application of previously established (legal) normative rules, principles, or standards. In spite of this difference, however, the legal and political systems could be viewed as working in harmony, with law—perhaps in the form of a constitution—framing the structure of the political. At the same time, law could also be interpreted as complementing the ad hoc compromises of politics with the resolution of conflicts pursuant to previously set legal rules, standards, or principles. Moreover, in view of the apparent complementarity of law and politics in this universe marked by the breakdown of the vertical unity of justice, it would seem that the fusion of law and politics rather than their uncoupling (with a view to establishing two autonomous social spheres) would be most likely to lead to a greater stabilization of expectations.

From the standpoint of autopoietic theory, however, the stabilization of expectations in a complex society with interweaving communal and noncommunal spheres of interaction might be best achieved through a process of increasing functional differentiation that requires uncoupling the legal (sub)system from the political (sub)system. In the context of noncommunal dealings among strangers, legal interaction would promote greater stabilization of expectations than would political interaction, to the extent that the former would have less of an "ad hoc" nature than the latter. In other words, if people could predict their legitimate legal expectations with a higher degree of probability than their legitimate political expectations, then the operation of the two spheres as separate and independent from one another might well lead to greater overall stabilization of expectations than if both spheres operated in a closely integrated manner.[16]

Within the framework of an autopoietic conception of social systems, the autonomous legal subsystem would be distinguished from its political counterpart by its mode of functioning (Luhmann 1987b, 340–47). Each of these subsystems would provide a different mode of structuring communicative interaction between social actors. Moreover, although legal communication could always remain distinct and independent from political communication, the proportion of social conflicts submitted to the legal subsystem for resolution in relation to those submitted to the political subsystem would fluctuate depending on the circumstances.[17] Many different considerations may enter into the determination of whether a particular conflict should be dealt with in the political or in the legal arena. As already mentioned, the legal system seems generally better suited than the political system to stabilize expectations to the extent that it lacks the ad hoc character of its political counterpart. In one important respect, however, this may not be the case. If the political forces are so skewed that one faction can dictate the terms of ad hoc conflict resolutions at will, then expectations may well be less likely to be disappointed in the political arena than in the legal one. Moreover, even if the faction in question is powerful enough to impose laws at will, that faction would still be better off in the political arena to the extent that laws are sometimes susceptible of acquiring enough of a meaning of their own to allow that they escape from the full grasp of their proponents.[18] Consistent with these observations, submitting conflicts to an autonomous legal system rather than to the political sphere evinces a retreat from the purely power-based relationships in the hope of achieving more stable expectations. In the context of a complete differentiation be-

16. It is conceivable, if the uncoupling of the legal system from the political system were to result in a much expanded political domain and a much shrunken legal domain, that sharp differentiation between the two domains would not lead to greater stabilization of expectations. There seems to be no reason, however, for the assumption that such an uncoupling would result in dramatic shifts in the relative sizes of the domains involved.

17. This seems to follow from Luhmann's assertion that each social subsystem treats all other such subsystems as its environment and from his conception of the legal system as being normatively closed but cognitively open.

18. It may be objected that the absolute ruler can fare as well in both the legal and the political arena since he or she can simply repeal any law before any application of it that would place an unwanted constraint on him or her. In reply, one can point out that the unchecked use of repeated repeals of law at will results in ad hoc resolutions of legal conflicts that would be virtually indistinguishable from the ad hoc resolutions of political conflicts. Furthermore, government by decree issuing from an absolute ruler would not satisfy the conditions of a modern legal system.

tween the legal and political spheres, the commitment of a class of conflicts to the self-contained normatively closed realm of law signifies both a deferral and an equalization of power among the parties to the relevant conflicts. Power is deferred inasmuch as the would-be winner of a present political resolution of an ongoing conflict submits to a previously established legal norm that leads to an anticipated but less favorable outcome of the conflict in question.[19] On the other hand, power is relatively equalized to the extent that a rational decision to commit a certain kind of conflict for resolution within the legal sphere implies a willing loss of power by the strongest members of society coupled with some gain in power for its weakest members. Indeed, from the standpoint of society's strongest members, a change of venue from the political to the legal arena may be desirable even if it entails a loss in power, provided that loss is deemed outweighed by the increase in stability and security that recourse to the legal system would produce. Conversely, from the perspective of society's weakest members, it would make little sense to pursue greater stability unless that would increase (or at the very least not decrease) their power.[20] Ultimately, the equalization of power stemming from rational agreement to refer certain conflicts to an autonomous legal system may not be very different from the kind of equalization that would be achieved through a Hobbesian social contract.[21] There is, however, one key difference between a Hobbesian agreement and submission to an autonomous autopoietic legal system. In the latter case, the very mediation provided by the autonomous legal system would ensure against direct subordination to the will of any individual or group vested with the powers of the sovereign.

Based on the preceding analysis, the kind of justice according to law that could be secured through an autopoietic legal system would include not

19. Under these circumstances, power is deferred rather than simply lost to the extent that the party who has been a relative loser by having to settle in the legal rather than the political arena may have enough political clout to influence changes in legislation that are calculated to make him or her fare better in future legal conflicts.

20. Gaining security concerning further erosions of power—as modest as that may be—does represent some gain of power over one's future destiny. On the other hand, there would be no rational incentive for society's worst off simply to seek to lock in that status for the sake of living under conditions of greater certainty. Furthermore, it is important to stress that these calculations concerning probable increases or decreases in power as a consequence of turning to the legal system must take place *ex ante* and not ex post facto. Given the vicissitudes of political conflict, it is possible that over time some of the weakest actors on the political scene might gain considerable power. That, however, is irrelevant for present purposes. What is crucial is the probabilities of increasing or decreasing power through political as opposed to legal action, as measured *ex ante*—that is, prior to a particular choice between politics and law.

21. According to Hobbes, in exchange for securing a right to life, the parties to the social contract would be willing to relinquish all their other rights to an absolute monarch. See Hobbes 1972, 234.

only a corrective component but also a distributive component.[22] This distributive component emerges from the sharp differentiation implanted by autopoietic law and must be assessed in terms of the two distinct fundamental contrasts sustained by the unfolding of legal autopoiesis. The first of those contrasts is that between order and disorder (in Hobbesian terms, between civil society and the war of all against all characteristic of the state of nature); the second, that between the legal and the political sphere as autonomous autopoietic subsystems.

The order of autopoietic law must be contrasted to the disorder of unregulated noncommunal social interaction. By producing order—any order—autopoietic law differentiates itself from the potential chaos of unregulated noncommunal dealings and ensures a significant measure of stability in dealings between strangers. Furthermore, the presence of such stability results in a distribution of benefits and burdens that is arguably far preferable to, and more just than, that which would emanate from chaos. Accordingly, the order established through the process of differentiation set in motion by autopoietic law secures, at the very least, what may be referred to as "minimal distributive justice."

Insofar as the process of differentiation that sustains the legal sphere's autonomy from the political sphere produces greater stability of expectations, it too contributes to the establishment of minimal distributive justice. Beyond that, moreover, as discussed above, the process that functionally differentiates an autopoietical legal system from its political counterpart tends to lead to the production of greater equalization (of power) in the legal sphere than in the political one; that is, assuming that the same conflict would be equally amenable to either legal or political resolution, then its legal resolution would most likely take place in the context of a smaller disparity of power among the parties to the conflict than would its political resolution. Consistent with this difference in disparity of power, commitment of a conflict to an autonomous legal rather than political system would result in a *relatively* more equitable allocation of relevant benefits and burdens.[23] Hence, in addition to producing minimal distributive justice, legal

22. The normative closure of the legal system ensures the availability of corrective justice as a necessary means to continued stabilization of normative expectations. In the face of inevitable disappointments of legitimate expectations through the transgression of legal norms, the continued stability of normative expectations depends on the availability of compensatory remedies. Moreover, to the extent that an autopoietic legal system internally generates the means necessary to dispense corrective justice, it is also bound to produce some form of procedural justice.

23. It is important to stress the relative nature of the equalization attributable to legal autopoiesis. It is of course possible to have very egalitarian political norms and highly inegalitarian legal norms. All that is claimed here is that relative to the actual political system that

autopoiesis further promotes distributive justice through an, albeit relative and modest, equalization of benefits and burdens among strangers engaged in noncommunal exchanges.

While all legal systems presumably satisfy minimal distributive justice, autopoietic legal systems are supposed to do more. Indeed, legal autopoiesis is poised not only to wrest order out of disorder but also to furnish some kind of insurance through the use of normative closure to stabilize expectations of expectations (Luhmann 1985, 31–40; 1990, 14–15, 232–33). To reduce complexity, social actors seek to achieve greater certainty concerning their expectations, and especially concerning their expectations of the expectations of others. The greater the certainty that a social actor has concerning the expectations of all concerned, the more insurance that actor has concerning the consequences of his or her dealings with others. Particularly when dealing with strangers in noncommunal settings, however, *cognitive* expectations are subject to constant revision as they are likely to be frequently disappointed due to error or miscalculations (Luhmann 1987a, 19–20). In contrast, *normative* expectations can be stabilized counterfactually, with the consequence that they need not be revised even if they are disappointed (ibid.).

For example, if I happen to expect all my business appointments to be punctual, and they frequently happen to arrive late, I would be better off by revising my (cognitive) expectation in order to minimize the aggravation I experience as a result of counting on punctuality. On the other hand, if the law provides that those who buy goods must pay for them, I need not revise my (normative) expectation that my customers should pay for the goods they buy, even if many of them fail to pay. So long as the law remains in force, I am entitled to hold on to my normative expectation. Moreover, to the extent that the law provides remedies for the disappointment of legitimate normative expectations, it provides insurance to legal actors.[24] Finally, although this is not logically required, the stabilization of normative expectations through law is also likely to lead to a significant decrease in the fluctuation of cognitive expectations. Indeed, it seems reasonable to expect that in the long run a vast majority of people will tend to behave in conformity with their legal obligations.[25]

---

launched the legislation implemented by a particular legal system and functionally constituted as part of the actual social environment of that legal system, a legal resolution of a conflict would tend to be more egalitarian than a contemporaneous political resolution of the same conflict.

24. I may be uncertain that my customers will pay me, but if the law provides for damages in case of nonpayment, I will, in most cases, be assured of payment for the goods I sell.

25. If, for example, I am fairly certain that failure to honor my contractual obligations will result in liability to pay damages, I am not likely to have any reasonable incentive to break

In the context of dealings among strangers, the kind of insurance that autopoietic law can provide in a complex, functionally differentiated society amounts to a benefit that enhances the distributive justice that may be dispensed through justice according to (autopoietic) law. Furthermore, by adding this latter enhancement to the minimal distributive justice and the relative equalization discussed previously, we get a fair picture of the kind of distributive justice that is implicit in justice according to (autopoietic) law. This distributive justice is purely procedural in the sense that (in light of the presumed breakdown and fragmentation of justice beyond law) it does not matter what the substantive content of valid legal norms may be so long as these norms are regularly applied and capable of marking the distinction between what should count as legal and what should be deemed illegal. In the last analysis, the modest measure of distributive justice compatible with autopoietic law seems to rest on two principal assumptions: a normative vacuum or hopeless struggle relating to justice beyond law and the vindication of the claim of normative closure in the realm of legal communications.

As to the first of these two assumptions, it is important to note that autopoietic law does not merely come to occupy an existing vacuum brought about by the retreat of justice beyond law, but it also constantly endeavors to actively maintain and even expand this vacuum through the proliferation of its self-enclosed and self-referential processes. Autopoietic law not only offers a means to resolve existing conflicts but also continuously generates conflict in order to secure a permanent medium for the recursive application of the legal norms embedded in justice according to law (Luhmann 1985, 12, 27). But by manufacturing conflict and by channeling social interaction into conflict only to resolve such conflict according to its own self-generated, self-referential, and self-enclosed normative scheme, legal autopoiesis confines legitimate legal discourse to a very narrow domain. That domain is circumscribed by the dichotomies between order and disorder, uncertainty and insurance, and ad hoc political accommodation and the relative equalization of autonomous law. The confinement of law to such a narrow domain may well seem artificial and contrived and therefore fairly raises the question of whether contemporary legal practice could be more faithfully captured by leaving aside the seemingly undue restrictions imposed by autopoietic law.

To be in a better position to answer this last question, it is necessary to take a closer look at the second assumption that underlies the conception of distributive justice linked to autopoietic law; namely that the system of

---

my contracts. My expectation would therefore most likely be to honor my contracts, and my actual and potential fellow contractors would have grounds to be relatively secure in their (cognitive) expectations of my expectation.

(autopoietic) legal communication is inescapably subject to the constraints of normative closure. The task of assessing the validity of this assumption is complicated by the highly abstract nature of Luhmann's discussion. Nevertheless, as we shall see, useful parallels can be drawn between the functioning of legal autopoiesis and Luhmann's description of the phenomenon of monetarization, which he presents as driving the process of economic autopoiesis.

In a nutshell, the core function of legal communications, according to Luhmann's autopoietic theory, is to provide information concerning the meaning of events and, in particular, actions in relation to the binary code legal/illegal (Luhmann 1990, 229–32). This information is not simply the product of the enactment and application of legal rules but rather emerges from the circular interplay between rules and decisions (ibid., 231).[26] Moreover, because the validation of legal norms hinges on a process of unfolding circularity (ibid.), neither the substantive values embodied in particular legal norms nor the intentions projected by actors engaged in the legal arena can in any direct or significant way inform determinations dependent on use of the binary code legal/illegal. This is merely a further elaboration of the notion of normative closure. On the other hand, the internally sealed circular interplay between legal rules and decisions by no means forecloses expanding (or for that matter shrinking) the domain of that which can be rendered legally meaningful through submission to the binary code legal/illegal. This seems to follow from the very notion of cognitive openness.

This highly abstract description of the work of an autopoietic legal system can be made perhaps easier to grasp by briefly concentrating on the analogy—drawn by Luhmann—between autopoietic economics and autopoietic law (ibid., 230–31). The autopoietic economic (sub)system, Luhmann maintains,

> operates openly with respect to needs, products, services, etc., and it is closed with respect to payments, using payments only to reproduce the possibility of further payments. Linking payments to the exchange of "real" goods interconnects closure and openness, self-reference and environmental references. General purpose money provides for closure and remains the same in all hands. Specifiable needs open the system toward its environment. Therefore, the operations of the system depend upon a continuous checking of one in terms of the other. This linkage is a prerequisite for the differentiation and self-regulation of the economic system. (Ibid.)

In essence, then, according to Luhmann's description, self-regulation of the economic system is based on the connection between needs (which

26. In other words, rules are validated by the decisions that invent or elaborate them and (to complete the circle) decisions are validated by the rules that use them as the medium through which they acquire a more definite shape.

fluctuate depending on factors located in the economic system's environment) and a closed monetarized exchange process that systematically mediates the complex interrelationship between the totality of existing needs and the network of products and services susceptible of contribution to satisfying those needs.

In the context of a free market economy, at least, the modernization of all exchange relationships provides a self-regulating system that structures an order for meeting needs under conditions of moderate scarcity. Monetarization, moreover, promotes and sustains a sharp differentiation between use value and exchange relationships beyond the subjective will of economic actors.[27] Accordingly, so long as (and to the extent that) market exchanges are considered to furnish the best possible means to satisfy needs for goods and services, maintenance of the self-regulating economic system relying on the universal language of monetarization is essential. In other words, unless the autonomy of the economic system is maintained, the avowed purposes of economic interaction will undoubtedly be frustrated. Indeed, replacement of the autonomous mechanism of competition by a subjectively crafted economic order would frustrate the economy's clearly differentiated function of maximizing the satisfaction of needs through a most efficient allocation of goods and services.

Taking at face value both claims, the need for autonomy in the economic sphere and the same need in the legal sphere, may lead to the conclusion that there is a fundamental analogy between the ways in which these spheres respectively achieve differentiation. Monetarization seems to provide for the internal regulation of economic relationships, and the binary code legal/illegal for the analogous ordering of legal relationships. On closer analysis, however, the analogy is merely superficial. Indeed, the closure of an economic system that relies on monetarization is plausibly meaningful,[28] while taken alone, the closure maintained by means of the appli-

27. The differentiation between use and exchange value is a function of the systematization of the relationship between supply and demand through the communicative effects produced by monetarization as an abstract and universally applicable code of quantification. Neither those who supply goods nor those who wish to acquire them can impose an exchange value on them because they depend on one another and on all others involved in the supply and demand of such goods for the determination of that value which is neither subjective nor objective, but intersubjective. For a more extended discussion of this last point, see Rosenfeld 1985, 832–39. Rational market exchanges cannot proceed without information concerning intersubjective exchange values that can only be systematically communicated in monetary terms.

28. I say "plausibly" because I am not convinced that a conceptualization of the process of monetarization as autonomous and circular is preferable to other plausible conceptualizations that place greater emphasis on the connection between the economic sphere and other spheres of social interaction. This raises important issues that remain beyond the scope of this book.

cation of the binary code legal/illegal remains essentially trivial. Economic closure through monetarization conceivably fulfills a substantive function that cannot be otherwise equivalently performed. Legal closure through application of the binary code legal/illegal, in contrast, appears to play a purely formal role and (at least standing alone) does no more than sustain an empty tautology (as opposed to a circular but meaning-enhancing or information-producing one).

At least in the context of certain plausible conceptions of the role of the economy, the autonomous process of monetarization fulfills a function that is substantively (as opposed to merely definitionally) necessary and sufficient to propel the economic system toward achievement of its intended social task. Thus, for instance, economic efficiency may well be only achievable through the systematic coupling of the closure of monetarization with openness to all needs, products, services, and so on. Take away the work performed by monetarization—namely providing a common measure to otherwise incommensurable needs, products, services, and so on—and the possibility of achieving economic efficiency through an independent economic system disappears.

From the standpoint of a complex modern legal system, on the other hand, the binary code legal/illegal may be necessary, but it is not sufficient to account for the normative characteristics of law, except in a trivial tautological sense. Even conceding that ex post facto every legal communication may be interpreted as having designated the actions to which it refers as being either legal or illegal,[29] legal practice can hardly nontrivially be reduced to the classification of actions as either legal or illegal.[30] As pointed out above, autopoietic law promotes the values of order, insurance, and equalization relative to the ad hoc compromises of its political environment. These values are not, however, the only ones pursued by law as a distinct contemporary practice. For example, the contemporary movement toward the juridification of human rights and constitutional guarantees extends beyond mere order or insurance. Actually, such juridification often appears to open the legal system to contested conceptions of justice beyond

---

29. Hubert Rottleuthner has argued against this last proposition. As a counterexample, he refers to instances in which adultery while itself strictly speaking neither legal nor illegal may have important consequences for the determination of legal conflicts, such as in the case of divorce. See Rottleuthner 1989, 792.

30. It may always be countered that whereas it may be socially useful or meaningful, anything beyond the autonomous and self-referential process of using the interplay of rules and decisions to communicate whether actions relating to conflicts are legal or illegal is not, strictly speaking, encompassed within the legal system. While such an argument may be defensible from a strictly logical or purely semantic point of view, nevertheless, due to its extreme reductionism, it projects a distorted image that does not capture the full richness of contemporary law as a practice.

law that transcend mere communalism inasmuch as they are specifically oriented toward the domain of noncommunal interaction. Moreover, to the extent that constitutional jurisprudence wrestles with fundamental values associated with justice beyond law, it is more likely to undermine than to promote the kind of predictability necessary to provide insurance.[31]

The problems posed by the reductionism of the autopoietic conception of legal practice are compounded by the fact that order, insurance, and equalization are by no means the exclusive preserve of justice according to (autopoietic) law. Indeed, order and insurance can also be provided by the allopoietic law decreed by Hobbes's absolute monarch, or even through political means. Similarly, greater equalization may be equally or better pursued in the political arena than through the modest standard of justice according to law that emerges from legal autopoiesis.

In conclusion, the analogy between the economic process of monetarization and legal practice viewed as an autonomous and self-regarding autopoietic system does not hold sufficiently to justify the claim of normative closure in the case of law. As a matter of fact, in certain fields like constitutional law at least, it seems more accurate to describe law as a practice as being normatively open to the extralegal norms that underlie justice beyond law. Moreover, to the extent that contemporary law as a practice is not restricted to the exclusive pursuit of order, insurance, and relative equalization, the autopoietic thesis seems defective as it unduly and arbitrarily narrows the domain of legitimate contemporary legal relationships.

IV. AUTOPOIESIS AND THE CONTEMPORARY STRUGGLES FOR JUSTICE

If autopoiesis fails to provide an accurate picture of contemporary legal practice as a whole, it nevertheless captures the essence of one of the two principal tendencies of modern law. Notwithstanding initial appearances to the contrary, modern law does not simply consist of the emancipation and triumph of justice according to law in the face of some final collapse of justice beyond law. Instead, the ascendance of justice according to law is accompanied by a movement toward the reconstitution of justice beyond law.[32] More precisely, contemporary law appears to be the product of an on-

31. As an example of significantly unpredictable areas of constitutional interpretation involving fundamental values relating to justice beyond law, one can mention substantive due process and equal protection rights under the Constitution. Concerning substantive due process, see, e.g., *Bowers v. Hardwick* (1986); *Griswold v. Connecticut* (1965); and *Roe v. Wade* (1973). As for equal protection, on the other hand, there is perhaps no greater unpredictability than in affirmative action. See Rosenfeld 1991a, chap. 7; 1991b.

32. The tendency toward legal autonomy is manifested in, among other things, the proliferation of process-based and procedural rules. Law's tendency toward extralegal norms, on

going clash between two contradictory drives: the drive toward autonomy and that toward the reestablishment of the vertical unity of justice.[33] One of the dynamic functions of contemporary legal actions and communications is to continuously produce sufficient normative differentiation to avert the dissolution of the legal sphere through absorption into the theologico-ethical or political sphere. On the other hand, clashing against this relentless pursuit of differentiation is contemporary law's insatiable need to work toward the recovery of the lost vertical unity of justice. Accordingly, the first of these two drives fuels contemporary law's tendency toward autopoiesis and autonomy while the second, on the contrary, pulls law away from autopoietic self-referentiality.

Contemporary law cannot genuinely resolve the tension between its conflicting tendencies without losing either its identity or its legitimacy. Paradoxically, contemporary law is more likely to fulfill its role by seeking to maintain an equilibrium between its conflicting tendencies than striving to minimize contradiction through a disproportionate development of one of these basic tendencies at the expense of the other. Moreover, the reason why the unrelenting pursuit of such an equilibrium is essential is because—contrary to Luhmann's assertion—the function of contemporary law is not merely one of differentiation but also one of unification. Finally, the justification for contemporary law's simultaneous pursuit of both unification and differentiation is extrinsic rather than intrinsic to law. Contemporary law's tendency toward autopoiesis may be justified as part of a larger whole, but only in terms of extralegal norms. In other words, it is legitimate for law to turn inward, but only because that tends to promote the integra-

---

the other hand, becomes apparent in legal doctrines that rely explicitly on extralegal values. In American constitutional law, the interplay between these two tendencies is exemplified in the contrast between procedural and substantive due process rights under the Fourteenth Amendment's due process clause. The tendency toward extralegal values, however, is not limited to public law. Several legal scholars, for example, have sought to account for contemporary contractual relationships in terms of extralegal norms. See, e.g., Atiyah 1979; Fried 1981; Gilmore 1974; Macneil 1980.

33. The constitutional jurisprudence of due process provides a clear glimpse of this clash. Indeed, the interplay between procedural and substantive due process illustrates how the search for legal autonomy through procedural due process rights collides with the recurring need to appeal to extralegal norms through substantive due process. The recognition of substantive rights has repeatedly prevented due process from becoming exclusively procedural. See, e.g., *Griswold v. Connecticut* (1965) (due process implies a fundamental right of privacy); *Lochner v. New York* (1905) (due process implies certain fundamental economic rights). However, the very determination of purely procedural due process rights may often be impossible without reference to substantive rights grounded on fundamental extralegal values. See, e.g., *Paul v. Davis* (1976) (determination of procedural due process rights depends on conceptions of liberty and property that are ultimately traceable to fundamental extralegal norms); *Board of Regents v. Roth* (1972).

tion of law in the larger social matrix in accordance with extralegal norms poised to permeate social life as a whole.

The paradox presented by contemporary law's turning inward as part of its bid to recover the vertical unity of justice can be unraveled by reference to the social forces that shape contemporary legal relationships. The function of these relationships is not simply to produce differentiation or, on the contrary, to foment the unification of legal and extralegal norms. Instead, the function of contemporary law is to produce differentiation and promote unification *simultaneously* as prevailing circumstances make the possibility of reconciling legal norms and extralegal values conditional on carving out a distinct sphere of differentiation.

The meaning of the movement toward legal autonomy is prone to being misinterpreted to the extent that law's turn inward is overdetermined and that the full reason for it is likely to remain dissimulated. Contemporary legal relationships are inscribed in a normative universe animated by the necessity to eliminate communal norms from the sphere of noncommunal relationships and to replace them with noncommunal—or more precisely, transcommunal—norms. Accordingly, on the one hand, law must turn inward to escape from both the grasp of past parochialisms and from the temptations of future parochialisms.[34] But, on the other hand—and this is much more likely to escape notice—the law must also turn inward as a means to the reconstitution of justice beyond law consistent with the establishment of extralegal norms with transcommunal appeal. At the very least, the differentiation produced by law's inward turn should serve as a communicative vehicle designed to dispel the notion that the extralegal norms sought to be given transcommunal validity are but the old parochial norms bent on venturing beyond their legitimate territorial boundaries.[35]

How contemporary law might seek to reconcile its inward thrust with its outward projection toward extralegal norms to strike a proper balance between unification and differentiation, or between integration and fragmentation, will not be pursued any further here. I shall return to this issue in Part Three below, in the course of my discussion of pluralism. For now, suffice it to emphasize that the promise of Luhmann's legal autopoiesis to

34. As an example of such an inward turn, one may cite the evolution of the English and American law of contract between the eighteenth and nineteenth centuries. This evolution saw the replacement of substantive contract rules based on custom by process-oriented rules relating both to contract formation and to the measure of damages. Moreover, the development and use of those process-oriented rules not only permitted abandoning locally rooted past customs but also made it possible to shield contractual relationships from future intermeddling in the name of extralegal norms. For a more extended discussion of this aspect of the evolution of contract law in the nineteenth century, see Rosenfeld 1985, 821–27.

35. In other words, preservation of the tendency toward legal autonomy protects against relapses into communal factionalism while reaching out for transcommunal extralegal norms.

bring an end to the quest for just interpretations cannot be fulfilled. Strictly speaking, even if law could be reduced to a closed, self-referential system, there would still be questions of interpretation in relation to determinations conforming to the binary code legal/illegal. But these latter interpretations would be strictly confined in scope and would not call for any reliance on, or reference to, extralegal norms. Accordingly, Luhmann's legal autopoiesis fails to put an end to the need for just interpretations inasmuch as it is unsuccessful in its attempt to shield law from the influence of extralegal norms.

In the last analysis, Luhmann's legal autopoiesis represents an advance over positivism, but it ultimately fails to erect an impregnable barrier between justice according to law and justice beyond law. Self-referential autopoietic law guarantees minimal distributive justice, relative equalization, and the benefits of greater order and insurance. Contemporary legal systems, however, are not confined to the pursuit of order and insurance through the stabilization of expectations. Contrary to the thrust of Luhmann's fundamental assumptions, contemporary legal systems must remain normatively open to the ever-greater juridification of human and constitutional rights squarely grounded on extralegal norms. As we have seen, contemporary legal systems tend toward autonomy, but that represents only part of the story. Indeed, contemporary law's tendency toward autonomy and justice according to law seems to be accompanied by (the often concealed but nevertheless always present) contrary tendency toward extralegal norms and justice beyond law. The dynamic interlocking of these contrary tendencies appears as the product of a quest to reconstitute the vertical unity of justice without bringing about a parochial rerooting of extralegal norms. Whether these extralegal norms turn out in the end to be parochial or transcommunal, however, it is clear that reliance on legal autopoiesis does not afford legitimate grounds for proclaiming the end of interpretation.

CHAPTER FIVE

Overcoming Interpretation through Dialogue

A Critique of Habermas's Proceduralist Conception of Justice

I. PROCEDURALISM AS A BRIDGE BETWEEN DEMOCRACY AND JUSTICE

The failure of legal autopoiesis to put an end to the need for interpretation should not be taken to imply that all forms of proceduralism are bound to be inadequate. As we saw in chapter IV, proceduralism that purports to do away with the need for justice beyond law cannot successfully deal with the crisis in interpretation. This does not foreclose, however, that a proceduralist approach that allows for a reintroduction of ethics and politics within the precincts of legal discourse might prove equal to the task of promoting justice while putting an end to interpretation.

In the crudest terms, recourse to any unbiased procedure can put an end to interpretation and to divisive disputes concerning law, ethics, and politics. For example, resolving a conflict through the flip of a coin dispenses with the need for further interpretation, curtails what has proven a fruitless and frustrating debate, and settles matters in an unbiased way—in the sense that it does not inherently favor any of the contending positions or parties. The only problem with the use of a coin flip to resolve legal disputes is that it is arbitrary. But if a procedural approach that is not arbitrary could be devised, then justice could be achieved without interpretation and without reliance on contested conceptions of the good. This precisely is what Jürgen Habermas seeks to achieve through the proceduralist paradigm of law that he derives from his discourse-theoretical approach to ethics, law, and politics.

Habermas agrees with Luhmann that law must stabilize expectations but goes further and insists that legal interpretations must be right (1996, 197–98). In other words, for Habermas justice according to law must be predictable but also consistent with justice beyond law. Moreover, what drives

Habermas toward legal proceduralism is his conclusion that alternative approaches to legal interpretation cannot successfully overcome the crisis in legal interpretation. Noting that natural law is not a viable option for a society with competing gods and demons (ibid., 197–99), Habermas also finds legal hermeneutics, legal realism, and legal positivism inadequate (ibid., 197–203). Legal hermeneutics is objectionable because it deals with the problem of indeterminacy through reliance for meaning on the ethos of the judge, which in a pluralist society is but one ethos among many. In other words, hermeneutics holds that the meaning of a text can only be cogently grasped if that text is placed in its proper historical, cultural, and normative context. In a society such as ours, marked by a clash among various competing sets of value preferences, a judge must necessarily draw on her own value preferences, to the exclusion of others, in rendering her opinion. Accordingly, hermeneutical judicial interpretation cannot lead to societywide acceptance or consensus. Legal realism, on the other hand, is fully aware of the contingency of any particular ethos in a pluralist society, and accordingly focuses on external factors, such as a judge's politics, psychology, or ideology to account for judicial decisions. For Habermas, however, the realist thesis is unacceptable as it wipes out the structural difference between law and politics and hence cannot explain how law stabilizes expectations (ibid., 200–201). Legal positivism, for its part, tries to account for law's role in stabilizing expectations, but it does so by considering it as impermeable to extralegal principles. In so doing, legal positivism unduly sacrifices law's rightness to its certainty (ibid., 201–3).

Consistent with the preceding observations made by Habermas, legal interpretation in contemporary pluralist democracies seems caught between the parochial justice of hermeneutics or legal realism and the democratically generated predictability of legal positivism. Legal hermeneutics and legal realism are thus essentially undemocratic and only just from the perspective of some, whereas legal positivism may well be democratic but it is not inherently just.

Proceduralism affords a way out of the vicious cycle circumscribed by parochial justice and arbitrary democracy. But to avoid arbitrariness, proceduralism must be just on its own terms, which means that it must conform with the requirements of pure procedural justice.[1] Moreover, it bears emphasizing that even if they satisfy pure proceduralism, most kinds of proceduralism will not do. After all, democratic lawmaking can be viewed as a form of pure proceduralism based on universal suffrage and majority rule. It fails to achieve justice in a pluralist democracy, however, as it allows disregarding those conceptions of the good that do not command majority

---

1. For a definition of the Rawlsian concept of "pure procedural justice," see chapter III, above.

support. Nevertheless, conceivably there might be a proceduralism capable of overcoming the residual arbitrariness of democratic lawmaking while at the same time maintaining a neutral stance toward the conflicting conceptions of the good found within the polity.

Habermas's proceduralist paradigm of law seems to be an attractive candidate for purposes of establishing the legitimacy of law through pure procedural justice. Based on communicative action, Habermas's proceduralist approach deals with the residual arbitrariness of democracy by relying on dialogical consensus as the source of law's legitimacy. On the other hand, Habermas's proceduralism affords fundamental rights a *legal* grounding that seemingly obviates any need to justify such rights in terms of any conception of the good not equally shared by all the members of the polity. Moreover, not only does Habermas's proceduralist approach to law offer a way to resolve the conflict between democracy and justice, but it also aims at establishing an internal connection between popular sovereignty and human rights, thus providing a normative underpinning for a legal regime that is poised to satisfy both democracy and justice.

In the last analysis, the possibility of achieving pure procedural justice depends on the background assumptions and the material conditions surrounding the insertion and deployment of the relevant procedural devices and practices. Consistent with this, Habermas's proceduralist paradigm of law ultimately fails to generate pure procedural justice and falls short of affording a comprehensive resolution of the conflict between democracy and justice. Nevertheless, Habermas appears to have taken proceduralism as far as it can go, and through his discourse theory has made great progress over the proceduralism that has emerged from the works of his major predecessors, namely Hobbes, Kant, and Rawls. Even Habermas's more nuanced and versatile proceduralism ultimately confronts the need to embrace contestable substantive normative assumptions in order to contribute to the resolution of conflicts that divide the members of the polity. As we shall see, however, notwithstanding its limitations, Habermas's proceduralism provides us with many rich and valuable insights that can be profitably incorporated into the search for a satisfactory solution to the problems posed by the quest for just interpretations.

To be in a better position to provide a principled assessment of Habermas's proceduralism, I shall first attempt to put it in context. Accordingly, in section II, I briefly examine some of the most salient general features of proceduralism as a means to establish normative legitimacy. In section III, I concentrate on the background assumptions, material conditions, and tasks that give shape to Habermas's proceduralism and provide a critical assessment of certain problems it raises. In section IV, I take a close look at a type of feminist objection that seems to go to the heart of Habermas's discourse-theoretical justification of law. In section V, I conclude that

Habermas's discourse-theoretical approach to law, while incapable of generating pure procedural justice, nonetheless can play an important constructive role in determining the normative legitimacy of contemporary law.

II. THE NATURE AND SCOPE OF PURE PROCEDURAL JUSTICE

As we saw in chapter III, procedural justice—of which pure procedural justice is but a limiting case—is a necessary component of any complex system for dispensing justice. Procedural justice, moreover, has an essentially twofold role in a contemporary constitutional legal system: first, it is supposed to ensure the just *application* of substantive norms belonging to the realm of distributive, corrective, or retributive justice; and second, it is meant to protect the worth and dignity of persons whose legal entitlement and obligations are subject to determination or modification by instrumentalities of the state. While these two roles of procedural justice are often intertwined in practice, they remain conceptually distinct. Thus, for example, in the context of the adversarial criminal law system prevalent in the United States, the criminal defendant's right to counsel and to cross-examine witnesses for the prosecution can be viewed both as an important tool in the pursuit of the truth, which is essential to the fair application of the substantive norms embodied in the relevant criminal statues, and as a means of recognizing the defendant's inherent dignity by guaranteeing his or her right of participation in a proceeding that may result in a drastic change in his or her legal status. Conceptually, however, as a means of application, procedural justice is generally parasitic on the substantive norms it is designed to implement. Accordingly, the adversary system's suitability as a vehicle of procedural justice depends on whether it provides a reliable means to ascertain the guilt or innocence of the accused, which is essential to the implementation of the relevant substantive norms of justice embodied in the criminal code. In contrast, as a means to vindicate the dignity of the accused, procedural justice is largely independent from (though it cannot squarely frustrate the application of) the above-mentioned relevant substantive norms. Consistent with this, even when the evidence against a criminal defendant is so overwhelming that guilt is obvious beyond any reasonable doubt, the defendant is still entitled to have "his day in court."[2]

---

2. What is more, to the extent that its ability to ferret out the truth is what makes the American adversary system of criminal justice procedurally just as a means of application of relevant substantive norms of retributive justice, some of its key features as guarantor of human dignity—such as the Fifth Amendment's privilege against self-incrimination, which allows the criminal defendant not to testify against himself or herself—seem somewhat at odds with its role as a procedural vehicle for the application of substantive justice.

Accordingly, procedural justice at once depends on and transcends particular substantive norms of justice.[3] It does not follow from that, however, that by virtue of transcending a *particular* substantive norm (or a particular set of substantive norms) procedural justice transcends *all* substantive norms. In fact, even inasmuch as it vindicates human dignity, procedural justice depends on substantive norms, except that the latter operate at a higher level of abstraction than the particular substantive norms sought to be applied in a just manner. Furthermore, because it is likely that there would be a greater consensus regarding substantive norms operating at higher levels of abstraction, *compared* to the less abstract substantive norms sought to be applied in a just manner, the more abstract norms may well *appear* to be universal or beyond conflicting conceptions of the good. In other words, from the perspective of the level of abstraction at which the conflict of particular substantive norms unfolds, the more abstract norms may well be perceived as remaining beyond dispute.

To illustrate this last point, let us consider the following example. Suppose that a state guarantees a certain minimum standard of living to every citizen and entitles everyone who can prove that he or she cannot reach this standard through his or her own means to receive public assistance. To implement this policy, the state erects a welfare administration charged with the responsibility of processing applications for public assistance, of determining whether to award public assistance to particular applicants, and whether to terminate such assistance on a finding that a particular recipient no longer needs it. Suppose further that the state's constitution requires that a citizen be given an opportunity to be heard before the revocation of any statutory entitlement.[4] In assessing the administrative procedures designed to carry out the state's public assistance program in accordance with its above-mentioned constitutional obligation, reference must be made to the following two norms: each citizen has a right to a state-guaranteed minimum standard of living; and every citizen is entitled to be treated with dignity and respect—which in this case requires that he or she be afforded an opportunity to be heard before the termination of public assistance payments. Although both of these norms are substantive and contestable, the first, which is more concrete, is much more likely to generate controversy than the second. Thus, whereas libertarians, utilitarians, and egalitarians would undoubtedly all endorse the second norm, they

3. Actually, the dependence between procedural justice and substantive norms of distributive, corrective, or retributive justice is mutual rather than one-sided. Indeed, as already pointed out, if a substantive norm is not susceptible of being applied in a procedurally just manner, it is altogether not suitable as a legitimate *legal* norm, although it may still well qualify as a legitimate ethical norm. See chapter III, above.

4. Cf. *Goldberg v. Kelly* (1970) (due process clause of the Fourteenth Amendment to the Constitution requires affording a hearing prior to termination of welfare payments).

would most certainly disagree concerning the legitimacy of the first norm, with the libertarians strongly objecting against welfare rights (Nozick 1974). Also, from within the trenches of the conflict over welfare rights, the equal dignity norm may well be perceived as being universally valid or at least as being settled beyond dispute.

The importance of procedural justice for modern legal systems and its structure enabling it to fulfill the twofold role identified above are no accident. Given modern law's strong tendency to cast relationships among legal subjects as relationships between strangers, it is hardly surprising that matters of procedure should be brought to the forefront, often predominating over matters of substance.[5] Perhaps less obvious, but equally important, is the fact that the flight to procedure can never be completely successful, with the consequence that matters of substance persist but are often either concealed or displaced. Moreover, a particularly important example of how substantive norms can be concealed by procedural ones emerges through a closer look at pure procedural justice.

Rawls suggests gambling as an example of pure procedural justice. In his own words, "If a number of persons engage in a series of fair bets, the distribution of cash after the last bet is fair, or at least not unfair, whatever this distribution is" (1971, 86). In other words, *any* distribution resulting from a series of fair bets is just, so long as the bets remain fair. If there is no tampering with the betting procedure, such as there would be in a case of cheating, then the outcome of the betting is purely procedurally just (or purely procedurally not unjust). Moreover, since gambling is a means to distribute or redistribute money or goods, gambling consisting exclusively of a series of fair bets produces, in a purely procedural manner, outcomes that further (or at least do not contradict) the requirements of distributive justice.

If we look more closely at the proposition "any distribution resulting from a series of fair bets is just" we can discern two different plausible interpretations, one narrowly focused on gambling as a procedure and the other more broadly focused on gambling as a distributive device. Under the narrow interpretation, fair gambling is just, in contrast to unfair gambling, to the extent that all participants in fair gambling obtain everything they are entitled to expect, namely an equal opportunity (in the sense of an equal probability) (Rosenfeld 1991a, 42) to become the winner. From

---

5. An extreme example of the uses of procedural issues to mask conflicts among parties with widely divergent conceptions of the good is provided by the protracted discussions concerning the shape of the negotiating table at the onset of certain peace talks. See, e.g., Thomas L. Friedman, "Third Round of Mideast Talks Closes with Scant Progress," *New York Times*, 17 January 1992, A4; Jackson Diehl and David Hoffman, "Participants Gather for Mideast Peace Talks," *Washington Post*, 29 October 1991, A16.

the broader perspective, however, fair gambling can only be just—or, more much more likely, not unjust—if certain material conditions and certain normative assumptions are present. Thus, if fair gambling only involves individuals who risk small amounts of discretionary income, in the context of a normative setting where random allocations of discretionary income would not contravene prevailing norms of distributive justice, then any outcome of fair gambling is not unjust. If, on the other hand, fair gambling were to involve large sums of money, including what for some gamblers would count as sums necessary for purposes of their subsistence; and if it were to take place in a setting in which according to prevailing substantive norms of distributive justice, redistributions of income that cause any of those affected to fall below the subsistence level are deemed to be unjust; then even such fair gambling would clearly be (distributively) unjust.

As the example of gambling indicates, pure procedural justice depends on substantive norms of justice as much as the other forms of procedural justice, with the only difference that under the confluence of certain material conditions and certain substantive norms of justice, application of a given procedure is bound to produce a just (not unjust) outcome or one of many equally just (not unjust) outcomes. Moreover, the perception that pure procedural justice remains independent from substantive norms of justice is made possible by a twofold abstraction: first, the legal subjects who avail themselves of the relevant procedure are abstracted from (in the sense of being lifted out of) the lifeworld of their daily existence; and second, the relevant procedure is abstracted from the concrete material conditions and the particular substantive norms on which it depends for its ultimate justification—this latter abstraction being performed through lifting the relevant procedure from its broader legitimating factual and normative context, and then through focusing on this procedure so narrowly as to leave its factual and normative setting out of the resulting picture frame.

The processes of abstraction present in both procedural and purely procedural justice, while operating somewhat differently, are ultimately relied on to perform largely similar tasks. On the one hand, abstraction is supposed to detach legal subjects from the totality of their concrete trappings sufficiently to place the spotlight on similarities among such subjects while downplaying the differences that set them apart. Accordingly, in the example of gambling, the individuals involved are considered in relation to their placing bets and not in terms of their differing wealth, education, social class, or family status. Similarly, in the context of the economic marketplace or of contract as a legitimate tool of procedural justice, individuals are considered in their capacities as producer, buyer, seller, or consumer rather than as men or women, rich or poor, or members of an ethnic majority or minority.

In addition to lifting legal subjects out of their concrete sociopolitical circumstances, abstraction serves to minimize or to conceal reliance on contestable substantive norms in the course of attempting to settle conflicts among legal subjects. Moreover, these two different tasks performed by abstraction are not independent from one another but rather closely connected. As already mentioned, the principal normative function of law in complex modern societies is to provide for just intersubjective dealings among legal subjects who relate to each other as strangers. And, as between strangers, justice would seem to require above all that all those involved be treated as equals and that the customs, normative beliefs, and ethical commitments of some not be favored over those of others. Also, because one is most likely to perceive a stranger in terms of the ways in which he or she differs from the members of one's own group, justice among strangers seems to require conceptualizing the realm of intersubjective transactions at a level of abstraction that optimizes awareness of what strangers share in common.

Where legal subjects relate to each other as strangers, procedural justice acquires major importance and promotes a brand of equality that clusters around similarities. As we have seen, however, genuine equality requires taking into account *relevant differences* as well as relevant similarities.[6] Accordingly, procedural justice seems prone to overemphasize similarities while underemphasizing differences. Because of this, from the standpoint of aiming at complete justice, every move in the direction of the greater abstraction required by procedural justice should be paired with a move in the opposite direction to prevent the eradication of relevant differences. This latter move, moreover, may either be set in motion automatically in the context of pure procedural justice operating under propitious material conditions and normative assumptions, or it may be triggered by the application of substantive norms that counter the flight toward abstraction promoted by procedural justice. In short, the task of justice is to account for, and to reconcile, relevant identities and relevant differences. At the level of law as a medium, this means that the formal equality derived from law as conforming to procedural justice must be reconciled with the substantive equality that properly incorporates differences. Moreover, this latter equality can be promoted through the content of legal norms.

Before turning to an examination of Habermas's proceduralist paradigm in light of the preceding observations, there are two further points about proceduralism in general that must be briefly mentioned. First, it does not necessarily follow that although proceduralism cannot do away with the need to embrace substantive norms, pure procedural justice is

6. Inequality results as much from treating those who are different as inferior as it does from conditioning treatment as equals on the disregard or suppression of relevant differences. See Rosenfeld 1991a, 222–24.

impossible. To be sure, proceduralism cannot rise above substantive norms. However, this does not preclude reliance on uncontested or contestable substantive norms to the extent that the latter are implicitly or explicitly embraced by all those confronted with the necessity of interacting with others, as legal subjects having to relate to each other as equals and as strangers. In other words, proceduralism may be acceptable in the context of substantive norms. This is true provided that the latter norms cannot be legitimately contested by those who come under the sweep of the background assumptions and material conditions underlying the proceduralism under consideration.

Second, a distinction must be drawn between what may be called "primary proceduralism" and what may be referred to as "derivative proceduralism." Under primary proceduralism, deployment of the relevant procedure is both indispensable to and determinative of any outcome that may count as legitimate. Under derivative proceduralism, on the other hand, outcomes are ultimately determined and legitimated by something more fundamental than, or logically antecedent to, the relevant procedure, and the latter is relegated to an auxiliary or essentially rhetorical role. As an illustration, one can cite the difference between "pure" or "primary" social contract theory and "derivative" social contract theory: "Pure social contract theory posits that the ultimate justification of all legitimate social and political institutions lies in the mutual consent of the individuals affected by such institutions. . . . Derivative . . . social contract theories, on the other hand, recognize the social contract device, but do not rely at the deepest level on mutual consent as the source of the legitimacy of social and political institutions" (Rosenfeld 1985, 857). Consistent with this distinction, Hobbes is an exponent of pure social contract theory whereas Locke is an exponent of derivative social contract theory (ibid.). In Locke's theory, the ultimate source of legitimacy is not the social contract itself but rather the natural right to property, which both prompts the passage from the state of nature to civil society and delimits the scope and function of the social contract (ibid., 857–58). More generally, pure procedural justice requires primary proceduralism and is ultimately inconsistent with derivative proceduralism. In other words, derivative proceduralism is not genuine proceduralism but rather substantive theory in procedural garb.

III. HABERMAS'S PROCEDURALISM IN CONTEXT

Habermas's proceduralism rooted in his discourse theory emerges against the background of Hobbesian contractarianism, which satisfies the requirements of primary proceduralism but remains morally arbitrary, and of Rawlsian contractarianism, which incorporates the standpoint of Kantian morality but which proves ultimately to belong to the realm of derivative proceduralism (Habermas 1996, 449–50). Moreover, all there proceduralisms rely on procedural devices that are counterfactual rather than actual. Accordingly, before assessing how proceduralism might pave the way toward overcoming the crisis in interpretation, it is necessary to take a brief look at the nature of and possible justifications for counterfactual proceduralism.

Unlike a coin flip or a lottery, Hobbesian social contract, Rawlsian hypothetical contract concluded behind a veil of ignorance, and Habermasian dialogical consensus predicated on communicative action do not involve any actual procedural devices. They are counterfactual constructs centered around a hypothetical or imaginary procedure. This is perhaps best illustrated by comparing an actual legal contract with an imaginary social contract in cases in which both can be legitimately viewed as vehicles of pure procedural justice. At least under certain background assumptions and material conditions, an actual legal contract may produce pure procedural justice.[7] As pointed out in chapter IV, this occurs where the terms of a particular contract can be said to be just *because* the parties to that contract mutually agreed to be bound by them. Thus, for example, a contract price agreed to between a buyer and a seller of certain goods would be just because they both freely assented to it, rather than because of any criterion external to, or independent from, the contract. In contrast, in a case in which an imaginary social contract is invoked as a legitimating procedural device, no actual agreement has taken place between the relevant parties. Therefore, in the case of an imaginary social contract, the *fact* of agreement cannot function as an essential legitimating factor.

In the imaginary social contract setting, in addition to the requisite background assumptions and material conditions, it is necessary to appeal to imagined facts and to an imagined agreement between actual or imagined parties. Thus, for Hobbes, the issue is what kind of agreement actual persons would reach if, contrary to fact, they found themselves in an imagined state of nature dominated by an imaginary war of all against all (Hobbes 1962, 63–66). For Rawls, on the other hand, the issue is what kind of agreement imaginary persons behind a veil of ignorance would conclude in an imagined gathering for purposes of establishing the basic structure of a fair society (Rawls 1971, 11–12). In either case, for the social contract device to have any legitimating credibility, the construct on which it depends must be susceptible of justification. And that requires at the very least providing a plausible justification for introducing contrary-to-fact "facts" and a contrary-to-fact "agreement," supplemented in a case such as Rawls's with a further justification for the introduction of contrary-to-fact "selves" or "persons."

7. For an extended discussion of this point, see Rosenfeld 1985, 884–94.

The difficulties associated with justifying counterfactuals seem compounded in the case of counterfactual proceduralism. Indeed, if actual devices such as lotteries, coin flips, or legal contracts produce pure procedural justice, actual implementation of the device in question looms as indispensable. A simulated lottery or contract will simply not do inasmuch as the fact of conducting the lottery or of negotiating and entering into the contract seems to be a necessary condition for the achievement of pure procedural justice. Accordingly, how could a counterfactual social contract construct ever lead to pure procedural justice?

To answer this last question, it is first necessary to understand that the aim of reconstruction through counterfactuals is not to furnish a replacement for things as they happen to be but to supplement images of the way things are in order to establish a perspective from which useful critical evaluation becomes possible. The point of counterfactual reconstruction is to furnish an imaginary picture bearing at once sufficient similarities and contrasts to "realistic" pictures of actual practices to facilitate meaningful critiques or justifications of the status quo. Thus, the counterfactual reconstruction must be far enough from prevailing reality to serve as a point of reference against which proposed changes from the status quo may be evaluated, and yet close enough to the way things stand to allow for a determination of whether proposed changes are plausible or merely chimeric. Furthermore, to ensure that a counterfactual reconstruction is not too distant from the actual institutional setting it is designed to evaluate, such counterfactual must either remain within a horizon of reasonably conceivable changes from the status quo or be consistent with the logic and normative assumptions inherent in prevailing institutional arrangements or practices.

On realization of the critical evaluative function of counterfactual reconstruction, the hypothetical or imaginary nature of counterfactual proceduralism ceases to be inherently problematic. This is perhaps most clearly demonstrated in cases in which counterfactual proceduralism is invoked to gauge an actual procedurally grounded institutional setting. For example, the counterfactual construct of a pristine market economy with evenly matched competitors, perfect information, and no transaction costs can be useful either to critique existing markets as self-legitimating procedural mechanisms or to vindicate such real-life markets because of their greater proximity to their counterfactual counterparts than any plausible alternative. In this example, both the counterfactual and the actual are procedural in nature and the difference between them illustrates the degree to which actual markets tend to deviate from the type of pure procedural justice that would be produced by perfect markets. In the case of Hobbesian social contract theory, on the other hand, only the counterfactual is procedural in nature, but that does not detract from its usefulness as an evaluative device. Thus, the actual institutional setting to be assessed in terms of the Hobbesian social contractarian device may have been the product of the imposition of particular institutions derived from parochial substantive conceptions of the good. Nonetheless, the justification for such actual institutional setting may be profitably evaluated in terms of its deviation from that which would have been produced by the Hobbesian social contract procedure under similar background assumptions and material conditions. In other words, it may be that the actual institutional framework in question was imposed by the fiat of an absolute monarch. This notwithstanding, it may still be legitimate if it could have been plausibly adopted by autonomous social contractors operating in a Hobbesian state of nature.

Consistent with the preceding observations, counterfactual proceduralism should not be measured in terms of whether it approximates an actual, historically implanted procedure, but in terms of whether it remains within the horizon of possibilities derived from the status quo or within the logic and normative assumptions inherent in prevailing institutional arrangements. Moreover, the counterfactual "facts," "persons," or "agreements" associated with any particular formulation of counterfactual proceduralism should also be evaluated by the same standard.

With this in mind, let us now turn to Hobbesian contractarianism where the contractual device both shapes and legitimates the contract of association that marks the passage from the state of nature to civil society.[8] The contractual device, moreover, performs a critical intersubjective task by both mediating between the conflicting wills of individual contractors and yielding a common will, which differs from every individual will involved, but which is nothing but the product of a voluntary compromise among all the contractors.[9]

Also, in the context of Hobbesian contractarianism, the state of affairs resulting from implementation of the contract may comport with the requirements of pure procedural justice, provided certain particular material conditions and normative assumptions are satisfied. Those conditions and assumptions are the ones that underlie Adam Smith's conception of a market society in which the "invisible hand" of competition transforms the

---

8. For a more detailed discussion of Hobbes's social contract theory, see Rosenfeld 1985, 849–50, 852–55, 858–59.

9. In a paradigmatic legal contract between a buyer who wishes to obtain a coveted good as cheaply as possible and a seller who wishes to sell that good as expensively as possible, the contract price will be set at a level that is higher than what the buyer wishes but lower than that wished for by the seller. Moreover, the contract price has to be such that neither the buyer nor the seller prefers to walk away from the contract rather than entering into a contract with the other. Thus the conflict between the will of the buyer and that of the seller is settled on agreement on a contract price that becomes the joint (intersubjective) will of buyer and seller but that transcends each of their (initial) individual wills.

clash of private interests into realization of the public interest.[10] In the context of the kind of atomistic competition envisaged by Smith, contract serves to transform the products emanating from the arbitrary wills of individuals into building blocks for the emergence of the public interest.

Absent atomistic market competition, and on rejection of the Smithian conception of the relationship between pursuit of private self-interest and promotion of the public interest, however, contract alone cannot serve to bridge the gap between private and public interest. Contract, accordingly, loses its ability to produce pure procedural (distributive) justice. Furthermore, while still a medium for mediation of conflicting wills, contract no longer serves as a means to transcend the arbitrary individual wills of the contractors. Finally, whereas in the context of atomistic competition each contractor presumably has an equal opportunity to influence the shaping of the common will generated through their joint and mutual contract, in the absence of rough material equality among contractors, the superior bargaining power of some contractors allows them to have a significantly greater influence than other contractors on the configuration of the inter-subjective will produced through contract.[11] In short, cut loose from its Smithian moorings, Hobbesian contractarianism is in the end both morally arbitrary and partial toward some among all of the contractors.

Rawlsian contractarianism proposes to resolve both of the defects that plague its Hobbesian counterpart. To overcome moral arbitrariness, Rawls infuses his social contractors with Kantian moral universalism. Unlike Hobbesian contractors, who are motivated to enter into the social contract to secure indispensable social cooperation on terms that are most favorable to the furtherance of their own arbitrary will, Rawlsian contractors seek to establish principles of justice on which they could all equally agree (Rawls 1971, 11–12). Moreover, to avoid the pitfalls caused by differences in power among contractors and by partiality, Rawls places his hypothetical contractors behind a veil of ignorance designed to make it possible for them to

10. For a more extended discussion of the relationship between Adam Smith's conception of a market society and the achievement of pure procedural justice through the implementation of contracts, see Rosenfeld 1985, 873–77.

11. Whereas it is obvious that the mere *fact* of contracting tends to lose its legitimating role in the context of a legal contract between two contractors with widely different bargaining power, it is not immediately apparent that an analogous change takes place in the context of the counterfactual social contract. On reflection, however, the analogy seems to hold to the extent that once the "invisible hand" premise is dropped, not all different conceptions of the good are likely to fare equally well when subjected to the social contract device. Thus, for instance, communitarian and feminist conceptions of the good are much less compatible with the ideology of contract than are individualistic and atomistic ones. Pateman 1988, 2, 108 (social contract establishes a "fraternal patriarchy" through which men rule over women). Accordingly, if differences *had to* be settled through reaching a contractual agreement, atomistic individualists would have a built-in advantage over communitarians or feminists.

agree on principles of justice without taking into account either their social position or their conception of the good (ibid., 11).

The veil of ignorance secures equality by allowing strangers to ascend to a higher level of abstraction, from which they can discover the core of their common identity, unhampered by the power struggles and the clashing differences of their daily existence. Based on that newfound equality predicated on their common identity, moreover, strangers can, through reciprocal recognition, discover fair principles of justice to govern all their intersubjective dealings. Rawls's use of the contract device at a higher level of abstraction, however, comes at too high a cost. Indeed, in the course of establishing abstract equality behind the veil of ignorance, Rawls has sacrificed difference, reduced the social contract from a dialogical to a monological device, and unwittingly paved the way for the predominance of some perspectives that cannot be justified as being superior to others with which they compete.[12]

Rawls's abstract equality behind the veil of ignorance is objectionable to the extent that it drastically downplays difference in its search for a solid common core of identity. Genuine equality requires taking into account relevant differences as much as relevant similarities, but Rawls's contractors have been deprived of the means to perceive diversity, and are thus unable to factor relevant differences in their elaboration of fair principles of justice. Differences are also essential to the proper functioning of the institution of contract, as only contractors with different needs, desires, motivations, and resources are likely to seek out one another to negotiate a contractual exchange. Ultimately Rawls's contractors behind the veil of ignorance are reduced to the position of mere abstract egos.[13] And since abstract egos are interchangeable, as identically constituted and uniform in perspective, individual conclusions concerning legitimate principles of justice would not differ from those reached collectively. Under these circumstances, the contract device seems altogether superfluous, thus rendering Rawls's principles of justice monological rather than dialogical[14] and his brand of contractarianism derivatively proceduralist at best.

The most serious defect of the Rawlsian process of abstraction is that it

---

12. For an extended discussion of these shortcomings of Rawls's contractarianism, see Rosenfeld 1991a, 233–37.

13. "Under Rawls' original position . . . common principles emerge after all differences in life plans and in natural and social assets have been set aside. Under these circumstances, common principles are reached, not from a diversity of perspectives that incorporates the multitude of existing differences, but from the mere abstract identity that equalizes all individual perspectives after having neutralized all the possible sources of individual differences" (ibid., 234–35).

14. This analysis is consistent with Habermas's assessment of Rawls's theory. See Habermas 1990, 66.

ultimately makes it possible, under the guise of remaining neutral among different perspectives, for some perspectives to gain the upper hand over others. This results from the very means of abstraction that Rawls sets into motion in order to transform the totality of everyday individuals embedded in the norms, institutions, customs, and practices of their particular socio-political setting into the collection of pure abstract egos acting as social contractors behind a veil of ignorance. In looking closely at this process of abstraction, a distinction can be drawn between physical differences and differences in perspective. For example, there is a difference between racial identity as a function of skin pigmentation and racial identity as the prod-uct of a distinct historically and culturally based perspective. Now, we can accept that the veil of ignorance conceals differences based on skin pig-mentation just as we can readily imagine a society that is not made up of differences in skin color. However, if historical events such as slavery and racial apartheid have fashioned distinct perspectives that, by and large, cor-respond to differences in skin color, then how can we go beyond these dif-ferences in perspective at the same time that we do away with differences in skin pigmentation? Either there is a universal perspective that transcends all particular perspectives, in which case proceduralism is entirely super-fluous or merely trivial. Or there is no universal perspective, in which case the abstract egos behind the veil of ignorance would have to adopt either a racial minority or a racial majority perspective in order to arrive at any common principles sufficient to sustain fair principles of justice. Under these circumstances, a racially influenced perspective becomes a material condition that is bound to have an impact on the selection of principles of justice but that remains concealed behind the erasure of differences relat-ing to skin pigmentation.[15]

Habermas's discourse theoretical proceduralism provides the means to overcome the particular limitations of both Hobbesian and Rawlsian con-tractarianism. By relying on communicative action—that is, action ori-ented toward reaching understanding[16]—as a means to generate consensus, Habermas furnishes a procedural approach that makes for a clear demar-cation between the *generation* of intersubjective norms and their *use* to one's own advantage. Consistent with this demarcation, and as a consequence of excluding "strategic action"[17] from the process designed to lead to the con-

---

15. For a more extended discussion of the role of race in shaping different perspectives in the context of American society, and on the relation between such perspectives and norms of justice, see Rosenfeld 1991a, chap. 9.

16. For a comprehensive discussion of communicative action, see Habermas 1984, 1987.

17. According to Habermas, in strategic action "the actors are interested solely in the *success*, i.e., the *consequences* or *outcomes* of their actions, [and] they will try to reach their ob-jectives by influencing their opponent's definition of the situation, and thus his decisions or

sensual adoption of intersubjective norms, Habermas provides a way to surmount the arbitrariness and lack of impartiality inherent in Hobbesian contractarianism. Indeed, contract is above all *the* institution of choice to channel peaceful and orderly interaction among strategically oriented social actors. Accordingly, the use of contract to generate intersubjective norms seems bound to subordinate the perspective of the rule maker to that of the strategic actor who wishes to press his advantage as far as the rules permit. From the standpoint of communicative action, where the focus is on reaching a consensus, on the other hand, both the arbitrary will and the thirst for success of the strategic actor seem sufficiently isolated and neutralized to move beyond the constraints inherent in Hobbesian contractarianism.

Communicative action also provides the means to overcome the two principal defects of Rawlsian contractarianism, namely its inability to properly account for differences and its unwitting privileging of certain perspectives over others. Not only is everyone supposed to participate in Habermas's discursive procedure for generating and validating intersubjective norms, but there is no veil of ignorance and everyone is free to introduce any matter of concern for discussion. Accordingly, differences are not eliminated *ex ante* but taken into full account, with the ultimate decision as to which differences ought to count as relevant and which not, to be reached by consensus, after full and uninhibited discussion. Moreover, Habermas's dialogical approach, unlike Rawls's contractarianism, is not reductive when it comes to taking different perspectives into account. Indeed, not only does Habermas envisage taking all different perspectives into account, but he insists that his discursive procedure calls for the complete reversibility of the perspectives of all participants in communicative action (Habermas 1990, 122). In other words, Habermas's proceduralism requires that conflicts presented for discursive resolution be considered by all participants from each and every perspective involved as a prerequisite to reaching a legitimate consensus.

Having thus set the procedural path free from unwarranted Hobbesian and Rawlsian constraints, Habermas proposes his proceduralist paradigm. According to this paradigm, the legitimacy of law is to be gauged counterfactually from the standpoint of an ideal collectivity of strangers who mutually recognize each other as equals and who jointly engage in communicative action to establish a legal order to which they could all accord their unconstrained acquiescence. In other words, on the basis of a reconstructive process relying on communicative action, the legitimacy of law is tested

---

motives, through external means by using weapons or goods, threats or enticements" (1990, 133; emphasis in original).

in terms of whether an ideal group of strangers representing the full pano-
ply of relevant perspectives would all agree both to enact it as autonomous
legislators and to obey it as law-abiding subjects.

Habermas's counterfactual proceduralism yields a deviation from the
actual settings against which it is erected that boils down essentially to the
difference between communicative action and strategic action. Actual legislators and actual interpreters of law are likely to push their own perspective and interests as hard and as far as they can. Counterfactual legislators
and interpreters committed to abide by the constraints built into communicative action, on the other hand, will only approve those laws and interpretations that prove consistent with all the relevant asserted interests and
represented perspectives. Consistent with this, moreover, Habermas's counterfactual proceduralism appears to track quite closely the counterfactual
construct established by Kantian morals. Indeed, Kant proposes universally
applicable moral norms that are self-imposed. In the Kantian counterfactual construct, every autonomous individual freely assumes the duties flowing from universally encompassing categorical imperatives deduced from
the premise that individuals should treat each other as ends in themselves
(Kant 1969, 53–54). The realm of universal rights and duties transcends
all parochial conceptions of the good, thus yielding a perspective that incorporates universal morality, self-imposed normative duties, and impartiality toward competing conceptions of the good.

Notwithstanding his affinity to Kant, Habermas refuses to fully endorse
the Kantian construct for two principal reasons.[18] Kant's theory is predicated on a dichotomy that sunders the realm of morals, free will, and duty
from that of inclinations, subjective interests, and sociopolitical institutions
(Habermas 1990, 203). Second, Kant's approach is monological rather
than intersubjective, with each individual solipsistically deriving his or her
moral duties on the basis of solitary reflection (ibid.). As a consequence of
that schism, universal morality that transcends competing conceptions of
the good becomes impotent in dealing with the sociopolitical realm of legal
relationships.

One of the chief virtues of Habermas's dialogical proceduralism is that it
incorporates the best qualities of the contractarian and Kantian constructs
by positing a perspective from which legal subjects may jointly determine
which laws could be genuinely imagined as being ultimately self-imposed.
Moreover, consistent with this proceduralism based on communicative action, democracy and rights can not only be reconciled but also apprehended
as internally connected and mutually dependent.[19] Indeed, absent the safe-

18. For a succinct discussion of the main differences between Habermas's discourse ethics
and Kant's moral theory, see Habermas 1990, 195, 203–4.

19. As Habermas states, "A legal order *is* legitimate to the extent that it equally secures

guards built in through communicative action, democracy and rights remain at loggerheads to the extent that the only guarantee against oppression by legislative majorities would come from antimajoritarian rights limiting the scope of legitimate democratic lawmaking. From the standpoint of communicative action, however, the very same rights (which those in the minority would otherwise grasp as shields against the majority) would loom as part and parcel of the same bundle of rights and freedoms that enables each member of the legal community to become integrated with every other member of that community in the dual yet concurrent capacity of author and addressee of the law.

In addition to reconciling rights and democracy from the standpoint of communicative action, Habermas's proceduralist paradigm of law also offers innovative means to pursue the purely procedural achievement of justice. Indeed, as Habermas indicates, the principal task of the strangers who relate to each other as equal consociates under law, in the context of communicative action, is to reconcile the requirements of legal equality with those of factual equality (Habermas 1996, 415–16). In other words, through communicative action, legal actors are supposed to reach agreement among themselves as to which factual similarities and which factual differences ought to be taken into account by the law. As we have seen, Hobbesian contractarianism shortchanges the demands of justice to the extent that its proceduralism favors recognition of the identities and differences dear to the most powerful. Likewise, Rawlsian contractarianism also proves inadequate, because among other things, its removal of certain differences *ex ante* render it only derivatively procedural. In addition, Kantian morals suffer from being too abstract and from remaining monological. Finally, substantive resolutions of the problem of justice necessitate recourse to justice beyond law, thus becoming bound to favor certain conceptions of the good over others. In light of these alternatives, Habermas's procedural proposal seems particularly attractive for a least two important reasons: first, it allows all identities and differences to be considered while weeding out strategic uses of them; and second, it requires subjecting all the identities and differences to every one of the perspectives represented by participants in communicative action. Accordingly, Habermas's proceduralism promises to reconcile legal and factual equality, in a way that not only accounts for all existing identities and differences but also takes into consideration the importance of every asserted identity and difference for each of the different perspectives represented in communicative action.

---

the co-original private and civic autonomy of its citizens; at the same time, however, it *owes* its legitimacy to the forms of communication in which alone civic autonomy can express and prove itself. This is the key to a proceduralist understanding of law" (1996, 409; emphasis in original).

The reconciliation of legal and factual equality is a paramount task for postmetaphysical justice. As Habermas notes, however, the two postmetaphysical legal paradigms—namely the liberal-bourgeois paradigm and the social-welfare paradigm—which he seeks to replace with his proceduralist paradigm, have not satisfactorily dealt with the nexus between legal and factual equality (Habermas 1996, 418–19). The liberal-bourgeois paradigm, which is the first of these two, reduces justice to the equal distribution of rights and thus basically ignores factual equality (ibid.). The social-welfare paradigm, on the other hand, seeks to remedy this deficiency, by zeroing in on the eradication of factual inequality, and in so doing reduces justice to distributive justice (ibid., 418). As a consequence of this, the dignity and autonomy of those who must be clients of the welfare state in order to achieve factual equality become substantially undermined (ibid., 418–19). Furthermore, from an interpretive standpoint, the liberal-bourgeois paradigm tends toward rigid formalism, which leads to predictable adjudications and a clear distinction between the legislative and judicial functions. Interpretation under this paradigm, however, is too inflexible to account for relevant equities. On the other hand, interpretation under the social-welfare paradigm is not hampered by such a limitation, but it tends to become reducible to policy making, thus blurring the divide between legislation and adjudication.

The material conditions underlying the emergence of Habermas's proceduralist paradigm of law reflect both the successive existence and the successive failures of the liberal-bourgeois and the social-welfare paradigms. The liberal-bourgeois paradigm, moreover, relies primarily on a formal conception of equality that clearly places identity above differences.[20] The social-welfare paradigm, in contrast, fosters a material conception of equality that places differences and the need to account for differences in the forefront, leaving equality as identity in the background.

From the broader perspective of the struggle for equality originating in the repudiation of the feudal order, one can observe an intertwining dialectic between identity and difference and between equality and inequality. A brief look into this dialectic is warranted at this point, in order to place the struggle to reconcile legal and factual equality and the three paradigms of law discussed thus far in a broader context. This, in turn, should make for a more thorough picture of the background and normative assumptions and of the material conditions surrounding Habermas's proceduralist paradigm of law.

20. In other words, in the liberal-bourgeois paradigm, inasmuch as every individual is considered identical to every other individual as a being who is inherently entitled to have rights, rights are distributed equally to everyone. But inasmuch as (material) differences among individuals tend to be downplayed, inequalities in the capacity to exercise rights are disregarded.

In the struggle against feudal hierarchy, equality as identity achieved predominance, as clearly evinced in the American Declaration of Independence's famous dictum "All men are created equal." Moreover, the emergence of equality as identity as a rallying point for bourgeois revolutionaries of the eighteenth century is set against the feudal order's association of difference with hierarchical social relations. In other words, in this particular setting, equality goes hand in hand with identity, whereas difference is coupled with inequality. Consistent with this, the pursuit of equality as identity is set to promote the establishment of the equal dignity of every citizen regardless of status or birth.

There are, however, other contexts in which equality as identity can be used as a weapon against treating all members of society as equals.[21] This is what occurs when equality has to be purchased at the price of giving up cherished differences, such as when equal membership in a polity is conditioned on adoption of an official religion, which may require repudiating or suppressing one's own religious preferences. More generally, in terms of the dynamics among identity, difference, equality, and inequality, whether equality as identity ultimately contributes to, or frustrates, treating every member of society as an equal depends on whether equality as identity is pursued in a setting that is best characterized by the metaphor of the master and the slave or by that of the colonizer and the colonized. Indeed, the master treats the slave as inferior because he is different, whereas the colonizer offers the colonized equal treatment provided that the latter give up his own language, culture, and religion in order to adopt those of the colonizer.[22] Accordingly, in a master-slave setting, equality as identity is a weapon of liberation, whereas in a colonizer-colonized setting, it is a weapon of domination.[23]

The dialectic between equality as identity and equality as difference unfolds in the context of the struggle for equality against the backdrop of commitment to *prescriptive* equality—that is, of acceptance, as a normative proposition, that all persons are inherently equal autonomous moral

21. Following Dworkin's distinction, equal treatment—to each the same thing—must be contrasted with treating persons as equals—as possessors of the same inherent worth and dignity. See Dworkin 1977, 227.

22. For a more extended discussion of these issues, see Rosenfeld 1991a, 222–24.

23. A clear example of this contrast is furnished by the constitutional treatment of racial differences in the United States. At the time when racial apartheid was constitutionally sanctioned, the slogan "the Constitution is color-blind" was a weapon against the denial of equal dignity to African-Americans. See *Plessy v. Ferguson* (1896) (Harlan, J., dissenting). In the context of modern-day claims to entitlement of affirmative action as a remedy against the lingering effects of past discrimination, however, "the Constitution is color-blind" has become the rallying point for those who refuse to redress lingering inequities against African-Americans. See, e.g., Paul Craig Roberts, "The Rise of the New Inequity," *Wall Street Journal,* 6 December 1995, A20.

agents. Moreover, there is a discrepancy between the ideal of prescriptive equality, which requires a reconciliation of legal and factual equality that accounts for *all* relevant identities and differences, and the conception of equality embraced by active combatants in the struggle for equality. To the extent that the full realization of the ideal of prescriptive equality remains elusive, combatants in the struggle for equality seem bound to embrace positions more tilted to identity or to difference, according to whether they are waging their fight against particular inequalities grafted on particular differences or, on the contrary, against inequalities maintained through exploitation of certain identities. But, inasmuch as the particular tilt required to combat inequality unduly sweeps ideally relevant identities or differences, the struggle for equality forces its protagonists to temporally forgo recognizing certain identities or differences that would ultimately have to figure in any lasting legitimate reconciliation between legal and factual equality. Finally, under these circumstances, the dialectic between identity and difference can be counted on to promote compensations for deviations tilting too far toward identity or difference, without ever fully aligning the path of the struggle for equality with the path carved out by the ideal of prescriptive equality.

Regardless of whether questions of justice can ultimately be settled apart from questions concerning conceptions of the good, from the standpoint of those engaged in the struggle for equality, *how much* equality there should be and *for whom* is always embedded within the limited horizon of a concrete conception of the good. Also, to the extent that the struggle for equality is likely to involve more than two protagonists, a protagonist's tilt toward identity or difference to deal with one antagonist may come back to haunt that same protagonist when confronting another antagonist. Thus, for example, from the perspective of the generation that carried out the American Revolution and that adopted the American Constitution, the tilt toward identity reflected in the phrase "All men are created equal" was undoubtedly useful in the struggle against the British monarchy. That same tilt, however, proved to be a nuisance, if not a downright obstacle, when it came to establishing a constitutional democracy that recognizes the institution of slavery as lawful.[24] Admittedly, this last example is extreme in that the perspective embraced by the founding generation in America leads to a blatant contradiction, lest one is prepared to proceed as if the African

---

24. It is noteworthy that the United States Constitution of 1787 implicitly recognizes the legal validity of slavery, see, e.g., U.S. CONST. art. I, §§2, 9, and contains no equality rights, thus remaining at odds with the 1776 Declaration of Independence. It would not be until the 1860s, and after the Civil War, that the Constitution would repudiate slavery, see U.S. CONST. amend. 13, and establish equality rights, see U.S. CONST. amend. 14. For a thorough and enlightening discussion of these issues, see Richards 1993.

slaves were less than human—which, shamefully, is exactly what the United States Supreme Court did in its infamous *Dred Scott* decision.[25] But even in more mundane cases, there is likely to be a tension, if not a contradiction, between the tilt one is forced to assume in one's struggle for equality and the optimal interplay between legal and factual equality consistent with one's perspective as grounded in one's own conception of the good. In sum, in view of the fact that the struggle for equality is waged from many different perspectives and against many differently positioned antagonists, the dialectic between equality and inequality generates both tilts (in the direction of identity or difference) that call for correction and overly sweeping claims that require adjustment in order to become better (without ever becoming fully) reconciled with the comprehensive perspective from which they are made. In other words, the dialectic between equality and inequality finds expression in a dialectic between rhetoric and understanding. Thus, the interplay between identity and difference must be treated as a dynamic process that significantly affects both the configuration and the scope of equality at any given time and place.

Consistent with the preceding analysis, from the standpoint of every perspective shaped by a particular conception of the good, which is compatible at the highest levels of abstraction with prescriptive equality, the reconciliation between legal and factual equality must satisfy two distinct, and at least to some degree, incompatible requirements. First, such reconciliation should satisfy the optimal relationship between identity and difference *within* the conception of the good espoused by the relevant perspective. And second, such reconciliation should level the playing field of the existing tilts and excesses that are the product of the ongoing struggle for equality among representatives of different perspectives. Indeed, unless such leveling takes place, the optimal mix between identity and difference could not be properly set in motion in order to become *effective*. On the other hand, the achievement of the desired leveling requires reliance on certain identities and differences that are bound to upset, or at least to postpone, the implementation of the optimal mix.

The three paradigms of law discussed by Habermas can now be put in context, both in terms of the dynamic struggle for equality and in terms of competing perspectives on equality and justice. In terms of the struggle for equality, there is a dynamic progression from the tilt toward identity of the liberal-bourgeois paradigm to the tilt toward difference of the social-welfare

25. In his opinion, Chief Justice Taney stated that at the time of the Declaration of Independence and of the adoption of the 1787 Constitution, African-Americans "had been regarded as beings of an inferior race, and altogether unfit to associate with the white race . . . and so far inferior, that they had no rights which the white man was bound to respect" (*Dred Scott v. Sandford* [1857], at 407).

paradigm and finally to the attempt to incorporate, reconcile, and balance the virtues of liberal identity and social-welfare difference within the proceduralist paradigm proposed by Habermas. Therefore, as against the two paradigms that it seeks to replace, Habermas's proceduralist paradigm appears to have significantly leveled the field on which the battle for the optimal reconciliation of legal and factual equality must be fought. This, however, does not necessarily imply that Habermas's paradigm levels the field sufficiently *as between* the competing perspectives it encompasses, or that it can yield any reconciliation of legal and factual equality that would be acceptable to *all* the encompassed perspectives.

Focusing on the issue of the perspectives encompassed within Habermas's proceduralist paradigm, three important questions arise. First, does Habermas's proceduralist paradigm, by the very nature of communicative action, *effectively* exclude certain perspectives? Second, does the proceduralist paradigm provide a *workable* means of achieving a genuine consensus among the competing perspectives it encompasses concerning the optimal mix of identities and differences, in relation to the legitimate reconciliation of legal and factual equality? And third, does the proceduralist paradigm provide an adequate means of leveling the field on which the perspectives it encompasses compete for justice and equality? Phrased somewhat differently, these three questions can be restated as (1) *which* perspectives can expect justice under Habermas's proceduralism? (2) can such proceduralism produce justice *among* different perspectives? and (3) can such proceduralism yield equal justice as gauged from *within* each of the encompassed perspectives?

Consistent with Habermas, in answering the first question, it is clear that some perspectives are effectively excluded from the discursive resolution of questions concerning justice. Thus, all perspectives that could be broadly characterized as metaphysical perspectives—including those framed by religious dogma and ideology—would effectively be excluded, or more precisely, would effectively exclude themselves, from any dialogical process designed to settle issues of justice. To be sure, this is not problematic for Habermas's proceduralist paradigm, since he makes it clear that his paradigm is designed for postmetaphysical conflicts over justice. The exclusion of metaphysical perspectives is noteworthy nonetheless, as it underscores that communicative action is not neutral as between *all* conceptions of the good, even if, in the last analysis, it remained neutral among the different conceptions of the good that are not incompatible with it.

Communicative action effectively excludes not only metaphysical perspectives but also nonmetaphysical ones that reject adherence to prescriptive equality. Indeed, there seems to be little point, from the standpoint of adherents to a nonmetaphysical perspective that maintains that some persons are *inherently* superior, to submit their views concerning justice for discussion with those whom they do not consider as equals. Even if convincing the unworthy is not deemed futile, communicative action by its very structure would still remain manifestly unfavorable toward blatantly inegalitarian ideologies that altogether reject prescriptive equality. In short, it remains to be seen whether Habermas's proceduralism is neutral as between the perspectives it encompasses. However, the exclusion consistent with Habermas's proceduralism of metaphysical and nonmetaphysical hierarchical perspectives indicates that it is ultimately tied to certain substantive normative assumptions, albeit negative ones.

The answer to the second question—whether communicative action can carve out a common ground for justice consistent with all the perspectives it encompasses—depends both on the nature of the procedural devices involved in communicative action and on the existence of material conditions making it plausible for the reversal of perspectives (undertaken by actors engaged in communicative action) to generate fruitful consensuses or compromises. As conceived by Habermas, communicative action requires each participant to have an equal opportunity to present claims for consideration and a commitment by all to be swayed only by the force of the better argument based on relevant information (Habermas 1984, 273–337). Thus, the only legitimate normative regulations under Habermas's proceduralist paradigm would be those that had been assented to by all the participants in rational discourses who might be affected (Habermas 1996, 459–60). Moreover, in the context of legal as opposed to moral norms, Habermas stipulates that assent could be based on bargaining and compromise as well as on consensus (ibid., 460). Finally—and this is an important advance over Rawlsian contractarianism—the needs, wants, and interests of participants in communicative action are not taken by Habermas to be immutable but instead as subject to evolution and transformation pursuant to dialogical exchanges. Because communicative action, as conceived by Habermas, can contribute to opinion and will formation (ibid., 461–62), it is not simply relegated to finding overlapping interests but is also equipped to harmonize interests through dialogical transformation.

In view of the characteristics of Habermas's proceduralism, there are at least three significant impediments to the goal of achieving an accord on justice among representatives of the diverse perspectives engaged in communicative action. First, the reconciliation of perspectives might ultimately prove to be a purely contingent matter. In that case, Habermas's proceduralism would prove inadequate because under many plausible circumstances it would altogether fail to lead to any legitimate reconciliation of legal and factual equality.

One way to avoid this latter possibility is by placing great weight on the requirement of rationality. Indeed, if communicative action called for rationality in the selection of ends, as well as rationality in dealing with the means toward one's ends, and in dealing with existing conflicts among persons who pursue different ends, then the reaching of an accord on justice may no longer be contingent. But that leads to the second problem. If the requirement of rationality is made strong enough to foreclose the contingency of an accord, then that accord is dependent on the operative norm of rationality rather than on dialogical reciprocity. Consequently, Habermas's proceduralism would become essentially derivative.

Relying on bargaining and compromise, as well as on consensus coupled with emphasis on the transformability of needs, provides an alternative way to minimize the chance that the proceduralist paradigm will fail to yield an accord. This last alternative, however, leads to the third problem. If the pressure to reach an accord is very intense, then bargaining and compromising—even if they remain free of strategic action—may favor certain perspectives over others (as contrasted with certain individuals over others). If that were the case, Habermas's proceduralism would fail to remain neutral as between the perspectives it encompasses (much like Hobbesian contractarianism proved unable to remain neutral as between all contractors).

The preceding observations fail to identify any definitive answer to the second question. However, they raise significant doubts whether Habermas's proceduralism alone, unsupported by substantive norms, can reliably lead to a common accord on justice among different perspectives without favoring some of those perspectives.

The last of the three questions—can the proceduralist paradigm level the field on which competing perspectives vie for justice?—as with the second, cannot presently be given anything nearing a definitive answer. To the extent that proceduralism's search for a common accord on justice leads to the favoring of some perspectives, the third question would seem to require a negative answer. However, assuming that an accord could be reached without having to favor any of the relevant perspectives, the success of Habermas's proceduralism to level the playing field would appear to depend on whether the requisite leveling could be achieved through dialogue or whether it calls for predialogical or extradialogical adjustments. To further clarify these matters, the following section addresses an important feminist objection to Habermas's proceduralism.

IV. THE FEMINIST CHALLENGE TO DIALOGICAL PROCEDURALISM

The feminist challenge to Habermas's proceduralism is a particularly serious one since it is launched from a perspective that is neither metaphysical nor hierarchical in nature. Moreover, the feminist challenge attacks Habermas's proceduralism on at least two different levels. On one level, feminists can argue that, even assuming that communicative action remains neutral as between feminist and male-oriented perspectives,[26] needs, wants, and interests are given such disparate interpretations under these opposing perspectives that it is not realistic to expect any general agreement on how to reconcile legal and factual equality. On another level, feminists can argue that discursive proceduralism cannot level the playing field, which has traditionally heavily tilted toward male-oriented perspectives. Additionally, feminists could press the more radical claim that, by its very structure, communicative action favors male-oriented perspectives over feminist ones. Consequently, no purely dialogical determination of the relation between legal and factual equality could ever prove genuinely acceptable to feminists.

Habermas agrees with the feminists that both the liberal-bourgeois and the social-welfare paradigms evince biases against women (Habermas 1996, 419–20). He parts company with the feminists, however, when it comes to the proceduralist paradigm. Essentially, Habermas's response to the feminist challenge is that since gender differences are constructed rather than preestablished, conflicts between feminist and male-oriented views should be amenable to dialogical resolution just as are other interperspectival conflicts (ibid., 425–27).

To determine whether Habermas's proceduralism can successfully overcome the feminist challenge, it is first necessary to take a closer look at some of the principal characteristics of that challenge. Moreover, since there is by no means unanimity among feminists, I shall take a reconstructive approach and combine various elements that have figured in feminist critiques while advancing the most effective good faith feminist challenge possible. Also, as gender-related issues may vary from one culture to another, I will only refer to gender-related issues as they arise in the United States.

The feminist challenge in the United States is premised on a constitutional, legal, cultural, and social tradition that has repeatedly used and/or constructed differences between men and women to the detriment of the latter, in order to perpetuate a male-dominated society. In that society, with its male-oriented institutions, the best women can hope for is that gender differences will not be used against them. In other words, women's only

26. It is important to remember that what distinguishes feminist perspectives from male-oriented ones are primarily gender-related differences, which are largely sociocultural constructs, rather than differences merely based on sex. Furthermore, while feminist perspectives may be more likely to be embraced by women than by men, certain men are genuinely feminists just as certain women clearly side with the antifeminists.

realistic escape from being subordinated has required them to settle for the role of the colonized[27] in a male-run colony. From the standpoint of the relationship between legal and factual equality, women have generally experienced two different regimes during the course of American history. Initially, the relationship between legal and factual equality unfolded in a setting tilted toward difference, with differences being, for the most part, weighed against women.[28] More recently, the tilt has shifted toward identity, but women still have been significantly disadvantaged, inasmuch as identity has, by and large, meant conformity with male identity.[29]

Against this background of exploited differences and coerced identities, feminists may construct a comprehensive perspective with a vision of the good based on a recasting of identities and differences in ways that are likely to be liberating and enriching for women. Inspired by Carol Gilligan's vision, feminists might construct a conception of the good stressing intimacy, attachment, interdependence, care, concern, responsibility, and self-sacrifice (1982, 12, 73–74, 132).[30] Such a feminist conception of the good would sharply contrast with its typical male-oriented counterpart propelled by its emphasis on separation, competition, and achievement.[31]

Let us suppose, now, that representatives of the above-sketched feminist perspective (whom I shall refer to as "the feminists") confront representatives of the typical male-oriented perspective (whom I shall refer to as "the masculinists"), and that they jointly endeavor to reach a dialogical consensus on a mutually acceptable reconciliation of legal and factual equality. Let us suppose, further, that, from the outset, the feminists stipulate that they concede that the proceduralist paradigm is neutral as between masculinist and feminist perspectives. Under these circumstances, the feminists will start by recounting the history of sex discrimination and will argue for the adoption of legal norms that would enhance care, responsibility, and meeting the needs of concrete others. The masculinists, on the other hand, while acknowledging past inequities, will propose legal norms emphasizing

27. See the distinction between master/slave and colonizer/colonized relationships in section III, above.

28. See, e.g., *Bradwell v. State* (1873) (state refusal to allow women to practice law held constitutional on grounds that a woman's proper role was that of wife and mother).

29. See Minow 1987 (arguing that Supreme Court adjudication on sexual discrimination and pregnancy has posited men's experience as the "norm" against which women are measured).

30. Gilligan is concerned with morals, not law. Her views, however, have influenced feminist legal theorists. See, e.g., Dubois et al. 1985. For a critique of Gilligan by a feminist legal theorist, see Schroeder 1990, 1141–43 n. 12.

31. Habermas has rejected the validity of Gilligan's challenge in relation to issues in the theory of moral development. See Habermas 1990, 175–84. That controversy, however, has no direct bearing on the use of Gilligan's work to outline the contours of a plausible feminist conception of the good.

autonomy and fair competition which would preclude gender-based discrimination.

Assuming that no legal norm capable of equally satisfying the masculinists and the feminists was to emerge at that point, our protagonists could proceed to engage in a reversal of perspectives. This would allow them not only to achieve greater empathy toward their antagonists' plight but also to become aware of the relative importance of each particular claim *within* the comprehensive perspective from which it originates. Being aware of the relative importance of conflicting claims within their respective perspectives might actually prove quite helpful, to the extent that it would be rational to sacrifice a claim of lesser importance within one's own perspective in order to accommodate a claim that is much more important within another perspective. Such a sacrifice would be rational (in the sense of rationality of means rather than rationality of ends) considering the potential for reciprocal gestures that would ultimately inure to the benefit of all those involved.

Now, let us assume that even after ranking all wants and interests, and abandoning the pursuit of those that rank lower in the hierarchy, in order to facilitate the realization of those that rank higher, the masculinists and the feminists still have not been able to settle on equally acceptable legal norms. At that point, one could imagine that each would try to convince the other to change their needs and wants. Thus, the feminists would argue that competition is not everything and that greater connectedness could enrich the lives of the masculinists. The masculinists, for their part, would try to impress on the feminists that competition is not as bad as they think, particularly if it is scrupulously rid of all vestiges of gender discrimination.

At that point in the dialogue, it is *possible* that a consensus regarding legal norms might be reached. But it is *equally possible* that a consensus on equally acceptable legal norms might never be reached. The failure to reach a consensus would not occur because of any strategic behavior, but simply because the honestly held divergent conceptions of the good, even after accounting for all the concessions and adjustments mentioned above, would still remain too far apart.

Thus far I have assumed that the feminists do not challenge the proposition that the proceduralist paradigm is neutral as between the feminist and the masculinist perspectives. There are, however, several plausible reasons that would lend support to such a challenge. Furthermore, the feminists could bring either a moderate or a radical challenge against the claim regarding proceduralist neutrality.

For the moderate challenge, the feminists would argue that the procedural guarantees afforded by dialogical proceduralism are insufficient to level the playing field since public discourse has historically been heavily titled toward masculinist perspectives as well as the liberal-bourgeois paradigm, the social-welfare paradigm, and most existing legal norms. Given that masculinist views are so entrenched in the ideology and the institutional structures of the polity, having an equal opportunity to present one's claims and to attempt to launch a transformation of needs, wants, and interests seems fairly unlikely to put the conflicting positions on an even keel. Again, this is true not because of any strategic conduct by the masculinists but rather because they are so deeply set in their ways.

Even assuming its validity, the moderate challenge may not be fatal to proceduralism, since even deeply entrenched positions could change over time. However, time is not a trivial matter when it comes to legitimating legal norms. If meaningful changes in opinion and will formation can be expected to take several generations, then exclusive reliance on dialogical proceduralism would seem both undesirable and inadequate.

Much more threatening to discursive proceduralism is the radical feminist challenge. That challenge takes as its point of departure Gilligan's view that men's ethics are oriented toward rights, equality, and fairness but women's are oriented toward responsibilities, equity, and the recognition of differences in need among "concrete others" (1982, 164). Suppose the masculinists and the feminists incorporate as part of their conceptions of the good the views that Gilligan ascribes respectively to men and to women. Feminists could launch the following attack. By its very structure—which is designed to lead to justice, equality, and rights—the proceduralist paradigm is inherently biased in favor of masculinist perspectives, against feminist perspectives. Ironically, because it provides for a reversal of perspectives, the proceduralist paradigm does not exclude expression of the needs, interests, or desires of feminists and even allows for masculinist empathy toward feminist claims. But those virtues are eventually nullified, in that, by its very nature, the proceduralist paradigm channels all intersubjective conflicts toward resolutions that must comport with justice, equality, and rights. Although the proceduralist paradigm gives the impression of treating feminists as full partners in the dialogical process, the very structure of that process forces feminists to suppress their most fundamental differences in order to obtain a measure of recognition that does not seriously threaten the hegemony of masculinist perspectives. In short, the proceduralist paradigm makes it possible for an individual feminist claim to be given priority over a competing masculinist claim, but it forecloses something much more fundamental from a feminist perspective—the replacement of "the hierarchy of rights with a web of relationships" (ibid., 57).

In defense of the legitimacy of the proceduralist paradigm, it could be argued that if the radical feminist challenge proves anything, it proves too much. Because its targets include justice, equality, and rights as such rather than any particular conception of them, the radical feminist challenge implies that law itself cannot possibly be justified as a medium for legitimate intersubjective interaction. Therefore, the radical feminist challenge would ultimately lead to a social universe devoid of law, in which feminists would either forcibly convert those who would oppose the implementation of their conception of the good or their antagonists would go their own separate ways.

Feminists, however, could argue that their radical challenge does not necessarily have the dire implications mentioned above. Viewed more closely, the radical feminist challenge is not against law itself but against a paradigm of law that is buttressed by a particular conception of law and rights. Indeed, a brief focus on Habermas's conception of rights reveals that, while he is open as to the *content* of legal rights, he clearly embraces a "static" rather than a "dynamic" conception of law as a medium of intersubjective interaction.[32] In Habermas's view, legal rights (as opposed to moral rights) are above all entitlements, which are logically prior to the duties they trigger.[33] Therefore, such rights carve out boundaries that tend to separate the rightholder from those who must assume a duty as a consequence of his or her entitlement. In the context of a dynamic jurisprudence such as the common law, however, because of the presence of greater flexibility, open-endedness, and indeterminacy, rights and duties become the product of interaction among legal actors; they are thus always susceptible to further perfection through cooperation.[34]

With the distinction between static and dynamic jurisprudences in mind, the feminists can argue that their radical challenge does not demand the abolition of law, justice, equality, and rights. It calls only for the replacement of the proceduralist paradigm and its static conception of rights with an alternative paradigm generating a dynamic conception of rights. This alternative paradigm would alter the *importance* of justice, equality, and rights, by balancing them against normative standards designed to enhance promotion of the "web of relationships." Moreover, any alternative paradigm

32. I borrow the distinction between "static" and dynamic" jurisprudence from Arthur Jacobson (1989b, 1990). For present purposes, the key distinction between these two jurisprudences is that dynamic jurisprudences are open ended and primarily concerned with the realization and development of legal personality, whereas static jurisprudences are primarily concerned with instituting legal order and accordingly draw sharp lines between legal relationships and other intersubjective relationships that remain essentially beyond the reach of law.

33. In Habermas's own words, "whereas in morality an inherent symmetry exists between rights and duties, legal *duties* only result as consequences of the protection of *entitlements*, which are conceptually prior" (1996, 451; emphasis in original).

34. See Jacobson 1989b, 890 (in the common law system persons cannot interact without generating rights and duties, but cannot know what those rights and duties are until after having interacted).

of law designed to be consistent with the radical feminist challenge could neither be exclusively dialogic nor merely procedural. It would have to press substantive feminist norms against masculinist objections, thus having to rely on predialogical or extradialogical sources of legitimacy.

Proponents of legal proceduralism may object to any alternative feminist paradigm that would countenance the imposition of feminist norms over masculinist objections, arguing the paradigm would be arbitrary or inconsistent with a commitment to prescriptive equality. Feminists, however, could counter, arguing that their proposed alternative paradigm would neither be arbitrary nor in violation of the dictates of prescriptive equality. Focusing on the dialectics between identity and difference, and between equality and inequality, feminists could claim that progress toward an optimal reconciliation of legal and factual equality has always been achieved through a series of thrusts that overshoot their intended target, thereby tilting legal paradigms toward certain conceptions of the good to the detriment of other conceptions. This state of affairs requires compensation, which necessitates generating a tilt pointed toward the opposite direction. Therefore, the feminist alternative paradigm, with all its bias, is thus but a logical moment in the ongoing struggle to reach an optimal reconciliation of legal and factual equality. Accordingly, this alternative feminist paradigm is neither arbitrary nor contrary to prescriptive equality.

Based on the above examination of the feminist objection to Habermas's proceduralist paradigm of law, it is now possible to give a more complete answer to the two questions left open at the end of section III. First, unaided by additional substantive norms, legal proceduralism cannot be expected to produce justice *among* different perspectives that clearly come under its sweep. Second, proceduralism alone fails to yield equal justice as gauged from *within* each of the encompassed perspectives.

V. THE LIMITS OF HABERMAS'S PROCEDURALISM AND THE RELATIONSHIP AMONG LAW, MORALS, AND POLITICS

The preceding analysis of the feminist objection to Habermas's proceduralist approach suggests that his proceduralism is ultimately derivative. It may seem that settings characterized by conflicts among competing conceptions of the good offer the most fertile grounds for the success of pure procedural justice. However, closer scrutiny demonstrates that proceduralism is not neutral as between competing conceptions of the good. Accordingly, contrary to initial expectations, as the gambling example discussed above indicates, pure procedural justice's legitimacy seems to be confined to settings in which there is accord over shared substantive norms.

Habermas's proceduralism fails to generate pure procedural justice be-

cause of its Kantian bias. To be sure, as mentioned above, Habermas's dialogical approach and refusal to draw a sharp boundary between the realm
of duty and that of interests amount to significant departures from the Kantian model. Nevertheless, Habermas remains essentially a Kantian in his
embrace of universal morals conceived as transcending all communally
grounded ethics. Consistent with this, moreover, Habermas's proceduralism can be reconciled with his conception of universal morals and accordingly can be regarded legitimately as capable of producing pure procedural
justice. However, that does not solve the problem concerning Habermas's
legal proceduralism, either because Habermas's conception of universal
morals is unpersuasive or because law cannot be ultimately derived from
universally applicable moral norms. Furthermore, these conclusions can be
buttressed by a consideration of the relationship among law, morals, ethics,
and politics from the standpoint of Habermas's dialogical proceduralism.

In general terms, Habermas's discourse theory approaches legal, moral,
and political conflicts in the same way—providing an impartial discursive
procedure, which, if followed by communicatively engaged actors, will yield
legitimate solutions acceptable to all affected. Accordingly, the differences
among law, morals, and politics boil down to differences concerning their
relevant domains and concerning the kinds of arguments that are appropriate in relation to each of these domains. Thus, for example, Habermas
asserts that the proper moral domain spans all social space and historical
time, whereas law's domain is that of a particular society living in a circumscribed historical time frame. Similarly, discursive moral arguments must
be universal in scope, whereas discursive legal arguments can also include
ethical arguments tied to conceptions of the good that are only prevalent
in the relevant society, as well as pragmatic arguments. Also, whereas moral
arguments can only be settled by consensus, legal arguments can also be
resolved through compromise and bargaining, and political arguments
through majority rule. Yet for all these differences, Habermas claims that,
in the context of discourse theory, morals, ethics, law, and politics are mutually consistent and that law and morals actually complement each other
(Habermas 1996, 451–53). On close examination, however, these claims
are not necessarily borne out.

Following the Kantian tradition, Habermas regards morals as the domain of universal justice, establishing correlative rights and duties transcending all particular conceptions of the good. Accordingly, as applied to
the realm of morals, discourse theory must be impartial as among different
conceptions of the good. On the other hand, even in a pluralist multicultural society, only a fraction of the various conceptions of the good formulated throughout the history would be represented. Discursive validation of
law in such a society would therefore not require impartiality as among all

conceptions of the good but only as among those conceptions actually represented. Thus, for example, moral norms must be impartial as among all religions, but legal norms need be impartial only as among those religions with adherents within the relevant society. There might conceivably be a continuum between the absolute impartiality of morals and the relative impartiality of law. But, as we shall see, it seems just as plausible that the relative impartiality of law would clash with the absolute impartiality of morals.

Even if one does not concede the latter possibility, there is another, potentially more vexing, problem. Certain issues, such as abortion, raise serious moral and legal questions, but they cannot be approached from any perspective indifferent to competing conceptions of the good. In Western societies, for example, abortion is viewed as anything from murder to a fundamental right inextricably linked to a woman's autonomy, privacy, and equality. Consequently, to determine whether abortion is morally or legally unjust requires reference to contestable conceptions of the good[35] and to the value preferences that they engender.[36]

Whereas moral consensus on the abortion issue seems impossible in contemporary societies, a discursive legal resolution of the issue might still seem plausible to the extent that, in the context of law, the discourse principle finds room for compromises and fair bargains. Compromises, consistent with the discourse principle, are legitimate, provided they are acceptable in principle to all communicative actors (Habermas 1996, 119–20). But unlike discursive consensuses, discursive compromises may be acceptable to different actors on the basis of different reasons (ibid., 119–20, 151–52). Furthermore, Habermas asserts that in the context of law, the discourse principle extends to ethical and pragmatic questions (ibid., 452). Ethical questions ask who we are and what our goals are, or, in other words, raise concerns relating to the authenticity and the collective self-realization of a particular ethical community. Pragmatic questions, on the other hand, aim at reaching an equilibrium between competing value preferences and competing interests (ibid., 119–20).[37]

Even with the greater flexibility surrounding operation of discourse theory in the realm of law, it is most unlikely that the proceduralist paradigm of law would yield any satisfactory legal resolution of the abortion issue.

---

35. Strictly speaking, if morals are conceived as not encompassing questions relating to the good, abortion would not be susceptible to any moral judgment.

36. According to Habermas, value preferences are intersubjective and they derive from the ethical norms associated with a particular conception of the good (1996, 255–56).

37. Whereas different value preferences derive from different ethical norms, there are likely to be different interests even in the context of shared value preferences and ethical norms. Thus, for example, even if management and labor share an equally strong commitment to the value preferences associated with a market as opposed to a command economy, at times the interests of labor may be at odds with those of management.

Lurking beneath the abortion controversy, there is such a sharp clash in value preferences and interests that no dialogical compromise or balancing seems plausible. Indeed, subjecting all existing perspectives on abortion to the reversal of perspectives process may result in better mutual understanding and empathy but would not afford any persuasive rationale for either pro- or anti-abortion advocates to change their position.

The abortion issue would not be resolved any more easily as a political matter under Habermas's discourse theory of political democracy. Assuming that there is an internal relation between popular sovereignty and fundamental rights, discourse theory projects a picture of democracy as a lawmaking process in the hands of communicative actors dialogically engaged in the task of joint rational opinion and will formation (ibid., 102–4, 114–18). Consistent with Habermas's approach, the dialogical process must establish the fundamental rights that make popular sovereignty among communicative actors and the political objectives that may legitimately shape laws acceptable under the proceduralist paradigm of law. Fundamental rights under this conception would seem, moreover, to come within the ambit of constitutional norms, whereas discursively validated political objectives would result in legitimate legal norms.

In view of existing divisions on the abortion issue, there seems to be no principled basis for dialogical agreement on the status of abortion either at the level of fundamental rights or at that of majoritarian lawmaking. Indeed, for someone who is sincerely persuaded that the right to abortion is central to a woman's autonomy, privacy, and equality, the absence of a constitutional right to abortion would vitiate the very possibility of Habermasian deliberative democracy, because women could not be genuinely counted as equal participants in the relevant discursive process. Conversely, for someone who sincerely maintains that abortion is murder, the absence of a constitutional ban on abortion would negate the possibility of the kind of mutual recognition and respect that Habermas invokes in connection with his dialogical approach to democracy. Finally, leaving the abortion issue to the will of the majority would also be unsatisfactory because it seems highly unlikely that rational discourse among communicative actors would change the minds of those who sincerely believe that abortion should be dealt with at the constitutional level.

It follows from the preceding observations that, at least with respect to certain issues, moral norms that are impartial as among all conceptions of the good seem impossible; that moral norms appear more likely to be in conflict with ethical norms than in harmony with them;[38] and that value

---

38. It is conceivable, for example, that the value preferences of one community would legitimate protecting abortion rights while those of another would, on the contrary, legitimate a complete ban on abortion. Accordingly, whatever may emerge as a discursively valid norm

preferences within the polity may be so polarized as to preclude uncoerced political compromise or balancing of interests. Hence, Habermas's counterfactual rests on a conception of the relation among morals, ethics, law, and politics that leads to an impasse on certain important and bitterly divisive issues within contemporary pluralist societies. Moreover, to the extent that it leads to such impasses, Habermas's counterfactual fails to engender constructive criticism of existing institutional arrangements or to suggest creative solutions to divisive social conflicts.

In the last analysis, Habermas's proceduralism proves incapable of satisfactorily reconciling legal and factual equality for two separate reasons. First, Habermas's discursive proceduralism would amount to pure proceduralism if his embrace of universal Kantian morals were persuasive. But, as the above-discussed case of abortion indicates, contemporary pluralist societies do not seem to afford fertile grounds for the implementation of universal morals capable of transcending the various biases of existing communally grounded competing conceptions of ethics. In other words, in contemporary ethically diverse polities, there seems to be no meaningful room for a neutral universally acceptable moral perspective that would make possible a genuine purely procedural just resolution of ethical and legal conflicts. Moreover, in the absence of such a universal moral perspective, any procedural reconciliation between legal and factual equality is bound to remain biased, and hence illegitimate, as amply illustrated in the course of our discussion of the feminist challenge to Habermas's legal proceduralism.

Second, even if the postulation of a universal moral perspective remained unchallenged, Habermas's legal proceduralism would still prove unsatisfactory. This follows from Habermas's assertion that legal proceduralism relies on ethical and pragmatic arguments combined with rejection of his conclusion that discursive ethical arguments and discursive moral arguments are mutually consistent. Indeed, inasmuch as morals and ethics clash, legal proceduralism boosted by ethical arguments cannot lead to unbiased reconciliations of legal and factual equality. Accordingly, to remain purely procedural, Habermas's legal proceduralism would have to risk becoming morally arbitrary. Conversely, to avoid such risk, Habermas's proceduralism would have to become merely derivative, and resolutions of legal conflicts would have to depend ultimately on application of universal moral precepts rather than on any discursive procedure.

Although we cannot count on Habermas's discursive proceduralism to put an end to legal interpretation—or, more precisely, to divisive and contestable legal interpretation—there is much in his approach that is highly instructive and valuable. Most obviously, Habermas's counterfactual recon-

---

regarding abortion could not, obviously, be neutral as between the conflicting conceptions of the good underlying, respectively, the pro- and anti-abortion ethic.

structive method provides, as already emphasized throughout this book, a versatile and useful tool of critical analysis. Furthermore, perhaps less obviously, Habermas's discursive paradigm based on communicative action and his endeavors to draw a counterfactual picture in which rights, democracy, and justice can be internally connected and made mutually consistent offer promising possibilities in the quest for just interpretations. Habermasian communicative action aptly carves out the important distinction between the joint perspective of citizens seeking to establish commonly acceptable norms to regulate societywide interactions within the polity and the individual or intracommunal perspectives of those who seek to maximize their own advantages within the bounds of existing institutional arrangements. What remains to be seen, and will be further explored below, in Part Three, is whether this distinction can be profitably invoked in the absence of a universally applicable moral perspective. On the other hand, the Habermasian construct that makes for drawing internal bonds between rights, democracy, and justice is particularly attractive in light of the current crisis in legal interpretation, especially inasmuch as the latter hinges on a blurring of the distinction between the legislative and judicial function, and on a seemingly insurmountable split between democracy and rights, and between justice according to law and justice beyond law. In short, the Habermasian construct based on the unity of rights, democracy, and justice looms as a potentially powerful counterfactual critical tool. However, it remains to be demonstrated that such construct is preferable to other constructs and that it is capable of helping in the determination of what ought to count as just interpretations in a pluralist universe deprived of moral universals. These issues will be postponed until Part Three, in order to focus now on yet another plausible path toward the end of interpretation. That path, which requires us to lower our sights in order to downsize the importance of the interpretive subject, is the one laid down by pragmatism.

CHAPTER SIX

Using Pragmatism to Downsize the Interpretive Subject

Posner's and Rorty's Justice without Metaphysics Confronts the Hate Speech Controversy

I. PRAGMATISM OR PRAGMATISMS?

Pragmatism promises to circumvent the thorny path to a just legal interpretation. Indeed, by cutting through the dichotomy between subject and object and by rejecting the need for foundations, pragmatism is supposed to eliminate the problematization of the interpretive subject. Characterized chiefly by its orientation toward the future, its adaptability, its fluidity, and its "down to earth" quality, pragmatism purports to offer practical solutions to concrete problems. By confining legal interpretation to the concrete and by orienting it toward practical consequences, moreover, pragmatism raises the possibility of settling questions of justice according to law without the necessity to appeal to justice beyond law, or to take sides in the contest among competing conceptions of the good.

Pragmatism, which originated in the United States and which counts the nineteenth-century American philosopher Charles Sanders Peirce as its first major proponent,[1] has been the dominant philosophy in the United States ever since (Diggins 1994, 3). Pragmatism has also made important inroads in Europe, where it has influenced many philosophers, most notably Habermas.[2] Moreover, by giving pragmatism a "linguistic turn,"[3] America's most celebrated neopragmatist, Richard Rorty, has instigated a further *rapproche-*

---

1. See Posner 1991, 29–46, 30. Posner points out that Peirce maintained that he got the idea of pragmatism from a lawyer friend.

2. For Habermas's discussion of Peirce and pragmatism, see Habermas 1971, 90–139. See also McCarthy 1978, 293, 299 (discussing affinities between Habermas and Peirce); Diggins 1994, 476 (referring to Habermas as a "neopragmatist").

3. See Rorty 1991, 91: "we new pragmatists talk about language instead of experience or mind or consciousness, as the old pragmatists did."

ment between American pragmatism and contemporary European theory, to wit, poststructuralism and deconstruction (ibid.).

At this point, pragmatism radiates so far afield over the philosophical and the legal landscape as to risk becoming devoid of any determinate meaning. Indeed, if in philosophy pragmatism regroups such diverse figures as Peirce, William James, John Dewey, and Rorty, in contemporary American legal theory it arguably encompasses everyone but the most rigid of formalists.[4] Consistent with this overly broad sweep, pragmatism would appear to embrace any practical, result-oriented approach, as opposed to any systemic approach rooted in fundamental principles. In the words of Cornel West, the "common denominator" of pragmatism amounts to "a future-oriented instrumentalism that tries to deploy thought as a weapon to enable more effective action" (1989, 5).

By shifting the focus from foundations to results, pragmatism invites all members of a pluralist society to turn away from their disputes concerning conceptions of the good in order to join in the common pursuit of practical results. Thus, under pragmatism, justice according to law would depend neither on particular conceptions of the good, nor on finding an Archimedean point between these conceptions, nor on systematically severing law from other normative or social endeavors. Instead, justice according to law would be measured by its practical consequences, by the actual results to which it leads.

So far, so good, but a nagging question emerges. Assuming that different laws (or different interpretations of the same law) would lead to different practical consequences, can recourse to pragmatism determine which of the available alternatives ought to be pursued? In short, is pragmatism self-sufficient, or is it merely *parasitic* on certain contestable conceptions of the good?

This last question is crucial for our purposes, for if pragmatism turns out to be merely parasitic on contestable conceptions of the good, its attractiveness would be very limited. Under those circumstances, pragmatism could help us avoid normative disputes when no demonstrable practical consequences are at stake but otherwise could do little to overcome clashes between conceptions of the good. To illustrate this point, let us suppose that a society is equally divided among those who maintain that wealth maximization is the summum bonum and those who assert that society ought to pursue social solidarity above all. Let us suppose further that a

4. See Rorty 1991, 89–91 (according to Rorty, Judge Richard Posner, the neoconservative leader of the "Law and Economics" school, Ronald Dworkin, and Roberto Unger, one of the leading figures in the Critical Legal Studies movement, can all be considered to be pragmatists).

judge in that society is confronted with the task of interpreting a broad, generally phrased constitutional equality provision, and that he or she knows that one plausible interpretation would foster wealth maximization to the detriment of social solidarity while another would lead to the opposite result. In that case, there is no question that both of the plausible interpretations would lead to palpable empirically verifiable effects, but pragmatism would appear to offer no help to a judge having to choose between the two alternatives. Accordingly, the judge would have to fall back on contested values in order to justify either of the two available alternatives.

It is *conceivable*, though highly unlikely, that pragmatism, if properly and consistently followed, could rise above dependence on contestable conceptions of the good. What makes this particularly unlikely is the wide span of political ideologies embraced by various proponents of pragmatism and the great divergence between old pragmatist and new pragmatist conceptions of "what works." For old pragmatists, like Peirce and Dewey, "what works" was understood in terms of scientifically grounded experience (Peirce 1956, 5–22; Dewey 1938, 345; Diggins 1994, 235). For neopragmatists like Rorty, on the other hand, "what works" is conceived in terms of a "linguistic redescription" susceptible of gaining widespread acceptance primarily on account of its aesthetic appeal (Rorty 1989, 7–22).

A pragmatism completely freed from the grip of contestable conceptions of the good, then, is highly unrealistic. A pragmatism entirely parasitic on such conceptions is largely uninteresting. The possibility of a pragmatism that falls between these two extremes, however, is worth investigating, and will thus provide the principal focus of the remainder of this chapter. Such a pragmatism may be termed "intermediate pragmatism" to distinguish it from a "comprehensive pragmatism" that would do away with the need to rely on contestable conceptions of the good and from a "mere pragmatism" that is but a parasite. Unlike mere pragmatism—which amounts to a pragmatism of means—and comprehensive pragmatism—which is a pragmatism of means and ends—intermediate pragmatism purports to be a pragmatism of means and *some* ends (or, at the very least, a special pragmatism of means allowing for a different perspective on ends).

The possibility of intermediate pragmatism is worth exploring in relation to concerns regarding just interpretations in a pluralist society. Indeed, such concerns presuppose commitment to certain ends, most notably the promotion of social cooperation and peaceful coexistence without having to do away with diversity predicated on the legitimate pursuit of competing conceptions of the good. Assuming that the latter end is not itself a product of pragmatism,[5] then intermediate pragmatism may well furnish the prac-

5. If it were, then we would be dealing with comprehensive pragmatism. But that would

tical means to realize the desired end so long as it does not mandate the achievement of any inconsistent ends.[6]

The search for intermediate pragmatism is complicated by the fact that pragmatists have tended to treat the relationship between means and ends with a remarkable lack of concern.[7] One critic has even suggested that the very success of pragmatism in the United States can be explained in terms of a pervasive uncritical acceptance of a Lockean conception of ends (Hartz 1955, 10). In light of this, and in order to sharpen the contrast between means and ends, I shall explore the possibility of intermediate pragmatism on the basis of a comparison between two very different versions of pragmatism, namely Richard Posner's brand of old pragmatism and Richard Rorty's neopragmatism. Moreover, what makes a comparison between Posner, who is on the right of the American political spectrum, and Rorty, who is on its left, particularly apt for our purposes is that they both agree that pragmatism justifies extensive freedom of expression rights (Posner 1991, 36–37; Rorty 1989, 60; 1982, 69–70). Actually, Posner goes so far as to assert that the scope of protection of free speech is one—and perhaps the only—legal question to which pragmatism is "directly applicable" (1991, 36).

One may object that given the universal embrace of freedom of speech in contemporary democracies, its derivation from pragmatism and the agreement between Posner and Rorty may ultimately be merely trivial. To avoid reaching misleading conclusions, therefore, I shall test the respective pragmatisms of Posner and Rorty against the divisive issue of extremist or hate speech. Extremist speech, which gives rise to what Karl Popper has called "the paradox of tolerance,"[8] has been afforded protection in certain constitutional democracies like the United States but banned in others.[9] Accordingly, pragmatism's production of a resolution to the paradox of tolerance and an inquiry into whether both Posner and Rorty would agree to it promise to shed light on the possibility and potential of intermediate pragmatism.

Before taking a closer look at Posner and Rorty, however, an important

---

simplify rather than complicate the task, for the problem would then be reduced to the selection of adequate means. Accordingly, if intermediate pragmatism can do away with the need to pursue the quest for just interpretations, a fortiori so can comprehensive pragmatism.

6. Of course, if such intermediate pragmatism turned out to be completely indifferent as between all ends, it would collapse into mere pragmatism and would prove useless inasmuch as it would be *equally* compatible with pluralistic diversity and with its destruction.

7. Thus, for instance, "Dewey saw no troubling dualism between means and ends because he regarded ends as given" (Diggins 1994, 242).

8. See Popper 1966, 265 n. 4. Popper suggests resolving the paradox by limiting tolerance to the tolerant (ibid., 266 n. 4). For further discussion of the paradox, see section V, below.

9. See section V, below.

question must be addressed: What links, if any, can be established between pragmatism in philosophy and pragmatism in law? As already mentioned in chapter II, above, although law and philosophy constitute two distinct practices, they overlap in certain instances. But from this it does not necessarily follow that there is any common ground between *pragmatism* in law and in philosophy. In other words, it is conceivable that legal pragmatism is reducible to a mere parasitic pragmatism. If that were the case, then the possibility of intermediate pragmatism in philosophy would be of no help in establishing plausible links between justice according to law and justice beyond law. With that in mind, let us now take a closer look at how pragmatism in law stacks up against pragmatism in philosophy.

II. PRAGMATISM IN LAW VERSUS PRAGMATISM IN PHILOSOPHY

Neither Rorty nor Posner sees any intimate relationship between philosophical pragmatism and pragmatism in law. Rorty states, "I agree with Posner that judges will probably not find pragmatist philosophers—either old or new—useful" (1991, 92). This is not to say, however, that Posner, Rorty, and other pragmatists see *no* relationship between pragmatism in philosophy and in law. According to them, pragmatist philosophy performs a useful task that facilitates the practice of legal pragmatism, but that task involves the removal of obstacles—or, to use Posner's metaphor, "clear[ing] the underbrush" (ibid., 44)—rather than building a philosophical framework affording backing to legal practice. According to this view, pragmatist philosophy's antifoundationalism has a liberating effect on law, by freeing the legal theorist from having to justify practical solutions to legal problems under any comprehensive theory. In the words of Thomas Grey, "pragmatism is freedom from theory-guilt" (1991, 10).

The apparent liberation afforded to law by pragmatist philosophy may have at least three different meanings. First, it may mean that pragmatist philosophy frees law from the need to have any ties to philosophy or any other comprehensive theory. Second, it may mean that pragmatist philosophy makes it possible for law to pick and choose whatever it may find useful among all available philosophies, without regard for consistency or comprehensiveness. Or, third, it may mean that, while law need not derive something positive from pragmatist philosophy, legal pragmatism depends on pragmatic philosophy for purposes of keeping at bay any encroachments from foundationalism or comprehensive theory. In the first case, philosophical pragmatism would make the case that legal pragmatism has altogether no need and no use for philosophy. In the second case, legal pragmatism would emerge as a mere pragmatism that could be engrafted on any philosophy of one's choosing without concern for consistency or comprehensiveness. Finally, in the third case, philosophical pragmatism and legal pragmatism would have a mutual connection making it possible for them to combine into some version of intermediate pragmatism.

All three of these cases have at least some plausibility. The plausibility of the first case stems above all from the sense that law is a practical endeavor that must aim for workable solutions that make a real difference in the empirical world. Accordingly, there ought to be a clear division of labor between philosophy and law. Thus, for instance, a philosophically grounded theory of justice may well justify holding a party to a contract to his or her original promise as he or she intended it and understood it at the time of entering into the relevant contract. However, with no practical way to verify what a person actually intended or understood some time in the past,[10] a legal rule relying on past subjective intent to settle contractual disputes would be impractical and could well lead to more harm than good. In short, holding contract promisors to their actual subjective intent may constitute a compelling ethical norm but an unworkable legal norm.

That law raises pragmatic questions that neither philosophy nor ethics can answer is consistent with the discussion of the relationship between law and ethics in chapter III, and thus hardly surprising. Actually, even certain comprehensive theories that are not reducible to pragmatism, such as Habermas's discourse theory examined in chapter V above, recognize the legitimacy of pragmatic justifications in law but not in morals (Habermas 1996, 452). Indeed, there is nothing *logically* inconsistent about embracing Kantian morals and adopting a pragmatic approach when it comes to law.[11] Accordingly, the crucial question raised by the first of the three cases discussed above is not whether there is a split between philosophy and law but rather whether, as a consequence of being unavoidably steeped in pragmatic considerations, law ultimately proves to be independent of philosophy.

Unless one adheres to an extremely reductive conception of law as being purely instrumental, and as having no role whatever in establishing any kind of ends, the answer to the last question must be in the negative. In any complex advanced legal system, law must determine at least some ends. Such determinations, moreover, cannot always be achieved by mere reference to law or to the political process resulting in the enactment of positive law. For example, whether a broadly articulated constitutional equality right

10. Even if a promisor is scrupulously honest, his or her recollection of what he or she intended months or years ago when the contract now in dispute was entered into may well be distorted or vague.

11. As a matter of fact, Kant himself advocates a prudent course of action in law and politics even if that results in postponing compliance with the dictates of morals. See Kant 1970, 118–19.

should be construed to prohibit discrimination against homosexuals, or whether a generally phrased constitutional privacy right requires protecting a woman's right to an abortion, is unlikely to be cogently addressed without any reference to ethical norms or other broader philosophical concerns. Thus, unless pragmatism is made synonymous with preservation of the status quo, or unless particularly extreme circumstances are at hand, the consequences alone cannot supply a principled answer to the relevant question confronting the constitutional judge.[12] Indeed, protecting homosexual lifestyles is likely to have *certain* practical consequences, and refusal to do so *certain other* practical consequences. Because of this, a judge may not be able to arrive at a cogent resolution of the question of constitutional equality rights for homosexuals on the basis of a legal pragmatism that is completely severed from ethics or philosophy. More generally, the first of the three cases described above looms as unpersuasive. Adherence to legal pragmatism, therefore, does not, in the last analysis, justify a complete emancipation of justice according to law from justice beyond law any more than does reliance on Luhmann's legal autopoiesis discussed in chapter IV.

The second of the three cases stems from an understanding of the liberating effect of pragmatist philosophy on law that, in effect, reverses the respective positions of philosophy and law. In a conventional foundationalist setting, philosophy can be viewed as preceding, and standing above, law. For example, one may embrace a Lockean theory of property and assess the legitimacy of laws in terms of their compatibility with the relevant precepts of Lockean theory.[13] In case of conflict, Lockean theory would unquestionably control, and inconsistent laws or interpretations of laws would have to be cast aside to make room for suitable substitutes. In the antifoundationalist setting carved out by pragmatist philosophy, in contrast, practical solutions to actual legal problems would become paramount and philosophical justifications would play a subsidiary role. Thus, the principal objective would be to find an acceptable and workable practical solution to an actual legal problem and then resort to philosophy only to refute

12. As an example of "extreme circumstances," one could imagine a situation in which a majority of the population is so inflamed against homosexuality that a mere extension of rights to homosexuals is almost inevitably guaranteed to result in a campaign of terror and violence against them. In that situation, it would seem plausible to argue that refusal to extend rights to homosexuals is morally wrong but pragmatically justified to avoid dire consequences. It is important to note, however, that even in such an extreme situation, pragmatism itself does not, strictly speaking, require bowing to the status quo or giving in to the threat of violence. Indeed, it is by no means logically inconsistent for a pragmatist to argue that the practical consequences of a violent revolution are preferable to the practical consequences of continuing to condone an intolerable status quo.

13. This does not mean, of course, that to be a competent judge one would have to be a Lockean scholar. Rather, Lockean norms would be embedded in prevailing legal standards and Lockean reasoning would permeate legal arguments.

charges that the adopted solution is arbitrary or unethical. Putting law before philosophy, while linked to the pragmatist philosopher's skepticism
(Posner 1995, 6), is by no means an exercise in cynicism. Indeed, practical
legal problems confronting a judge may be so particularized as to defy any
neat classification in terms of any general philosophical conceptions. In a
complex situation, there may be a widely shared intuition on how to reach
a just result in a particular case. A systematic philosophical justification of
such an intuition may seem hopelessly elusive, even as some plausible, albeit
partial and incomplete, philosophical justification serves to dispel the sus-
picion that the result is merely arbitrary.

In certain other situations, there may be a clear link between a particular
legal solution and philosophically grounded support for it, but two legal
solutions widely believed to be just may lead to competing and perhaps
even inconsistent philosophical justifications. For example, one can imagine that there is widespread consensus that equality in relation to medical
benefits should be interpreted to mean equality based on need, whereas
equality in relation to employment should be construed as being limited
to formal equality of opportunity.[14] Equality according to need would be
justified under an egalitarian but not a libertarian theory of justice, while
formal equality of opportunity would be called for under a libertarian but
not an egalitarian theory of justice.[15] In short, so long as law remains in the
forefront and philosophy in the background, and so long as philosophical
pragmatism frees those who seek to determine justice according to law from
the need to be philosophically comprehensive or consistent, legal pragmatism can apparently flourish as a form of mere pragmatism. But the latter
mere pragmatism—which we may refer to as "mere legal pragmatism"—
differs significantly from the mere pragmatism that we discussed above—
which we may refer to, by way of contrast, as "mere philosophical pragmatism." Actually, mere legal pragmatism stands mere philosophical pragmatism
on its head. Under mere philosophical pragmatism, pragmatism serves as
a screen for some nonpragmatic ultimate end or justification. Under mere
legal pragmatism, philosophy furnishes an attractive wrapping for a prac-

14. Formal equality of opportunity means that "X and Y have equal opportunity in regard
to A so long as neither faces a legal or quasi-legal barrier to achieving A the other does not
face" (Fullinwider 1980, 101).

15. To be sure, equality according to need in one area and formal equality in another
could easily be made consistent by subsuming them under a suitable comprehensive theory
of justice, such as utilitarianism. Thus, it is plausible that the greatest good of the greatest
number would best be promoted by dispensing medical benefits according to need and employment positions through competition equally open to all. Nevertheless, there appears to
be no inherent contradiction in adhering to egalitarianism regardless of utilities in the context
of medical benefits and at the same time to libertarianism, even in the face of disutilities, in the
realm of employment.

tical solution to a concrete problem that stubbornly refuses to be neatly subsumed under any comprehensive theory.

The mere legal pragmatism that emerges in the second case does not do away with philosophy in the way that legal pragmatism under the first case does. Nevertheless, mere legal pragmatism deflates and relativizes the role of philosophy; seemingly places all ethical norms on an equal footing regardless of the conception(s) of the good that sustain(s) them; and thus reduces philosophy (in relation to justice according to law) to a parasitic role.

Subordinating philosophy to law may seem more appealing than altogether severing philosophy from law. But the question remains whether making philosophy parasitic on law can ultimately lead to a satisfactory solution of the problem of just interpretations. As we shall now see, the answer must be in the negative, as becomes obvious from consideration of situations in which there is sharp disagreement concerning the ends to be served by a particular law or legal interpretation.

On close examination, mere legal pragmatism only proves attractive when set against a background of widespread consensus on relevant values. Such consensus need not be philosophically comprehensive or consistent. For instance, there is nothing anomalous about a consensus based in part on libertarian ideas and in part on egalitarian ones. Moreover, so long as the consensus holds, there may be no awareness of prevailing philosophical inconsistencies and no felt need to fill existing theoretical gaps. In short, broad agreement on ends obviates the need to examine or justify them and allows for concentration on means, to wit, on legal solutions that work.

Another possibility that has the effect of relegating philosophical issues to the background is that a particular practical legal solution to a problem happens to be consistent with several otherwise inconsistent philosophical positions. For example, the legitimacy of freedom of expression can be predicated on different philosophical justifications. Thus, in the United States, free speech rights have been variously defended under a democratic self-government theory,[16] a marketplace of ideas theory,[17] and an individual self-expression theory.[18] All three of these theories justify protecting political speech, although arguably only the latter two require protecting artistic expression[19] and only the self-expression theory may cogently extend pro-

---

16. The foremost proponent of this theory was Alexander Meiklejohn. See Meiklejohn 1948.

17. This theory, which will be further explored in section V, below, has its judicial origins in Justice Holmes's famous dissent in *Abrams v. United States* (1919) and its philosophical origins in Mill (1859).

18. According to this theory, the right to self-expression is essential in relation to individual autonomy and dignity. See, e.g., Dworkin 1977; Richards 1974.

19. See Bork 1971 (advancing a narrow view of the self-government theory that condones refusing to protect works of fiction).

tection to pornography.[20] Consistent with this, proponents of all three of these theories can set their differences aside when dealing with political speech. Under these circumstances, pragmatism merely counsels not to jeopardize the pursuit of legal objectives consonant with one's philosophy, by engaging in unproductive theoretical debates that might as well be postponed.[21]

Whether complacence, confusion, or overlap is responsible for philosophy's low profile, that is not likely to last once background consensus dissolves in the face of a sharply divisive issue, such as, for example, abortion. Indeed, when dealing with an issue like abortion, the luxury of relegating theoretical concerns to a secondary plane quickly vanishes, conflict between proponents of different practical ends seems bound to erupt, and the advocates of each contending position are called on to justify their preferences. Moreover, as the debate sharpens, it becomes increasingly necessary to develop a more consistent and more comprehensive position to counter the attacks of adversaries bent on exploiting every possible inconsistency or weakness. Unless one concedes that selection among contending legal avenues is merely a matter of politics, one must reach back to find the best possible theoretical support for one's preference. In sum, when dealing with genuinely divisive issues susceptible of competing practical solutions, neither mere legal pragmatism nor mere philosophical pragmatism hold up. Accordingly, legal pragmatism can neither do away completely with philosophy nor consistently confine itself to a purely parasitic relationship to philosophy.

That leaves the third case according to which legal and philosophical pragmatism combine to yield some kind of intermediate pragmatism. In this last case, pragmatic philosophy's liberation of legal pragmatism from the constraints of comprehensive theory does not mean liberation from all philosophy or freedom to pick and choose among all philosophies. It means, instead, freedom from all philosophies other than pragmatism on the condition of submitting to the constraints dictated by pragmatist philosophy. And if these constraints are often hard to discern, it is because they seem to be primarily negative ones. But we are getting ahead of our story. Before further exploring the possibility of intermediate pragmatism, we must take a closer look at the rather different versions of pragmatism advocated respectively by Posner and Rorty.

---

20. The marketplace of ideas theory can reject protecting pornography on the grounds that it is unlikely to contribute anything to the discovery of the truth. See Schauer 1979, 605, 608 n.14; Sunstein 1986, 616–17.

21. Unlike in the case of tacit consensus, in the latter case of philosophical overlap we are dealing with mere philosophical pragmatism rather than with mere legal pragmatism.

III. POSNER'S BLEND OF SCIENTIFIC PRAGMATISM, LAW AND ECONOMICS, AND LIBERAL INDIVIDUALISM

A. Posner and Intermediate Pragmatism

Richard Posner's pragmatic jurisprudence emerges in the context of his distinguished career as a legal academic and judge. He is the preeminent exponent of the Law and Economics school, and has been for some time one of the leading federal judges in the United States.[22] His unique blend of unusually broad theoretical interests[23] and practical experience as a judge have led him to acknowledge the limitations of the economic approach to law (Posner 1995, 22–23) and to embrace philosophical pragmatism (Posner 1990, 454–69). Moreover, Posner purports to blend his philosophical pragmatism with his commitment to the economic approach to law and to liberal individualism (Posner 1995, 22–29).

Posner's pragmatism is particularly interesting for our purposes in that it seems a good candidate for an intermediate pragmatism. Indeed, Posner rejects the proposition that law is autonomous (1990, 428–53) and asserts that it is pragmatism that justifies the economic approach to law (1995, 15–21) and adherence to liberal individualism (ibid., 23). Furthermore, since Posner maintains that neither the economic approach to law nor individualistic liberalism is comprehensive (ibid., 23–25), his pragmatism calls for some but by no means all ends.[24]

Posner's brand of pragmatism is scientific in the tradition of Peirce and Dewey. In his own words:

> Pragmatism in the sense that I find congenial means looking at problems concretely, experimentally, without illusions, with full awareness of the limitations of human reason, with a sense of the "localness" of human knowledge, the difficulty of translations between cultures, the unattainability of "truth," the consequent importance of keeping diverse paths of inquiry open, the dependence of inquiry on culture and social institutions, and above all the

22. See Stephen B. Presser, "A Kinder Posner: The Master of Legal Controversy Becomes Ecumenical," *Chicago Tribune*, 23 April 1995, 2; Posner 1977, 1981.

23. In addition to his prolific contributions in law and economics, Posner has written on many diverse subjects. See, e.g., Posner 1988, 1992, 1995.

24. What should count as means and what as ends is no simple matter, for certain ends may properly be regarded as means toward other ends. Thus political liberalism may be regarded as a desirable political end but, consistent with the ideology of individualism, may also be regarded as a means toward the ultimate end of allowing each individual the greatest opportunity to pursue his or her own self-interest consistent with an equal opportunity for all. Whereas the dialectics between means and ends will be further explored below, for now suffice it that liberalism can be properly conceived as a political end and law as molded through the economic approach as a practical means necessary to promote the end of maximizing the welfare of society.

insistence that social thought and action be evaluated as instruments to valued human goals rather than ends in themselves. These dispositions, which are more characteristic of scientists than of lawyers (and in an important sense pragmatism is the ethics of scientific inquiry), have no political valence. (1990, 465)

On its face, Posner's pragmatism is thus antifoundationalist and anti-Cartesian, experimental and culturally relativistic, and open to a seemingly unlimited array of ultimate value preferences and conceptions of the good. Posner insists, moreover, that his pragmatism is antidogmatic and skeptical without being radically or dogmatically so (1995, 6). Posner regards pragmatism as sufficiently skeptical to foreclose the finality of any scientific insight or hypothesis, but not so thoroughly skeptical as to raise serious doubts about the existence of the outside world or the belief that some propositions are more sound than others (ibid.).

On more exacting scrutiny, however, Posner's pragmatism does not prove as flexible, culturally relativistic, and antidogmatic as he believes. Specifically, while Posner's pragmatism remains open-ended regarding ultimate ends, it turns out to be much more rigid than might be expected when it comes to means. To be sure, rigidity concerning means may merely result from proper focus on practical consequences. If, regardless of which of many possible ends is pursued, the same means are called for, then a singular set of means is consistent with a plurality of ends, and conditions are presumably propitious for intermediate pragmatism to thrive. But rigidity concerning means may also result from dogmatism concealed through a shift in focus from ends to means. In the latter case, what appears to be intermediate pragmatism turns out to be mere pragmatism in disguise. To determine where Posner's pragmatism fits in the last analysis, it is therefore necessary to look into its relation to the economic approach to law and to liberal individualism and to its handling of the nexus between means and ends.

Because of his openness to a wide array of diverse value preferences and goals among members of the polity, Posner seems agnostic concerning ultimate ends. Consistent with this, moreover, his economic approach to law and his liberal individualism are but means in the overall scheme of maximizing the opportunities for everyone to pursue his or her own conception of the good. And, since under pragmatism particular means become justified on proof that they afford the *best* practical path to a desired end, commitment to the economic approach to law and to liberal individualism implies that no better practical alternative has yet been found.

It seems anomalous that agnosticism regarding ends should go hand in hand with firmly entrenched means. Plausibly, in such a case, what on the surface appears as a progression from means to ends, is at bottom the product of a reversal between means and ends concealed by the vicissitudes of the dialectic that connects sequences of events into relationships of means to ends. In terms of that dialectic what should count as means, and what as ends, depends on the perspective from which a relevant sequence is approached. Thus, for example, from the perspective of achieving justice according to law, the economic approach to law emerges as a means toward the end of achieving just interpretations. By contrast, from the perspective that posits maximizing the welfare of society as the targeted end, achieving justice according to law emerges as a means. Accordingly, anything that is best characterized as an end under certain relevant perspectives, and as a means under others, can at most be a relative or intermediate end. By the same token, only something that counts as an end from the standpoint of every relevant perspective can be genuinely considered as a final end.[25] Furthermore, under pragmatism, means and intermediate ends are to be evaluated in terms of their practical contribution toward final ends. Agnosticism concerning final ends, therefore, casts a serious doubt on any preference among means or intermediate ends.

A reversal between means and ends, on the other hand, occurs when a temporal means/end sequence is juxtaposed against a conceptual, ideologically grounded means/end relationship pursuant to which the temporally anterior event constitutes the end while the temporally posterior one amounts to the means. As an illustration, consider the following example involving a lottery to dispose of a sum of money coveted by a large number of potential recipients. An obvious interpretation would be to regard the lottery as the (temporally anterior) means to a (subsequent) fair distribution of the relevant sum of money to one of the equally deserving potential recipients. But, in the context of an ideology that seeks to portray allocations of wealth as arbitrary and uncertain, it seems quite plausible to frame the lottery as a desirable or inevitable institution and to treat the actual distributions that it yields as means to reinforce a sense of arbitrariness and insecurity.[26] In the latter case, moreover, by preaching indifference as to the actual distributions resulting from the lottery, one can mask the overriding objective of legitimating the lottery as an end in itself (at least in relation to the distributions that it actually yields) by concealing the relevant conceptual sequence under the more obvious and more superficially appealing chronological sequence.

25. "Final" should be understood here as implying that the end in question cannot assume the role of a means pursuant to a shift in relevant perspective, but not as implying that it may not be legitimately substituted by another (nonintermediate) end.

26. Strictly speaking, it is the recollection of past arbitrary distributions or the projection of anticipated future ones that serves as means to cast the lottery as a desirable or inevitable institution.

To assess fairly whether Posner's pragmatism ultimately rests on a reversal of means and ends, I shall first explore to what extent his combination of agnosticism regarding ends, advocacy of the economic approach to law, and embrace of liberal individualism can be cogently defended as yielding intermediate pragmatism. To this end, I should first point out that agnosticism regarding ends can mean two different things depending on whether it is the consequence of dogmatic skepticism or of pragmatic skepticism. In the first of these cases, all ends are literally equivalent, meaning that they all stand on the same plane and that adoption of any one of them is no better or worse than adoption of any other, or of a scheme that makes for the peaceful coexistence of as many diverse ends as possible. In short, dogmatic skepticism renders all ends equally contingent and arbitrary, thus making pragmatism practically useless.

Under pragmatic skepticism, however, agnosticism regarding ends may take on an altogether different meaning. Indeed, pragmatism's antifoundationalism results not in the equivalence of all conceivable ends but rather in the belief that no conception of the good could ever be definitively established as superior to all of its rivals. Consistent with this, moreover, the pragmatist can justify putting one end on a different plane than all the others, namely the end of maximizing equal freedom to pursue other ends. This special end thus becomes a second-order end while all other ends remain in principle on the same plane as first-order ends. Under pragmatic skepticism, therefore, agnosticism regarding ends should be understood as being limited to first-order ends.

In a sense, the second-order end appears to be but a means toward first-order ends, or in other words, merely an intermediate end that must be reached to preserve the widest possible choice of final ends. But because the pragmatic skeptic can give no definitive endorsement to any first-order (final) end, he or she must rely on the second-order end as the only constant objective against which the practicality of all available means must be eventually tested. Furthermore, inasmuch as Posner views himself as a pragmatic skeptic, his agnosticism implies commitment to the second-order end. Accordingly, Posner may well prove to be an intermediate pragmatist in spite of his agnosticism. What remains to be seen, however, is whether his economic approach to law and his liberal individualism can be successfully defended as the best possible practical means toward the achievement of the predominant second-order end.

B. Pragmatism and Posner's Law and Economics

Even as tempered by his pragmatic skepticism, Posner's ambitions for the economic approach to law can hardly be characterized as modest. In his own words: "The most ambitious and probably the most influential effort in recent years to elaborate an overreaching concept of justice that will both explain judicial decision making and place it on an objective basis is that of scholars working in the interdisciplinary field of 'law and economics' as economic analysis of law is usually called" (1990, 353). Thus, if law and economics can fulfill its promise, the problem of just interpretations would largely disappear. Legal interpretation would be taken out of the hands of limited, partisan, biased, and self-interested interpretive subjects and become entrusted to the objectively grounded and empirically testable norms and instrumentalities of economic science. In a nutshell, relying on the assumption of instrumental rationality,[27] economics—in its two dimensions as a positive science that purports to explain the behavior of instrumentally rational self-interested human actors and as a prescriptive science oriented toward wealth maximization—furnishes objective (in the sense of scientifically testable) criteria for the evaluation and interpretation of laws. Thus, for example, assuming that a particular law may be susceptible to a number of different interpretations, law and economics prescribes that the interpretation best suited to lead to wealth maximization be adopted. The emphasis on wealth maximization, moreover, seems pragmatically justified as consistent with agnosticism concerning first-order ends. As Posner asserts, "wealth maximization may be the most direct route to a variety of moral ends" (ibid., 382). In other words, wealth maximization may be best suited to lead to maximization of equal freedom to pursue the widest possible range of first-order ends.

From the perspective of law and economics, justice according to law is bounded by instrumental rationality and the scientific pursuit of wealth maximization. This allows for the elimination of formalistic and subjective approaches to legal interpretation. To use an example furnished by Posner, suppose a common law judge must decide whether the finder of a lost cat is entitled to a reward on its return to an owner under the following circumstances. The owner had posted notices offering a reward for the return of the cat, but the actual finder, being unaware of such notices, did not expect any reward when he decided to bring the cat to its owner (Posner 1995, 423). Pursuant to some formalistic conception of contract law, justice would not require the owner to pay the reward, for there was no conceivable "meeting of the minds" between him and the finder. Under law and economics, however, awarding the reward to the finder would be just if enforcement of a legal rule extending rewards in all similar cases would be wealth maximizing.[28]

27. Posner 1990, 367 (economics "assume that human beings behave rationally").
28. Posner 1995. Curiously, if the common law judge follows the prescriptions of law and economics, he or she must decide the case at hand in terms of future consequences that may

As law and economics becomes ever more pervasive in its scope, it raises the question of whether in the end law might not become completely subsumed under economics. If that were to occur, then justice according to law would give way to economic justice. More generally, law and politics would become increasingly peripheral in a social world factually and normatively ruled implacably by economics. In other words, in a world in which wealth maximization is perceived as a precondition to the achievement of a plurality of ends, there is a serious danger that attention to wealth-maximizing means would overshadow the pursuit of moral ends. Accordingly, although in theory wealth maximization would only serve as means, in practice it would force all other ends to be continuously postponed or relegated to a lesser plane.[29]

One of the most vexing issues raised by law and economics is not *whether* economics should figure in contemporary determinations of justice according to law but rather *how much* or *how far* it should figure. It would be absurd to pretend that economics has nothing to contribute to just interpretations. But in some areas of law it is difficult to see what relevance, if any, economics might have in the search for just interpretations. For example, economics seems of little or no relevance in determining whether constitutional liberty, equality, or privacy should be interpreted as justifying a woman's right to an abortion.[30] Actually, even if economics could prove that a right to abortion would be wealth maximizing—which as Posner indicates it cannot, as there is no scientifically cogent way to determine the "cost" of an abortion to the aborted fetus (1995, 22)—that would hardly seem to be an important consideration for adopting or rejecting a constitutional right to abortion.

---

have no bearing on solving the dispute concerning retrospective justice that brought the parties to the present case before the court. To come back to Posner's example, there is no issue concerning wealth maximization as between the cat owner and the finder who has returned the cat. The only issue between them is one of just distribution to be determined in relation to past conduct. In terms of distributive justice, it may make a difference whether the owner or the finder ends up with the reward. From a wealth-maximization standpoint, however, the outcome of the lawsuit is indifferent, for—all other things remaining equal—overall wealth is neither increased nor decreased by a transfer of the reward from the owner to the finder. If it makes no difference, from the standpoint of distributive justice, which way the case is decided, the common law judge can both properly adjudicate the dispute at hand and further the aims of law and economics. But if distributive justice in the present case and wealth maximization in similar future cases pull in opposite directions, then to remain true to law and economics, the common law judge would, for all practical purposes, have to abdicate the role of adjudicator to embrace that of purely future-oriented legislator.

29. Cf. Smith 1976a, 477–78: "By pursuing his own interest [the individual] frequently promotes that of society more effectually than when he really intends to promote it. I have never known much good done by those who affected to trade for the public good."

30. See *Roe v. Wade* (1973).

To his credit, and true to his commitment to pragmatism, Posner has acknowledged the limits of law and economics in his more recent works.[31] But once law and economics is no longer conceived as potentially all-pervasive, the question of limits becomes highly unsettling. Does a chastened law and economics still replace the interpretive subject in many though not all cases? Or does it merely make a partial contribution to just interpretations which must be further processed and incorporated with other partial insights by an interpretive subject? To get a better handle on these questions, it is first necessary to look somewhat closer at the nexus between economics and law; to explore whether the usefulness of the economic approach to law is confined to market situations or whether it extends to nonmarket activities; and to assess the limits of normative economics as a prescriptive guide in the realm of legal relationships.

Even under the most optimistic scenario, law as a distinct practice would never give complete way to positive and normative economics. Indeed, assuming all intersubjective dealings were reducible to uninhibited fully competitive market transactions, it would still seem impossible to sustain a functioning market society without a legal regime—albeit a limited one confined to the protection of property and contract rights.[32] Moreover, it also seems highly unlikely that applications and interpretations of laws would in each and every case boil down to a straightforward economic assessment of the unmediated demands of wealth maximization. In other words, even in the best of law and economics worlds, it is hard to imagine that at least some legal rules would better serve the overall aim of wealth maximization by refraining from seeking to promote wealth maximization in the context of each individual case.[33]

In contemporary societies, the relationship between law and economics is bound to be complex and multifaceted. With respect to efficient markets, legal regulation should be limited to the minimum required to prevent

31. Compare Posner 1977 with 1990 and 1995.

32. See Unger 1983, 625: "A regime of contract is just another legal name for a market."

33. See footnote 28, above. Moreover, this argument is analogous to that made in the context of utilitarianism, according to which overall utility may be better achieved through application of a uniform rule to a whole range of cases rather than taking each case individually and acting so as to maximize utilities in that case, or in other words, that "rule-utilitarianism" is preferable at least in certain cases, to "act-utilitarianism." For a discussion of the distinction between act-utilitarianism and rule-utilitarianism, see Smart and Williams 1985, 9–11. As Posner observes, there are striking similarities between normative economics' wealth-maximization objective and that of utilitarianism. The two do not completely overlap, however, to the extent that some utility-maximizing outcomes may not be wealth maximizing. For example, if a thief enjoys a stolen object more than its rightful owner, then the theft would be utility maximizing assuming the added pleasure experienced by the thief outweighs the added pain suffered by the owner as a consequence of the theft. Condoning such theft, however, would not be wealth maximizing as it would discourage productivity. See Posner 1990, 357, 390–91.

interference with uninhibited market transactions. To the extent that markets prove inefficient, however, positive legislation becomes indispensable to make up for the imperfections of existing markets. In other words, in the context of efficient markets, the law performs a *facilitative* role, whereas in that of inefficient ones, the law must fulfill a *regulative* role aimed at correcting market deficiencies.

In theory there ought to be no significant difference whether law plays a facilitative or a regulative role. In either case, the legitimacy of a law or the justification of a particular legal interpretation would be subject to the same test, namely whether the consequence of the law or legal interpretation in question is to promote wealth maximization. In practice, however, one cannot remain within the frictionless world of perfect markets in which law is merely facilitative and outcomes automatically wealth maximizing. Instead, frictions are inevitable, littering the path to wealth maximization with serious obstacles, making it necessary to appeal to regulative law, and raising for the first time significant questions concerning distributive justice.

In the imaginary world of perfect markets, everyone enjoys unlimited access to all relevant information so that freedom of contract (relying on the modest facilitative legal regime on which it depends) guarantees the proliferation of wealth-maximizing transactions among individuals with a propensity to "truck, barter and exchange one thing for another" (Smith 1976a, 17). If we imagine, moreover, a lack of significant material disparities among contractors in such a world of perfect markets,[34] distributive justice is not likely to become a matter of concern. But once the ideal of perfect markets is left behind, distributive issues are bound to arise even if all intersubjective transactions could be subsumed under a contract paradigm. This can be illustrated by reference to the Coase theorem (Coase 1960), which furnishes some of the central ideas animating the economic analysis of law (Polinsky 1983). According to the Coase theorem, in cases with zero transaction costs,[35] a wealth-maximizing or efficient outcome will be reached regardless of the legal rule selected. If there are positive transaction costs, on the other hand, not every rule is likely to be efficient, accordingly calling for the adoption of a preferred legal rule capable of minimizing the effects of transaction costs (ibid., 13). In either case, the choice of a relevant legal rule has palpable and significant distributive effects.

---

34. This last assumption is unnecessary from the standpoint of law and economics, in view of its single-minded pursuit of wealth maximization. Nevertheless, it may make the perfect-market construct more palatable to others and may better approximate Adam Smith's vision of an atomistic market society in which no one is powerful enough to dominate competition. See Smith 1976a, 165, 382–83.

35. "In general, transaction costs include the costs of identifying the parties with whom one has to bargain, the costs of getting together with them, the cost of the bargaining process itself, and the cost of enforcing any bargain reached" (Polinsky 1983, 12).

These distributive effects become clear on consideration of the following example.[36] Suppose a factory emits smoke that damages the laundry
hung outdoors to dry by five residents who have properties adjacent to the
factory. Suppose further that if no action is taken, each resident will suffer
a loss of $100, for a total of $500. To eliminate the smoke damage, two
alternatives are available: the factory can buy a smokescreen for $150, or
each resident can buy an electric dryer for $50. The efficient solution is
obviously to buy the smokescreen, because it eliminates damages in the sum
of $500 for $150 rather than for the $250 that the five dryers would cost.
Now, assuming zero transaction costs, the same result would be reached
regardless of whether there is a legal rule making polluters responsible for
the consequences of their polluting activities or a legal rule granting factories a right to pollute, and thus placing the burden of obtaining adequate
protection on those who are affected by the pollution. Under the first rule,
the factory would have to spend the $150, whereas under the second, each
resident would have to contribute $30 to buy the smokescreen. Although
both rules are equally efficient, their distributive effects are clearly different. As a consequence of this, moreover, if a common law judge were confronted with the need to adjudicate a suit by the five residents against the
factory, wealth-maximizing considerations would be insufficient to suggest
which of the two equally efficient legal alternatives should be adopted. If
justice according to law should only be concerned with the size of the economic pie, this indeterminacy would be of no concern; if it is also to deal
with how the economic pie ought to be divided, however, then even in the
idealized world of no transaction costs, law and economics would fail to
solve a large number of legal problems.

The distributive problem is likely to be compounded in cases involving
positive transaction costs, as the efficient legal options are likely to dwindle.
Returning to our example, suppose it would cost $60 for each resident to
get together to discuss the problem and to decide on a common course of
action ($60 representing transportation and lost time costs). In that case,
under a clean air rule, the factory would still buy the smokescreen for $150,
thus producing the most efficient outcome. But under a right to pollute
rule, it would cost each resident $90 to obtain the smokescreen, which
would prompt each of them to act individually and purchase a $50 dryer.
Accordingly, the right to pollute rule would be less efficient than the clean
air rule, thus requiring the conscientious common law judge to apply the
latter rule.

Because one may tend to regard factories as more economically powerful
than individuals, the more efficient clean air may also seem better suited
to satisfy the demands of distributive justice. But by adding an additional

36. This example is provided by Polinsky (ibid., 11–13).

transaction cost to our example, we can readily see how the reduction of options when it comes to adopting efficient legal rules is likely to exacerbate the tension between wealth maximization and distributive justice. Suppose that installing the smokescreen would cost the factory an additional $120 in lost productivity as the smokescreen would require the factory to reduce somewhat its rate of production. In that case, the most efficient solution would be for each resident to purchase a dryer (thus spending $250 rather than $270 to prevent a loss of $500), and for a common law judge to apply "a freedom to pollute" rule. But what if the factory owner is more than twenty times wealthier than each of the five residents, and if the price of the factory products to the consumer would be only negligibly increased as a consequence of a reduction in productivity due to the smokescreen? Would it then be *fair* to impose a $50 cost on each resident to save the factory owner $270? Arguably, in that case efficiency and fairness are on a collision course.

Posner envisages a division of labor designed to keep efficiency issues by and large separate from issues of distribution. He stresses that distributive issues are best handled by legislatures that are well equipped to redistribute wealth through their taxing and spending powers (1990, 360). He goes on to argue, "An efficient division of labor between the legislative and judicial branches has the legislative branch concentrating on catering to interest-group demands for wealth distribution and the judicial branch on meeting the broad-based social demand for efficient rules governing safety, property, and transactions" (ibid.).

Given this framework, moreover, problems of distribution would be relegated to the political realm, with interest groups competing for influence over legislatures and legislators competing to ensure sufficient interest-group support to optimize their chances of reelection (ibid., 354–55). Consistent with this, law, as opposed to politics, would consist essentially in the interpretation and application of statutes embodying politically mediated interest-group deals concerning redistribution (ibid., 355) and in the elaboration of means for efficient dispute resolution in areas not covered by statutes. Within this perspective, to use Posner's own words, "many of the law's doctrines, procedures, and institutions can usefully be viewed as responses to the problem of transaction costs, being designed either to reduce those costs, or, if they are incorrigibly prohibitive, to bring about the allocation of resources that would exist if they were zero. The law tries to make the market work and, failing that, tries to mimic the market" (1995, 416).

Even with the division between legislative and judicial function and between politics and law suggested by Posner, the problem of distributive justice is far from being satisfactorily handled. The most persuasive pragmatic argument in favor of the marriage between the politics of wealth redistribution and the law of wealth maximization suggested by Posner seems to be that it is the best that we can realistically hope for, given a lack of consensus on ends in the context of the prevailing and current allocation of wealth in the United States (Posner 1990, 388). But that argument appears circular in that it seems to assume the inevitability of the status quo and the impracticality of any departure from it. Indeed, on the assumption that it is the most powerful interest groups who will be in the best position to influence legislatures, the combination of legislative wealth redistribution and judicial wealth maximization would seem inevitably headed toward ever-increasing disparities in wealth.[37] Posner seems mindful of the danger of giving *Homo economicus* unconstrained latitude in the realms of politics and law, as he appeals to the U.S. Constitution to curtail the most objectionable political redistributions and to rule out the most ethically reprehensible uses of wealth maximization in common law adjudication (ibid., 387–88).

Constitutional constraints may be envisioned as setting a floor above which the economics of wealth redistribution and wealth maximization would be left alone to mold legislative and judicial outcomes. For example, a constitutional prohibition against slavery would preclude legislation imposing slavery or enforcement of a contract of self-enslavement but beyond that would allow economics to shape legislation and adjudication in the field of labor relations. On further consideration, however, the above picture looms as overly mechanistic and static. Constitutional constraints embedded in a long-standing historical tradition, such as those arising under the U.S. Constitution, are likely to be evolving ones with a propensity to permeate through the legislative and judicial process rather than merely delimiting it through the deployment of bright-line boundaries. One need only recall the broad sweep of certain constitutional protections such as the Due Process Clause or the Equal Protection Clause of the U.S. Constitution[38] to realize that there is an evolving process of interpenetration between constitutional norms and other legal norms.[39] Moreover, once it is clear that constitutional norms are quite often neither transparent nor merely external to the remainder of the realm of legal relationships, then

---

37. In this respect, it is noteworthy that there is an increasing gap between rich and poor in the United States. See Keith Bradsher, "America's Opportunity Gap," *New York Times*, 4 June 1995, sec. 4, p. 1; James K. Glassman, "The Income Gap: Where's the Problem?" *Washington Post*, 25 April 1995, A17.

38. See U.S. CONST. amend. 14, §1.

39. Compare, e.g., *Lochner v. New York* (1905) (Due Process Clause forbids state from limiting the number of hours that bakery employees may work) with *West Coast Hotel v. Parrish* (1937) (minimum-wage law is not violative of the Due Process Clause), and *Plessy v. Ferguson* (1896) (racial apartheid in public accommodations permissible under the Equal Protection Clause) with *Brown v. Board of Education* (1954) (mandated racial segregation in public schools held violative of the Equal Protection Clause).

problems of constitutional interpretation may not be neatly detachable from other problems concerning legal interpretation. In other words, if constitutional interpretation is not reducible to law and economics, neither is interpretation of any law that might be plausibly subject to constitutional challenge.

The problem posed to law and economics by the need to rely on constitutional constraints is compounded on rejection of the adequacy of the economic approach when it comes to dealing with nonmarket transactions. For Posner, all human activity can be profitably understood in terms of the economic model, which postulates that all social actors are rational instrumentalists (Posner 1995, 15–16). There are serious questions, however, as to whether analogous cost/benefit considerations are equally likely to motivate a profit-seeking merchant and a would-be adulterer or a religious zealot. And the more nonmarket activities stray from the economic model, the looser becomes the grip of law and economics over the optimization of law and legal interpretation.

In the last analysis, Posner's law and economics fails the pragmatist test as it cannot secure achievement of the second-order end that emerges as the necessary correlate of agnosticism regarding first-order ends. Moreover, law and economics does not merely fall short of its intended target but squarely proves inadequate to assume a leading role in the delimitation of pragmatically justifiable legal relationships to the extent that it cannot carve out a domain free of constitutional or other nonmarket reducible constraints. Furthermore, it is possible to launch an even more radical critique of law and economics from the standpoint of intermediate pragmatism. Indeed, it is by no means self-evident that law and economics provides the best practical means—or even good practical means—toward the second-order end associated with intermediate pragmatism. For example, it is certainly not obvious that wealth maximization is more likely than utilitarianism[40] to bring us closer to the desired end. As a matter of fact, if a wealth-maximizing policy leads to greater overall unhappiness than some other policy, it is difficult to imagine why the latter policy would not be clearly preferable from a pragmatist standpoint. In short, from a pragmatist perspective, there seems to be no *ex ante* justification for embracing wealth maximization as an intermediate end. Even if in some cases it proved optimal based on an evaluation of its consequences, that would still not justify singling out wealth maximization for privileged status. Finally, a similar argument can be launched against privileging liberal individualism. Again, nothing inherent in liberal individualism makes it more suitable to bring about intermediate pragmatism's second-order end than participatory democracy, civic republicanism, or welfare liberalism, for example. Also, in

---

40. For a statement of the principal difference between the two, see footnote 33, above.

the view that wealth maximization is not automatically desirable, even proof that liberal individualism best promotes economic efficiency would not justify placing it above all other political alternatives.

Given its limitations when it comes to initial rights allocations or to non-market activities, the usefulness of positive economics in guiding our understanding of legal relationships is, at best, limited. Moreover, given that wealth maximization is far from necessarily pragmatically justified, the legitimate reach of normative economics is even more limited. As a consequence of this, Posner's pragmatism is perhaps best understood as an adjunct to his commitment to the principle of wealth maximization rather than the other way around. From this latter perspective, wealth maximization is not primarily a neutral engine designed to optimize choices for everyone. Instead, wealth maximization is part of a way of life that encompasses a value system and a conception of the good that competes with several others. What is deceiving about wealth maximization is that it does not foreclose the pursuit of certain first-order ends and is thus easily confused as being part and parcel of a second-order end. For example, wealth maximization privileges individualism and competition over communitarianism and solidarity and is accordingly much more amenable to conceptions of the good predicated on the former than on those dependent on the latter. It does not follow, however, that wealth maximization completely precludes the pursuit of preferences based on solidarity or that it must necessarily take sides among competing conceptions of the good rooted in individualism. Nevertheless, the essential points remain that wealth maximization is not neutral and that the fate of other conceptions of the good are subordinated to it rather than the other way around.

Once wealth maximization is posited as the predominant pursuit, agnosticism regarding other conceptions of the good can be mobilized to thwart the thrust of attacks launched from ideological standpoints inimical to the law and economics ethos. Similarly, under those circumstances constitutional constraints supply useful means to appease potential opponents of wealth maximization by tempering its harshest tendencies. Most important for our purposes, pragmatism can be invoked to deflect the sting of revelations concerning wealth maximization's limitations and contradictions. Accordingly, not only would Posner's pragmatism prove to be mere pragmatism rather than intermediate pragmatism, but also its principal usefulness would derive from its ability to deflect attention from dogmatic idealization of wealth maximization. Consistent with this, moreover, pragmatism as a vehicle for the justification of wealth maximization is at best merely parasitic and at worst pernicious.

The preceding analysis reveals that Posner's commitment to wealth maximization and liberal individualism is difficult to reconcile with intermediate pragmatism. That does not, however, preclude Posner from entering into the ranks of intermediate pragmatism through his defense of freedom of speech. But before tackling that issue, it is time to examine Richard Rorty's rather different brand of pragmatism.

IV. RORTY'S NEOPRAGMATISM: USING THE LINGUISTIC TURN TO REINVIGORATE IRONY, LIBERALISM, AND SOLIDARITY

The philosopher Richard Rorty is the preeminent proponent of neopragmatism, a postmodern reformulation of the pragmatist project by means of a shift in focus from experience to language.[41] Rorty's pragmatism is shaped by his radical reinterpretation of the meaning and implications of the rejection of foundationalism. For Rorty, antifoundationalism not only requires rejection of Cartesianism and Kantian moral theory (Rorty 1982, xxxvii); it also demands that we refrain from according science and "the scientific method" any special deference (Rorty 1989, 52) and that we abandon viewing language as a medium of expression or of representation (ibid., 9–10). In other words, according to Rorty, it is not useful to regard language as referring to, or corresponding to, a reality beyond it, or as connecting a subject to an object (ibid., 7, 10–11). Rather, language is most profitably conceived in Wittgensteinian terms, as a game making possible the use of alternative vocabularies relating to one another more "like alternative tools than like bits of a jigsaw puzzle" (ibid., 11). Rorty warns us, however, that language tools are in one important respect unlike other tools. For example, the tools of a craftsman are made or chosen with knowledge of the particular task for which they are intended. Language tools, by contrast, must be chosen or developed before that for which they will be used is fully known, for its very definition is dependent on the actual language tools being put into use (ibid., 12–13). In a nutshell, Rorty invites us to turn away from the interpretive subject and its elusive objects and to accept that the human self makes its mark by the use of a vocabulary (ibid., 7). Moreover, choices among alternative vocabularies are supposed to be evaluated in terms of their practical consequences—that is, in terms of whether they are likely to lead to a greater and more fruitful consensus among members of the polity.

Consistent with the place of language games in Rorty's vision, justice is more likely to emerge out of the poet's imagination than out of the philosopher's search for normative coherence (Rorty 1991). Thus, as Rorty emphasizes, there is a prophetic side to justice (ibid., 92–93). But it is an open question whether the prophetic quality of justice has anything to do with pragmatism other than that pragmatism's removal of foundations may do away with cumbersome constraints on the uses of imagination and

41. See footnote 3, above.

prophecy. Arguably, there is no intrinsic connection between Rorty's pro-phetic strand and his pragmatism.[42] Furthermore, Rorty himself has not been consistent in his own pronouncements on the relationship between pragmatism and recourse to prophecy.[43]

On the assumption that there is no intrinsic connection between proph-ecy and pragmatism, the poetry of justice would belie any nexus between justice according to law and justice beyond law, and would confine the for-mer to the realm of aesthetics. Legal interpretations could only be mean-ingfully evaluated in terms of their appeal, and judges would have to rely on their imaginations with the hope that their opinions will be able to kindle a favorable and uplifting response. In this scenario, justice would be entirely liberated from philosophy, and the legitimacy of legal interpreta-tions could only be measured by the lasting power of their aesthetic appeal.

There is another plausible reading of the link between pragmatism and prophecy which allows bringing Rorty's contribution closer to intermediate pragmatism. Under this alternative reading, antifoundationalist philosophy and the turn to language do not merely play a negative role but also bestow legitimacy on certain particular positive undertakings. In other words, in this alternative, pragmatism not only clears away obstacles that stand in the way of prophecy but also furnishes positive backing for certain crucial ele-ments in the prophetic vision. With this in mind, let us now focus on the potential of Rorty's pragmatism for forging plausible links between the critical work stemming from antifoundationalism and the constructive task of the prophetic poet.

Rorty's antifoundationalism is closely connected to an inevitable existen-tial confrontation with contingency. If we focus on the starting points of our reflection, we notice that it is contingent, that we find ourselves where we are as a consequence of chance rather than necessity (Rorty 1982, 166). Confronted with our contingency, moreover, we can either seek to escape from it or accept it and cope with it as best we can (ibid.). Those who seek to escape are likely to turn to the philosophical tradition rooted in Kant that conceives of truth as a vertical relationship between representations and what is represented (ibid., 92). To overcome the contingency of their existential predicament, they will accordingly seek to approach the latter from the vantage point of a truth anchored somewhere high above. Those willing to accept contingency, on the other hand, are likely to link up with a philosophical tradition issued from Hegel that regards truth as a horizontal process consisting in the "reinterpretation of our predecessors' reinterpre-

---

42. See Baker 1991, 99–119 (arguing that Rorty's utopianism and call for social change bears no intrinsic connection to his pragmatism).

43. Compare, e.g., Rorty 1990a ("if you had the prophecy, you could skip the pragma-tism") with Rorty 1990b (feminist prophets "might profit from thinking with the pragmatists").

tation of their predecessors' reinterpretation" (ibid.). Unlike their Hegelian predecessors, however, those who are prepared to confront contingency do not believe that successive reinterpretations will progressively approximate any comprehensive truth, albeit an immanent one. The point of reinterpretation is not discovery or realization of any transcendent or immanent truth but redescription in the hope of finding ways better suited to handle our contingency on the realization that it is fruitless to attempt to escape from it.

The justification for choosing redescription as opposed to appeal to vertical truth is pragmatic. Indeed, to be concerned with vertical truth is unproductive in much the same way as it is not helpful to become bogged down with questions about the existence or the nature of God. Just as the secularist maintains that we should not dwell on questions beyond our capacities to resolve, so too the pragmatist insists that we should not waste our time worrying about the truth, since we are not in a position to ascertain its existence or precise nature (ibid., xiv).

By refusing to look beneath or beyond language, Rorty comes close to Derrida's insistence that we regard all texts—written or unwritten—as writings referring to other writings (ibid., 94; chap. I, above). Moreover, whereas Rorty admires Derrida—and in particular later Derrida (Rorty 1989, 124 n. 6)—he has certain reservations about the Derridean enterprise.[44] Without delving further into Rorty's assessment of Derrida, it suffices for our purposes to emphasize that the principal difference between the two is that Rorty is more directly concerned with practical consequences and is more squarely future oriented than is Derrida. Indeed, whereas Rorty embraces the Heideggerian notion that "language speaks man" and acknowledges that "human beings cannot escape their historicity," he nevertheless stresses that they can "manipulate the tensions within their own epoch in order to produce the beginnings of the next epoch" (Rorty 1989, 50).

Not only does Rorty have important affinities to Derrida, but his pragmatism also relies on a dialogical proceduralism reminiscent of Habermas. Indeed, for Rorty, the legitimate resolution of conflicts among competing redescriptions vying for general acceptability is by means of an undistorted dialogue (Rorty 1982, 164–65, 173–74). Like Habermas,[45] Rorty maintains that contested alternatives be submitted to others for consideration and discussion and that the normative validity of an alternative derives from its ability to generate a consensus among all those who are engaged in the relevant dialogue. Significantly, however, Rorty parts company with Habermas when it comes to defining "undistorted" dialogue. In explaining what

---

44. See Rorty 1982, 99 (warning against Derrida's tendency to succumb to nostalgia and to engage in system building).

45. See chapter V, above.

should count as "undistorted," Habermas, according to Rorty, "goes transcendental and offers principles. The pragmatist, however, must remain
ethnocentrist and offer examples" (ibid., 173). In other words, in contrast
to Habermas's Kantian dialogical proceduralism, in Rorty's version of undistorted dialogue, the participants are aware of their contingent starting
points, conscious that they cannot transcend the imprints of their own culture, and mindful of the fortuity and fragility of any consensus that they
might happen to reach (ibid., 173-75).

The critical side of Rorty's antifoundationalism leads to the same conclusion as does Posner's: no one can prove that his or her conception of
the good—or in Rorty's characterization, his or her "final vocabulary"[46]—is
superior to any other. Moreover, agnosticism concerning final vocabularies calls for a split between first-order ends and the second-order end of
maximizing freedom to develop and of choosing among final vocabularies.
Consistent with this, within the confines of an intermediate pragmatist
framework, Rorty's prophetic vision seems a good candidate to complement
critical antifoundationalism and furnish the requisite positive component
needed to elaborate a coherent practical approach for dealing with the contingency, diversity, and volatility of first-order ends. It remains to be seen
whether Rorty's prophetic vision can be integrated into a workable conception of intermediate pragmatism. As we will now see, however, it is clear
that the positive side of Rorty's theory differs very significantly from that
of Posner.

What drives Rorty's positive contribution is the redescription of the liberal project consistent with the practical implications of his critical analysis.
The protagonist of Rorty's prophetic journey is the "liberal ironist." To be
"liberal," in Rorty's redescription, is to think that "cruelty is the worst thing
we do" (1989, xv); to be an "ironist" is to recognize the contingency of
one's innermost beliefs and desires (ibid.). Accordingly, the liberal ironist
seems bound to be committed to the pursuit of two distinct ends: eradicat-
ing cruelty and combating against the forceful imposition of any final vocabulary. Both these ends, moreover, appear consistent with the concept of
intermediate pragmatism in that they can be plausibly integrated into a
project to secure a second-order end to allow for maximization of equal
opportunities to pursue first-order ends.

Rorty's prophetic agenda combines an individualistic objective with a
collective one, namely self-creation with solidarity (ibid.). On the one hand,
everyone should be given as much room as possible to use his or her imagination to devise a final vocabulary better suited to his or her needs and

---

46. See Rorty 1989, 73: "All human beings carry about a set of words which they employ
to justify their actions, their beliefs, and their lives. . . . I shall call these words a person's final
vocabulary."

desires. Moreover, from a political standpoint, all that opportunity for self-creation requires, according to Rorty, is peace, wealth, and the standard "bourgeois freedoms" (ibid., 84). On the other hand, the collective pursuit of solidarity also involves reliance on imagination, in this case to foster an ever more broadly encompassing mutual perception as fellow sufferers who are vulnerable to humiliation (ibid., xvi, 91).[47]

Given the predominant role Rorty envisions for imagination with respect to both the individualistic and the collective component of his prophetic conception, it is not surprising that he advocates a shift in emphasis from science and rationality to poetry, literary criticism, and utopian politics (ibid., 52–53). Indeed, it is the strong evocative powers of the poet and the literary critic that can foster greater awareness of and greater sensitivity toward the suffering and the vulnerability to humiliation of fellow humans whom we may have thus far approached as outsiders, strangers, or outcasts. Similarly, an imaginative utopian politics may be useful to unfasten entrenched prejudices, to expose settled political institutions and practices inimical to self-creation and solidarity, and to suggest new ways of incorporating the marginalized. The pursuit of poetic imagination and the evocation of utopian politics may thus unite to further two interrelated practical objectives: to enlarge as much as possible the space for idiosyncratic individual self-creation and to narrow as much as possible the (perceived) differences that stand as obstacles to achieving greater solidarity.[48]

The two objectives of making more room for individual idiosyncrasy and of fomenting greater solidarity may well appear to be at loggerheads. Arguably, following the threads of one's idiosyncratic imagination is a rather solipsistic endeavor, whereas developing sufficient empathy toward other human beings to perceive them as fellow sufferers, on the contrary, requires a certain measure of self-abnegation and an altruistic gesture of openness toward the other. Within the confines of Rorty's prophetic vision the tension between the individualist and the collective objective can be productively harnessed to further the agenda of the liberal ironist. From a less utopian standpoint, however, this tension raises serious questions concerning whether Rorty's positive conception can be ultimately reconciled with intermediate pragmatism. This last question is best postponed until after completion of our examination of the promise of Rorty's prophetic vision. For the moment, suffice it to note that the difficulties in the case of Rorty concern means and intermediate ends rather than final ends.

47. As Rorty emphasizes, the liberal ironist "thinks that recognition of a common susceptibility to humiliation is the *only* social bond that is needed" (ibid., 91; emphasis in original).

48. See ibid., 192 (moral progress toward greater solidarity depends on "the ability to see more and more traditional differences [of tribe, religion, race customs, and the like] as unimportant when compared to similarities with respect to pain and humiliation").

From within Rorty's own perspective, what binds individualism and solidarity closer together is not logic but the consequences of contingency. Because of the precariousness and vulnerability of the individual who cannot ground any final vocabulary on a solid foundation, everyone is relegated to projecting into the future a plausible hope of redemption that will make up for the painful limitations inherent in his or her present predicament (ibid., 86). Rorty emphasizes that this hope is a common one. He writes, "What binds societies together are common vocabularies and common hopes. The vocabularies are, typically, parasitic on the hopes—in the sense that the principal function of the vocabularies is to tell stories about future outcomes which compensate for present sacrifices" (ibid.). We should not infer from this passage, however, that Rorty preaches subordinating individualist aspirations to collective undertakings. Indeed, as he emphatically indicates, for the liberal ironist "human solidarity is not a matter of sharing a common truth or a common goal but of sharing a common selfish hope, the hope that one's world—the little things around which one has woven into one's final vocabulary—will not be destroyed" (ibid., 92). In sum, the nexus between individualism and solidarity depicted by Rorty appears to be a pragmatic one based on recognition of the inevitability of contingency. Accordingly, solidarity may be imaginatively promoted through poetic narrative, but what predisposes the individual to remain open to it is fear of being trivialized and humiliated and the desire to give free rein to his or her own idiosyncratic imagination in order to develop future hopes that might be usefully pitted against present insufficiencies.

Rorty's focus on future hopes admittedly bears a parallel to religious promises of redemption in the afterworld as compensation for the inevitability of present sacrifices (ibid., 86). Rorty's promise of redemption differs in a crucial respect, however, from its religious counterpart. Redemption in a secular society, according to Rorty, depends "on the existence of reasonably concrete, optimistic, and plausible *political* scenarios, as opposed to scenarios about redemption beyond the grave" (ibid., 86; emphasis in original). In other words, what Rorty the prophet offers is political redemption that somehow weaves together overlapping individualistic and collective concerns (ibid., 92–93). To be sure, how the requisite blend between individualism and solidarity is to be achieved is never clearly spelled out. Nevertheless, Rorty's prophetic vision seems quite amenable to being incorporated into a framework comprised of a second-order (primarily) collective objective allowing for the maximization of opportunities to pursue the widest possible array of (primarily) individually grounded first-order preferences.

The political means Rorty considers necessary to render his hopes for redemption in this world realistic are startlingly simple and familiar. He

states, "I think that contemporary liberal society already contains the institutions for its own improvement. . . . Indeed my hunch is that Western social and political thought may have had the last *conceptual* revolution it
needs. J. S. Mill's suggestion that governments devote themselves to optimizing the balance between leaving people's private lives alone and preventing suffering seems to me pretty much the last word" (ibid., 63; emphasis in original). Moreover, the principal difference between Rorty's
postmodern liberal ideal and its Millian counterpart stems from Rorty's
insistence on privileging the role of language and narrative to the exclusion
of anything that may lie behind or beyond language. In Rorty's ideal liberal
society, change is the result of persuasion rather than force, reform rather
than revolution (ibid., 60). Also, since the best hope for liberal society is
that it will foster useful redescriptions, uninhibited freedom of expression
ranks among its paramount objectives.

It is true that freedom of expression already occupied a similar promi-
nence in Mill's vision. But Mill, who unearthed the philosophical roots of
the marketplace of ideas justification of freedom of speech, was convinced
that uninhibited discussion afforded the best possible means toward discovery of the truth (Mill 1859, 15–52). Rorty, by contrast, values discussion
for its own sake and preaches freedom of expression as the best hope to
lead to more speech instead of the use of force (Rorty 1989, 52). In short,
the paramountcy of freedom of expression is doubly justified in Rorty's
prophetic vision. On the one hand, it enlarges the horizon for redescription; on the other, it serves to channel conflicts toward resolution by means
of discussion as opposed to force. It is Rorty's hope that in a liberal society
committed to freedom of expression the poet and the innovator will prevail.
And if that makes life harder for others, Rorty reassures us that we need
not worry, for it will be harder "only by words, and not deeds" (ibid., 61).

In the last analysis, Rorty's critical analysis and his prophetic vision can
be plausibly combined to yield a seemingly coherent version of intermediate
pragmatism. Moreover, since Rorty's philosophy is driven by at least one
constant objective, namely the hope for more useful redescription, the intermediate pragmatism to which it apparently leads would qualify as a pragmatism of ends, at least with respect to one end. That (second-order) end
is the maximization of opportunities for imaginative redescriptions, and it
calls for at least one legal norm, namely affording the greatest possible protection to freedom of expression. Accordingly, in spite of their otherwise
significant differences, Posner and Rorty both concur that pragmatist philosophy lends support to freedom of expression. It is now time to take a
closer critical look at this common conclusion, by inquiring whether the
pragmatist defense of freedom of expression can overcome the challenge
posed by extremist and hate speech. Also, after this inquiry, we will be in

a better position to answer the question raised but left open above, that is, whether Rorty's prophetic vision is ultimately unpragmatic because of its shortcomings regarding means rather than ends.

V. PHILOSOPHIC PRAGMATISM, FREEDOM OF EXPRESSION, AND THE PARADOXES OF EXTREMIST AND HATE SPEECH

A. *Pragmatism and the Free Marketplace of Ideas*

There is a strong affinity between the pragmatist justifications of freedom of speech propounded respectively by U.S. Supreme Court Justice Oliver Wendell Holmes, Posner, and Rorty and the utilitarian justification elaborated by John Stuart Mill. Significantly, the philosophers Mill and Rorty display a much more optimistic outlook concerning the virtues of freedom of expression than do the judges Holmes and Posner. Nevertheless, the views of all four converge when it comes to the question of truth in that they all reject the Kantian conception of truth as a vertical relationship. Accordingly, all four of them advance a justification of freedom of expression predicated on the impossibility of complete or immutable truth.

Mill's strong defense of freedom of expression is rooted in his individualism and in his optimism concerning the possibility of social progress. Operating within a utilitarian framework, Mill embraces the general principle that society can limit the individual's freedom to promote the common good whenever an individual's *action* is not purely self-regarding—that is, when it is likely to have a direct impact on the well-being of others (Mill 1859, 73–74). That general principle is largely inapplicable, however, in the context of *expression*. Indeed, in Mill's view, even an expression that is directly harmful to others should remain beyond regulation unless it amounts to an *incitement* to violence.[49] Moreover, underlying Mill's opposition to regulating harmful speech is his firm belief that free discussion is indispensable to the discovery of incremental truth and to social progress.[50] Thus, stripped to its utilitarian essentials, Mill's broad justification of freedom of expression boils down to the following: the long-term benefits (in relation to truth and social progress) of uninhibited discussion are bound to outweigh the sum of harms attributable to (noninciting) expression.

---

49. See Mill 1859, 53 (opinions lose their immunity when their expression amounts to "a positive instigation to some mischievous act"). Cf. *Brandenburg v. Ohio* (1969) (speech that "incites" to violence rather than merely "advocating" violence is not constitutionally protected).

50. See Mill 1859, 50–52. Suppressing expression that incites to violence is consistent with Mill's view that the broadest possible uninhibited discussion offers the best means toward truth and progress. Indeed, inciting speech by its very nature seems more likely to lead to violence than to more speech. See Redish 1984, 191.

Holmes imported Mill's broad justification of freedom of expression into constitutional jurisprudence and gave birth to the marketplace of ideas justification of speech,[51] which has been influential in the United States ever since (Schauer 1982, 15–16). Although Holmes's *justification* of free expression is very similar to Mill's, the respective *reasons* that led the two men to embrace the same principle are in sharp contrast. Indeed, whereas Mill is led by optimism and belief in progress, Holmes is driven by skepticism and pessimism. In particular, Holmes is quite skeptical about the possibility of truth. In one of his letters, Holmes writes, "When I say a thing is true I mean that I can't help believing it—and nothing more. But as I observe that the Cosmos is not always limited by my Cant Helps, I don't bother about absolute truth or even inquire whether there is such a thing, but define the truth as the system of my limitations."[52] Consistent with this view, Holmes endorses a free marketplace of ideas on pragmatic grounds. Because most wrongly held views eventually prove false, any limitation on speech is most likely to be grounded on a false idea. Accordingly, a free marketplace of ideas is likely to reduce harm in two distinct ways: it lowers the probability that expression will be needlessly suppressed on account of falsehoods; and it encourages most of us, who are prone to stubbornly hold on to worthless or harmful ideas on the belief that they are true, to develop a healthy measure of self-doubt.[53]

What unites Mill and Holmes in spite of their differences—and what links Posner to both of them—is the belief that constraining the marketplace of ideas would do more harm than good. Posner's pragmatic rationale in favor of the marketplace of ideas actually straddles a middle course between Mill and Holmes. Like Holmes, Posner is wary of objective truth, but coming closer to Mill he is rather optimistic about the possibility of scientific progress (Posner 1991, 36–37). Moreover, having had the benefit of the extensive American debate on freedom of speech since the days of Holmes, Posner adopts a broader, more encompassing view of the marketplace of ideas than his two illustrious predecessors. Unlike them, Posner is not constrained by the model of scientific discussion and thus refuses to draw any sharp boundaries between rational and emotive expression, such as artistic expression, or symbolic action with a predominant expressive content—for example, draft card or flag burning (Posner 1990, 467). In short, Posner maintains that any expression, whether rational or emotive, factual or fictional, that may lead to consequences in the world of facts should be protected within the framework of the marketplace of ideas

51. See *Abrams v. United States* (1919), at 630 (Holmes, J., dissenting).
52. Oliver Wendell Holmes to Learned Hand, 24 June 1918, cited in Gunther 1975, 757.
53. See *Abrams v. United States* (1919), at 630.

(ibid.). Also, by emphasizing the importance of emotive expression and fiction, Posner's justification of freedom of expression displays an important affinity to that of Rorty.

Posner's endorsement of his expanded version of the marketplace of ideas is not unlimited, however. In what appears to be a departure from the Millian ideal, Posner indicates that certain restrictions on the marketplace of ideas may be warranted when the failure to impose them is likely to impose too high a cost on society (ibid.). In his most recent writings, Posner seems to retreat even further from an unqualified endorsement of the free marketplace of ideas. He writes, "Nothing in pragmatism teaches that the harms caused by speech should be ignored; nothing justifies the privileging of freedom of speech over other social interests" (1995, 396).

Whether Posner's apparent recent retreat from the Millian ideal is ultimately attributable to his pragmatism or to his commitment to wealth maximization is a question that is best deferred until after consideration of the case of extremist and hate speech. In the meantime, suffice it to reiterate that whereas their respective reasons may differ somewhat, and whereas their respective attitudes to the relation between freedom of expression and discovery of the truth vary significantly in scope and emphasis, Holmes, Posner, and Rorty all strongly embrace the Millian ideal of a free marketplace of ideas because of their conviction that it comports with the practical dictates of pragmatism. Accordingly, it is time to turn to the problems raised by extremist and hate speech in order to evaluate the pragmatist justification of freedom of expression, and to be in a better position to offer a cogent critical assessment of the viability of the concept of intermediate pragmatism.

B. Theoretical and Practical Problems Raised by Extremist and Hate Speech

Constitutional provisions affording protection to speech and expression tend to be uniformly sweeping and indeterminate (Schauer 1994, 356–57). These free speech provisions, moreover, give rise to widely diverging interpretations (ibid.), thus squarely raising questions concerning the criteria of legitimacy in constitutional interpretation. Perhaps nowhere are these questions more acute than in the context of extremist and hate speech in which American jurisprudence stands in sharp contrast to that of many other Western democracies.[54]

Extremist speech, as already mentioned, gives rise to what Karl Popper

---

54. See, e.g., 3 R.S.C. c. 46, §319 (1985) (Canada); Public Order Act, 1986, chap. 64, §§17–29 (United Kingdom); and Convention on the Elimination of All forms of Racial Discrimination (1965), U.N.G.A. Res. 2106 Axx, 600 U.N.T.S. 195 (1969).

has called the "paradox of tolerance."[55] Briefly, the paradox arises as a consequence of tolerating the intolerant. In a tolerant society, the intolerant can take advantage of the broad protection of speech to spread extremist views. And if these views prove persuasive to a large enough audience, the intolerant may well be in a position to ascend to power and to eradicate tolerance. Hence the quandary: to remain tolerant, must a society be consistently tolerant toward all? Or must it, to protect itself, be intolerant of the intolerant?

The paradox raised by hate speech is analogous to that triggered by extremist speech.[56] Indeed, just as a tolerant society depends on the willingness to live in peace with those who do not share one's outlook and views, a free marketplace of ideas seems viable only so long as it affords a fair forum for the uninhibited examination and free discussion of all ideas and viewpoints. To be sure, not all ideas or viewpoints that reach the marketplace are likely to fare equally well. Undoubtedly, at any time, some ideas will be widely embraced while others will be roundly rejected. But there is a crucial difference between rejecting an idea based on an assessment— even an erroneous one—of its merits and rejecting an idea based on prejudice or hatred against its proponent. Thus, if hate propaganda succeeds in vilifying its target group by fomenting contempt among nonvictims coupled with self-doubt and withdrawal among victims, the marketplace is in grave danger of becoming thoroughly corrupted.

At first, it seems that recourse to pragmatism affords the best means to deal with the paradoxes raised by extremist and hate speech. Indeed, no systematic solution looms as wholly satisfactory as it cannot solve numerous theoretical and practical problems posed by extremist or hate speech. For example, a complete ban would sweep much too broadly, equate hatred of the oppressor and the oppressed,[57] blur the distinction between endorsement of and satirical reference to reprehensible views,[58] and generate dif-

55. For a more extended analysis of the constitutional implications of this paradox, see Rosenfeld 1987.

56. Extremist and hate speech are distinguishable even though they often go hand in hand, as in the case of Nazism where political totalitarianism was combined with systematic hate propaganda against Jews. It is possible, however, to embrace totalitarian political extremism without harboring any hatred on the basis of race, sex, ethnic origin, religion, or sexual orientation. Thus, for example, one could conceivably adhere to a radical, antidemocratic, communist vision predicated on rigid forced egalitarianism. By the same token, it is possible to reject political extremism in favor of a certain conception of democracy and yet hate, vilify, and demean the members of certain racial, ethnic, or religious groups.

57. See, e.g., Skillen 1982, 142 (noting the irony of the fact that the first person to be convicted under the British 1965 Race Relations Act for uttering a racially derogatory expression was a black).

58. For example, in the late 1960s, an American fictional television series was based on

ficult line-drawing problems.[59] The complete absence of any ban, on the other hand, would facilitate the imposition of oppression and its perpetuation, would encourage violence in certain circumstances, and would stand in the way of implementing a policy of equal dignity and equal respect for every member of society.[60] In contrast, a pragmatic approach focusing on likely actual consequences might seem best suited to avoid undesirable extremes without having to be sacrificed to satisfy impractical demands of theoretical coherence.[61] Thus, for example, American legal commentators have argued that tolerance of extremist speech is justified in the United States although it may not be in Germany, because the respective historical experiences of both countries make the United States much less vulnerable than Germany to the perils of Nazism (Bollinger 1986, 198–99; Schauer 1994, 365–67).

On further reflection, however, the pragmatist approach to extremist and hate speech proves to be seriously deficient. Beyond requiring the obvious caveat that theoretical coherence does not justify accepting practical consequences contrary to those sought to be achieved, pragmatism's contribution regarding extremist and hate speech looms as largely circular. Because of the complexities inherent in the dialectic between tolerance and intolerance,[62] the practical consequences of different approaches to extremist and hate speech are likely to be varied and nuanced rather than clear-cut. Accordingly, focus on practical consequences would at best be inconclusive, thus triggering the need to choose among different sets of similarly plausible practical consequences. To a significant degree, moreover, the practical consequences of tolerance or intolerance toward certain views may be simply unpredictable. It does not follow from this that choosing between tolerance and intolerance should no longer be considered a matter of concern. But it may well follow that the choice in question, while normatively important, does not depend, by and large, on practical consequences.

---

a satire meant to ridicule Archie Bunker, an unenlightened racial bigot. Significantly, however, public surveys indicated that a (sizable) portion of the viewers identified with, not against, Archie Bunker. See Key 1973, 159.

59. For example, should the ban encompass advocacy but not a sympathetic depiction of an extremist position in the course of a classroom discussion? Should the ban extend to a true statement exploited for purposes of propagating racial hatred? Cf. sec. 319 (3) of the Canadian Criminal Code (truth is a defense to criminal charges for propagating hatred against an identifiable group pursuant to sec. 319 [2]).

60. See *Regina v. Keegstra* (1990) (majority opinion of Supreme Court of Canada upholding constitutionality of statute criminalizing hate propaganda).

61. See, e.g., Grey 1991, 22–26 (advocating a pragmatic solution to the problem of hate speech on university campuses by borrowing from the theories that respectively buttress constitutional liberty and constitutional equality without attempting to reconcile the two).

62. For a more extended examination of this dialectic, see Rosenfeld 1987, 1460–66.

To illustrate these last points, one need only consider briefly certain aspects of the dialectic between tolerance and intolerance. There is a significant asymmetry between tolerance and intolerance (Rosenfeld 1987, 1461– 67). Intolerance implies disapproval, but tolerance, depending on the circumstances, may communicate approval or disapproval. Thus, a religious person with a profound aversion to abortion may nonetheless consistently maintain that he feels politically obligated to tolerate abortion, although he cannot endorse it, and is prepared to argue against it in front of anyone who still has an open mind on the issue. On the other hand, whereas tolerance implies disagreement, it does not necessarily require disapproval. For example, a scientist may disagree with the theories of a colleague and yet approve of the latter as a worthy member of the scientific community. Furthermore, there are cases in which a plea for tolerance not only involves approval but also an intent to mask agreement. For example, white students who defend the right of a member of the Ku Klux Klan to be a featured speaker at the university in the name of tolerance may be motivated by tacit agreement with the proposed speaker's racist message.[63] Finally, tolerance bears a different connotation whether it results from a genuine act of self-restraint—such as when someone powerful refrains from taking available measures against less powerful people whose conduct he strongly disapproves—or from conditioning by more powerful outside forces, thus corresponding to what Herbert Marcuse labeled "passive toleration" (1965, 85)—such as when a benefit to a much-victimized group is conditioned on the exercise of stoic self-restraint in the face of demeaning treatment by members of other groups.

The above examples suffice to make it clear that, depending on the circumstances, tolerance and intolerance are likely to have very different practical consequences. Whether tolerance is inclusionary or exclusionary depends on the relevant context, and whether a policy of inclusion or exclusion is more desirable under given circumstances seems more a matter of substantive value preferences than one of predominantly pragmatic considerations.

That no single pragmatic course of action emerges in the context of extremist and hate speech is well illustrated by the contrast between the respective constitutional jurisprudence of Canada and the United States. Although neither Canada nor the United States affords unqualified protection to speech,[64] the constitutional jurisprudence of the United States has

63. As noted by one commentator, the appeal to tolerance in this last case may amount to a "form of vicarious aggression" (Bollinger 1986, 233).

64. In the case of Canada, see, e.g., *Regina v. Keegstra* (criminalization of hate speech held constitutional); in that of the United States, see, e.g., *Chaplinsky v. New Hampshire* (1942) ("fighting words" are not protected speech).

displayed much greater tolerance toward extremist and hate speech than that of Canada. Indeed, toleration of hate speech is a divisive issue on both sides of the border,[65] but in more recent times, American courts have come down on the side of toleration of hate speech,[66] and Canadian courts on the opposite side.[67] The dominant position in the United States, consistent with a marketplace of ideas approach, is that content-based regulations of speech pose a serious threat to the ideal of an "uninhibited, robust and wide open" debate on public issues[68] which lies at the core of the American commitment to free speech. Accordingly, extremist or hate speech that falls short of "fighting words" or of triggering an incitement to violence ought to be tolerated and fought with more speech rather than with censorship. In contrast, the position adopted by a majority on the Supreme Court of Canada is that some sacrifice in the scope of public debate is warranted in order to deal with the serious harm threatened by hate speech.[69] Stressing Canada's commitment to equality and to multiculturalism, the Supreme Court upheld the ban on hate speech because of its serious potential for humiliating and degrading those whom it targets and for gradually prejudicing the remainder of society against members of the targeted group.[70]

Once one realizes that the United States and Canada have certain different priorities, it becomes obvious that nothing inherent in either approach makes it more pragmatic than the other. If one is concerned with the gradual yet potentially devastating effect of hate speech on self-esteem and on respect for others, then the Canadian approach looms as more pragmatic than the American one. Indeed, by allowing restrictions on speech only if it poses a "clear and present danger" to society[71] or if it amounts to an incitement to violence,[72] American constitutional jurisprudence is

65. The Supreme Court of Canada decided the *Keegstra* case by a four to three majority. Meanwhile the refusal of American courts to exclude hate speech from constitutional protection has been surrounded by an often strident and bitter polemic. See, e.g., Bollinger 1986, 14–15 (discussing upheaval and dissent within the American Civil Liberties Union [ACLU] pursuant to its decision to represent neo-Nazis bent on marching in full uniform including swastika in a suburban area heavily populated by Jewish survivors of Nazi concentration camps); Matsuda 1989 (arguing that severe impact of hate speech on its victims justifies criminalization).

66. See, e.g., *Brandenburg v. Ohio* (1969) (Ku Klux Klan "advocacy" of [as opposed to "incitement" to] violence against Jews and blacks is constitutionally protected); *Collins v. Smith* (7th Cir. 1978), cert. den. (1978) (neo-Nazi march in Jewish neighborhood is constitutionally protected); and *R.A.V. v. City of St. Paul, Minnesota* (1992) (statute criminalizing hate speech held unconstitutional as applied to Ku Klux Klan-style cross burning).

67. See *Regina v. Keegstra* (upholding constitutionality of criminalization of anti-Semitic hate propaganda).

68. *New York Times Co. v. Sullivan* (1964), at 270.

69. See *Regina v. Keegstra* (1990), at 795.

70. Ibid., at 746–48.

71. See *Schenck v. United States* (1919).

72. See *Brandenburg v. Ohio* (1969).

poorly adapted, from a practical standpoint, to deal with speech that produces humiliation instead of provoking violence and that gradually undermines the very fabric of social cohesion instead of immediately threatening to tear it to shreds. Conversely, of course, if the object is to foster the greatest dissemination of available views, limited only by avoidance of imminent danger and violence, then the American approach clearly seems more pragmatically suited than its Canadian counterpart.

It may also be that the Canadian approach exaggerates the harms of hate speech while the American one underestimates them.[73] More generally, it seems quite plausible that there is no reliable way to predict the practical consequences of tolerating extremist and hate speech, as the number and complexity of relevant factors and as the full gamut of contextual variations far exceed our grasp. In the latter case, pragmatism would be of little help in selecting a constitutional approach to extremist and hate speech, but that would by no means obviate the need for one. Accordingly, the choice would have to depend on conceptions of the good and value preferences rather than on practical considerations. Consistent with this, the Canadian approach would be better suited for those with a more egalitarian and multicultural outlook while the American one would seem preferable for those with a libertarian bent. In sum, there is no pragmatist solution to the paradoxes of extremist and hate speech. At best, there are different pragmatist means suited to different nonpragmatist ends. At worst, the role of pragmatism is reduced to the negative task of preventing nonpragmatic designs from leading to consequences that are diametrically opposed to those that were originally intended.

C. Critique of the Pragmatist Justification of Freedom of Expression

The preceding observations concerning extremist and hate speech suggest that the pragmatists' trust in the Millian ideal is misplaced. As the Supreme Court of Canada has stated, "The successes of modern advertising, the triumphs of impudent propaganda such as Hitler's, have qualified sharply our belief in the rationality of man. We know that under the strain and pressure in times of irritation and frustration, the individual is swayed and even swept away by hysterical emotional appeals. We act irresponsibly if we ignore the way in which emotion can drive reason from the field."[74] Thus, assuming that uninhibited discussion is insufficient to ward off the evils threatened by hate speech, and that hate speech can cause serious incre-

---

73. In this connection, it seems quite remarkable that in the United States with its long history of slavery, racial segregation, and ruthless violence against African-Americans, the criminalization of Ku Klux Klan cross burnings should not survive a constitutional challenge on free speech grounds. See *Brandenburg v. Ohio* (1969).

74. *Regina v. Keegstra* (1990), at 744.

mental harm, leaving the marketplace of ideas open to hate speech would most likely lead to more harm than good.

Rejection of the Millian ideal seems most damaging to Rorty's prophetic vision of a society devoted to persuasion and redescription. To be sure, Rorty, unlike Mill, is not concerned with advancing the cause of truth. Nevertheless, very much in the tradition of Mill, Rorty assumes that harms perpetrated by words are less serious than those perpetrated by deeds. To the extent that extremist and hate speech belie that assumption, however, persuasion and redescription may inflict harms that are comparable to those flowing from evil deeds. Indeed, it would not be surprising if a protracted verbal hate campaign proved more painful, more demeaning, and more humiliating than an occasional physical drubbing. Moreover, precisely because Rorty admonishes us that there is not much use to being overly concerned with the truth, there would seem to be virtually no constraint against using one's creative power of imagination to generate redescriptions that are more humiliating and demeaning than uplifting.[75] Consistent with this, pragmatism can offer no assurance that Rorty's prophetic utopian dream of solidarity among poets will not turn into a harrowing nightmare of hate propaganda and humiliation. In short, even if Rorty's objective of making room for more useful redescription can be fully justified under pragmatism, the Millian marketplace of ideas fails the pragmatist test for qualifying as a suitable means toward that end.

On the surface, it may seem that rejection of the Millian ideal does not deal as severe a blow to the pragmatic defense of the marketplace of ideas advanced by Holmes. Holmes harbors no prophetic dreams or misplaced optimism. He resorts to the marketplace of ideas because of his distrust of the state's ability to distinguish between useful and harmful speech and because of his distaste for the unwarranted hubris of those who stubbornly hold on to their erroneous ideas. Accordingly, even if hate speech is harmful, trusting the state to decide when speech should be protected might in the end prove worse.

On further consideration, however, Holmes's argument for the marketplace of ideas may be more persuasive than Rorty's, but it is hardly convincing or compelling from the standpoint of pragmatism. On the one hand, if it is much more likely that any given idea will prove false rather than true, then it is by no means obvious that a certain measure of unwarranted state suppression of views would be worse than an unimpeded flow

---

75. Rorty could argue that this pessimistic scenario is unrealistic in view of the liberal ironist's aversion to cruelty. To the extent that Rorty would open the Millian marketplace of ideas to everyone, however, the self-imposed constraints of the liberal ironist would be plainly insufficient to turn away harmful redescriptions. Thus even if the liberal ironist is legitimated by intermediate pragmatism, the Millian marketplace of ideas need not be.

of extremist views and hate propaganda. Moreover, it is not clear that misplaced confidence in one's most likely erroneous views will lead to more harmful consequences than constant insecurity and self-doubt. Indeed, intolerance may well be caused more often by self-doubt and insecurity than by overconfidence (Bollinger 1986, 86).

On the other hand, even if we were to agree that the benefits to be gained from the unimpeded flow of all ideas (except those that provoke an imminent danger of violence) far outweighed the harms of extremist or hate speech, it still would not be obvious that the American approach to hate speech would be superior, from a *practical* standpoint, to the alternative adopted in Canada. There can be no absolute protection of the flow of ideas so long as judges are required to uphold constraints on "fighting words" and on communications that pose a "clear and present danger" because of their message. And without absolute protection, there can be no guarantee of absolute neutrality, with the consequence that the unconscious, implicit, or hidden biases in an approach predicated on the American model may ultimately prove more harmful than the publicly acknowledged and openly discussed restrictions adopted in an approach based on the Canadian model. In this connection, it is particularly noteworthy that, while arguably consistent on a doctrinal level, American First Amendment jurisprudence has fairly consistently resulted in suppression of extremist speech coming from the left and in toleration of hate propaganda perpetrated by the extreme right.[76] Thus, in the end, skeptical and pessimistic premises fail to afford a convincing pragmatic justification for a marketplace of ideas approach. But even if they did furnish such a justification, the American approach to hate speech would not necessarily emerge as pragmatically superior to plausible alternatives.

Inasmuch as Posner's reasons for supporting the marketplace of ideas

76. Compare, e.g., *Debs v. United States* (1919) (conviction of longtime leader and presidential candidate of the Socialist party for speech opposing World War I, in an opinion by Justice Holmes); *Gitlow v. New York* (1925) (criminal conviction of member of Socialist party for advocating in general terms the violent overthrow of the government upheld on grounds that such advocacy is sufficient by itself to meet the "clear and present danger" requirement; Justice Holmes dissented); *Whitney v. California* (1927) (conviction similar to that in Gitlow upheld; Justice Holmes concurred); *Dennis v. United States* (1951) (criminal conviction for organizing the Communist party and advocating the violent overthrow of the government upheld); and *Communist Party v. SACB* (1967) (requirement that Communist party register with attorney general and furnish membership lists based on legislative finding that the communist movement presents a "clear and present" danger upheld over objection on freedom of association grounds); with *Brandenburg v. Ohio* (1969) (Ku Klux Klan advocacy of violence against Jews and blacks held constitutionally protected); *Collins v. Smith* (1978) (march in Nazi uniforms including swastikas and advocacy of Nazism constitutionally protected) and *R.A.V. v. City of St. Paul, Minnesota* (1992) (statute making cross burning in the manner of the Ku Klux Klan criminally punishable expression held unconstitutional).

fall somewhere between Mill's and Holmes's, his most recent retreat seems consistent with the conclusion reached here—namely that neither pragmatist ends nor pragmatist means necessarily call for approaches to free speech spanning the spectrum bounded by the respective theories of Mill and Holmes. As Posner emphasizes, the harms of hate speech impose costs that must be empirically ascertained. And it is only on the basis of those costs, and of other relevant costs and benefits, that a legitimate decision can be made on whether hate speech should be tolerated or prohibited (Posner 1995, 396). Moreover, the "costs" and "benefits" in question may be determined in terms of a wealth-maximization criterion or some other substantive normative criterion such as libertarianism or egalitarianism. In any event, consistent with Posner's own recent remarks, pragmatism itself can offer no justification for or against tolerating extremist or hate speech.

VI. CONCLUDING REMARKS: THE LIMITS AND DANGERS OF PRAGMATISM IN LEGAL INTERPRETATION

The last conclusion concerning hate speech can be extended to cover freedom of speech in general. Indeed, whether we tackle freedom of speech at its core or at the margins, any cogent justification for it ultimately depends on linkage to ends that are not reducible to pragmatism. This may be less apparent at the core than at the margins, because of the availability of a large number of overlapping normative justifications. For example, at the core free speech may be justified from democracy, truth, self-expression, equal dignity, solidarity, and so on, but at the margins many, if not most, of these justifications would in all probability be unavailable. Also, where a large number of overlapping ends afford justifications to freedom of expression, there may be no practical need to focus on ends. But that should not be mistakenly interpreted to imply that ends do not matter. Thus, it may be possible sometimes to pick and choose among suitable ends, but inescapably all purportedly pragmatic justifications of free speech will ultimately prove to be parasitic on some nonpragmatic end. In short, to the extent that it makes sense to speak of pragmatist justifications of free speech, such justifications would fall under the rubric of mere pragmatism rather than under that of intermediate pragmatism.

Given the high hopes that the pragmatic justification of freedom of expression would bolster the case for intermediate pragmatism, its failure to do so calls into question whether the very notion of intermediate pragmatism is devoid of any practical consequences. To resolve this question, it is necessary to focus briefly on the distinction between critical and constructive pragmatism. As will be remembered, critical pragmatism refers to antifoundationalism, skepticism, and contingency, whereas constructive pragmatism designates whatever positive aims or programs may derive their justification from pragmatism. Assuming for the moment that critical pragmatism is generally unproblematic, the question boils down to whether anything remains to constructive pragmatism after the conclusion that there is no cogent purely pragmatic justification for freedom of expression.

Arguably, the only constructive prescription to which critical pragmatism leads is the necessity to embrace as a second-order end the maximization of equal freedom to pursue first-order ends. At first, it appeared that the promotion of freedom of speech could be subsumed under this second-order end. That did not prove to be the case but is not necessarily dispositive of the question. Under further consideration, however, it becomes apparent that while critical pragmatism *does not foreclose* pursuing the above-mentioned second-order end, it by no means requires it. After accepting that antifoundationalism, skepticism, and contingency lead to the conclusion that no conception of the good can be convincingly established as superior to others, the pragmatist must confront the need to determine the best practical course to follow under the circumstances. With this in mind, suppose that embracing the conception of the good shared by a majority would lead to greater peace and stability, whereas adopting the second-order end would lead to greater freedom and sense of fairness. In that case, is either of the two options preferable to the other from a pragmatist standpoint? The answer is clearly no, as the first option offers the best practical means toward the (nonpragmatic) end of stability whereas the same is true for the second option with respect to the nonpragmatic objective of greater freedom. At least when it comes to constructive pragmatism, therefore, the concept of intermediate pragmatism ultimately proves empty.

What about critical pragmatism? Can it escape the fate of being ultimately relegated to mere pragmatism? In other words, do antifoundationalism, contingency, or moderate skepticism have anything peculiarly pragmatic about them? Here again, the answer seems to be clearly in the negative. Antifoundationalism is typical of the postmetaphysical era and even more of the postmodern era and counts among its many advocates some, like the deconstructionists, who are not necessarily pragmatists.[77] The same can be said of contingency, which is by no means within the exclusive preserve of the pragmatists. Indeed, the notion of contingency has been invoked and extensively used by others, such as the existentialists.[78] Finally, skepticism is hardly an invention of pragmatists,[79] and "moderate skepticism," to the

77. See chapter I, above.
78. See, e.g., Sartre 1956, for an extended existentialist treatment of the notion that the individual's existence is contingent.
79. Skeptical thinking has historical roots going as far back as the pre-Socratic philoso-

extent that it is a feature of pragmatism, seems far from coherent. Specifically, once the hope of constructive pragmatism is cast aside, what is
there to constrain skepticism? If the answer is, "what we cannot help but
believe in," it is purely circular. In that case, "moderate skepticism" either
dissolves into a mere tautology—"I believe in what I believe in and I doubt
what I cannot believe"—or it ends up amounting to an arbitrary refusal to
ride skepticism to its logical conclusion.

Critical pragmatism thus seems as parasitic as constructive pragmatism.
Nevertheless, it may still be preferable to alternatives to the extent that it
is biased toward practical concerns, makes room for theoretical inconsistencies, and is oriented toward the future. To determine whether that can
be borne out, we must ask ourselves whether legal interpretation ultimately
stands to gain or lose from adherence to critical pragmatism.

Critical pragmatism's orientation toward practical concerns can make a
positive though limited contribution to legal interpretation. At the legislative level, it can help to weed out unworkable or counterproductive legislation. This help, however, is likely to remain relatively modest, to the extent
that pieces of legislation have multiple purposes and that the practical implications of legislation are often not clear-cut. Similarly, at the judicial
level, critical pragmatism may help judges recognize and reject legal interpretations that are practically unworkable or that would clearly lead to practical consequences inconsistent with what was intended. But in the great
many cases in which different judicial interpretations would lead to different practical results, critical pragmatism could only play a minor role. As
already mentioned, in those cases, judicial interpretation must rely on nonpragmatic normative considerations, with the consequence that critical
pragmatism cannot be relied on to furnish a just interpretation.

The much-touted room for theoretical inconsistency, which philosophical critical pragmatism affords to legal pragmatism, proves in the end to be
as dangerous as it is convenient. In cases in which there is a consensus concerning legal interpretation, but the theoretical reasons for agreement vary
among various parties to the consensus, as already pointed out, convenience clearly outweighs any plausible danger. Indeed, because of inherent
differences between philosophy and law as distinct practices, and because
everyone who gives his or her assent to the legal interpretation that is the
subject of the relevant consensus does so because the interpretation in
question is consistent with his or her own theoretical outlook, putting theoretical differences aside looms as both practical and harmless.

In cases in which there are genuine theoretical inconsistencies, however,
critical pragmatism may often do more harm than good, by masking con-

---

phers. See Popkin 1967. Also, among twentieth-century skeptics must be included such diverse
philosophers as Albert Camus and George Santayana. See ibid., 458.

flicts and tensions that would benefit from being tackled in the open. Thus, for example, along the lines suggested by Thomas Grey (1991), one may attempt to solve the thorny legal problem raised by hate speech by devising an approach that borrows from both libertarianism and egalitarianism without being consistent with either of the two. Accordingly, let us assume that to placate egalitarian concerns regarding the harms of hate speech, a libertarian marketplace approach is somewhat modified through criminalization of hate propaganda that falls within the definition of "fighting words."[80] From a libertarian standpoint, this solution might be dangerous in that it undermines (what the libertarian considers) "content-neutrality" and opens the door to an initially nearly imperceptible and gradual, but nonetheless ultimately potentially devastating, corruption of the free marketplace. From the egalitarian standpoint, on the other hand, this compromise is also dangerous, for "fighting words" hate speech may only represent the tip of the iceberg, and it may actually be less harmful than less strident alternatives that are likely to cause more profound and more permanent injuries. The compromise solution, moreover, may not only conceal the relative potential for harm of different kinds of hate speech but also, by conveying the impression that it imposes a balanced and reasoned standard, may make it more difficult to combat the evils of hate speech than if the clash between libertarians and egalitarians were fully spelled out in the open. Finally, enthusiastic endorsement of theoretical inconsistencies would seem to make it easier for greater judicial manipulation. In other words, concerns of theoretical consistency are likely to impose some constraints making for greater judicial integrity than if theoretical inconsistency could be exploited to shield judicial biases. Accordingly, for all these reasons, the likely consequences of theoretical inconsistency do not appear to enhance the cause of critical pragmatism.

Critical pragmatism's orientation toward the future is linked both to its antifoundationalism and to its concern with practical consequences. Stated in conventional terms, pragmatism is designed to allow us to rid ourselves of cumbersome historical baggage and to concentrate on what works as measured by actual future consequences. On the level of common sense, this certainly sounds like a useful and practical, even if very banal, approach. From a more critical theoretical perspective, however, combining pragmatism's antifoundationalism with its future orientation leads to a vex-

---

80. This solution comes close to that advocated by Grey. See Grey 1991, 25. Moreover, while this solution may seem consistent with the libertarian approach, it is actually not, to the extent that it only criminalizes "fighting words" that also qualify as hate speech and thus engages in content discrimination. See *R.A.V. v. City of St. Paul, Minnesota* (1992) (criminalization of racist and gender-based "fighting words" but not other kinds, such as those based on hatred of homosexuals, held to amount to constitutionally impermissible content discrimination).

ing contradiction. Consistent with this latter perspective, it is pragmatism's orientation toward the future that shapes and sustains its antifoundationalism. This is most obvious with respect to metaphysics. Indeed, in the postmetaphysical age, there is no practical future-oriented use for metaphysics in the sense that metaphysics does nothing to help us solve the problems we must confront in the course of shaping our future. Furthermore, the case of metaphysics is easy, because in the postmetaphysical age most of us believe that, and behave as if, science rather than metaphysics helps solve practical problems. But from the standpoint of pragmatism, the proof of any theory or hypothesis lies in its consequences, and since the future cannot ever be known *ex ante,* strictly speaking, no action could ever be pragmatically justified before or at the time of its occurrence without recourse to some unwarranted foundation. Consequently, the old pragmatists were foundationalists who relied on science and experience to justify their future-oriented actions. Neopragmatists like Rorty, on the other hand, reject empirical science as incompatible with pragmatism's antifoundationalism but replace it with arbitrary foundations of their own. Thus, to the extent that Rorty goes beyond claiming that use of language and redescription are inevitable facts of our past and present lives, and prophesies about future self-creation and solidarity, he falls into the foundationalist trap. Indeed, without any foundations, there is no reason to believe that any particular future consequence, as opposed to any other, would follow from any present use of language or from any past or present effort at redescription. In sum, if pragmatism's antifoundationalism and its orientation toward the future are taken together and taken seriously, they logically lead to only one outcome, namely complete paralysis. Therefore, not only does pragmatism's failure to deal with ends condemn it to a purely parasitic existence, but also, when logically interpreted, its antifoundationalism combined with its future orientation deprive it of any legitimate basis for dealing with means.

Based on the preceding analysis, pragmatism cannot solve the problem of just interpretations or eliminate the need for the interpretive subject. Whereas the intellectual journey of pragmatism has left us with useful lessons and modest gains, pragmatism offers no viable solution to the crisis concerning legal interpretation in a pluralist society. Because of the failure of the promise of pragmatism, the split between justice according to law and justice beyond law cannot be overcome through a mere rejection of foundations or through exclusive focus on means to the exclusion of ends. As a matter of fact, pragmatism's propensity to draw attention to means is not only inadequate but can also be downright harmful. Submersion or concealment of ends most often boosts the status quo and thus exacerbates the obstacles encountered by those who are disfavored by prevailing institutional arrangements. On the other hand, pragmatism's antifoundationalism is so paralyzing in its logical implications that pragmatists have been prone to preach it much more than to practice it. There is, however, a useful lesson to be drawn from pragmatism's attacks on foundations. Foundations are necessary and unavoidable, but in this postmodern age, they cannot be drawn from metaphysics, the Enlightenment's conception of scientific reason, or Kantian morals. The challenge posed by the intellectual journey of pragmatism, therefore, is to discover foundations consistent with contingency and a plurality of conceptions of the good and, at the same time, capable of reconciling justice according to law with justice beyond law in a way that provides a satisfactory handle on the problem of legal interpretation. In Part Three, I attempt to deal with that challenge by elaborating a theory of comprehensive pluralism suited to mediate between the need for foundations and the current predicament involving contingency and plurality.

Substantive Commitments, Partial Interpretations, and Imperfect Justice

CHAPTER SEVEN

Partiality and Comprehensive Pluralism

Strategies against the Mutual Eradication of Individual and Community

Systems theory, discursive proceduralism, and pragmatism have all failed to justify proclaiming an end to interpretation. Accordingly, it now becomes imperative to return to interpretation in a last-ditch effort to determine whether the crisis in interpretation may be nonetheless overcome and whether justice according to law might be after all susceptible to reconciliation with justice beyond law. In this last part of the book, I explore whether there might be a path toward just interpretations that might steer clear of the many obstacles encountered thus far.

The challenge of clearing a path to just interpretations is daunting. Not only must a suitable way be found to close the gap between self and other without undermining the diversity that stems from the coexistence of a plurality of conceptions of the good; but this must be done in a way that fully accounts for the conclusions reached throughout the preceding analysis, including those concerning contingency, lack of a workable neutral moral standpoint, impossibility of successfully relying on pure proceduralism, and impracticability of completely severing law from ethics or politics. These obstacles notwithstanding, I believe that a path to just interpretations may be found through reliance on pluralism—or more precisely, on pluralism understood in substantive normative terms. I call the latter kind of pluralism "comprehensive pluralism." I define it and indicate how I believe it might open a path toward just interpretations in the remainder of this chapter. In chapter VIII, I close the inquiry into just interpretations by focusing on significant practical applications of interpretive norms derived from comprehensive pluralism.

I. FROM PLURALISM IN FACT TO PLURALISM AS NORM:
THE ROAD TO COMPREHENSIVE PLURALISM

Throughout this book, I have referred to pluralism to denote societies whose members adhere respectively to a multiplicity of diverse conceptions of the good. Such societies experience "pluralism in fact." The fact of pluralism taken by itself, however, does not tell us anything about how we ought to deal with conflicts arising within pluralistic societies, including conflicts regarding just interpretations. Depending on one's normative commitments, there are many possible ways of approaching conflicts within such societies. For example, one might prefer to tackle the problems of a pluralistic society in a way that maximizes freedom, or equality, or that best conforms to the fundamental tenets of a majority religion. There is, however, one plausible normatively grounded approach to these problems that stands out as different from the rest. This approach is predicated on the conviction that pluralism itself is desirable and should therefore be endorsed and promoted. According to this approach, which I call "pluralism as norm," the conflicts in a society that is pluralistic in fact ought to be handled in a way that is designed to preserve and enhance pluralism. Furthermore, the thesis I defend in this chapter is that normative pluralism—or, more precisely, comprehensive pluralism—affords the *best* possible means to deal with the conflicts within a society that is in fact pluralistic, consistent with an ethic of reconciliation between self and other and with an eye to minimizing the violence inflicted on the self or the other. This thesis, which can be encapsulated in the slogan "pluralism as norm is best for pluralism in fact,"[1] can be summarized in its essentials as follows.

Legal interpretation cannot avoid reliance on substantive normative commitments, and that precludes genuine neutrality as between competing conceptions of the good. Comprehensive pluralism, in turn, is a conception of the good, but while admittedly non-neutral, it is different from other such conceptions inasmuch as it is dependent on the latter for its own survival. Indeed, the aim of comprehensive pluralism is to encompass, and to foster peaceful coexistence among, as many competing conceptions of the good as possible. Moreover, comprehensive pluralism must be prepared to accept the norms produced by other conceptions of the good, but only to the extent that such norms do not interfere with its encompassing design.

---

1. Normative pluralism could be pressed further to extend even to homogeneous societies. Thus, one could claim that promoting the values of pluralism, tolerance, and diversity would be beneficial to a homogeneous society. Although the position I defend is not necessarily inconsistent with this claim, I remain agnostic as to whether it is desirable to extend normative pluralism beyond factually pluralist settings. In any event, given the broad conception of factual pluralism that I adopt, all modern constitutional democracies would qualify as being pluralistic in fact.

Accordingly, the normative apparatus associated with comprehensive pluralism's integrating mission can be conceived as consisting of second-order norms that are distinguishable from first-order norms—that is, all the other norms associated with one or more of the remaining conceptions of the good. In short, comprehensive pluralism's principal aim is to negotiate the tension between first-order and second-order norms without thereby compromising the latter, all the while remaining as inclusive as possible with respect to the former.

From the standpoint of legal interpretation, comprehensive pluralism requires the legal interpreter to be guided by second-order norms while urging those who submit claims calling for legal interpretation to remain as true to the first-order norms to which they are committed as is possible consistent with genuine acceptance of the dictates of legitimate judicial adjudication. Moreover, even allowing for the fact that every person can be both legal claimant and legal interpreter and that, as we shall see below, promotion of second-order norms is likely to have spillover effects on the evolving configuration of first-order norms, comprehensive pluralism maintains a split between demands for justice predicated on first-order norms and legitimate endeavors to dispense justice, which must look, above all, to second-order norms. In short, to the extent that comprehensive pluralism amounts to yet another conception of the good, it is clearly distinguishable from contemporary Kantian visions such as those of Habermas or of Rawls in *A Theory of Justice.* On the other hand, to the extent that comprehensive pluralism is more than yet another conception of the good, in that it unleashes an inevitable but ultimately unresolvable dialectic between first-order and second-order norms, it differs markedly from theories based on building an "overlapping consensus," such as that elaborated by Rawls in *Political Liberalism,* and from all theories ultimately reducible to mere relativism.

Before further exploring comprehensive pluralism, it is necessary to provide a somewhat fuller account of the distinction between "pluralism in fact" and "pluralism as norm." The picture drawn of pluralism in fact thus far is one of a society composed of diverse ethnic, religious, cultural, or ideological groups who do not see eye to eye concerning at least some fundamental ethical, legal, and political issues. To complete this picture, in terms of a phenomenology of pluralism—conceived as the product of any plausible division of the relevant policy along the axes of self and other— reference must be made to pluralism among individuals. Indeed, individuals within a polity may have different values and objectives, or, in the words of Rawls, different "plans of life" (1971, 92–94). Moreover, whereas an individual standing alone may not be able to develop a full-fledged conception of the good, he or she may certainly decide to opt out of an existing conception, thus lending an individual dimension to the conflict between conceptions of the good. Consistent with this, we can distinguish between group and individual pluralism in fact or between "communal pluralism" and "individualistic pluralism." Furthermore, so long as both of these are incorporated within the definition of pluralism in fact, all contemporary constitutional democracies can be deemed to be in fact pluralistic.

Although communal pluralism and individualistic pluralism are conceptually distinct, they need not actually conflict with one another. Individuals do not customarily live apart from communities, and virtually never without significant communal ties. As a matter of fact, individualistic pluralism can often be protected through endeavors to safeguard communal pluralism and vice versa. For example, an individual's interest in practicing his or her religion may be adequately protected through group rights accorded to every religion within the polity. Conversely, a religious group may find sufficient protection in individual rights to freedom of assembly and freedom to worship. It follows from this, that the distinction between individualistic and communal pluralism only becomes crucial when group rights cannot be recharacterized as individual rights and vice versa, and that occurs most notably when the individual becomes alienated from his or her own group. For example, if a group's integrity and survival depended on maintaining a prohibition against divorce, and if a married member of that group wanted to divorce another such member, then either the group would prevail under a collective right to survival as a group or the individual would prevail under an individual right to divorce. In this case, however, it would be impossible to recharacterize the collective right involved as an individual right or vice versa. For one committed to promoting pluralism, that would mean that a choice would have to be made between furthering communal pluralism at the expense of individualistic pluralism or vice versa.

Communal pluralism can be conceivably destructive of individualistic pluralism and vice versa, but actual tensions in a pluralistic contemporary polity are more likely to be reflective of the tendency of individuals to have affiliations with a number of distinct groups, which may be in conflict with one another. Consider, for instance, the difficult group identification issues that may confront a contemporary African-American woman in the United States. As a woman, she may be drawn to feminism and be critical of all forms of sexism, including those prevalent among certain African-American men. As a member of a group that has long been the victim of violent and pervasive racial hatred, however, an African-American woman may be loathe to further fuel the fires of racism as a consequence of acting on her feminist convictions.[2] On the other hand, a racist woman who also happens to be a feminist may be more prone to identify with men of her own race

2. For an extended discussion of the dilemma confronting black feminists in the United States, see Crenshaw 1993.

than with women of other races when it comes to dealing with any issue in relation to which she regards race as a factor. More generally, the split into self and other, which constitutes an essential feature of pluralism in fact, should not be regarded as necessarily fixed or permanent. More probably this split is multiple, fragile, and context dependent. Accordingly, this split is better understood in *relational terms* as a consequence of alliances and divisions, prone to shift over time, and likely to intensify or abate depending on the political climate or particular issues involved (Rosenfeld 1994, 4,13–14).[3] In short, in a contemporary setting, pluralism in fact is most likely to reflect the citizen's many evolving ties to a multiplicity of different types of communities as well as the sense that each citizen has that he or she is entitled to carve out a personal path to happiness and fulfillment.

In addition to there being a split between self and other between individuals, between the individual and the group, and between different groups, there are also likely to be manifestations of such a split within the individual (Lacan 1966, 655, 839–40; Rosenfeld 1995, 1056–59). Furthermore, consistent with pluralism in fact, individuals and groups may at times embrace contradictory value preferences or lack a coherent conception of the good. What is more, they may partially buy into many different conceptions of the good, or even be unaware of some of their allegiances or value preferences.

These difficulties arising at the level of the individual or at that of an actual group are likely to disappear at the level of society as a whole, and are certainly overcome in the context of counterfactual reconstruction. In other words, whereas it may be impossible at any given moment to determine who can be counted as an adherent to a particular conception of the good, or how much a person may be committed to the conception in question, it should be readily apparent which are the main competing conceptions of the good within the polity as a whole. Similarly, from the standpoint of counterfactual reconstruction, what is of foremost importance is to construct a picture that is representative of actual conflicts and potential avenues of resolution rather than a detailed depiction of the actual predicament of every person within the polity.[4]

3. This is not to deny that some splits along self and other can become rigid and endure over several centuries, as history has painfully demonstrated in several cases. The point is rather that the latter type of split ought to be regarded as the exception rather than the rule from the standpoint of a phenomenology of functioning constitutional democracies that are pluralistic in fact.

4. Whereas no quantitative method is available to sort out what is purely idiosyncratic from what has broader intersubjective significance, the context should usually make matters sufficiently clear. Thus, for example, an individual's obsessive quest for simultaneous fulfillment and violation of a religious duty could be safely ignored in the process of counterfactual reconstruction. In contrast, a widespread tension among a significant segment of the popula-

In light of the preceding observations, a few further remarks concerning conceptions of the good, value preferences, perspectives, vantage points, and interests are required for purposes of rounding out the broad outlines of pluralism in fact. As will be remembered, a conception of the good is a particular ethic, and, at least from the standpoint of counterfactual reconstruction, it amounts to a comprehensive integrated perspective. A conception of the good may be primarily religious, ethnic, cultural, or ideological. Thus, for example, Catholicism, Zionism, Marxism, and John Stuart Mill's liberalism all yield their own distinct conception of the good. Moreover, the integrated perspective framed by a conception of the good prescribes certain value judgments and certain value preferences. As Habermas emphasizes, value preferences are intersubjective, and they derive from the ethical norms associated with the particular conception of the good of a given ethical community (1996, 255–56).

A value preference may be grounded in more than one conception of the good. For example, both a religious conception of the good and a capitalist ideology revolving around the family as the optimal unit of production and consumption may generate a value preference for the zealous preservation of traditional family life. The contours of a given value preference may be different, however, depending on which of the numerous conceptions of the good susceptible of affording it adequate grounding is relied on by particular proponents of that value preference. Moreover, differences in the contours of value preferences tied to different conceptions of the good are most likely to emerge in the context of conflicts or rankings among diverse value preferences. Two important consequences follow from this: first, the full import of an asserted value preference can only be adequately gauged from its relation to the conception of the good on which it is actually grounded; and second, particular value preferences can furnish areas of convergence or overlap for proponents of different conceptions of the good.

Like value preferences, ethical norms are susceptible of being grounded in more than one conception of the good. Actually, certain ethical norms, such as the prohibition against murder, appear to be embraced by all conceptions of the good. However, which homicides qualify as murder is likely to vary depending on one's conception of the good. Thus, for instance, certain abortion opponents consider abortions to be murder and the killing of physicians who perform abortions, justified homicide. Supporters of abortion, on the other hand, regard such killings of physicians as murder while maintaining that abortion in no way involves murder. Consistent with

---

tion arising from a simultaneous partial adherence to a religious and to a secular ideology would certainly appear to warrant being taken into proper account.

this, moreover, even universal embrace of the prohibition against murder as an ethical norm does not convert the latter into a moral norm (transcending all conflicts among conceptions of the good) in any but a purely formal, and hence vacuous, sense. Moreover, agreement concerning an ethical norm, such as the prohibition against murder, coupled with disagreement over what the ethical norm in question actually proscribes, may well be the source of some of the most intense conflicts among proponents of rival conceptions of the good.

It is only when it is grasped from the perspective of the conception of the good to which it happens to be linked that the full import of an assertion of a value preference or ethical norm can be properly evaluated. Furthermore, whereas a developed conception of the good frames a comprehensive integrated perspective, to the extent that such conception promotes role differentiation, its adherents will most likely embrace respectively different vantage points. For example, even if labor and management both subscribe wholeheartedly to a capitalist ideology, the vantage point of labor would still differ in significant respects from that of management.

Within this framework, interests loom as flexible, adaptable, and transformable. Informed by needs and desires, interests can be molded by conceptions of the good and vantage points, through education and other intersubjective dealings. Moreover, particularly in dynamic pluralist settings characterized by a high level of intercommunal interaction and fluid boundaries between internal and external others, interests are also likely to assume an active role in the construction and transformation of conceptions of the good and vantage points. Within the dialectic dynamic of a constantly evolving pluralist setting, interests can serve both to guide their proponents' participation within established games with fairly well defined rules and to prompt their proponents to seek new games or to change the rules of existing games. In other words, in the absence of any neutral moral standpoint, the pursuit of interest presumably involves both maximizing one's advantage within the existing institutional arrangement and promoting institutional changes that would optimize one's chances to realize one's objectives. For example, consistent with the discussion of the feminist challenge to Habermas's discursive proceduralism in chapter V, in a setting with rules devised by men, feminists can strive both to better the lot of women within existing rules and to press for rules that are better suited to women's interests.

Although conceptions of the good, value preferences, vantage points, and interests are never likely to remain rigid or immutable within a setting that is pluralist in fact, their actual degree of elasticity ultimately depends on the kind of pluralist polity involved. Greatest elasticity is likely to occur under "melting pot" conditions in highly interactive societies typified by a broad-based intertwining of individualistic and communal pluralism. At the other end of the spectrum, least elasticity is likely to occur in societies that are predominantly communally pluralistic and that experience a very low level of intercommunal interpenetration.

In the broadest terms, pluralism as norm, to which we now turn, stands for the proposition that pluralism in fact is good and that it ought therefore to be encouraged and protected. Normative pluralism is distinguishable from both monism—roughly defined as the view that there is a single conception of the good that is correct and that all value preferences are to be judged in terms of that conception—and relativism—the view that all value preferences are ultimately purely subjective and so contextually bound to the conception of the good from which they emerge that it would be meaningless to seek to gauge them from the standpoint of any other perspective.[5] In other words, against monism, normative pluralism holds that the good extends beyond any single conception of the good; against relativism, that not all conceptions of the good are equivalent as the mere projections of contingent perspectives. As we shall see below, normative pluralism can be viewed as mustering relativistic tendencies against monism and monistic tendencies against relativism while carving out a path that remains distinct from both monism and relativism.

Before pursuing these matters further, there are a couple of distinctions that must be briefly addressed. The first of these is that between "methodological pluralism" and "substantive pluralism"; the second, that between "limited pluralism" and "comprehensive pluralism." Methodological pluralism can be characterized as a strategic tool of limited scope, whose main function is to combat the tendency to hegemony of conceptions of the good vying for dominance in settings that are pluralistic in fact. As a strategic tool, methodological pluralism may embrace any position that might help weakening the grip of the most dominant conceptions of the good. Accordingly, methodological pluralism may align itself with relativism or with particular conceptions of the good positioned as significant rivals of the dominant ones. In short, methodological pluralism encompasses all weapons and strategies that may be profitably put to use for purposes of undermining monism.

Substantive pluralism, on the other hand, embraces a particular conception of the good that prescribes inclusion and accommodation of as large a plurality of conceptions of the good as possible. Consequently, substantive pluralism is definitely antirelativistic inasmuch as relativism would be indifferent as between inclusion or exclusion of a plurality of conceptions of the

5. For a more nuanced, thorough, and extended discussion of the relationship among pluralism, monism, and relativism, see Kekes 1993, 13–14, 34–35, 118–38.

good. In its antirelativism, however, substantive pluralism appears to come perilously close to becoming monistic in its own right. Indeed, like monistic conceptions of the good, substantive pluralism asserts its superiority over its rivals. Nevertheless, as will become clear below, substantive pluralism remains unlike its monistic rivals in that it both acknowledges the value of other conceptions of the good and cannot dispense with them.

Substantive pluralism may be pursued with moderation or systematically with unrelenting determination. In cases of moderate pursuit, we have what I refer to as "limited pluralism," whereas in cases of systematic pursuit, we have "comprehensive pluralism." Both limited and comprehensive pluralism embrace the normative objectives of substantive pluralism. Comprehensive pluralism, however, is much more radical than its limited counterpart, in that it seeks to level all existing hierarchies among conceptions of the good. Limited pluralism, on the other hand, is prepared to accept existing hierarchies, or to recommend relatively modest changes, while mainly preaching tolerance of a plurality of conceptions of the good and peaceful coexistence among proponents of different such conceptions. In short, comprehensive pluralism calls for *equalization* of all conceptions of the good, whereas limited pluralism mainly aims for *acceptance* of a plurality among such conceptions.

Actual constitutions in established democracies tend to promote limited pluralism inasmuch as they make room for tolerance without dislodging certain deeply entrenched traditions. Comprehensive pluralism, on the other hand, is unlikely to be embraced in actual constitutional practice owing to its radical implications but looms as an apt normative standard for counterfactual reconstruction. In other words, comprehensive pluralism affords a critical ideal that allows for a principled determination of how a polity that happens to be pluralistic in fact might be better stirred toward the objectives of substantive pluralism.

Consistent with the preceding observations, the thesis I promote—that pluralism as norm is best for pluralism in fact—can now be further specified as follows. Comprehensive pluralism as a critical counterfactual ideal yields the best possible normative criterion for the reconciliation of self and other within a pluralistic in fact society, in a way that maximizes the potential for justice while minimizing that for violence. Thus, equalization, and inclusion, of all conceptions of the good furnishes the normative yardstick against which the call for justice, the reach to the other, and the quest for just interpretations must be set. But before going any further, it is necessary to deal with an apparent contradiction that lurks within the very core of the ideal of comprehensive pluralism. Indeed, the requirement of equalizing all conceptions of the good seems squarely at odds with that of being all-inclusive. Or, put somewhat differently, how can substantive pluralism's call for inclusiveness prevail over rival claims for exclusiveness when all different conceptions of the good are supposed to be placed on a strictly equal footing?

II. THE DIALECTICS OF COMPREHENSIVE PLURALISM

The apparent contradiction between pluralism's thrust toward equalization and its commitment to inclusiveness is reminiscent of the paradox of tolerance discussed in chapter VI. Just as tolerance of the intolerant ultimately jeopardizes tolerance, equalization of all conceptions of the good eventually casts pluralism and antipluralism as equally legitimate. Moreover, if that proves to be the case, then comprehensive pluralism dissolves, in the last analysis, into relativism. On the other hand, if comprehensive pluralism places itself above rival conceptions of the good—in ways that are analogous to Popper's suggested resolution of the paradox of tolerance through intolerance of the intolerant—then comprehensive pluralism may, in the end, prove to be but monism in disguise. In sum, either pluralism is limited or it seems impossible for it to be genuinely pluralistic.

Further inquiry reveals, however, that comprehensive pluralism need not be relegated to a monistic or a relativistic fate, provided it is properly understood in terms of the dialectic that it unleashes. Indeed, viewed as a counterfactual ideal rather than as a realizable end-state, comprehensive pluralism serves to launch a coordinated two-pronged attack against both hierarchy and exclusion. As already indicated, comprehensive pluralism figures, in part, as a conception of the good that claims superiority over its rivals, but only for the limited purpose of minimizing exclusion of other conceptions of the good. Conversely, comprehensive pluralism's systematic leveling of conceptions of the good does introduce some measure of relativism, but it is a limited and narrowly targeted one, whose only aim is to undermine the pretensions to superiority of certain conceptions of the good. Strictly speaking, therefore, comprehensive pluralism is not relativistic as between conceptions of the good; it is merely skeptical concerning any claim to a hierarchy among them.

To better grasp the dialectic that gives shape to comprehensive pluralism, we must refer again to the distinction between the norms emanating from comprehensive pluralism as a conception of the good and those deriving from other conceptions of the good. The former, as we have seen, constitute *second-order* norms, whereas the latter amount to *first-order* norms.[6] Accordingly, the privileging of comprehensive pluralism as a conception of the good without falling into monism can be recharacterized as follows:

6. This distinction is analogous to that drawn between first-order and second-order ends in chapter VI.

privileging comprehensive pluralism over other conceptions of the good boils down to affording second-order norms priority over first-order norms since that is a prerequisite to achieving equality among first-order norms.

As a counterfactual ideal, comprehensive pluralism becomes operative in settings marked by historical contingency and perspectival partiality. Thus, it is largely a historically contingent matter which first-order norms are favored and which disfavored or even banished at any particular time and place. Similarly, prevalent conceptions of the good and the nature of the interaction among them inevitably shape and constrain the scope of actual and potential perspectives capable of playing a relevant role in a given spatiotemporal setting. Consistent with this, moreover, the aim of comprehensive pluralism is to overcome the very contingency and partiality with which it is confronted, for purposes of clearing a path leading to equality among first-order norms. Specifically, comprehensive pluralism confronts the status quo through a dialectical process that involves two distinct *logical* moments that combine to delimit the quest for equality among first-order norms.

Set against a competition among a multiplicity of first-order norms vying for predominance, comprehensive pluralism's first logical moment is a negative one characterized by a strict refusal to endorse or favor any of the competing first-order norms. Thus, in its negative moment, comprehensive pluralism imposes strict equality and neutrality among all existing first-order norms and the conceptions of the good from which they derive.

Carried to its logical conclusion, however, comprehensive pluralism's first moment leads to self-destruction. If all first-order norms are completely neutralized through a leveling negation, then the very pursuit of pluralism would become meaningless. In the absence of a plurality of viable conceptions of the good, no first-order norms would remain for pluralism to protect. Accordingly, to avoid self-destruction, comprehensive pluralism must supplement its negative moment with a positive one. The object of that positive moment is to foster readmittance of previously leveled and equalized conceptions of the good into the pluralist universe.

In its positive moment, however, comprehensive pluralism must confront a major problem. Not all conceptions of the good excluded in the course of comprehensive pluralism's negative moment can gain readmission in its positive moment. For example, a crusading religion, for which conversion of the infidel, by force if necessary, is a sacred duty that admits of no exceptions, has no place under comprehensive pluralism. Moreover, even those conceptions of the good that can be slated for readmission cannot occupy the same position under comprehensive pluralism as they did prior to its deployment. Thus, religions that depend for their survival on radical intolerance can only be readmitted on condition that they pose no serious threat to other religions or to nonreligious conceptions of the good. This could be accomplished, for example, by relegating readmitted religions to the private sphere.[7]

Because comprehensive pluralism cannot equally readmit in its positive moment all the conceptions of the good that it has equally excluded in its negative moment, it inevitably falls short of its ideal of equal accommodation for all conceptions of the good. At best, comprehensive pluralism can undertake to better approximate equality among all first-order norms without ever reaching its goal of providing for full equality among all first-order norms. Moreover, because of this, comprehensive pluralism, once unleashed, becomes engaged in a ceaseless dialectic marked by a constant succession of negative and positive moments, without ever reaching a final resting point.[8] Indeed, since at the completion of every positive moment deriving from comprehensive pluralism some first-order norms are altogether left out and others included but displaced, there are bound to be calls for greater inclusiveness and equality, and hence a need for further negative leveling. Furthermore, the constant leveling and repositioning of first-order norms not only affect their location in relation to the center of gravity of the relevant normative universe but also make them more susceptible to internal alterations and reconfigurations.[9]

There is a strong parallel between comprehensive pluralism and comprehensive justice in that they both underscore the ever present opportunities for amelioration within settings that can never fully escape from imperfection. Although comprehensive pluralism cannot eradicate uncertainty or anxiety, it does nurture hope of progress and of better and more mutually enriching avenues of reconciliation between self and other. But before attempting to make the case for comprehensive pluralism any further, it is necessary to focus on a couple of important consequences that follow from its logical structure.

The juxtaposition of comprehensive pluralism's two logical moments underscores the asymmetry between its negative and its positive moment. In its negative moment, comprehensive pluralism reaches for, and achieves, radical equality. Moreover, such equality is reached procedurally as existing hierarchies among first-order norms are routinely struck down. In terms of

---

7. Cf. Marx 1967 (arguing that religious emancipation can only be obtained at the cost of relegating religion to the private sphere).

8. It should be emphasized that the succession in question is strictly a logical one and not necessarily a temporal one. Logically, every negative moment must be followed by a positive one and vice versa. Historically, the leveling and reinstating functions may be amalgamated or out of logical sequence provided they remain susceptible to reconstruction in the proper logical order.

9. The susceptibility of first-order norms, value preferences, and conceptions of the good to internal changes under the aegis of comprehensive pluralism will be explored in greater detail in the course of the next chapter.

counterfactual reconstruction, comprehensive pluralism, in its negative moment, pictures all first-order norms as strictly equivalent and through projection of this construct against prevailing hierarchical arrangements, fashions a powerful yet interpretively unproblematic means of critique. For example, in the context of a religiously pluralist society in which the state has singled out a particular religion for purposes of official endorsement, comprehensive pluralism's negative moment makes for a simple, immediate, obvious, and swift critique.[10] Furthermore, comprehensive pluralism's achievement of complete (albeit purely formal and fleeting) equality in its negative moment affords a systematic way to characterize the difference between limited and comprehensive pluralism. Indeed, unlike its comprehensive counterpart, limited pluralism fails to fully level all first-order norms in the course of its negative moment. In other words, limited pluralism fails to distinguish consistently and systematically between first-order and second-order norms. In contrast, in its positive moment, comprehensive pluralism aims at equality, but equality at the end always eludes its grasp. Accordingly, the best that can be hoped for is that in its positive moment, comprehensive pluralism will eradicate *some* inequalities while leaving others in place. Or more precisely, taking into account that repositioning first-order norms may lead to changes within their internal configuration, comprehensive pluralism is poised in its positive moment to wipe out certain inequalities but only at the cost of triggering others. Furthermore, since reintegration of first-order norms in the course of its positive moment is not automatic, but instead contingent on their compatibility with second-order norms and with other first-order norms, comprehensive pluralism's positive moment, unlike its negative moment, is not reducible to proceduralism. Also, not only must comprehensive pluralism in its positive moment fall back on substantive norms, it cannot avoid reliance on contestable interpretive practices. Indeed, application of substantive criteria to determine which first-order norms ought to be readmitted is not reducible to purely formal or quantitative procedures.

Since comprehensive pluralism in its positive moment can neither fully reconcile legal equality with factual equality nor obviate the problem of just interpretations, it seems fair to ask whether it is altogether worth pursuing. A positive answer to this last question seems reasonable, provided one makes a persuasive case concerning the priority of second-order norms

10. This does not mean that comprehensive pluralism automatically condemns state endorsement of a particular religion regardless of the circumstances. Ultimately, any legitimate verdict under comprehensive pluralism must fully account for both its negative and its positive moment. Although the circumstances that would warrant this might be exceedingly rare, it is not inconceivable that in its positive moment comprehensive pluralism would reinstate a state religion to the position it held prior to its demotion in the course of comprehensive pluralism's negative moment.

over first-order norms and provided reliance on the dialectic promoted by comprehensive pluralism significantly increases the chances for greater inclusiveness and reduced inequities. In short, going through comprehensive pluralism's positive moment seems justified so long as it leads to a more inclusive and more equitable accommodation of diverse first-order norms. Moreover, the inner reconfiguration of first-order norms in the context of comprehensive pluralism is only objectionable if it limits rather than expands opportunities, and if it constrains rather than broadens the scope for self-fulfillment and reconciliation with the other.

Comprehensive pluralism must rely in its positive phase on substantive norms and contestable interpretations, but these need not produce interpretive hurdles leading to arbitrariness or excessive indeterminacy. Indeed, the priority of second-order norms mandates certain clear-cut results, such as the repudiation of actively antipluralistic conceptions of the good and limited acceptance of less activist ideologies that are nonetheless intolerant. In addition, in other cases, the priority of second-order norms can provide guidance without fully determining the most desirable outcome.

More difficult situations arise when the pursuit of one conception of the good that is not inherently objectionable impedes the pursuit of another such conception. However, even in those cases, satisfactory solutions may often be available, through the deployment of a reversal of perspectives along the lines contemplated by Habermas.[11] Thus, after being considered successively from the standpoint of each of the perspectives involved, conflicting pursuits could be ranked according to their respective importance in relation to the particular conception of the good that provides them with normative grounding. In some cases, such rankings would establish clear orders of priority that should prove equally acceptable to all proponents of the reversal of perspectives test. Moreover, inasmuch as such a test leads to greater inclusiveness of the other without undue sacrifice of diversity, it ought to include comprehensive pluralists among its most loyal supporters. Because of the lack of a neutral perspective transcending all communal biases, the reversal of perspectives consistent with comprehensive pluralism cannot be expected to lead to a determinate resolution of all difficult cases. Nevertheless, by supplementing the priority of second-order norms, the reversal of perspectives enables comprehensive pluralism to chart a distinct course toward a better integration of an increasingly diverse range of first-order norms. Further discussion of the interpretive implications that follow from this will be postponed until the next chapter, but two important points deserve mention at this point. First, all interpretation deriving from comprehensive pluralism is bound to be intersubjective and dialogical rather than monological. Second, all such interpretation is not

11. See chapter V, above.

only intersubjective but also intercommunal in its reach, as it takes into serious account all others and all communities within the polity.

To recapitulate: the promise of comprehensive pluralism is considerable. From the standpoint of its negative moment as a counterfactual construct, comprehensive pluralism furnishes a crisp and reliable means to criticize prevailing inequities. From the standpoint of its positive moment, on the other hand, comprehensive pluralism generates counterfactual models suggestive of ways in which existing inequities might be plausibly overcome and greater inclusiveness and diversity achieved. These characteristics certainly make comprehensive pluralism attractive. It remains to be seen, however, whether the claim that comprehensive pluralism offers the best hope for societies that are pluralistic in fact can be persuasively substantiated.

III. THE CASE FOR COMPREHENSIVE PLURALISM

To assess the virtues of comparative pluralism as compared to those of its most likely rivals, it is necessary to take a closer glance at what it stands for. Above all, by only claiming that comprehensive pluralism is best in the context of settings that are pluralistic in fact, it is not necessary to embrace the proposition that pluralism itself constitutes the ultimate good. This is certainly advantageous, for if pluralism itself were postulated as the summum bonum, then the case for comprehensive pluralism would become purely circular. This circularity is avoided, however, if the ultimate good is deemed to be the reconciliation of self and other in the least coercive and least confining manner possible. In that case, moreover, the strongest case for comprehensive pluralism would consist in proving that it is best suited to lead to the desired reconciliation.

By conceiving such reconciliation in the widely encompassing relational terms stressed throughout this book, it is possible to cast a far-reaching normative net that bridges most of the many divides long associated with polities that are pluralistic in fact. Indeed, inasmuch as self and other are conceived as cutting across individual and communal divides, as somewhat malleable and prone to evolve, and as capable of simultaneously expressing complex identities and multiple alliances, the traditional oppositions between the individual and the group and between liberals and communitarians tend to lose much of their grip. Because of this, as we shall see, comprehensive pluralism seems particularly well suited to harmonize the perspectives and vantage points of individual and group and of liberals and communitarians in a large number of situations.

Consistent with regarding the reconciliation between self and other as the ultimate good, autonomy, reciprocity, empathy, dignity, and diversity rank among the highest values and occupy the place of second-order norms within the perspective of comprehensive pluralism. Autonomy and dignity are closely intertwined with the notion of selfhood and occupy a prominent place in connection with the self's capacity for ethical choice and commitment. Reciprocity, on the other hand, cements the bonds between self and other, by prescribing that the other be recognized as another self (Hegel 1977, ¶¶178–96). Moreover, a distinction can be drawn between "mere reciprocity" and "reversible reciprocity."[12] As a norm, mere reciprocity prescribes recognition of the other as possessing a perspective or vantage point, without concern for actual differences among perspectives or vantage points. In contrast, reversible reciprocity requires not only recognition that the other has a perspective but also empathy for the other, based on a proper recognition of differences in perspectives. Finally, diversity emerges as a key value to the extent that it makes for less confining and less coercive avenues toward reconciliation between self and other. Without diversity, reconciliation would only be possible through self-constraint to the point of yielding to the identity of the other, or through coercing the other to fit within the mold of the self's own image. With diversity, on the other hand, not only is there greater room for more satisfactory reconciliation between self and other, but every self can rely on a much wider array of choices toward self-fulfillment.

Comprehensive pluralism confronts two different kinds of rivals, which may be characterized respectively as "metaphysical" and "postmetaphysical." Much like Habermas's discourse ethics discussed above, comprehensive pluralism rejects the position of metaphysical rivals typified by comprehensive religious conceptions of the good. Specifically, comprehensive pluralism opposes its metaphysical rivals' claims to the truth and to hegemony, and subsumes them under the dictates of its second-order norms. From the perspective of comprehensive pluralism, metaphysically grounded religious and ethical systems are reduced to the level of first-order norms subject to exclusion to the extent that they are antipluralistic. Thus, metaphysical perspectives cannot be accepted on their own terms and are reduced to becoming one among many vehicles of self-expression and self-fulfillment. In other words, within the framework of comprehensive pluralism, metaphysical perspectives lose their grip on the ethical to become absorbed into the rich and varied aesthetics that gives expression to pluralistic ethics.

Comprehensive pluralism thwarts the intercommunal aspirations of metaphysical perspectives but does not seek to interfere with their intracommunal pursuit. Nevertheless, by uprooting all hierarchies among firstorder norms, and by promoting the spread of avenues of intercommunal interaction, comprehensive pluralism vastly increases the pressures for internal reconfiguration of metaphysical perspectives. Accordingly, even if

12. For an extended discussion of reciprocity and of the progression from mere reciprocity to reversible reciprocity, see Rosenfeld 1991a, 242–49.

proponents of metaphysical perspectives are willing to withdraw from the public square, they are unlikely to prevent external influences from penetrating within their own community and from eventually prompting some of their fellow members to seek internal changes. For example, a religion with a clergy open only to men may withdraw from the affairs of the state and still face pressures from within its ranks for admitting women to its clergy as a consequence of the spread of feminist ideas. In short, for the militant proponent of a metaphysical conception of the good, comprehensive pluralism poses an unacceptable double threat: it relativizes a cherished and revered conception of the good, and it also exposes such conception to internal erosion.

Whereas there is very little common ground between comprehensive pluralism and its metaphysical rivals, matters seem quite different when it comes to the relationship between comprehensive pluralism and its postmetaphysical rivals. What unites all major postmetaphysical perspectives, including comprehensive pluralism, is the search for a reconciliation of self and other without reliance on metaphysics. Consistent with this broad definition, postmetaphysical perspectives span a spectrum that extends from liberalism to republicanism and to communitarianism and find expression in the views of such diverse thinkers as Locke, Rousseau, Kant, Mill, Marx, Habermas, Rawls, Sandel, Rorty, Raz, and Dworkin. Some of these views have already been examined and found wanting from the standpoint of just interpretations in the course of the preceding analysis. Accordingly, comprehensive pluralism can be deemed superior to the perspectives respectively emanating from the latter views, provided it leads to a reasonable resolution of the problem of just interpretations.

Pluralism has been frequently associated with liberalism, but the two are by no means coextensive.[13] Although liberalism encompasses a wide variety of different views, and lacks any commonly accepted definition (Raz 1986, 1), it nonetheless seems inextricably linked to limited pluralism. Beyond that, however, at least some versions of liberalism rely on certain overriding values, such as liberty (ibid., 2), equality (Dworkin 1978, 125), or justice (Rawls 1971, 3–4), and thus appear incompatible with comprehensive pluralism.[14] Furthermore, in contrast to liberalism, republicanism and communitarianism are not customarily linked to pluralism, and even, on occasion, are deemed altogether inconsistent with pluralism.[15] This notwithstanding,

13. See Kekes 1993, 199–217, for an excellent discussion of the relationship between pluralism and liberalism. The following discussion relies significantly on his analysis.

14. Cf. Kekes 1993, 199 (arguing that "there are good reasons for supposing that pluralism and liberalism are incompatible").

15. See, e.g., Sunstein 1993, 26–27, 38–39 (arguing that deliberative representative democracy predicated on republicanism is incompatible with "interest-group pluralism").

as we shall see, in the context of a pluralistic in fact polity, neither republicanism nor communitarianism is inherently incompatible with pluralism. Consistent with this, I will now argue that, in the presence of pluralism in fact, comprehensive pluralism is better suited to further the respective principal objectives of liberalism, republicanism, and communitarianism than the overriding values customarily associated with any of the three.

A. Comprehensive Pluralism and Liberalism

In spite of the significant differences noted above, Anglo-American liberalism encompasses a family of conceptions of the good, which, for our limited purposes, can be distilled to the following essentials. The individual is the subject of moral choice, and the purpose of society is to optimize the opportunities for individual self-realization by striking an appropriate balance between individual autonomy and individual welfare. Within this framework, moreover, individual interests ultimately prevail over group interests, and groups—including the polity taken as a whole—conceived as associations or aggregations rather than as organic units are justified in terms of their suitability for advancing individual interests. To put it in terms of the distinctions drawn above, for liberalism, the polity is individualistically pluralistic in fact, and its principal objective is to promote the most extensive possible equal opportunity for individual self-realization.

From the standpoint of the present discussion, the most important division among proponents of liberalism is over how best to strike a balance between autonomy and welfare and how best to secure equal opportunity for individual self-realization. Thus, for example, libertarians insist that liberty is paramount, and trust that by maximizing liberty, individual self-realization will naturally follow.[16] Liberal egalitarians, on the other hand, tend to stress that equality is paramount (Dworkin 1978, 115, 125). More generally, whatever a particular proponent of liberalism deems paramount as a function of personal theoretical convictions and prevailing contextual considerations, he or she is likely to postulate as an overriding value. As already mentioned, liberty, equality, and justice have been advanced as overriding values, to which can be added fundamental human rights (Berlin 1969, 165). Furthermore, the face of liberalism is likely to change depending on which values it embraces as overriding, and the possible variations are numerous, since liberalism may treat as overriding any one of these values, or certain combinations of them.

---

16. The libertarian position is rooted in the philosophy of Locke (see Locke 1960) and counts among its best-known contemporary exponents, Robert Nozick (see Nozick 1974). For a more extended discussion of the libertarian belief that liberty leads to an optimal balance between autonomy and welfare, see Rosenfeld 1991a, 58–59, 224–25.

From the perspective of comprehensive pluralism, liberalism's key weakness lies in its need to lock in any of the above-mentioned values as overriding. Leaving aside any pluralistic critique of liberalism's individualistic bias, pluralism proves to be better suited to advance liberalism's chief objectives than any combination of liberal values enshrined as overriding. This may seem paradoxical at first but should become plain on further inquiry. Thus, one can recharacterize the liberal ideal as the reconciliation of the individual self and the individual other in a way that best maximizes their respective opportunities for self-realization. Moreover, it seems fair to assume that conceptions of one's individual good and of one's self-realization are likely to vary from one individual to the next, and that, consistent with the preceding analysis, no neutral Kantian moral perspective is available. Under these circumstances, a flexible approach—that is, the ability to appeal to different values to varying extents, depending on the material conditions and the conceptions of self-realization actually involved—would seem far preferable in terms of the requisite reconciliation than would unbending commitment to certain values taken as overriding. The liberal may object that overriding values are required as a prophylactic to prevent the self from trampling on the other. The pluralist would reply, however, that a pluralist mindset is the best guarantee against intentional interference by the self against the other. Thus, even if the same values happened to be stressed by pluralists and liberals, the pluralist approach would still be preferable, both because of its greater adaptability and because of its sharper focus on reconciling self and other in the most mutually satisfactory manner possible. Moreover, as conceptions of autonomy, of welfare, and of plausible ways to strike an acceptable balance between them are likely to evolve significantly over time, the superiority of the highly flexible pluralistic approach over its liberal counterparts should become increasingly apparent.

B. Comparing Liberalism, Republicanism, and Communitarianism from a Pluralistic Perspective

The cases for pluralism's superiority over republicanism and communitarianism bear certain resemblances to but also certain significant differences from the case concerning the preferability of pluralism over liberalism. As in the case of liberalism, both republicanism and communitarianism encompass a broad array of different views, and respectively lack any commonly accepted definition. Unlike liberalism, which seems inextricably tied to limited pluralism, however, republicanism and communitarianism need not be pluralistic in any way. Thus, for example, classical republicanism based on the paramountcy of civic virtue was thought to "flourish only in small communities united by similar interests and by a large degree of homogeneity" (Sunstein 1993, 20). Similarly, communitarianism can invoke the image of a tightly woven organic whole encompassing a single community with a unanimously shared conception of the good.[17]

Republican and communitarian visions steeped in conceptions of the polity as essentially homogeneous need not concern us to the extent that they take no account of pluralism in fact. That leaves only those republican and communitarian conceptions that purport to account for heterogeneity. Although critics have expressed skepticism (Fallon 1989, 1717–18, 1725–33), republicanism and communitarianism are not inherently incompatible with some degree of pluralism.[18] Indeed, one could imagine a version of republicanism in which citizenship and civic virtue remain the principal focus, but in which the common good would account for differences in perspectives rather than remaining monolithic. In other words, the republican ideology under consideration would still place the civic duties of the public citizen ahead of the interests of the private person but would allow for differences over which civic duties and which configurations of public citizenship would best serve the common good of the polity. Furthermore, assuming communitarianism is ultimately distinguishable from liberalism and individualism because of its commitment to the primacy of the community over the individual, then communitarianism should be compatible with communal pluralism even if it precludes individualistic pluralism. Consistent with this, within a communally pluralistic communitarian setting, solidarity could function as the overriding value, provided it encompassed intracommunal bonds as well as intercommunal ones.

For purposes of considering the advantages of comprehensive pluralism over republicanism and communitarianism, it suffices to bear in mind the most salient features of the latter two. Accordingly, I gloss over differences among various republican and communitarian perspectives and concentrate on those among their respective principal features that accentuate their contrast with pluralism. Moreover, I treat republicanism and communitarianism as distinct, even though they often seem linked. Or, more precisely, whereas it is obvious that not all communitarians are republican, all contemporary versions of republicanism are arguably ultimately communitarian in nature. Be that as it may, the following discussion is predicated on acceptance of the possibility of noncommunitarian republicanism.

---

17. Cf. Sandel 1982, 151 (contrasting the unity of community in a constitutive sense to the plurality envisioned by Rawlsian liberalism).

18. There is a revival of republicanism among certain contemporary constitutional theorists in the United States. These theorists have sought to reconceptualize republicanism so as to take pluralism in fact into proper account. See Michelman 1988; Sunstein 1988.

C. Comprehensive Pluralism and Republicanism

At the core of the republican vision is a conflict between private man (woman) and public citizen. This conflict shifts the center of gravity of the struggle between self and other from the realm of interpersonal relations to that of each person's inner universe. This shift, moreover, emerges particularly clearly in Jean-Jacques Rousseau's republican conception of self-government driven by adhesion to the general will. Rousseau's republicanism is rooted in his conception of the social contract as a pact between each individual qua individual, on the one hand, and society as a whole (of which each individual member is but a part), on the other.[19] Furthermore, as a consequence of having been a party to Rousseau's social contract, every individual assumes a dual role: on the one hand, the individual is one among the many who are governed; on the other hand, the individual is an integral part of society as an indissoluble whole in its capacity as governing sovereign (Rousseau 1947, 16–18). Within this vision, the divide between the governed and the governors is correlated to the split between the individual interests and particular will of the private person and the common good embodied in the general will that informs the civic virtue of the self-governing public citizen (ibid., 14–16).

The notion of the general will propounded by Rousseau remains somewhat mysterious and does not always seem fully consistent. Rousseau characterizes the general will as the sum of differences between all the individual wills, or as the "agreement of all interests" that "is produced by opposition to that of each" (ibid., 26, n. 2). Thus, the general will is not reducible to any individual will, nor is it the will of the majority envisioned as a mere aggregate of individual wills. Nevertheless, under at least one plausible reading, Rousseau's general will accounts for pluralism in fact inasmuch as it takes clashing individual wills into account in the course of its formulation.

Consistent with these remarks, it is now possible to see how the individual comes to occupy the center stage with respect to the conflict between self and other in the context of Rousseauian republicanism. From the vantage point of the private person, the self is embodied in the particular will, and the other, in the general will. Conversely, from the vantage point of the public citizen, the self becomes identified with the general will, and the other, with the individual interests that inform the particular will. It follows from this that self-identity either as a private person or as a public citizen necessarily involves some measure of self-alienation—some degree of incor-

19. See Rousseau 1947, 16–17. For a discussion of the contrast between Rousseau's conception of the social contract and those of Hobbes and Locke, see Rosenfeld 1985, 863–67.

poration of the other as part of oneself and some degree of repudiation of one's self (identity) for purposes of severing (part of) the self that must be cast away as other. Moreover, although within this perspective the focus of the conflict between self and other becomes predominantly internal, it also has important external repercussions. Indeed, definition of the self from the vantage point of the public citizen requires building bridges toward others in their capacities as fellow citizens in order to ferret out the "agreement of all interests" that is constitutive of the general will. At the same time, the public citizen must repudiate not only his or her particular interests (inasmuch as they cannot be incorporated into the general interest) but also the particular interests of others. Conversely, from the vantage point of the private person, the other is not only the internalized communal identity of oneself as public citizen but also all of one's fellow citizens in their capacities as private persons with different particular interests. In short, the self of the republican public citizen is built on a combination of alienation from oneself and of internalization of the other.

Viewed from the standpoint of the relationship between self and other, there is much that is common between Rousseauian republicanism and comprehensive pluralism. Indeed, by subordinating first-order norms to second-order norms, comprehensive pluralism conditions self-realization on accepting some degree of alienation from one's own first-order objectives. Just as the Rousseauian individual must sacrifice purely particular self-interest for the sake of seeking reconciliation with the other under the guidance of the general will, so too the proponent of particular first-order norms, under comprehensive pluralism, must give up pursuing them on their own terms in order to reconcile his or her own pursuit of self-realization with those of others.

Focus on these similarities brings out two issues around which the key differences between republicanism and comprehensive pluralism revolve. These two issues, which are closely related, concern respectively the possibility of reaching agreement among all interests and the extent to which self-sacrifice might be warranted for purposes of seeking to reconcile the self and the other. Regarding the possibility of reaching an agreement, there seems to be a significant difference depending on whether one believes that there are universal interests shared by all members of the polity. If there were universal interests, and particularly if these were predominant, then emphasis on civic virtue and on adhesion to the general will could be justified as consistent with equity and with a tolerable degree of self-sacrifice. If, on the other hand, consistent with the conclusions reached above, no universal interests—other than perhaps the interest in the survival of the polity—are likely to be found in settings that are pluralistic in fact, then civic virtue and conformity to the general will would either be contrived or require an unconscionable degree of self-sacrifice and self-denial. In Rousseau's own case, moreover, republican virtue seems to extol much too high a price in terms of self-denial, as evinced by his famous dictum "Whoever refuses to obey the general will shall be compelled to it by the whole body: This in fact only forces him to be free" (ibid., 18).

Even if they were equal in all other respects, pluralism would still be preferable to republicanism, by refusing to enshrine civic virtue as an overriding value. Also, although contemporary republicanism may be less harsh than Rousseau's, inasmuch as it remains genuinely republican it must still adhere to the primacy of the public citizen over the private person. Comprehensive pluralism, in contrast, harbors no preference among the two and is thus better suited to less coercive means of reconciliation between self and other. In other words, by not requiring any a priori choice between public citizen and private person, comprehensive pluralism is less likely to exact excessive personal sacrifice for the sake of the self-governing polity's cohesiveness.

D. Comprehensive Pluralism and Communitarianism

Communitarianism, for its part, assigns overriding status to the values of solidarity and group loyalty. Moreover, as already pointed out, communitarianism need only be considered as a plausible rival to comprehensive pluralism inasmuch as it makes room for communal pluralism. Consistent with this, before it is possible to indicate why pluralism is preferable to communitarianism, it is necessary to take a closer look at a conceivable communitarian vision that might be compatible with the preservation of heterogeneity.

The kind of communitarianism that might rival pluralism would make room for polities composed of a plurality of diverse communities. Furthermore, a distinction must be drawn among those polities made up of essentially self-enclosed separate communities with a minimum of intercommunal dealings and those that include communities largely open to one another and linked together through a multiplicity of intercommunal undertakings. Polities consisting of largely self-enclosed communities are not much different from those constituting a single tightly knit community. Accordingly, only the communitarian model that encompasses a multiplicity of communities open to one another is relevant for present purposes.

An important question that arises in relation to the latter model is whether solidarity can play a significant role in intercommunal dealings. It seems reasonable to answer that question in the affirmative, since it is easily conceivable that intercommunal bonds calling for solidarity between members belonging to different communities would play a non-negligible role in a communally pluralistic polity. For example, intercommunal bonds of solidarity could develop among members of different religions who unite to promote the spirit of religion in the face of a mounting tide of secularism.

Given the possibility of intercommunal solidarity, the question becomes whether communitarianism in a communally pluralistic polity would be better off if solidarity is made into an overriding value. Returning to the example of intercommunal solidarity among members of different religions, it should be noted that each such member must have dual loyalty and solidarity with two different communities that do not completely overlap. Intracommunally, such member must achieve solidarity with those who adhere to his or her own religion. Intercommunally, on the other hand, that member must establish solidarity with adherents to other religions. Moreover, even if all the religions involved are in full agreement when it comes to dealing with secularism, there may well be certain matters over which these various religions differ sharply. In the latter case, the two loyalties involved would come into conflict with one another, and intracommunal and intercommunal solidarity would tend to pull in opposite directions.

Assuming solidarity and group loyalty are considered overriding values, then the above conflict and tension seem bound to strain the unity and cohesiveness of the communities involved. To ease this situation, these communities would seem to have to move in the direction of greater self-enclosure. Thus, a person with dual commitments that come into conflict with one another may only be able to maintain membership in the two communities involved by tempering his or her loyalty to each of them. To avoid diluting loyalties and weakening solidarity, therefore, there might be no other workable solution but to confine one's commitments to a single community.

In multicommunal settings where significant intercommunal dealings are virtually unavoidable, the communitarian ideal may be better served by a proliferation of overlapping communities than by a retrenchment into completely separate self-enclosed communities. Consistent with this, moreover, the communitarian ethos would seem best served by extending the reach of loyalty and solidarity to new frontiers, even if that would result in a diminution in the latter's intensity. Or, put more accurately, the communitarian ethos in communally pluralistic polities requires some loosening of loyalty and solidarity in order to allow for an expansion of the reach of communal interaction.

It follows from the preceding observations that pluralism is better suited than communitarianism—understood as prescribing solidarity and group loyalty as overriding values—to advance the case of the communitarian ethos in communally pluralistic settings. Indeed, proliferation of overlapping communities and multiplication of diverse communal commitments depend on the availability of a degree of flexibility and diversity largely lacking in the context of strict adherence to loyalty and solidarity as over-riding values. Pluralism, on the other hand, is more finely calibrated than communitarianism for purposes of fostering an optimal reconciliation of self and other without undermining the predominance of communal rela-tionships or *unduly* diluting communal bonds. As a matter of fact, pluralism is not inherently inconsistent with promotion of high degrees of loyalty and solidarity, and because of its flexibility it can broker a viable integration of overlapping communities by forging better distributive channels toward an optimal apportionment of solidarity and group loyalty.

E. The Superiority of Comprehensive Pluralism

Thus far, in building the case for the superiority of comprehensive plural-ism over liberalism, republicanism, and communitarianism, I have largely taken the latter's chief objectives at face value and on their own terms. From the perspective of reconciling self and other in the least coercive or confining manner possible, however, these objectives hardly impose them-selves as self-evident. Actually, as we shall now see, these objectives cannot be legitimately considered to be overriding from the standpoint of recon-ciling self and other. Moreover, as a consequence of this, the case for the superiority of comprehensive pluralism turns out to be much stronger than may be inferred from the preceding discussion.

Given the broad characterization of self and other that has emerged throughout this book, there appears to be no need for postulating any fun-damental primacy of the individual over the group or of the community over the individual. Similarly, whereas self-government figures as an impor-tant value in the context of enhancing the mutual autonomy and dignity of self and other, this hardly justifies elevating civic virtue into an overriding value. From the standpoint of reconciling self and other, all principal lib-eral, republican, and communitarian values appear to have a significant role to play. Accordingly, liberty, equality, human rights, justice, civic virtue, solidarity, and group loyalty are all worth pursuing, the only question being how they ought to be harmonized and combined to better reconcile self and other.

There is no single answer to the last question, because the right interplay among the above-mentioned values depends in part on contingent and con-textual factors. Thus, for example, pursuit of liberal values ought to pre-dominate in settings where communities are powerful, repressive, and rather self-enclosed. Conversely, communitarian values should be strongly stressed in the face of rampant individualism with consequent loss in social conscience and collective cooperation. More generally, as needs, interests, and circumstances vary, none of the values under consideration can claim any set entitlement to priority. Because of this, and because it molds the relationship among these values to suit the constantly evolving quest for reconciliation between self and other, comprehensive pluralism emerges as far superior to liberalism, republicanism, and communitarianism. Actually, because of its flexibility and broadly encompassing sweep, comprehensive pluralism can make use of what is best in liberalism, republicanism, and communitarianism while staying clear of their respective drawbacks.

IV. THE NEXUS BETWEEN COMPREHENSIVE PLURALISM, INTERPRETATION, AND THE DIVISION OF LABOR AMONG LAW, ETHICS, AND POLITICS

Liberalism, republicanism, communitarianism, and comprehensive pluralism each have interpretive consequences that can be assessed in terms of the quest for just interpretations. These interpretive consequences may not always be easy to pin down, as they tend to vary depending on the particular version of the comprehensive perspective from which they are drawn. For example, both Posner's law and economics supplemented by liberal individualistic constitutional constraints discussed in chapter VI and Dworkin's expansive liberal egalitarian conception of substantive constitutional rights supplemented by his theory of law as integrity mentioned in chapter I emanate from a liberal perspective. Posner and Dworkin part company, however, due in large measure to Posner's embrace of liberty and welfare maximization as overriding values as contrasted with Dworkin's commitment to equality as paramount. Nevertheless, distinctions *within* any of these three pale in comparison with the clear-cut differences *between* liberal, republican, and communitarian interpretations. Thus, the boundaries of fundamental rights are bound to shift depending on whether these rights are assessed from a liberal, republican, or communitarian standpoint. A Rousseauian republican conception of liberty, for instance, insists on freedom *through* the polity or positive freedom,[20] in contrast to liberal conceptions of liberty, which reserve a prominent place for freedom from the polity or negative freedom.[21]

As already mentioned, comprehensive pluralism derives distinct interpretive consequences from the operation of its two logical moments identified above. Because of comprehensive pluralism's refusal to embrace any first-order norm as overriding, however, the distinctness of its interpretive products is not always readily apparent. Indeed, to the extent that comprehensive pluralism draws on some of the values espoused by other compre-

20. For a discussion of Rousseau's conception of positive freedom, see Rosenfeld 1985, 870.

21. For a classical statement of the nexus between liberalism and negative freedom, see Mill 1859.

hensive perspectives—without ascribing the same weight to these values as competing perspectives do—there are inevitable interpretive overlaps between comprehensive pluralism and rival perspectives. Nevertheless, even when outcomes coincide, reconstruction pursuant to the dictates of its two logical moments is bound to reveal comprehensive pluralism's distinct interpretive imprint.

I have already briefly described the contrast between comprehensive pluralism's negative moment—a rather transparent process consisting in the systematic leveling of hierarchies among first-order norms—and its positive moment—a constructive effort at reintegration that falls inevitably short of its mark because of unavoidable contingency and limitations. The time has come now to inquire into how comprehensive pluralism might contribute to the quest for just interpretations. More particularly, it is necessary to focus on how comprehensive pluralism's logical split between its negative and its positive moment and its normative distinction between first-order and second-order norms may make use of the divide between law, ethics, and politics to generate just interpretations.

It should be emphasized from the outset that comprehensive pluralism's rejection of overriding values should not be misconstrued as meaning that it can dispense with justice. Indeed, so long as there is pluralism in fact, comprehensive pluralism is concerned with striking some balance among competing perspectives and must thus incorporate justice among its constellation of second-order norms. That does not mean, however, that comprehensive pluralism necessarily endorses any particular conception of justice or that it singles out justice as a first-order norm—that is, justice as it emerges from within the perspective of a given conception of the good vying for supremacy in the arena of first-order norms—for special treatment. Similarly, whereas comprehensive pluralism incorporates equality as part of its second-order negative leveling of all first-order norms, it does not inherently embrace any particular conception of equality or necessarily favor equality as a first-order value as against other such values. More generally, comprehensive pluralism contemplates that every value and (first-order) conception of the good will vary depending on whether it is considered from the standpoint of second-order objectives or from that of first-order ends.[22]

Inasmuch as selves tend to be more deeply anchored within the realm

22. Strictly speaking, the second-order conception of the good—that is, comprehensive pluralism—also varies depending on which of these two standpoints is embraced. Thus, from within any first-order perspective, comprehensive pluralism appears to be no different than any other rival (first-order) conception of the good. I do not pursue this any further here as it has no bearing on the search for the interpretive consequences that follow from the endorsement of comprehensive pluralism.

of first-order norms, the first-order norms that one identifies with will un-doubtedly be much more internalized than the second-order norms that one has agreed to honor. Accordingly, notwithstanding that prescriptively comprehensive pluralism requires internalization of second-order norms, phenomenologically valued first-order norms will tend to appear as inter-nal, and second-order norms, as external. But once the process of internali-zation required by comprehensive pluralism takes hold, then internalized first-order norms must be first recast as external. Indeed, I cannot adopt the perspective of comprehensive pluralism unless I first gain some distance from my communally grounded beliefs. Moreover, the negative moment of comprehensive pluralism fosters detachment from one's first-order com-mitments. On the other hand, after having carried such detachment far enough, comprehensive pluralism, through its positive moment, requires reintegration of communally grounded norms to the extent required to maximize diversity while minimizing confinement and coercion. Reintegra-tion, in turn, requires a reinternalization of first-order norms, but such reintegration needs to be partial rather than complete. Otherwise, the gains made through internalization of second-order norms would alto-gether dissipate. In short, under comprehensive pluralism, the interplay between first-order and second-order norms unleashes a dialectic revolving around internalization and externalization. This dialectic engages the es-sential components of each participant's shifting normative vantage point precariously anchored in a commonly shared perspective that remains in a perpetual state of construction.

Its constant need for internalization and externalization suggests that comprehensive pluralism could make good use of the division between eth-ics—the locus of internal normative relationships—on the one hand, and law and politics—characterized by external normative relationships—on the other. As discussed in chapter III, emphasis on the external links forged through law can defuse ethical conflicts among proponents of competing conceptions of the good, and therefore provide the breathing room neces-sary for peaceful coexistence among the members of an ethically divided polity. Consistent with this, comprehensive pluralism could presumably ap-peal to law to deal with first-order norms in the least intrusive manner pos-sible—that is, by limiting constraints on first-order norms to the realm of external relationships. From the standpoint of comprehensive pluralism's negative moment, law should provide for external relationships in a way that avoids, as much as possible, privileging certain first-order norms over others. From the standpoint of comprehensive pluralism's positive moment, moreover, law should furnish the space necessary for ensuring that the sac-rifices required for reintegration of first-order norms are largely confined to the realm of external relationships. Ideally then, from the perspective of comprehensive pluralism, law would promote equality among competing first-order perspectives through provision of a neutral area for external relationships, and liberty by circumscribing the space for constraints to an intercommunal sphere reserved for external relationships.

As just described, the ideal of comprehensive pluralism seems virtually identical to that of liberalism, with the one difference that unlike liberalism, comprehensive pluralism does not appear to be biased in favor of individualism. However, because actual neutrality cannot be achieved except in a purely (negative) formal sense, and because in any complex contemporary constitutional democracy the private preserve of intracommunal dealings cannot be neatly separated from the public sphere of intercommunal relationships, this ideal lacks sufficient counterfactual critical bite to yield sound interpretive criteria. In particular, this ideal is deficient in that it overemphasizes form over substance and essence or end-state over process. Instead of focus on neutrality and equality, the emphasis should be on neutralization and equalization; instead of on liberty, on liberation; and instead of on internal and external, on internalization and externalization.

The liberal ideal is insufficient for purposes of advancing the interpretive enterprise consistent with comprehensive pluralism, but that does not mean that this ideal ought to be altogether discarded. The problem with the liberal ideal is that it is one-sided. But so are the republican and the communitarian ideals. Indeed, the ultimate, unattainable, ideal of comprehensive pluralism maps out a vision of full integration through self-realization without sacrificing full differentiation. In accordance with this ideal, the self would not be merged into the other, but each would become transparent to the other, and they would jointly devise and maintain a unified and integrated communal setting in which each self could freely invent, develop, and pursue a conception of the good. This ideal enterprise would thus function much like a self-governing artists' community devoted to optimizing individual and collective opportunities for aesthetic creativity, satisfaction, and diversity. Moreover, within this ultimate ideal of comprehensive pluralism, the liberal, republican, and communitarian ideals would on one level mutually limit one another to sustain differentiation, while on another level they would become subsumed within the unified construct designed to lend support to integration. In other words, within the ultimate ideal of comprehensive justice, the respective ideals of liberalism, republicanism, and communitarianism loom as both antagonistic and complementary.

The ultimate ideal of comprehensive pluralism has much in common with the concept of comprehensive justice. Actually, the vision promoted by this ideal amounts to a representation of the state of affairs that would obtain if comprehensive justice could be fully achieved. Accordingly, just as comprehensive justice should figure in the determination of just interpretations, so too should its corresponding ideal. However, since both of them are impossible to achieve, their contribution to establishing just interpretations must be limited to providing a *sense of direction*. Thus, faced with an ever-changing process of confrontation and accommodation, the seeker of just interpretations must refer to these two impossible objectives to determine whether a proposed resolution to a conflict is likely to lead in the right direction (or where many different resolutions are proposed, whether any of them is more likely than the others to lead in the right direction). Moreover, this sense of direction should inform the backdrop against which criticism of an actual state of affairs is launched as well as the backdrop against which concrete proposals for change are articulated.

Set against the two impossible objectives discussed above are the two poles that must be reconstructed as if they were part of a progression toward greater perfection. These two poles are the actual state of affairs torn by a conflict calling for actual resolution and the plausible horizon of possible concrete resolutions of that conflict. Both of these poles, moreover, involve a significant element of contingency: the conflict itself is historically contingent, and the plausible horizon for its resolution is bound to be partially determined by the particular nature of the conflict as well as by cultural, technological, and institutional contingencies that constrict the range of available options. Beyond these contingencies, however, within contemporary constitutional democracies, conflicts and their plausible resolutions revolve around the antagonistic and complementary relationship among the liberal, republican, and communitarian strains associated with comprehensive pluralism. Thus, the conflicts between self and other which call for just interpretations seem amendable to recharacterization. They can be recharacterized as involving either infringements on liberty or equality, or frustration of self-realization, or the undermining of communal solidarity, or finally the placement of impediments on the convergence of integration, differentiation, and self-realization.

Just interpretations are thus circumscribed by the logics of comprehensive pluralism, on the one hand, and by the dialectics fueled by the concurrent antagonism between, and complementarity of, the liberal, republican, and communitarian tendencies within comprehensive pluralism, on the other. Within this framework, the division of labor among ethics, law, and politics might at first be attempted as follows. Ethics would preside over the internalization of both intracommunal and intercommunal norms, or, in other words, of both first-order and second-order norms. Politics, for its part, would provide external harmonization of intracommunal and intercommunal objectives through self-government. Finally, law would both secure the necessary conditions for the proper functioning of ethics and politics and provide interstitial regulation to cover gaps unfilled by ethics or politics. Moreover, this division of tasks would, by and large, place law under the liberal ideal, ethics under the communitarian ideal, and politics under the republican ideal.

The above division of labor is not only sharp and clear but also seems to allow the tensions between law, ethics, and politics to provide an expressive outlet for the antagonism between the liberal, communitarian, and republican strands of comprehensive pluralism. By the same token, this division apparently allows for expression of the complementarity of these three strands through the reconciliation and harmonization of law, ethics, and politics, or, in other words, of justice according to law and justice beyond law. Unfortunately, however, as will now be demonstrated, in spite of its great appeal, the above division must be rejected as inadequate. If ethics merely internalized first- and second-order norms, this would not lead to communitarian pluralism but rather to confusion. As we have seen, second-order norms are not on the same plane as first-order norms. Moreover, from a phenomenological standpoint, inasmuch as intracommunal norms are more deeply entrenched than intercommunal norms, genuine internalization of second-order norms only seems possible if accompanied by externalization of first-order norms. Such externalization, however, cannot be achieved by ethics alone, but requires recourse to law and politics. Indeed, unlike in a metaphysical perspective where ethics, law, and politics merely complement each other, from the perspective of comprehensive pluralism, law and politics are also, in part, antagonistic to ethics. In particular, law binds together the outer framework of a polity committed to comprehensive pluralism, through the leveling of all hierarchy among first-order norms and through reintegration of such norms in a way that precludes them from gaining readmission on their own terms. Law's leveling thrust introduces a contradiction between the self's internal commitment to certain first-order norms and the self's external commitments based on the proposition that these same first-order norms are no better than any others. To put it in terms of the operative dialectic, the self may be initially drawn to law in order to place the other's first-order norms at a sufficient distance to create the space necessary for the self to attend to his or her own first-order concerns. But once the wide net of law is cast, the self's own first-order norms will also become caught in it, with the consequent alienation of the self from his or her own first-order norms. Finally, in yet another dialectic reversal the very distance that separates the self from his or her own first-order commitments allows for greater tolerance of the other's first-order norms. On the other hand, law's concentration on reintegration yields a cluster of first-order norms that is different—if not in configuration, then in weight and in its relationships to other norms—from those previously internalized by the self. To cope with this difference, the self must mediate its ethical commitments through law, and this involves essentially two separate steps: first, law's negation and displacement of the self's cluster of first-order norms allows for sufficient externalization of the latter to make room for internalization of second-order norms; and second, by mapping out the (external) norms designed to govern intercommunal dealings, law leaves space for intracommunal pursuits and thus makes for (partial) reinternalization of first-order norms.

It follows from this that within comprehensive pluralism, ethics is dependent on law, and because the two are antagonistic as well as complementary, they cannot be collapsed into one another. Moreover, just as ethics is dependent on law, so too is law dependent on ethics. Because law cannot achieve neutrality and equally accommodate all first-order norms in its positive thrust, it must remain open to ethical criticism and influence. Specifically, ethics is bound to call on law to create conditions for greater and better accommodation of diverse first-order norms. Furthermore, depending on the circumstances, the ethical call on law may be primarily steeped in the communitarian or in the liberal strand of comprehensive pluralism.

From the standpoint of ethics, politics plays a role similar to law. Broadly speaking, politics provides the arena for the democratic setting and pursuit of intercommunal objectives and thus fosters antagonism and complementarity regarding communal (first-order) norms. In its own way, politics tends to level all first-order norms, by forcing them to compete for approval by the majority.[23] On the other hand, political solutions in a pluralistically diverse polity are unlikely to satisfy many of the holders of different clusters of first-order norms whose value preferences become significantly frustrated. Inasmuch as politics fulfills an integrating function by pursuing a common base for intercommunal dealings, it can serve as a point of departure for internalization of second-order norms; inasmuch as it leads to division and fragmentation, it may foster externalization of first-order norms as well as retreat within communal bounds shielded from intercommunal strife.

In terms of just interpretations, it is the relationship between law and politics that warrants further exploration. Ideally, politics should provide an external medium for the reconciliation of self-government and self-realization, of public citizen and private or intracommunal person. In actuality, however, republican self-government and individual or communal self-realization are often at odds with one another. Moreover, even if the

---

23. Presumably, if a particular cluster of first-order norms is already endorsed by the majority, there might be no real competition, and the antagonism between ethics and politics might well be minimized. Majority endorsement, however, need not spell the end of competition. It is conceivable that a majority might be convinced that it would be politically advantageous to accommodate certain value preferences held by a minority, to ensure overall more advantageous and more harmonious intercommunal dealings.

sacrifices required to abide by the republican ideal were deemed legitimate no matter how severe, no "general will" in the *equal* interests of the entire citizenry could ever be devised. Accordingly, recourse to ethics for purposes of internalizing civic virtue, while necessary to prevent runaway fragmentation due to unmediated clashes of interests, would be inadequate to bring about a political balance between self-government and self-realization.

On the level of politics, pursuit of self-government may become reduced to attempting coercion of the other, through use of political leverage to force the other unduly to sacrifice self-realization in the name of a "common good" that leaves that other at a distinct disadvantage. On the other hand, in the relentless pursuit of self-realization, the political clash of self-interests may lead to such excessive fragmentation as to threaten the cohesion of the polity. Against these two dangers, law offers two kinds of safeguards: antagonistic counterweights and complementary relief.

Law's mediation can furnish a counterweight against excessively coercive politics,[24] through constitutional constraints. More specifically, constitutional constraints can play both an enabling and an antagonistic limiting role with respect to politics. On the one hand, constitutional provisions accorded the force of law function as constitutive rules that afford a measure of institutional stability to the game of democratic politics. On the other hand, constitutional constraints carve out part of the domain of external relationships in order to place it beyond the reach of everyday politics. Thus, constitutional constraints may antagonize politics by thwarting the latter's reach toward some of its objectives.[25]

Law also complements politics to the extent that the realm of external relationships is apportioned among the two of them, largely as a matter of convenience. It will be remembered that in chapter III a distinction was drawn between two distinct approaches toward a division of labor between law and politics. The first of these was the structural approach, which, roughly speaking, institutionalizes the divide between constitutional constraints, on the one hand, and politics—broadly understood to include laws inasmuch as these are the products of the will of a legislative majority—on the other. The second was the thematic approach, according to which certain matters are left to law and others to politics, primarily as a matter of convenience. Now, it is in the context of the thematic approach that law

24. I use the word "excessively" advisedly, as majoritarian politics, no matter how considerate, necessarily involves some measure of coercion.

25. It can be objected that constitutions are as much a subject to politics as ordinary laws and all other issues ordinarily dealt with in the political arena. Suffice it for now, in reply, to point out that acceptance of constitutional politics as a fact of life does not preclude asserting that counterfactually, and within the perspective of comprehensive pluralism, constitutional constraints on politics are more—or more precisely, other—than merely political. I shall discuss these issues in greater detail in the course of the next chapter.

and politics can be regarded as complementary. To the extent that out-comes in politics are more volatile and unpredictable than outcomes in law, and that a complex pluralistic polity lacks the resources to deal thoroughly and competently within the realm of politics with all issues conceivably amendable to political resolution, it makes sense to turn to law to unclog the channels of politics. Moreover, although the *fact* of apportionment may be a matter of convenience, the way in which such apportionment is achieved is often not a matter of indifference. Thus, depending on contextual factors, maintaining as much stability as possible in certain areas may be a prerequisite to viable politics within the constraints of comprehensive pluralism. In short, if law as complementary could be likened to frozen or decelerated politics, then its legitimacy would hinge on its ability to shield the political engine from overheating.

To recapitulate: the ethics of comprehensive pluralism is communitarian, but instead of addressing a single community, it seeks to provide the internal glue for a community of communities. This, however, cannot be achieved directly; it requires the mediation of law. Law makes for the externalization of certain norms, which, in turn, allows for the internalization of others, all of which is necessary to transform the priority of second-order norms into a working ethical principle. As indispensable to the survival of the ethics of comprehensive pluralism, law is ethical. But as necessarily other than ethics—remember it is law's propensity for generating external relationships that renders it indispensable—law must, on some level, remain distinct from ethics. On the other hand, from the standpoint of law, law must remain independent from ethics as the leveler of first-order norms but must fall back on ethics to make up for its failure to achieve neutrality and equality in the course of its reintegration of first-order norms. Moreover, to the extent that law must act independently from ethics, it clearly tends toward the liberal ideal. Nonetheless, because it needs to rely on ethics to compensate for its failure to achieve neutrality, law must remain open to communitarian influences. Finally, politics emerges as a medium for external reconciliation of self-realization and self-government. Inasmuch as such reconciliation can never be fully achieved, however, politics needs to be constrained by law and ethics to avoid the excesses of self-government to the exclusion of self-realization, and of self-realization for some at the expense of others. Furthermore, insofar as law and politics are properly regarded as complementary, the two remain on the same plane, and law can be subsumed, by and large, under the broader objectives of politics. Consistent with this, politics bears a close connection to law and ethics, but there remains, all the same, a limited area within which (democratic) politics ought to remain supreme. That area covers those instances in which all available options would neither materially advance nor set back self-realization. Indeed, in those instances, as all other relevant things remain equal, self-government looms as clearly superior to the alternative, and politics as the appropriate vehicle for self-government becomes paramount. Accordingly, with respect to the instances in question, politics ought to be driven by the republican ideal. Otherwise, politics should accommodate a combination of liberal, republican, and communitarian influences.

The preceding remarks concerning the division of labor among law, ethics, and politics, within the framework of comprehensive pluralism, touch on, in broad outline, some of the salient requirements for just interpretations. A more specific examination of the interpretive consequences of this division of labor will be addressed in the next chapter. However, there is one issue with very significant interpretive consequences that must be briefly examined now, before the close of this chapter. That issue concerns the nexus between *counterfactual* reconstruction of the division of labor among law, ethics, and politics and what *actually* happens to be embodied in law.

It is obvious that what is actually encompassed within law does not necessarily correspond to what ought to be counterfactually consistent with comprehensive pluralism. For example, actual constitutions may constrain actual politics in ways that seem unwarranted counterfactually, or actual laws may fail to complement ethics or politics as they should. In such cases, a question arises concerning the interpretive implications of the discrepancy between the actual and counterfactual domains of law.

Where a discrepancy is over the content rather than the domain of law, then reference to the appropriate counterfactual content seems entirely legitimate for critical purposes. Moreover, provided there is room for a range of plausible interpretations, then reliance on the relevant counterfactual seems fully warranted to interpret the actual law in ways that bring it as close as possible to its counterfactual counterpart. For example, if an antidiscrimination law that omits any reference to discrimination on the basis of homosexuality can be plausibly interpreted as either permitting or prohibiting such discrimination, and if the latter is counterfactually called for, then commitment to just interpretations would clearly seem to require interpreting the antidiscrimination law in question as prohibiting discrimination against homosexuality.

With discrepancies concerning the domain of law, in contrast, it is far from obvious that juxtaposition of the actual and the counterfactual would be productive *with regard to legal interpretation*. Undoubtedly, such juxtaposition would be highly useful from the standpoint of criticizing the actual law involved for trespassing beyond the legitimate bounds of legal relationships. But what interpretive use could possibly be derived from the conclusion that the matter addressed by an actual law ought legitimately be left to ethics or politics? Arguably, under those circumstances, no plausible legal interpretation of the actual law would in any way advance the cause of just interpretations.

On closer examination, that last conclusion is only warranted in some of the cases in which discrepancies concerning the proper domain of law are present. Indeed, if counterfactually a matter ought to be entrusted to politics, and if actual politics or the plausible horizon of possible politics can properly handle the matter in question, then the above conclusion holds. However, if counterfactual politics can in no way be approximated by actual politics (or possible politics within the relevant horizon of plausibility), then actual law (or possible law within the horizon of plausible law) might well turn out to be the best available means to approximate counterfactual politics. Consequently, in that case, juxtaposition of the actual and the counterfactual would yield significant consequences for legal interpretation notwithstanding discrepancies regarding the proper domain of law. Moreover, in such a case, it is the counterfactual division of labor among law, ethics, and politics, rather than its actual (or possible within the relevant horizon of plausibility) counterpart, that determines which values ought to inform the optimal legal interpretation under the circumstances. For example, if, counterfactually, a matter ought to be left exclusively to politics and be governed by the republican ideal, but if actual and foreseeably possible politics are so fragmented and self-centered as to preclude genuine republican self-government, then actual or foreseeably possible law interpreted in terms of republican values might well represent the best available approximation to just interpretations.

In conclusion, comprehensive pluralism has definite interpretive consequences, which, I have argued, are better suited than those of its rivals to lead polities that are pluralistic in fact to just interpretations. These interpretative consequences are, in part, procedural and, in part, substantive, and they hinge on juxtaposition of the counterfactual, the actual, and the possible within a plausible horizon of change. The interpretive consequences of comprehensive justice, moreover, depend on complex uses of the division of labor among law, ethics, and politics. Because of these intricacies, and because of the significant role of contingency, comprehensive pluralism rarely leads to direct or obvious interpretive outcomes. As a matter of fact, the interpretive consequences of comprehensive pluralism have proven to be above all *relational*. That is not surprising since comprehensive pluralism is primarily concerned about the relationship among diverse perspectives and between the actual, the foreseeably possible, and the counterfactual. Finally, although comprehensive pluralism's interpretive consequences loom as primarily relational, as I seek to demonstrate in the next chapter, it does not follow that they cannot be concrete or determinate.

CHAPTER EIGHT

In Pursuit of Meaning amid Partial Subjects, Elusive Others, the Open Texture of Law, and Imperfect Justice

I. MICRO-INTERPRETIVE VERSUS MACRO-INTERPRETIVE CONSEQUENCES OF COMPREHENSIVE PLURALISM

In the last chapter, I provided an overview of the interpretive consequences of comprehensive pluralism. Here, I seek to round out my examination of the interpretive implications flowing from comprehensive pluralism, by shifting the focus to salient particulars and reconstructing the quest for just interpretations from the "bottom up." In the last chapter, I dealt with "macro-interpretive" issues arising in connection with comprehensive pluralism; here, I start from a select number of "micro-interpretive" issues, with a view to determining how comprehensive pluralism might lead to sufficiently concrete and determinate meanings in its quest for just interpretations.

From a micro-interpretive standpoint, the starting point is the confrontation between self and other as mediated through law. Moreover, although the confrontation in question is multifaceted, given the present focus on legal interpretation, phenomenologically, the optimal starting point is the citizen's encounter with law—or, more precisely, with a particular law. To the extent that such a law is external to the citizen—that it imposes external constraints on him or her—it represents the other as against the citizen as a self. Conversely, to the extent that the citizen regards that law as the externalization of his or her will—or, in other words, the citizen views himself or herself as the author or coauthor of that law—the law in question becomes an expression of the citizen's self. Thus, the citizen finds the confrontation between self and other embedded *within* laws as well as permeating all intersubjective attempts at ascribing commonly shared meanings to laws.

The citizen is bound to encounter law in many different capacities, including those of lawmaker, law administrator, law enforcer, adjudicator, and law-abiding person. Also, the need to ascribe meanings to laws arises no matter in which of these capacities the citizen happens to approach the law. For our purposes, however, it suffices to concentrate on the quest for meaning from the standpoint of the law-abiding person and from that of the adjudicator.

The law-abiding person must focus primarily on the confrontation between self and other *within* the law, in contrast to the adjudicator, who must concentrate above all on the conflict between self and other over what meaning ought to be ascribed to a law implicated in a legal dispute between them. Although the focus of the adjudicator within the perspective of comprehensive pluralism is distinct from that of the law-abiding person, as we will see, their respective viewpoints are by no means unrelated. Actually, the standpoint of the law-abiding person must be incorporated as a building block in the construction of a vantage point suited to the needs of the adjudicator. Consequently, our inquiry into the micro-interpretive implications of comprehensive pluralism must begin with a quick glance at the interpretive predicament of the law-abiding person.

The citizen who takes the vantage point of a law-abiding person within the perspective of comprehensive pluralism is called on to indicate why he or she ought to be bound to obey a particular law. Ideally and in the most general terms, the answer should be that the law in question encapsules a legitimate reconciliation of self and other. Furthermore, even at this high level of generality, the boundaries of the duty to obey laws emerge rather sharply. If a given law lacks any plausible trace of either the self or the other, then the law-abiding person does not strictly speaking have a duty to obey it. Indeed, on the one hand, a legal duty that is exclusively owed to oneself is no duty at all, whereas, on the other, a law that completely lacks any trace of the self is not only patently unjust but also purely oppressive. Thus, in any pluralistic setting, any law reducible to a mere projection of the self (which from the vantage point of the other amounts to a mere extension of the other) is but an illusion or an instrument of tyranny.

Between these two extremes, every law can be construed as embodying some reconciliation between self and other, and the question becomes whether such reconciliation should be deemed legitimate by the law-abiding person. Again, in the most general terms, those laws should count as legitimate which can be reconstructed as aiming at a reconciliation wherein the self meets the other halfway. And that could be accomplished in one of two ways. First, a law would be legitimate if the law-abiding person could be viewed at once as its author and as a person properly subjected to it—or, in other words, could be regarded as the law's author notwithstanding the degree to which that law incorporates the aims of the other and at the same time considered properly subjected to that law, even after acknowledging that the law's content bears a significant imprint of the other. Second, a law would be legitimate if it could be reconstructed as seeking to apportion rights and duties in a way that provides equal consideration to both self and other.

From the vantage point of the law-abiding person within the perspective of comprehensive pluralism, then, laws can be roughly divided into three different kinds. First are purely oppressive laws imposed by a foreign occupier, or by an enemy within the polity bent on annihilation or complete subjugation, which properly call for rebellion or resistance rather than obedience. Second are laws that can be construed as striking the optimal possible balance between self and other, which must be obeyed, in part, because they are self-imposed and, in part, because by treating them as binding, one extends to the other the recognition needed for reconciliation through law. And third are laws that apportion rights and duties in a way that evinces equal consideration of both self and other, which must be obeyed either because they facilitate reconciliation between the two or because they block a path to greater subordination of one to the other.

There is likely to be much overlap between the second and the third kind of law described above, but the two must be kept distinct, for there are laws of the third kind that do not satisfy the requirements for laws of the second kind. Indeed, as a consequence of comprehensive pluralism's rejection of the viability of a neutral Kantian moral perspective discussed above,[1] there may be situations in which self and other are unable to find sufficient common ground for purposes of arriving at a mutually acceptable reconciliation. In such situations, a law that favors neither the self nor the other, but which might not be voluntarily embraced by either of them, might nevertheless be justified. The basis for such justification, moreover, could be either that the law in question prevents mutual eradication of self and other or that it preserves a status quo that precludes domination by one over the other pending potential overcoming of the current impasse.

Whereas the paradigm cases corresponding respectively to the three kinds of laws identified above demarcate counterfactual ideals around which legal discourse seems bound to revolve, actual laws will inevitably fall short of these ideals. Accordingly, the interpretive challenge consists, above all, in gauging how actual laws stack up against these ideals, with a view to either legitimating the status quo or justifying calls for changes. Moreover, from a micro-interpretive standpoint, the principal tasks are to endow the relevant ideals with semantic content suited to the particular context involved; to furnish credible depictions of the relationship between the challenged status quo and plausible alternatives; and to harmonize viable arguments for or against departure from the status quo with pertinent semantically

1. See chapter V, above.

cohesive depictions of the relevant counterfactual ideal(s) while remaining within the normative constraints of comprehensive pluralism.

From the vantage point of the law-abiding citizen, a particular law open to many different interpretations should, if possible, be construed as co-authored by the self and the other. The next best possibility would be to construe it as authored in part by the self and in part by the other, with both of them agreeing to be mutually bound to the extent that the law is traceable to the other. Finally, there is a third, less desirable, possibility that nonetheless allows for legitimate self-justification and for treating the law in question as binding.[2] According to this third possibility, if the law under consideration could be interpreted as being equally alienating from the standpoints of self and other, it could still be worthy of obedience to prevent intensifying discord among the two.

The kind of joint authorship relevant in the first of the three above-described cases involves an overlap of interests or value preferences between self and other.[3] For example, if self and other belong to different religions, but if each of these would be better served if the state withdrew from the private sphere, then self and other should welcome the opportunity to co-author a law confining state intervention to the public sphere. Although different particular aims and conceptions of the good would ultimately stand behind the respective support accorded by self and other to their coauthored law, so long as the operative overlap remains firmly in place the law in question should not give rise to significant interpretive disputes. This is hardly surprising, for in these cases self and other are assumed to have the *same* legal aims notwithstanding that they differ in their extralegal objectives. In a complex pluralistic polity, however, these cases are likely to be exceedingly rare, thus primarily serving as useful counterfactual markers.

The second kind of collaborative authorship mentioned above, on the other hand, is likely to be much more prevalent, but it is also bound to generate its fair share of interpretive disputes. The kind of coauthorship involved here is perhaps best exemplified by the writing of a private con-

---

2. In terms of prudential considerations, the scope of self-justification for abiding by a law would be much broader than when viewed from the perspective of comprehensive pluralism. Thus, submission to even a very oppressive law could be justifiable for prudential reasons if failure to comply could lead to dire consequences.

3. Cases in which more than an overlap underlies coauthorship, such as when self and other within a polity join forces to combat an external other, are best reconstructed as the product of a self rather than as the coproduct of a self and another. In such cases of self-legislation the resulting law is not reducible to a mere illusion, however, for the fragile self that binds fellow citizens together against a foreign other is most probably in constant danger of dissolution. In any event, so long as this precarious self holds together, interpretive difficulties are not likely to arise. Accordingly, there is no need for further examination of these cases.

tract to govern an exchange between two parties. As pointed out in chapter I, such a contract is an expression of the joint will of self and other which is to a certain extent contrary to the individual will of either of them. Although the contract is a joint writing, and the signatories to it adopt the same legal objective, they do not ordinarily share the same legal aims at the time of entering into contract negotiations. Thus, as already noted, a prospective buyer typically wants to pay as little as possible, while a prospective seller typically wishes to charge as much as possible. Initially then, buyer and seller are likely to bring somewhat conflicting legal aims to their contract negotiations. Consequently, contractors carve out a common scheme not because their interests and value preferences happen to overlap but because they decide that compromise affords the best available means toward their respective objectives.

A contract is thus a jointly authored law based on compromise. In the context of ordinary commercial transactions, moreover, there is no harm in seeing both parties as coauthors who assume joint responsibility for the actual text of their contract. In carrying the contract analogy to coauthorship based on compromise within the realm of intersubjective dealings among proponents of competing conceptions of the good, however, coauthorship is best conceived as several rather than joint. Indeed, out of concern not to be swept within the perspective of the other, self and other might be viewed as agreeing to string together a mutually acceptable text in which fragments authored by each of them are blended with fragments contributed by the other. As thus conceived, moreover, whereas the law represented by the contract is binding on both parties, it is, in part, binding as self-imposed self-legislation and, in part, as mutually coercive.

The contract analogy thus leads to the conclusion that, consistent with comprehensive pluralism, law is binding *because* it is self-imposed and *because* it is coercive—a conclusion that seems much like those reached by Habermas and by Hart (1961, 165–67). The justification regarding law's bindingness under comprehensive pluralism differs, however, from the respective justifications offered by Habermas's discourse theory and Hart's positivism. Unlike under these other theories, under comprehensive pluralism, self-legislation and coercion do not figure as alternatives, and neither of them could ultimately become subsumed under the other. Actually, under comprehensive pluralism, it is the very opposition between self-legislation and coercion that justifies adherence to laws that fall within the paradigm demarcated by the contract analogy. Paradoxically, within the perspective of comprehensive pluralism, coercion is not only constraining but also liberating: it allows the self to engage in a joint enterprise with the other without either of them being swept into the perspective of the other. In other words, so long as the contract analogy holds, law's coercive side allows the self to become enlisted in the pursuit of the other's objectives without having to express allegiance to the latter's conception of the good while, at the same time, assuring the other's cooperation in one's own projects without threatening to compromise the other's inner commitments.

The legitimacy of the paradigm modeled on contract hinges not only on opposition but also on balance between self-legislation and coercion. For self and other to meet halfway, each must find a balance between the gains and sacrifices resulting from their mutual compromise. Ideally, this means that the gains and sacrifices of each will be equivalent to those of the other and that each one's gains will be proportional to his or her own sacrifices. Failure to satisfy the latter requirement, however, does not preclude the self from meeting the other halfway. Thus, even if neither self nor other derives any positive gain from a law, such law could still be legitimate consistent with comprehensive pluralism if the sacrifices required of each of them were equivalent. In that situation, moreover, the law in question would fall under the third kind of case identified above.

The third kind of case is the micro-interpretive equivalent to the first logical moment of comprehensive pluralism, which as we saw in chapter VII consists in the leveling of all first-order norms. Indeed, in some cases a standoff between self and other may be the only way for them to meet halfway and thus the best alternative short of dissolving the unity of the polity.[4] Furthermore, the second kind of case, modeled on the contract analogy, corresponds, by and large, to the confluence of both logical moments of comprehensive pluralism and gives expression to the interplay between law and ethics, externalization and internalization, which is set in motion by attempts to harmonize competing first-order norms under the aegis of second-order norms.

Both of these latter cases, unlike the first case, are likely to raise vexing interpretive issues. Indeed, how can we tell whether self and other meet halfway, when there is no common measure to gauge their respective perspectives? Similarly, how can we compare their respective gains or sacrifices? Furthermore, are not these difficulties likely to be compounded as the lack of common measure may encourage self and other to argue that, in spite of appearances to the contrary, a particular law imposes a relatively heavier burden on them than on their counterpart?

In keeping with the contract analogy, many of these interpretive difficulties may be circumvented or minimized. As long as a contract represents the embodiment of the joint will of both contractors, then arguably the

4. Given that comprehensive pluralism is agnostic as to whether a polity that is not pluralistic in fact ought to be committed to normative pluralism (see chapter VII, above), it has nothing to say on the issue of whether secession would be preferable to continued association among conflicting communities. In any event, there are cases in which external factors, such as economic or political conditions, make secession impractical.

procedural constraints inherent in contract formation would appear to guarantee that self and other would meet halfway. As we have seen in the course of our discussion of proceduralism in chapter V, however, contract alone does not ultimately guarantee pure procedural justice. For one thing, background conditions and substantive concerns must be taken into account. For another, consistent with the fluid conception of self and other advanced throughout this book, it is by no means assured that the needs and objectives of self and other will remain essentially unchanged throughout the life of the contract. Thus, whereas a party to a contract may have meant one thing on entering into the contractual relationship, that party may in good faith subsequently believe that he or she meant quite a different thing. In short, the respective identities of self and other, which figure prominently in the determination of whether a particular contract allows them to meet halfway, may evolve sufficiently during the projected life of their mutual undertaking to raise serious doubts as to whether their contract amounts to joint self-legislation.

The interpretive difficulties confronting self and other as contractors are compounded in the case of the adjudicator charged with resolving contractual disputes. To a large extent, the adjudicator must put himself or herself in the shoes of the contractors to determine their respective contractual intent, and that task is complicated by epistemological difficulties above and beyond those confronted by the contractors themselves. But, in addition, the adjudicator is also responsible for factoring background constraints and substantive concerns into the reading—or rewriting—of the contract before him or her. In that latter capacity, moreover, the adjudicator must either directly apply substantive norms or counterfactually reconstruct the intent of each contractor as if the latter had acted as a fully cognizant and fully responsible agent operating within the perspective of comprehensive pluralism.

The contract analogy to self-legislation has thus helped identify three different interpretive tasks likely to figure in the quest for just interpretations consistent with comprehensive pluralism. First, an actual intent for self and other must be imputed. Second, their counterfactual intent must be reconstructed so as to conform with the dictates of comprehensive pluralism. And third, substantive norms derived from comprehensive pluralism must be readied for application through interpretation. Furthermore, the second and third of these tasks are to a significant degree overlapping, as substantive norms can be frequently, but not always, factored in counterfactual reconstruction.

The search for reconciliation between self and other in terms of the three tasks mentioned above suggests that, from a micro-interpretive standpoint, legal interpretation is likely to remain incomplete and tentative. Nevertheless, these three tasks and particularly counterfactual reconstruction and implementation of substantive constraints can contribute to a significant narrowing of available options, and thus to channeling legal interpretation *in the direction of* greater justice and more suitable reconciliation of self and other. In what follows, I briefly spell out how these tasks may be harnessed in the pursuit of just interpretations within the perspective of comprehensive pluralism. First, I explore from a micro-interpretive standpoint how counterfactual reconstruction might deal with antagonistic positions predicated on competing conceptions of the good, including clashes between proponents of different religious ideologies. Second, I examine the nexus between comprehensive pluralism and internal transformations of self and other. Third, I investigate how the three tasks above might contribute from a micro-interpretive standpoint to harmonizing competing first-order norms within the space made available for them by second-order norms. Finally, I focus on how interpretive insights deriving from comprehensive pluralism might contribute to resolution of difficult cases without leading to pathological suppression of difference.

II. MAKING INTERPRETIVE SENSE OF CLASHES AMONG PARTIAL SELVES AND ELUSIVE OTHERS: ON THE ROAD TO JUSTICE AS REVERSIBLE RECIPROCITY

Confronted with the task of interpreting a law open to many different meanings, the adjudicator must, on the contract analogy, seek to approach the law in question as a piece of coauthored self-legislation. Viewed on the surface, this seems rather banal, as it is a well-established judicial practice to elucidate the meaning of a statute by reference to the legislative intent of parliament, and that of a constitutional provision by reference to the intent of the framers of the constitution. Viewed in greater depth and in the context of comprehensive pluralism, however, the adjudicator's task is not only more difficult than merely ascertaining legislative intent but also rather different. Indeed, leaving aside the inherent difficulties in deciphering the intent of the parties to a contract from a reading of the coauthored writing that embodies their agreement, the adjudicator confronts partial selves, elusive others, and a series of extralegal constraints, all of which play crucial roles in the quest to settle on legitimate meanings. Moreover, whereas these additional concerns in some sense clearly complicate the search for just interpretations, paradoxically, in another sense, they can ultimately contribute to simplifying it. On one level, reconciliation of self and other in ways that fully account for all relevant identities and differences is a never-ending project fraught with significant interpretive uncertainties. Nevertheless, these very interpretive uncertainties, when properly embedded in a setting animated by partial selves and elusive others, call for gap-filling measures as a prerequisite to establishing any coherent meaning.

Furthermore, these gap-filling measures must be justifiable in terms of the dictates of comprehensive pluralism to be legitimate, and on counterfactual reconstruction, rather than on unavailable or unreachable factual conclusions, to be workable. On the level of gap filling consistent with comprehensive pluralism, therefore, the interpretive task is measurably simplified as a manageable counterfactual reconstruction based on a stable normative foundation replaces a never-ending factual search hampered by insurmountable interpretive hurdles.

For all their stabilizing potential, the normative constraints and counterfactual reconstructions associated with comprehensive pluralism cannot purge the interpretive enterprise of contingency. Actually, the very starting point in the quest for just interpretations is mired in contingency, as the self, the other, the law that purports to bind them together, and the plausible avenues to better reconciliation between self and other are all to a significant degree dependent on historical contingencies and thus bound to vary from one setting to the next. In contrast, the framework of normative constraints and the architectonic principles of counterfactual reconstruction linked to comprehensive pluralism are essentially invariable and thus furnish a set mold transportable from one setting to the next. Consistent with this, the interpretive enterprise circumscribed by comprehensive pluralism tends to organize the relevant material in sets of recognizable relational clusters. Furthermore, it is the very recurrence of these relational clusters that allows for the simplifying steps that render the interpretive enterprise manageable.

A. Comprehensive Pluralism's Interpretive Baseline: Equal Worth and Mere Reciprocity

Lying at the very core of comprehensive pluralism is a normative commitment to the equal worth of self and other.[5] Because of this, for a law to make it possible for self and other to meet halfway, it must consistently uphold their equal worth. Otherwise, a law would have to be considered oppressive. Furthermore, assessment of whether a law complies with the equal worth imperative would in some cases remain independent of the imputed objectives of the law-abiding person, while in other cases, it would have to factor in such objectives. In other words, on the contract analogy, the optimal interpretation of a law is likely to depend, in part, on extracontractual normative constraints and, in part, on historically contingent contractual objectives.

At a minimum, equal worth depends on what I have referred to in chap-

---

5. This commitment is derived from comprehensive pluralism and does not, therefore, imply any reliance on overriding values.

ter VII as "mere reciprocity" or recognition of the other as an other self. Some laws or legal interpretations, such as those that would make for subordination of a person or group to the will of another, would obviously fail to meet the criterion of mere reciprocity and ought therefore clearly be fought or avoided. Moreover, whereas repudiation of such laws or legal interpretations may often be recharacterized as originating in self-legislation or contract, this need not be the case. At bottom, arguments against unlimited subordination are ultimately buttressed by normative constraints inherent in comprehensive pluralism rather than by arguments from contract or self-legislation.

Beyond repudiating subordination, the interpretive implications of mere reciprocity defined as recognition of the other as another self remain largely unclear. Thus, consistent with that definition, mere reciprocity may equally plausibly be interpreted as merely requiring formal equality or, on the contrary, as imposing an impossible Kantian requirement to treat the other exclusively as an end. To avoid this kind of indeterminacy, it is useful to further specify mere reciprocity as requiring recognition that the other has—or is capable of having—a perspective or a vantage point of his or her own.[6] Consistent with this, the equal worth of self and other implies mutual recognition as possessors of a perspective or vantage point. This mutual recognition is essential to collective self-legislation and to the legitimacy of contract as a vehicle suited to the common need of self and other to meet halfway but is not itself a by-product of self-legislation or contract. It figures instead as a prerequisite to self-legislation and contract and lies beyond their respective bounds. Hence, mutual recognition as possessors of a perspective furnishes both the foundation to and the limits of self-legislation and contract. Furthermore, it follows from this that, ideally, such mutual recognition should be cast as a constitutional principle that adjudicators ought to use in shaping the course of law and legal interpretation in the direction prescribed by comprehensive pluralism.

Positing mere reciprocity as a constitutional principle leads to certain determinate consequences but proves insufficient to carry out the normative prescriptions of comprehensive pluralism. Adherence to mere reciprocity thus forecloses slavery and conscious subordination[7] and requires the self to recognize that the other is equally entitled to any right claimed by the self as the possessor of a perspective or vantage point. For example,

6. To avoid the difficulties presented by exceptional cases such as those involving the profoundly retarded or by very young children, I understand the capacity to have a perspective counterfactually. Accordingly, every human being and every identifiable group should be deemed normatively entitled to be treated as if he or she possessed the capacity to form and express a perspective.

7. For a more extended discussion of the implications of mere reciprocity, see Rosenfeld 1991a, 246–48.

if the self asserts entitlement to freedom of expression rights as the possessor of a perspective, then mere reciprocity would compel the self to recognize that the other is equally entitled to such rights. Mere reciprocity, however, is too limited from the standpoint of comprehensive pluralism, for it
fails to account for differences in perspective. Because of this, mere reciprocity stresses identities at the expense of differences and does so at the
highest levels of abstraction where self and other are reduced to mere possessors of a perspective or vantage point. Mere reciprocity thus promotes
bare tolerance but cannot prompt self and other to meet halfway as it lacks
the means to constrain a dominant self to acknowledge the needs and aspirations rooted in the perspective of the other as opposed to those traceable to the other possessing a perspective.

B. Linking Mere Reciprocity to Reversible Reciprocity

To avoid a regime tailored to dominant perspectives coupled with bare tolerance which would at best satisfy the minimum requirements of limited
pluralism, mere reciprocity must be supplemented by reversible reciprocity.
As mentioned in chapter VII, reversible reciprocity requires recognition of
and empathy for the perspective of the other and thus makes for proper
acknowledgment of differences and for accommodation of diversity. Reversible reciprocity relying on the reversal of perspectives allows for evaluation
of conflicts from the standpoint of each perspective and vantage point involved and thus opens the way to solutions that fairly account for differences in perspective and vantage point (Kohlberg 1979; Rosenfeld 1991a,
249–50).

Whereas mere reciprocity implies equality among subjects as possessors
of a perspective or vantage point, reversible reciprocity targets equality
among perspectives. If reversible reciprocity could guarantee full and equal
accommodation of all existing perspectives within a polity, then it would
prove interpretively sufficient for purposes of achieving the objectives of
comprehensive pluralism. However, as demonstrated with respect to the
logics of comprehensive pluralism in chapter VII, equal accommodation
of all competing conceptions of the good *in a positive sense* is impossible to
achieve. Accordingly, reversible reciprocity may be perfectly suited for purposes of equally leveling all conceptions of the good in the negative moment of comprehensive pluralism but is, standing alone, inadequate for
purposes of partial reintegration of first-order norms during comprehensive pluralism's positive moment.

To overcome this limitation, it is necessary to link mere reciprocity to
reversible reciprocity. Moreover, this link, which is meant to cast mere reciprocity and reversible reciprocity as antagonistic yet complementary, is essential. Indeed, strict and exclusive adherence to reversible reciprocity

would give no weight whatsoever to the fact that one is a proponent of a particular perspective and would require everyone to treat his or her own perspective as if it were that of another. Thus, the self would be forced to treat himself or herself as an other rather than being merely expected to treat the other as another self. In the last analysis, self-effacement to relate to oneself as an other seems equally likely to upset the equilibrium between self and other as the failure to acknowledge anything beyond that the other is the possessor of a perspective.

By pitting mere reciprocity against reversible reciprocity one maximizes the chances that self and other will be able to meet halfway. More specifically, it is the dynamic born out of the tension between pursuing one's own perspective within the bounds of mere reciprocity and deferring to the other out of empathy following from reversible reciprocity, which seems to lead self and other to meeting halfway. From the standpoint of the self, as a consequence of constantly alternating between self-assertion and empathy, mere reciprocity and reversible reciprocity emerge as complementary. Furthermore, such alternation closely tracks comprehensive pluralism's demand for allegiance to second-order norms coupled with its prompting proponents of previously leveled first-order norms to press for their reintegration within the prevailing normative order.

From the standpoint of the adjudicator, the dynamic tension between mere reciprocity and reversible reciprocity produces important interpretive consequences. These consequences relate both to the reconstruction of the respective positions of partial selves and elusive others and to the reconciliation of these positions. For purposes of reconstruction, the adjudicator must seek to harmonize the various partial selves of the law-abiding person as counterfactual contractor or self-legislator into a cohesive perspective or vantage point that the person in question could plausibly endorse as his or her own. In the course of carrying out this interpretive task, the adjudicator should accentuate the common elements that emerge from a conjunction of the various partial selves involved at the expense of the contradictions and inconsistencies encountered along the way. Moreover, the adjudicator should also identify the common core of various partial selves through a focus on the contrasts between the positions attributable to the latter and those espoused by those who constitute the relevant other. In short, the adjudicator can simplify the interpretive task by stressing the commonalities linking together partial selves and the oppositions that fuel the antagonism between self and other.

Mere reciprocity figures prominently in the adjudicator's efforts at reconstruction, but reversible reciprocity dominates the latter's quest for reconciliation. Indeed, for purposes of reconciling the respective positions of self and other, the adjudicator must develop equal empathy for the clashing perspectives and vantage points involved in the relevant conflict. Ideally, having given equal weight to all the perspectives and vantage points involved, the adjudicator would resolve the conflict at stake in a way that accommodates as much as possible as many as possible among the relevant perspectives and vantage points, without losing sight of the intensity with which each of the parties involved adheres to his or her position.

Rejection of Habermasian notions of dialogically redeemed universal morality, or of solutions in the equal interests of all, implies that an adjudicator's reliance on reversible reciprocity can never lead to complete justice or incontestable outcomes. Even if an adjudicator were to fully capture the positions of self and other, and to grant an absolutely equal weight to the respective perspectives and vantage points of all involved, the resulting adjudications would nonetheless most likely have a disparate impact on the respective interests in self-legislation and self-realization harbored by self and other. Conceivably, in some cases, adjudication could come very close to being in the equal interest of self and other. One such case would be where self and other largely share the same interests against a common external threat. Such cases are of limited interest, however, as they vastly differ from the large number of cases in which clashing interests give rise to demands for competing interpretations. Furthermore, at the other end of the spectrum, there may be cases in which the conflicting interests are so radically antagonistic that no plausible adjudication could conceivably carve out any common ground. For example, a conflict between proponents of two ideologies exclusively bent on destroying their rival could only be resolved, consistent with the dictates of reversible reciprocity, by completely frustrating all the parties involved.

Between these two extremes, it seems fair to expect that there would be room for certain overlaps, certain possibilities for compromise, certain resolutions dependent on mutual adjustments or on limited measures of self-restraint, and certain concessions based on relative orders of priority. Accordingly, the task for the adjudicator would be to identify these and to vie for solutions consistent with equal respect for all law-abiding persons involved and with equal consideration toward all represented perspectives and vantage points. Moreover, after having ascertained who stands for what in relation to the conflict at hand, the adjudicator should seek to craft a just resolution of the contested issues, primarily through reliance on the normative precepts of comprehensive pluralism and through submission of conflicting claims to the test of reversible reciprocity.

In principle, all first-order norms, interests, objectives, life plans, and self-realization aspirations stand on an equal footing from the standpoint of comprehensive pluralism. In the course of resolving conflicts, however, adjudicators need to parse out the clashing value preferences advanced by the various parties to the controversy. This has to be done in accordance with the norms imposed by comprehensive pluralism and with the precepts of reversible reciprocity. Significantly, after completion of this process, not all value preferences involved are likely to fare equally well. Consistent with adherence to comprehensive pluralism, second-order norms have priority over first-order norms, with the consequence, for example, that an intolerant (first-order) conception of the good is assured to fare much worse than one that is not intolerant. Thus, the ideal of giving equal weight to all perspectives is made subject, in the course of adjudication, to the normative constraints of comprehensive pluralism.

These normative constraints are non-negotiable and they limit self-legislation and the paths to self-realization.[8] Moreover, they include constraints that derive from adherence to mere reciprocity as well as others necessary to prevent subordination to any particular set of first-order norms. Ideally, these normative constraints ought to be constitutionalized to the extent that they are needed to carry out the objectives of comprehensive pluralism in the realm of external relationships. Indeed, because they transcend the bounds of self-legislation, these normative constraints ought to be elevated above the constant give-and-take of ordinary everyday politics.

The first task of the adjudicator, therefore, is to evaluate the conflicting positions before him or her in terms of their compatibility with second-order norms. In performing this task, however, the adjudicator should be vigilant against inhibiting the pursuit of first-order norms more than is necessary to uphold the priority of second-order norms. For example, while the pursuits of a crusading religion would have to be substantially curbed, comprehensive pluralism by no means automatically justifies complete frustration of all its pursuits. Thus, if such a religion's coercive proselytizing could be separated from its other pursuits, such as worshiping and spreading other aspects of its religious dogma among existing adherents, then only the former pursuit ought to be frustrated. To do more than that would actually run counter to the fundamental tenets of comprehensive pluralism as it would single out the pursuit of certain first-order norms not inherently incompatible with second-order norms for discriminatory treatment or eradication.

A far different situation is presented when the adjudicator confronts a conflict in which the pursuit of one set of first-order norms not inherently incompatible with second-order norms inevitably tramples on the pursuit

8. Alternatively, these constraints may, through recharacterization, become incorporated into self-legislation. To the extent that these constraints frustrate the actual objectives sought through self-legislation, however, it is preferable to view them as external to the process of self-legislation. Indeed, whereas for a proponent of comprehensive pluralism modifying one's objectives to conform with second-order norms may constitute an act of self-legislation, this would not be the case for those who reject comprehensive pluralism.

of another such set of first-order norms. This latter situation, which arises after the adjudicator has rejected those proposed alternatives that proved inherently inconsistent with second-order norms, calls for recourse to reversible reciprocity. Specifically, it requires an evaluation of the conflicting claims at stake according to what I have called elsewhere the principle of "justice as reversible reciprocity" (Rosenfeld 1991a, 7, 254–82).

C. Justice as Reversible Reciprocity

Building on the notion of reversible reciprocity, justice as reversible reciprocity allows for a ranking of conflicting claims not inherently incompatible with comprehensive pluralism in a hierarchical order, and requires that claims that rank higher in the hierarchy be given priority over those that rank lower. Such hierarchical ranking, moreover, is twofold: on the one hand, interests, value preferences, and objectives must be ranked in the order of importance that they have within a particular conception of the good; on the other hand, interests, value preferences, and objectives issuing from different conceptions of the good must be ranked based on a comparison of their relative importance within the conception of the good to which they are attached. Accordingly, in case it is impossible equally to accommodate two conflicting interests, value preferences or objectives, those that rank higher within the perspective of their proponents ought to prevail over those that rank lower within the perspective of theirs. For example, if two communities compete over a scarce resource but one demonstrates that the resource in question is essential to its very survival while the other concedes that it can survive without it, then justice according to reversible reciprocity requires that the resource be awarded to the first community. In short, when confronted with clashing claims that are not inherently incompatible with comprehensive pluralism, justice as reversible reciprocity prescribes satisfying the highest-ranking interests within each of the contending perspectives before turning to the next highest ranking interests within any of them. Finally, when it comes to equally ranked interests, justice as reversible reciprocity calls for satisfying first those that are most widely shared, thus placing reliance on the principle of majoritarian democracy.

From the standpoint of the adjudicator, the interpretive consequences derived from the normative constraints of comprehensive pluralism and from the dictates of justice as reversible reciprocity boil down essentially to three. First, for purposes of interpretation, laws ought to be treated as contracts or instances of self-legislation only to the extent that they do not contravene the priority of second-order norms over first-order norms. As already mentioned, ideally, the pertinent normative constraints will be constitutionalized, and the adjudicator will strike down nonconforming contracts and self-legislation as unconstitutional. In other cases, the adjudicator will interpret laws as far as possible as consistent with pertinent normative constraints notwithstanding any contractual or self-legislative intent to the contrary.

The second and third interpretive consequences for the adjudicator, on the other hand, derive from justice as reversible reciprocity. The second corresponds to those cases in which justice as reversible reciprocity leads to an order of priority among the interests, value preferences, and objectives involved; the third, to those cases in which justice as reversible reciprocity yields no such priorities. In the second case, the adjudicator must ascertain what each party to the controversy seeks, compare all the perspectives represented in the controversy, establish an order of priority among conflicting claims, and vindicate that order of priority in the course of settling the meanings of laws. Moreover, ideally, respect for the requisite order of priorities ought to be constitutionalized. This could be accomplished, for example, by shaping existing constitutional rights as requiring respect for proportionality in ways that assure that the relevant priorities will be respected.

In the third case, all interests, value preferences, and objectives involved are in themselves equal in importance, with the consequence that the adjudicator should be guided by the principle of majoritarian democracy. Accordingly, laws emerging from a majoritarian process ought to be treated as instances of self-legislation, and the adjudicator should scrupulously track the legislative intent (or reconstruct it to the extent that the actual intent is difficult to discern) behind them in the course of articulating their meaning. Furthermore, to the extent that laws falling within this third category are best analogized to contracts, the adjudicator should rely heavily on the actual or reconstructed intent and objectives of those who are properly considered to be the contractors. Finally, laws within this third category are best reconstructed as the products of ordinary everyday majoritarian politics, and distinguished from mere politics by stressing their potential for stability and predictability.

To recapitulate: ideally and counterfactually, laws in the first category should be constitutionalized, those in the second category shaped by constitutional constraints, and those in the third category left to the will of the majority as extensions of politics that remain on the same plane as ordinary politics. On closer scrutiny, the second category encompasses a gray area between constitutional and ordinary legal norms. This results, in part, because the second category is not as fully constitutionalized as the first and, in part, because the divide between what should be subjected to hierarchical considerations and what should be left on an even plane is often blurred and contestable.

D. Factoring the Difference between Constitutional Politics and Ordinary Politics in Reconstructive Adjudication

Based on these distinctions, it is now possible to draw a systematic distinction between constitutional politics and ordinary politics.[9] Indeed, constitutional politics is confined to the first of the three categories of law identified above and to part of the second category. Ordinary politics, on the other hand, underlies all laws falling in the third category and has some influence on those within the second category but ought to have none within the first category.

Before exploring the implications of this proposed systematic division between constitutional and ordinary politics any further, however, it is necessary to focus briefly on the possible role of constitutional *politics* within the context of comprehensive pluralism. At first, it may seem that there is nothing political about constitutionalizing the normative constraints inherent in comprehensive pluralism—or, in other words, about translating the priority of second-order norms over first-order norms into a constitutional principle. On further reflection, however, even if all concerned remain unanimous in their commitment to implement the priority of second-order norms, they may still disagree on how best to achieve their commonly shared objective. Specifically, to what extent the priority of second-order norms ought to become embedded in constitutional norms (as opposed to purely ethical norms) and what precise form the embodiment of second-order norms in constitutional principles should take loom as matters about which reasonable proponents of comprehensive pluralism might disagree as a matter of constitutional politics. Furthermore, constitutional politics also seem bound to figure in connection with the determination of the degree to which laws in the second category ought to be molded by constitutional concerns. Finally, constitutional politics and ordinary politics might be expected to overlap in the gray area within the second category wherein the blurred boundaries between constitutional and ordinary legal norms must be set. In contrast, laws in the third category ought to fall exclusively within the grip of ordinary politics.

The above division of labor between constitutional politics and ordinary politics is systematic and driven by normative considerations emanating

---

9. This distinction figures prominently in the work of Bruce Ackerman. See Ackerman 1991. Ackerman's account, however, is more intuitive than systematic. For him, constitutional politics occurs at extraordinary moments when the people become mobilized in pursuit of the common good. In contrast, in the context of ordinary politics, Ackerman argues that the people are motivated by narrowly drawn self-interest. Unlike Ackerman's distinction, the one offered here does not depend on particular historical events or on the mindset of the relevant actors within the polity. Instead, the distinction in question is normatively grounded in the perspective of comprehensive pluralism and systematized through counterfactual use.

from comprehensive pluralism. Moreover, the distinction between constitutional and ordinary politics is particularly important from a critical counterfactual standpoint. On the one hand, this distinction is useful for purposes of assessing constitution making;[10] on the other hand, for purposes of critically evaluating actual lawmaking and legal adjudication. Furthermore, the very acknowledgment of constitutional politics presupposes that there is some room for contingency in the context of normative assessments of constitution making. Wherever counterfactual reconstruction of constitutional constraints consistent with comprehensive pluralism leaves room for constitutional politics, available alternatives can be profitably narrowed down. This can be accomplished by reference to the design of the actual constitution makers and to relevant historical narratives that link together the constitution's origins with its current interpretive profile. In sum, by blending relevant contingent events into the mold carved out by comprehensive pluralism, the adjudicator can find meaningful ways of bridging the gap between partial selves and elusive others and measurably narrow down the legitimate interpretive alternatives. Also, the adjudicator seems poised to achieve all this without losing sight of the importance of maintaining a cogent demarcation between the proper realm of constitutional constraints and that which ought to be left to majoritarian legislation.

Two serious objections may be raised at this point against relying on justice as reversible reciprocity to adjudicate claims among proponents of conflicting conceptions of the good in accordance with the requirements of comprehensive pluralism. The first objection is that conceptions of the good should be regarded as cohesive and indivisible wholes rather than as mere aggregates that might be readily disassembled and reassembled to suit needs for a hierarchical ranking of interests, value preferences, and objectives. The second objection is, in turn, that even if the first objection could be successfully addressed, comparisons cutting across different perspectives are either impossible to carry out or highly unlikely to uncover enough common ground to lead to fair resolutions of conflicts.[11] I address these objections in order, starting with an examination of the case of clashing religions to determine whether it is necessary to treat conceptions of the good as indivisible wholes consistent with adherence to comprehensive pluralism.

---

10. To the extent that constitutions are living experiments subject to evolution and constant adaptation, constitution making need not be understood in the narrow sense as merely referring to the work of actual constitutional assemblies. It can also be profitably interpreted in a broader counterfactual reconstructive sense as encompassing significant steps leading to important evolutionary adaptations.

11. This last charge is reminiscent of the feminist challenge to Habermas's discourse theory of law discussed in chapter V. As we shall see below, however, comprehensive pluralism allows for a different response to this charge than does Habermas's discourse theory.

III. THE CASE OF CLASHING RELIGIONS AND THE LIMITS OF JUSTICE AS REVERSIBLE RECIPROCITY

Imagine a polity composed of two religious communities that are diametrically opposed to one another, not only on matters of religious dogma but also on all significant economic, social, and political matters. Imagine further that each of these religions holds that its beliefs, precepts, and practices are bound together in such an indissoluble bond that failure to abide by any of them constitutes mortal sin. Finally, imagine that neither of these two religions preaches the eradication of the other—thus not qualifying as a crusading religion—but that each requires that its precepts be fully carried by all its adherents in the public sphere as well as in the private sphere. For example, one religion may prescribe self-reliance and a free market economy while the other may command solidarity and a socialist economy. In such a situation, the best alternative would be to split the current polity into two and give each of the two religious communities complete control over its own destiny. But if for some reason that were not to prove a viable option, then justice as reversible reciprocity would indeed seem to lead to an impasse. Since, by definition, all interests, value preferences, and objectives within each of these religions are on an equal footing, and since all of them are of equal paramount importance for both religions, a reversal of perspectives fails to reveal any plausible course of action within the bounds of comprehensive pluralism.

On further thought, there might be a solution consistent with justice as reversible reciprocity, provided the two religious communities involved are not of the same size. If the majority of the citizens of the relevant polity belong to one of these religions, and the remainder to the other, then, arguably, majority rule ought to prevail, as all relevant interests, value preferences, and objectives are by stipulation on the same plane. Moreover, the consequences of this argument are far-reaching, for in every polity with a plurality of competing conceptions of the good, it seems fair to assume generally that proponents of one conception of the good are, by and large, as committed to it as proponents of other such conceptions are to theirs. But if this is true, then comprehensive pluralism seems essentially collapsible into majoritarianism.

In spite of its superficial appeal, the above argument is clearly wrong, as comprehensive pluralism, which is predicated on the inherent equal worth of all first-order perspectives as well as that of all persons, is certainly not reducible to majoritarianism. Indeed, as will be remembered, justice as reversible reciprocity is not supposed to be unlimited in scope but is instead made subject to the normative constraints imposed by comprehensive pluralism. Moreover, chief among these constraints is steadfast commitment to the priority of second-order norms over first-order norms, which requires placing great value in protecting the integrity of (first-order) perspectives. In other words, comprehensive pluralism prescribes mutual respect between self and other, to be understood as respect for the integrity of each other's perspective. Accordingly, from the perspective of comprehensive pluralism, for majoritarianism to be legitimate, it must be consistent not only with justice as reversible reciprocity but also with preservation of the integrity of all the (first-order) perspectives involved. Consistent with this, to return to our example, since majoritarianism would lead to complete capitulation of the minority religion to the majority religion, it would patently fail to uphold the integrity of the minority religion and would hence be clearly illegitimate.

The limitation of justice as reversible reciprocity by the requirement to preserve the integrity of the perspectives respectively embraced by self and other has interpretive implications that will be addressed briefly in section V below. For the moment, I wish to concentrate on two of the most salient consequences that follow from the rejection of majoritarianism as the means to resolve the clash between the two religions involved in our example. First, paradoxically, the only way to resolve the conflict between these two all-encompassing religions consistent with the prescriptions of comprehensive pluralism is by preventing both of them from gaining control over the realm of intercommunal dealings. This follows from the very logic of comprehensive pluralism, for any other solution would result in subordination of one first-order perspective to another. Now, if there were no room whatsoever left for intracommunal dealings, the proposed solution would lack any practical consequence. Also, if because of the comprehensiveness of the religious ideologies involved, it were impossible to map out an institutional framework for intercommunal dealings that would not be fully subsumed under either of the two clashing religions, then the proposed solution would prove impossible. But otherwise, comprehensive pluralism would require resolving the clash between our two all-encompassing religions by expelling them both from the public sphere. Furthermore, the very nature of this solution makes it plain that comprehensive pluralism is firmly grounded in a substantive normative vision rather than being merely reducible to a process-based perspective.

The second salient consequence that follows from the rejection of a majoritarian solution to the clash between the two religions of our example is that, even if our minority religion counted with but a single adherent, comprehensive pluralism would still call for refusing to regulate intercommunal dealings in conformity with the dictates of either of the two religions. This may seem an absurd result, but it is nonetheless clearly mandated by the fundamental normative tenets of comprehensive pluralism. Indeed, from the standpoint of the equal preservation of the integrity of each perspective within the polity, it makes no difference whether any such perspective is shared by nearly everyone or whether it is merely embraced by a single person.

If the last result is difficult to accept, it is not because it is at odds with the ethos of comprehensive pluralism but rather because recourse to comprehensive pluralism may be questioned under the highly rigid and artificial circumstances of our example. As already mentioned, I am agnostic as to whether it is desirable to promote the ethos of comprehensive pluralism in polities that are not in fact pluralistic. Moreover, even if we were to assume that comprehensive pluralism is intrinsically desirable in all circumstances, the case for it could still be much less compelling in some contexts than in others. Accordingly, the situation under consideration involving a completely homogeneous society saddled with a lone dissenter certainly presents close to the least compelling case for recourse to comprehensive pluralism.[12]

If we broaden our focus beyond the artificial example discussed above, however, we are bound to notice that the appeal of comprehensive pluralism is likely to increase as we move to polities that are increasingly pluralistic in fact. Thus, as we reach a typical contemporary pluralistic polity with many different religions that are hardly monolithic; with a wide array of partial selves connected to various degrees to several perspectives; with wide-ranging overlaps of value preferences; and with a significant measure of fluidity among communal groupings; comprehensive pluralism leads to outcomes that are likely to be considered appealing by vast majorities, including many who reject comprehensive pluralism as a persuasive conception of the good. For example, the Judeo-Christian heritage that has been so influential in Western civilization is hardly monolithic in several relevant respects. First, all three of the major religions linked through that common heritage share common elements; second, none of the three is internally monolithic, as each encompasses a plurality of different views concerning several religious issues; third, none of them is all-encompassing in the strong sense of dictating particular courses of action in all human endeavors;[13] and fourth, none of them rigidly places all its interests, value preferences, and objectives on the same footing.[14] Furthermore, many citi-

---

12. Actually, the minimum conditions necessary for comprehensive pluralism to make *any* sense are those of a completely homogeneous polity in which the possibility of opting out or dissenting from communal norms is at least acknowledged. If no such possibility were ever conceived, then the very notion of comprehensive pluralism would be altogether meaningless.

13. For example, each of these three religions seems relatively open to a wide array of options in the realms of economic and social policies ranging from laissez-faire capitalism to socialist interventionism.

14. Proponents of all three religions would thus presumably agree that adherence to

zens in a contemporary pluralist polity are likely not to identify with any religion, and even among those who do, a sizable number are likely to identify with religion only in part. Yet others are likely to opt out of the religion of their ancestors, or to convert from one of the religions within the polity to another. In short, under such circumstances, some kind of separation between church and state may seem quite wise and highly advisable, not merely from the standpoint of comprehensive pluralism, but also from that of other perspectives, such as liberalism.[15]

Complex and multifaceted ideologies seem clearly better suited than monolithic ones to offer fertile grounds for comprehensive pluralism. Moreover, the conjunction of respect for the integrity of perspectives with justice as reversible reciprocity is more likely to yield workable solutions if there is a fair degree of fluidity among the perspectives that contribute to the definition of the respective identities of self and other. In other words, there appears to be an increase in opportunities for mutually acceptable intercommunal regulation if communal boundaries are open and flexible rather than static or rigidly entrenched. But for the requisite openness and fluidity to be present requires that self and other be capable of internal transformation. Accordingly, I now briefly examine how comprehensive pluralism is poised to contribute to such transformation.

IV. COMPREHENSIVE PLURALISM AND THE INTERNAL TRANSFORMATION OF SELF AND OTHER

As a consequence of its stress on the equal worth of different perspectives and on accommodating as many of them as possible, comprehensive pluralism sharpens our awareness of the plurality of available conceptions of the good. Moreover, adherence to the priority of second-order norms is bound to distance us somewhat from our own first-order value preferences while at the same time getting us closer to those espoused by others. This, incidentally, is not without danger, for the insecurity resulting from alienation from one's own value preferences many well lead to intolerance and

---

monotheism ranks as a higher-order value than abiding by even the most minor of religious prescriptions. See, e.g., Peters 1990, 201–11, 356–57.

15. In a religiously pluralistic society, the separation of church and state may well count as a desirable objective from within the perspective of at least some of the religions involved. It is therefore hardly surprising that some religious leaders have been among the most avid supporters of the separation of church and state in the United States. See, e.g., *Testimony of J. Brent Walker, General Counsel and Assoc. Dir., Baptist Joint Comm. on Public Affairs Before the Senate Comm. on the Judiciary*, Federal Document Clearing House, 25 October 1995, available in LEXIS, Nexis Library, CURNWS File; Curtis 1995; "Dissenting from the Right—Religious Right," *Christian Century* 112:631, 21 June 1995.

outright repudiation of normative pluralism. But, by the same token, commitment to the priority of second-order norms affords opportunities for self-enrichment and for better reconciliation between self and other, through greater interpenetration between their respective perspectives. In short, openness to each other's perspective makes for an internal transformation of self and other in ways that may be both more fulfilling and more apt to carve out mutually acceptable common paths without having to abandon cherished differences.

The propensity of comprehensive pluralism to lead to internal transformation may be best captured through consideration of an example. Imagine, therefore, a society that proclaims allegiance to comprehensive pluralism but that bans homosexuality and is completely intolerant of homosexual lifestyles. To reconcile its embrace of comprehensive pluralism with its intolerance of homosexuality, this society would have to articulate a reason why conceptions of the good promoting homosexual lifestyles should not be tolerated in the same way as are other nonmajoritarian conceptions of the good. Imagine further that such a society argues that homosexuality is abnormal and deviant and, as such, a threat to the preservation of the social fabric.[16] If such an argument were accepted, then a society devoted to comprehensive pluralism would presumably be able to justify intolerance of homosexuality in the same way as it could justify intolerance of crusading religions.[17]

To overcome the belief that homosexuality poses a threat to society, and to make acceptance of homosexuals possible, requires a multifaceted approach to combat prejudice and alter perceptions. For our purposes, however, what is crucial is the need for recharacterization, leading in this case to a higher level of abstraction. Instead of focusing on homosexual practices and on traditional attitudes toward them, the aim should be to stress the need of every person, heterosexual and homosexual alike, for intimate sexual relationships and to insist that all adults should be equally entitled to

16. Cf. Chief Justice Burger's concurring opinion in *Bowers v. Hardwick* (1986) (referring to homosexuality as a "crime against nature" and as a "heinous act").

17. There is, of course, one crucial difference between the two that ought to be recognized even by those who claim that homosexuality is abnormal. Whereas crusading religions preach a duty to proselytize by force if necessary, partisans of homosexual lifestyles are most unlikely to seek converts among the heterosexual population. Nevertheless, from the standpoint of maintaining a viable comprehensively pluralistic society, it is indifferent whether a perceived threat to its integrity is voluntary or involuntary. For example, if a religion forbade its adherents from being vaccinated, and the latter's refusal would result in the spreading of a deadly disease, the pluralist state would be justified in disregarding their conception of the good to the extent necessary to order them to be vaccinated against their will, even though they had no intention to harm or influence fellow citizens who do not share their religious faith.

privacy to pursue consensual sex with another adult.[18] Obviously, the move to a higher level of abstraction in this case is designed to shift the focus from what is different about homosexuals to what heterosexuals and homosexuals share in common. But less obvious, perhaps, is that if the move is successful it will not merely result in adding the pursuit of homosexual lifestyles among the multiplicity of existing legitimate first-order conceptions of the good. The move will also undoubtedly have consequences *within* the latter conceptions of the good, such as further weakening beliefs in any necessary nexus between sex and procreation, or sex and marriage. Or the move may lead to calls for legitimizing homosexual marriages, causing a shift in attitudes toward marriage, and thus leading to transformations *within* groups adhering to conceptions of the good that place great value on traditional notions of marriage. Furthermore, increasing acceptability of homosexual lifestyles is also likely to have repercussions for particular religions traditionally opposed to homosexuality, as homosexual adherents become emboldened to seek changes within their religious community.[19] Finally, assuming that homosexuals succeed in their quest for initial acceptability, they might well push for additional changes in pursuit of broader equality capable of encompassing differences and thus lead to further internal transformation within groups adhering to more traditional conceptions of the good.[20]

One should not lose sight of the possibility that a push for greater acceptance of homosexuality might actually result in a hardening of positions and a backlash. Nevertheless, so long as the spirit of comprehensive pluralism prevails, moves toward greater inclusivity are likely to produce greater openness toward alien perspectives as well as internal transformations of self and other in enriching new directions. Indeed, such internal transformations may significantly broaden the possibilities for viable reconciliation of self and other in ways that remain protective of the integrity of all the relevant perspectives involved.

18. This is the position embraced by the dissenters in the U.S. Supreme Court's 5–4 decision in *Bowers v. Hardwick* (1986), at 218–19, in which the Court refused to recognize a constitutional right to homosexual sex among consenting adults.

19. See, e.g., Sullivan 1995 (arguing that the Catholic church should permit homosexual sex on the analogy of permitting heterosexual sex in the case of married infertile couples).

20. In the pursuit of equality-as-identity, homosexuals may search for official recognition of same-sex marriages. In the pursuit of equality-as-difference, in contrast, homosexuals are more likely to pursue public alternatives no longer geared to favoring traditional marital relationships and family values. Compare Sullivan 1995 (arguing for assimilation of homosexuals) with Bersani 1995 (arguing against assimilation and emphasizing implications flowing from affirmation of gay sexuality).

V. THE INTERPRETIVE QUEST TO ACCOMMODATE
THE PRIORITY OF SECOND-ORDER NORMS AND TO PROTECT
THE INTEGRITY OF PERSPECTIVES

Based on the preceding observations, accommodating diverse perspectives while protecting their integrity need not lead to undue fragmentation of conceptions of the good. This is, in part, because in complex pluralistic societies perspectives are not likely to be monolithic or rigidly bounded; and, in part, because external reorderings of existing conceptions of the good to achieve greater inclusiveness are likely to be accompanied by internal transformations driven by the search for unity and continuity within the self. Actually, it is the partial self confronting the elusive other who seems most vulnerable to increasing fragmentation. On the other hand, the self's gesture of reconciliation toward the other, through more inclusive reconstruction and internal transformation, aims at (re)unification and cohesion. In other words, fragmentation is the by-product of pluralism in fact, whereas unification and cohesion loom as the objectives of comprehensive pluralism.

When internal transformation and the search for cohesion through reconstruction are placed in their proper context, it becomes apparent that rankings of interests, value preferences, and objectives, in accordance with justice as reversible reciprocity, do not necessarily lead to the destruction of the identity or integrity of conceptions of the good. As we have seen in the last two sections, conceptions of the good can be sufficiently elastic and adaptable to withstand frustration and reorientation of relatively less important objectives, as well as some measure of internal transformation, without fundamental loss of identity or integrity. Moreover, consistent with the dynamic environment characteristic of complex pluralistic societies, the identity of conceptions of the good is perhaps best analogized to that of a person who evolves throughout his or her entire life without losing the sense of selfhood—that is, the sense that the same self somehow endures throughout all the changes.[21] Accordingly, the first objection raised at the end of section II—that conceptions of the good must be regarded as indivisible wholes that cannot be partially accommodated based on a ranking of their priorities—ultimately misses the mark, for it is predicated on a misconception of the relative positions of self and other within a complex and constantly evolving pluralistic setting.

The second objection raised at the end of section II—that comparisons across different perspectives are either too difficult to carry out or unlikely to uncover common ground—however, seems more troubling. On the one

---

21. See Ricoeur 1990 for a thorough and penetrating analysis of self-identity based on the contrast between identity derived from selfhood and identity derived from sameness.

hand, the transformability of self and other and of their respective perspectives appears to increase significantly the prospects for establishing common grounds. But, on the other hand, in order to achieve this, it is necessary to unleash potentially destabilizing interpretive strategies that raise at least two additional problems. First, as the example of the quest for inclusion of homosexual lifestyles discussed in section IV indicates, the kind of transformation required to open new common ground depends on reinterpretation of the implications of homosexuality. Such reinterpretation, moreover, relies on a shifting of levels of abstraction that upsets the clustering of identities and differences associated with the interplay of those perspectives granted accommodation within the status quo targeted by proponents of homosexual lifestyles. And, as already pointed out in chapter I, shifts in levels of abstraction tend to lessen the constraints that keep meanings relatively determinate and thus threaten to throw the interpretive enterprise into disarray. In particular, if comparisons across various perspectives tend to be complicated even without major shifts in levels of abstraction, then in cases involving wide fluctuations in such levels, fruitful use of the comparisons in question would seem much more difficult.

A. Intraperspectival Commitments, Interperspectival Comparisons, and Shifting Levels of Abstraction

The second problem, which is also related to the need for significant shifts in the levels of abstraction, is that proponents of change are prone to unleash transformations that they do not seek, or that they may even fear, but that they cannot control. Thus, challengers of the status quo may unwittingly destabilize settled meanings in ways that frustrate their own quest for inclusion or that provoke inclusions or exclusions they oppose. To illustrate this, let us return briefly to the example concerning homosexuality discussed in section IV. As indicated there, the key argument offered in support of tolerance for homosexuality is that decisions regarding intimate sexual relations among consenting adults should be left to the exclusive discretion of those concerned. This argument is pitched at a level of abstraction designed to draw attention to what heterosexuals and homosexuals share in common. However, this argument may also advance the purposes of others with whom proponents of tolerance for homosexuality might not wish to identify, including proponents of incest or of sadomasochistic sex. As a matter of fact, proponents of rights for homosexuals may be eager to differentiate homosexuality from incest or sadomasochism to the extent that the latter, which continue to convey connotations of deviance, had traditionally been lumped together with homosexuality.[22]

22. See Justice Harlan's concurring opinion in *Griswold v. Connecticut* (1965), at 499 (spe-

These two problems, while real enough, are not insurmountable. Departures from the status quo cannot be achieved without some prior loosening of established meanings, but inasmuch as desired changes point to definite new directions and are subjected to the constraints imposed by comprehensive pluralism, they appear more prone to reorienting meanings rather than merely rendering them overly indeterminate. Furthermore, any claim for or against greater inclusivity necessarily involves some shifts in levels of abstraction and some unintended consequences in the course of pursuing an optimal mix between relevant identities and differences. It follows from this that all moves involve certain risks and that progress is by no means assured. For example, as discussed in chapter III, women who have achieved equality-as-identity may wish to improve their lot and reach a more equitable equal footing with men by aiming for equality-as-difference. But in calling attention to differences, women may unwittingly rekindle suppressed support for inequality based on difference and thus jeopardize already acquired gains while struggling for additional gains. Notwithstanding these uncertainties, claims do not arise in a vacuum, but rather in a context of relatively settled meanings. Moreover, in most cases only a limited horizon of plausible changes from the status quo would arguably lead to improvements from the standpoint of comprehensive pluralism. In short, meanings are not fixed, but it does not follow that anything goes. So long as we do not lose sight of the relevant context and of the direction in which comprehensive pluralism points, meanings can become sufficiently determinate to indicate which interpretations are likely to bring us closer to justice.

Looking at this from the micro-interpretive standpoint of the adjudicator, the key to success lies in the ability to carry out reliable comparisons across diverse perspectives. As already pointed out, three tasks confront the adjudicator: imputing an actual intent for self and other regarded as contractors or self-legislators; reconstructing their counterfactual intent as shaped by comprehensive pluralism; and interpreting the substantive constraints emanating from comprehensive pluralism so as to make them applicable to legal disputes. The second of these three task depends on the above-mentioned comparisons, for the counterfactual reconstruction at stake is designed to best approximate what self and other would have intended had they been aware of, and determined to abide by, the relevant order of priority encompassing the various interests, value preferences, and objectives of all involved. Moreover, this second task is crucial because actual intents must be canceled out to the extent that they prove incompatible with their counterfactually reconstructed counterparts, and because limitations pursuant to the substantive constraints of comprehensive pluralism

cifying that the constitutional right to marital sexual intimacy should not be misconstrued as extending to homosexuality or incest).

tend to weigh heavier on interpretive outcomes on failure by justice as reversible reciprocity to yield concrete answers.

Establishing proper intraperspectival and interperspectival comparisons thus represents important yet difficult undertakings for which the adjudicator must take responsibility. With respect to intraperspectival comparisons, the adjudicator must rely, in the first place, on the input of the proponents of the perspective involved. Moreover, the adjudicator must be mindful that such proponents may have an incentive to exaggerate or distort the importance of certain values within their own perspective in the course of pressing their interests in conflicts with interperspectival implications. To counter this potential for distortion, the adjudicator can test intraperspectival claims for consistency, for integrity over time, and against the claims of other proponents of the same perspective. Although claims based on individual idiosyncrasies may be particularly difficult to evaluate, it seems reasonable to assume that a vast majority of intraperspectival claims are communally rooted and thus shared by fairly identifiable groups of individuals. Accordingly, in most cases, the adjudicator will be able adequately to carry out intraperspectival comparisons for purposes of interpreting laws consistent with the dictates of comprehensive pluralism.

Interperspectival comparisons, on the other hand, loom as more delicate. Nevertheless, there are certain distinctions that can help to make the adjudicator's application of the criterion of justice as reversible reciprocity more manageable and more reliable. Three such distinctions deserve further elaboration: that between primary and secondary goods; that between primary and secondary values; and that between subject-exclusion and benefit (burden) -exclusion.

B. Primary versus Secondary Goods

The distinction between primary and secondary goods is derived from Rawls (1971, 90–95; 1993, 178–87), but as I conceive it in the context of comprehensive pluralism, it differs in many significant respects from the conception developed by Rawls. As understood here, primary goods are goods that inhere in the second-order conception of the good, or goods considered as such *within each* of the various first-order conceptions of the good present in the relevant polity. Primary goods deriving from the second-order conception of the good shape the substantive constraints of comprehensive pluralism and need not therefore be subjected to interperspectival comparison. In contrast, the remaining primary goods—whether they inhere within each relevant first-order conception of the good as a matter of necessity or of contingency—do figure in interperspectival comparisons and have priority over all other goods, which are thus relegated to the status of secondary goods.

It may be objected, however, that according automatic priority to primary goods is not always warranted because the fact that a given good is valued *within* each of the perspectives involved does not automatically warrant that such good is equally important *for* each of these perspectives. Suppose, for example, that all relevant perspectives regard achieving a minimum of subsistence for each individual as an important good, but that such good ranks as the highest priority from the standpoint of certain perspectives but not from that of others. Suppose further that pursuant to one of the conceptions of the good involved, abiding by certain religious precepts is a greater good than securing enough food for all the members of the faith. Under these conditions, if the only way to feed all members of the polity is by producing food using means that contravene the religious precepts identified above, and if no other means would be adequate for purposes of feeding all but those who feel bound by the religious precepts in question, then it would appear that giving priority to primary goods would violate the precept commanding that the highest-ranking goods within each perspective be pursued before addressing the next highest good within any perspective.

C. Primary versus Secondary Values

To avoid the problems posed by cases in which a primary good proves to be one of relatively low priority for some of the perspectives involved, it is helpful to supplement the distinction between primary and secondary goods with that between primary and secondary values.[23] Primary values are those that rank the highest within a particular perspective, whereas secondary values are those that rank lower within that same perspective. Now, where primary goods and primary values tend to converge, there is a very strong case for the priority of primary goods. Moreover, whereas this is not logically required, it stands to reason that the two should often overlap. Thus, it would hardly be surprising if all the perspectives involved considered freedom from hunger and freedom from torture as goods, and if most of those perspectives considered these goods to be among their most highly valued ones. Consequently, if a primary good is involved and if it counts as a primary value for a vast majority of the perspectives involved, the adjudicator should be entitled to adopt the presumption that the primary good in question is entitled to priority.

This last presumption should be rebuttable, but only on a showing that, under the particular circumstances involved, giving priority to the primary

23. This distinction is also made by John Kekes (1993, 18–19), but I do not follow his definition, which comes close to equating primary values with what I have described as primary goods.

good involved would only marginally advance the objectives of those perspectives for which that good represents a primary value while disproportionately disadvantaging those other perspectives that view pursuit of that good as a secondary value. Take, for example, the issue of whether euthanasia ought to be legally permissible in a polity in which the protection and preservation of life is a primary good and a primary value for most but not all existing perspectives. In this case, there ought to be a presumption against the legality of euthanasia. But suppose further that the proponents of euthanasia specify that they only support it in cases in which responsible adults in the possession of their full mental capacities freely choose it for quality-of-life reasons, and that they believe euthanasia to be inextricably linked to the primary value of individual control over his or her destiny. Moreover, a reversal of perspectives would not settle this issue, for it seems safe to anticipate that opponents of euthanasia would be as intensely committed to its prohibition as would proponents of its legalization. Proponents may further argue, however, that whereas prohibition of euthanasia would deprive them of something essential from the standpoint of their own conception of the good, legalizing euthanasia would by no means have a like impact on their opponents. Indeed, the opponents may find euthanasia profoundly ethically repulsive, but they would remain free to rule it out for themselves and to seek to persuade others to do likewise. Accordingly, proponents of euthanasia could plausibly argue that the harm to them following from its prohibition would be much greater than that to its opponents in case of legalization.[24]

This last argument may seem very similar to the liberal argument made by John Stuart Mill that society has no business regulating the individual's purely self-regarding acts (1859, 73–74). In the context of comprehensive pluralism, however, the Millian distinction between self-regarding and other-regarding acts is generally considered to be untenable. This is consistent with the view that perspectives are fluid, open to external influences, and susceptible to internal transformations and that partial selves and elusive others are in a constant state of dynamic interaction. Accordingly, so long as any intracommunal practice is not devoid of any conceivable intercommunal consequence, it may not be deemed self-regarding. Viewed in this light, legalizing euthanasia is certainly likely to have repercussions on the perspectives of its opponents and on the membership of opponent groups. That does not mean that communities that oppose euthanasia should be granted a veto over the decision of other communities within the

---

24. See *Cruzan v. Director, Missouri Department of Health* (1990), at 314 (Brennan, J., dissenting) (the state's "general interest in life" is outweighed by a person's "particularized and intense interest in self-determination" in determining whether or not to continue receiving life support).

same polity to legitimate euthanasia for their own members, but comprehensive pluralism requires that this conflict be settled on the basis of something beyond the distinction between self-regarding and other-regarding acts.

D. The Distinction between Subject-Exclusion and Benefit-Exclusion

Before exploring any further how comprehensive pluralism might settle this conflict concerning euthanasia, it is time to introduce the third distinction mentioned above, namely that between subject-exclusion and benefit-exclusion. This latter distinction is primarily helpful when it comes to determining whether a law is consistent with respect for the equal worth of self and other, or, more precisely, whether a law complying with formal equality requirements derived from mere reciprocity is thus consistent.[25] All laws classify and as a consequence are prone to benefit members of certain classes in ways that members of other classes are not benefited. For example, a law that provides that no one under eighteen years of age can drive an automobile excludes a sizable portion of the population from the benefit of driving. Benefit-exclusions are not objectionable per se, particularly when they relate to matters properly left to majoritarian politics consistent with comprehensive pluralism. But some benefit-exclusions may become tantamount to subject-exclusion—that is, to exclusion from membership in the relevant community, or, in other words, to exclusion from equal membership in the polity in ways that are inconsistent with the equal worth of self and other.[26]

A further distinction must be drawn between a *per se* subject-exclusion and a *comparative* subject-exclusion. The former may either involve an outright denial of membership in the relevant community or a benefit-exclusion involving a primary good that is also a primary value. The latter, on the other hand, only involves a benefit-exclusion, but because others who are similarly situated are not thus excluded, it becomes an indirect means to achieve a subject-exclusion. For example, in a wealthy polity in which every citizen has the means to educate his or her own children, enactment of a law barring public expenditures for education would be reasonably deemed to produce benefit-exclusions without thereby becoming the

25. Although the distinction between subject-exclusion and benefit-exclusion is relevant in both these situations, cases involving a failure to meet formal equality requirements are more efficiently dealt with by means of direct reference to the dictates of mere reciprocity.

26. Not all departures from equal membership in the polity necessarily involve violations of the equal-worth principle. For example, at least arguably, denying short-term foreign transients full voting rights does not amount to a violation of their right to equal worth. On the other hand, denying women full voting rights would obviously be contrary to upholding their equal worth.

source of any subject-exclusion. Furthermore, if the state restricts free public education to those who could not otherwise pay for their children's education, the benefit-exclusion that would only affect the wealthier members of the polity would still not amount to subject-exclusion. But if free public education were only denied to a persecuted ethnic minority, then the resulting benefit-exclusion would be tantamount to subject-exclusion—or, more specifically, to comparative subject-exclusion—inasmuch as it is the *fact* of being singled out for different treatment than that reserved for others who are similarly situated, rather than the benefit-exclusion itself, which results in the denial of equal worth. From an interpretive standpoint, per se subject-exclusions can be weeded out through implementation of the mere reciprocity criterion. And so can *some* comparative subject-exclusions, such as, for example, those based on racial discrimination. But others cannot be thus eliminated, nor can they be brought to light through implementation of the reversal of perspectives in accordance with justice as reversible reciprocity. Moreover, the above example concerning euthanasia appears to fit within the latter pattern. Indeed, the conflict between proponents and opponents of euthanasia cannot be resolved at the level of mere reciprocity as they mutually recognize each other as possessors of a perspective, and as neither of them are bent on eliminating or suppressing the perspective of the other but are only determined to pursue their own conception of the good in a fair and open competition. Also, as we have seen, the conflict cannot be resolved at least with respect to value preferences by appealing to justice as reversible reciprocity since protagonists on both sides of the conflict advance primary values.

It is conceivable, however, that justice as reversible reciprocity might resolve the conflict through focus on the respective interests involved. Thus, pursuant to a reversal of perspectives, opponents of euthanasia might conclude that their interests in preventing others from choosing euthanasia because of fears about repercussions on the polity as a whole is somewhat less central vis-à-vis their own perspective than the proponents' interest in freedom to choose euthanasia happens to be in relation to theirs. But it seems equally plausible that the opponents of euthanasia would conclude that their own interests are just as strong from the standpoint of their perspective as the interests of the proponents of euthanasia is from theirs.

If justice as reversible reciprocity cannot settle the issue, it seems that we have reached an impasse: either the perspective of the proponents of euthanasia must prevail at the expense of that of its opponents or, conversely, the latter must be vindicated at the expense of the former. Moreover, unlike in the case of the clashing religions examined in section III, the conflict at hand cannot be settled by relegating the antagonists to the precincts of some walled-off private sphere. But also, unlike in the case of the clashing religions, the antagonists in the case of euthanasia are not otherwise completely at odds with each other.

Building on the commonly shared values by proponents and opponents of euthanasia, and relying on the asymmetry between their respective positions, the adjudicator can overcome the apparent impasse mentioned above through reliance on the distinction between benefit-exclusion and comparative subject-exclusion. As postulated above, all involved agree that protection of life is a primary good but disagree as to whether it is a primary value. If the views of the proponents of euthanasia are embedded in legislation applicable to the polity as a whole, opponents of euthanasia can still vindicate their primary values intracommunally though they are prevented from doing so intercommunally. On the other hand, if euthanasia becomes illegal, its proponents will be prohibited from implementing their primary values even within the limits of their own community. Also, without questioning the genuineness of the opponent's fear that recognition of euthanasia as legitimate might lead to erosion of the polity's commitment to the protection of life, the fact that the proponents of euthanasia embrace the protection of life as one of their value preferences seems to mitigate the dangers of the dreaded erosion. Under these circumstances, therefore, it seems fair to characterize frustration of the objectives of euthanasia's opponents as involving a benefit-exclusion and, in contrast, frustration of the objectives of euthanasia proponents as, *in comparison,* amounting to a subject-exclusion.

There may be other ways to establish that outright prohibition of euthanasia under the circumstances of the above example would be violative of the duty to uphold the equal worth of self and other. That does not detract, however, from the usefulness of the distinction between benefit-exclusion and subject-exclusion to the adjudicator charged with resolving legal conflicts in ways that are consistent with the precepts of comprehensive pluralism. More generally, the latter distinction together with those between primary and secondary goods, and between primary and secondary values, with the normative constraints emanating from comprehensive pluralism, and with the criterion of justice as reversible reciprocity, furnish a fairly comprehensive set of interpretive devices enabling the adjudicator to arrive at just interpretations. In many cases, this means that the adjudicator will be led to a determinate resolution of the conflict at hand, in a way that best promotes justice under the circumstances without ever fully reaching it. In other cases, the available interpretive tools may not enable the adjudicator to settle on a determinate solution but may point to a particular direction that provides the best means, under the circumstances, to lessen injustice and move closer to the reconciliation between self and other.

The actual solutions reached through deployment of the interpretive apparatus emerging out of comprehensive pluralism may often be similar or even identical to those that emanate from monistic conceptions of the good, such as liberalism. Thus, for example, the solution pursuant to comprehensive pluralism to the conflict concerning euthanasia could also be justified by reference to the Millian distinction between self-regarding and other-regarding acts. Nevertheless, it is crucial not to be lulled by the similarity of certain solutions into blurring the divide between comprehensive pluralism and other perspectives. For one thing, in spite of similarities, solutions under comprehensive pluralism may differ in scope; for another, solutions under comprehensive pluralism are context dependent and hence turn on the particular contingencies involved in ways that monistic solutions do not. Finally, solutions under comprehensive pluralism also differ from those under relativism, in that the latter are contextualized through and through, whereas the former are contextualized only to the extent consistent with adhesion to the mold carved out by comprehensive pluralism.

In the last analysis, the interpretive enterprise charted by comprehensive pluralism is characterized by the processing of an ever-changing flow of contingent inputs through a steady and fairly thoroughly defined mold. The functioning of this interpretive enterprise, moreover, is perhaps best captured by reference to the analogies between semantic value in intertextual exchanges and economic value in market exchanges discussed in chapter I. Focusing more particularly on market exchanges, the contingent inputs molded by the various perspectives and vantage points found throughout the polity are analogous to the contingent desires that motivate individuals to participate in market transactions. Furthermore, there is an analogy between the invisible hand mechanism, which allows the market to channel clashes between actors who seek to satisfy self-interest into the production of the common good, and the structured bundle of interpretive means, which allow the adjudicator to resolve conflicts in ways that lead to greater justice and better reconciliation between self and other. Of course, this last analogy is far from complete, as the adjudicator, unlike the rules of market competition, must wield a very visible hand charged with imposing substantive constraints as well as procedural ones. The fact remains, nonetheless, that so long as the adjudicator remains faithful to the interpretive enterprise defined by comprehensive pluralism, there is every reason to believe that he or she will be able to resolve conflicts in the best possible way. This conclusion is also reinforced if we realize that, in spite of all the contingencies in play over time, the plausible alternatives available to a good faith adjudicator at any particular moment in time are likely to be rather limited in number. Indeed, on the analogy to the values emerging from market exchanges and to the semantic values issuing from intertextual exchanges discussed in chapter I, the interplay between contingent factors and the enduring mold carved out by comprehensive pluralism will most likely yield a narrow range of legitimate semantic path openings and path closings, hence greatly reducing the number of potentially acceptable solutions. Accordingly, although meanings constantly change under comprehensive pluralism, such changes are likely to be both incremental and limited when gauged in terms of the passage from one moment to the next. Because of this, the conscientious adjudicator bears but a relatively small risk of being unwittingly led astray.

VI. DIFFICULT CASES AND PATHOLOGIES

A. *Revisiting Abortion*

That the amount of uncertainty or indeterminacy in ordinary cases may amount to less than meets the eye does not sufficiently indicate how comprehensive pluralism might fare in difficult cases. Moreover, the example involving euthanasia discussed above does not qualify as a truly difficult case, because it was carefully limited to consenting adults in full possession of their mental capacities making decisions in their own case. Abortion, however, does constitute a genuinely difficult case, if not *the* difficult case par excellence. Indeed, as pointed out in the course of the brief discussion of abortion in chapter V, neither universal morality, nor an ethics predicated on the reversal of perspectives, nor politics, can authoritatively resolve the profound and intense conflicts that abortion arouses in pluralist societies. The question that remains is whether comprehensive pluralism is suited to fare any better. Also, consideration of this question is likely to provide a fair sense of the limits of comprehensive pluralism and, in particular, of the outer bounds of its interpretive potential.

What makes abortion such a difficult issue to handle is that it combines religious and secular aspects, and, depending on one's perspective, it is either central to the equal worth of women and to the integrity of certain conceptions of the good or violative of the most elementary duty to the other as it inevitably results in the annihilation of an other. Certain opponents of abortion base their position on religious grounds and confront antagonists who embrace a secular perspective. Presumably, in such a case, the conflict over abortion cannot be resolved like that between clashing religions considered in section III. Other opponents of abortion may offer support for their position without relying on religion and thus trigger a secular conflict that seems no more amenable to legitimate resolution pursuant to comprehensive pluralism than that in which religious views are pitted against secular ones. Thus, secular opponents of abortion may claim that fetuses must be deemed to be persons from an ethical, constitutional, and legal standpoint[27] and that consequently abortion is inadmissible as violative of the minimum requirements of mere reciprocity. Against this, secular proponents of abortion would argue that personhood is contingent on birth and that, accordingly, prohibiting abortion signifies denial of the equal worth of women and disregard of the integrity of the perspective of those who view the right to abortion as essential for purposes of maintaining control over one's body and one's destiny.

Ronald Dworkin has proposed a more unusual approach to the problem centered on treating differences over abortion as the product of a clash among antagonistic religious ideologies (1993, 30–178). According to Dworkin, the clash over abortion is not primarily about whether the fetus ought to be considered as possessing the attributes of personhood but rather about which of two diametrically opposed conceptions of the sanctity of life is the right one. Opponents of abortion, claims Dworkin, view the sanctity of life in terms of reverence for the life-generating processes of nature (ibid., 11, 92). Proponents of abortion, on the other hand, conceive of respect for the sanctity of life as requiring a commitment to upholding a certain quality of life (ibid., 33, 97). Accordingly, when a fetus is defective with but a short and painful life ahead for it, or when carrying the pregnancy to term would have a significantly adverse effect on the quality of life of the mother or of her loved ones, then abortion would be consistent with respect and concern for the sanctity of life (ibid., 33, 97–100). What is particularly attractive about Dworkin's approach is that it allows the conflict over abortion to be resolved much like that between clashing religions considered in section III. As Dworkin sees it, inasmuch as the conflict over abortion is a religious one, the state ought to stay away from it, and allow each person to follow his or her conscience (ibid., 26, 164–65). Consequently, from a conceptual standpoint, the state should favor neither the proponents nor the opponents of abortion and should remove the issue of abortion from the agenda of the public intercommunal sphere. From a practical standpoint, however, prohibiting state intervention when it comes to abortion is tantamount to a constitutional injunction against banning abortions and thus appears to hand a clear victory to the proponents of abortion.

Even if the conflict over abortion were reducible to a clash among an-

---

27. This position is contrary to that adopted by the majority on the Supreme Court in *Roe v. Wade* (1973) in which it was decided that the fetus was not a "person" for constitutional purposes. Subsequent to the *Roe* decision, however, certain members of Congress advocated a constitutional amendment that would provide that the fetus must be considered to be a person for constitutional purposes, on conception. See S. 158, 97th Cong., 1st sess. (1981); H.R.J. Res. 62, 97th Cong., 1st sess. (1981); see also Westfall 1982, 97–102.

tagonistic religious perspectives, Dworkin's approach proves, on further consideration, to be ultimately unsatisfactory. This is because casting irreconcilable differences over abortion as a religious conflict does not eliminate the residual issue concerning the legality of abortion. Consistent with comprehensive pluralism, neither of the two religious perspectives involved ought to influence the determination of whether abortion should be legal or illegal. Moreover, if no relevant secular considerations were pertinent, then it would seem that comprehensive pluralism would require some determination of the legal issue, but would be indifferent as between making abortion legal or illegal. In any event, the residual issue would not vanish and would necessarily call for some kind of resolution.

To illustrate this consider the following example. A polity is equally divided among two religious groups, one of which requires the sacrifice of the firstborn child on his or her first birthday; and the other of which places the sanctity of life above all, and considers it a paramount divine command to intervene for purposes of saving the lives of those who are unable to protect themselves. It is obvious that, under these circumstances, the state must intervene to prevent a religious civil war and that regardless of the actual nature of such intervention, one of the two religious groups will be incidentally favored and the other frustrated. Thus, even something as seemingly neutral as imposing a strict physical separation between the two groups would favor the group that sacrifices babies and frustrate the other group.

Returning to abortion, not only is the legal issue unavoidable, but the matter is not essentially reducible to religion, notwithstanding Dworkin's argument. Dworkin seeks to bolster his position by noting that opponents of abortion, who nonetheless are prepared to lift the ban on abortion in cases of rape or incest or to save the life of the mother, can only justify their position by appealing to the sanctity of life, rather than to the proposition that personhood attaches at conception (ibid., 94–97). It is true that if the fetus is deemed entitled to full personhood rights, the fact that the pregnancy originated in rape or incest would not, in itself, justify altering the rights of the fetus. But if rights to personhood are not considered absolute, or if, in a universe of partial selves and elusive others, actual positions need not be expected to be consistent, then it does not follow that opponents of abortion must rely on the sanctity of life on the pain of logical or practical contradiction. In any event, there are opponents of abortion who allow for no exception, even saving the life of the mother, and who would thus remain consistent with the position that the fetus is entitled to the full rights of personhood even on Dworkin's own terms. Furthermore, there are arguments on both sides of the abortion issue that may be supported without any appeal to religion or religious aspirations. In short, in the context of a contemporary pluralistic polity, no matter how deeply the abortion debate happens to be immersed in religion, there are bound to remain residual secular arguments for and against abortion, as well as the inescapable residual secular issue concerning its legality.

Abortion drives comprehensive pluralism to the limit, because it cannot be confined within the realm of first-order norms. Inevitably, to the extent that it raises the question of whether personhood ought to be extended back to cover the unborn fetus on grounds that are arguably exclusively secular, abortion triggers second-order normative issues. Specifically, abortion problematizes the question of membership within the polity, which is a critical question on which the entire edifice of comprehensive pluralism rests. Indeed, as noted already, the chief objective of comprehensive pluralism is to lead to the best possible reconciliation between self and other in ways that minimize violence and subordination. Because of this, the integrity of comprehensive pluralism hinges on avoiding bias in determining who shall count as a self for purposes of implementing second-order norms and of according equal consideration to all first-order perspectives that happen to have a proponent within the polity. Moreover, the requisite integrity arguably depends on the determination that every person—understood broadly as encompassing individuals and communal groups—within the polity qualifies as a self. But as soon as personhood becomes contested, and especially if those involved advance conceptions of personhood predicated on particular first-order perspectives, the integrity of comprehensive pluralism becomes severely and even potentially fatally compromised. For if proponents of a first-order perspective can impose criteria for membership within the normative space carved out for the polity, they become empowered to subordinate or exclude other first-order perspectives and thus undermine the fundamental precepts of comprehensive pluralism.

To the extent that the conflict on abortion turns on the plausible secular limits of personhood, comprehensive pluralism cannot advance its resolution. Although it may seem on the surface that extending personhood to the fetus makes for greater inclusivity and ought therefore be prescribed by comprehensive pluralism, on closer inspection, this does not follow at all. Because of the unique dependency of the fetus on its mother, granting personhood to the fetus cannot be simply equated with the mere addition of yet another self or first-order perspective to the previously acknowledged total within the polity. *Erroneous* extension of personhood to the fetus would have second-order, not merely first-order, consequences for the mother, as it would deprive her of her fundamental right to equal worth. Consequently, comprehensive pluralism cannot provide an answer to the question whether personhood ought to extend to the fetus. And because this question exceeds its limits, the best that comprehensive pluralism can do is to deal with issues relating to abortion after the decision concerning personhood has been made. Or, in other words, from a logical standpoint, comprehensive pluralism enters the scene after the decision concerning extending personhood to the fetus has been made.

In view of this, it would seem preferable, as an interpretive matter, to enshrine a polity's initial decision on abortion in its constitution. If the constitution explicitly permits or prohibits abortion, the adjudicator is spared the need to confront an interpretively impossible task that would inevitably lead him or her to an arbitrary decision. Enshrining a provision dealing explicitly with abortion in the constitution, however, does not solve the problem from the standpoint of constitutional justice. Indeed, regardless of what the relevant constitutional texts actually provide, the problem posed by abortion cannot be definitively settled at the level of counterfactual reconstruction.

In spite of the ultimate impossibility of resolving the problem of abortion under present material and ideological conditions,[28] and in spite of the semantic indeterminacy to which this impossibility leads, there remains nevertheless an important interpretive contribution with respect to the conflict over abortion which can be made within the confines of comprehensive pluralism. Regardless of how the ultimate decision concerning whether to extend personhood to fetuses is made, there are at least two crucial interpretive tasks that are well within the purview of the adjudicator working within the bounds of comprehensive pluralism. The first of these is to weed out religious from secular arguments concerning abortion; the second, to explore to what extent divisions might be plausibly mended regardless of the outcome of the ultimate conflict.

With respect to the first of these tasks, it is imperative to sort out the religious from the secular grounds of arguments concerning abortion because only the latter may have second-order normative implications. To the extent that secular and religious considerations only relate to first-order norms, they stand on the same plane. But because of comprehensive pluralism's refusal to ground its normative universe on metaphysical foundations, only secular considerations may be taken into account for purposes of determining the scope of second-order norms. Consequently, notwithstanding that comprehensive pluralism cannot settle whether personhood should be extended to the fetus, it can, and does, rule out adopting any religious perspective on abortion and making it binding for the polity as a whole.[29] Conversely, within the relevant operative secular constraints, the

28. It bears emphasizing that to a significant extent the problem of abortion is contingent on the limits of available technologies. Thus, if acceptable means to end dependency of the fetus on its mother were in place, granting rights of personhood to the fetus would presumably not entail any threat to the mother's equal worth.

29. It follows from this that the adjudicator must weed out religiously grounded positions

adjudicator should endeavor to ensure that proponents of a religious perspective should be enabled, as far as possible, to act on their convictions about abortion within their own communities.[30]

Concerning the second task identified above, the adjudicator ought to take responsibility for ironing out contradictions and inconsistencies, as well as for locating potential areas for compromise, notwithstanding existing divisions. Moreover, in performing this latter task the adjudicator should be aided by comprehensive pluralism's rejection of monism and its rigid insistence on postulating overriding values or objectives (Kekes 1993, 19). For example, even against the most extreme opponents of abortion who refuse to recognize any exception whatsoever, the adjudicator may legitimately carve out an exception for cases in which the mother's life is endangered. Indeed, neither mere reciprocity nor justice as reversible reciprocity requires sacrificing one's own life to save another life. More generally, submitting conflicting claims to justice as reversible reciprocity may often result in narrowing the gap between the antagonists, regardless of whether rights of personhood have been extended to the fetus in the first place.[31] In short, comprehensive pluralism cannot resolve the conflict over abortion, but it can reduce the tensions that surround it.

B. Pathologies

Conflicts can be defused, either by avoidance or as a consequence of increased understanding and empathy. The preceding review of interpretive practices associated with comprehensive pluralism revealed that the latter makes use of both these approaches. Avoidance, however, proves to be a double-edged sword. On the one hand, in certain cases, such as that of the clashing religions explored in section III, avoidance appears to be the best available alternative. Indeed, when two religions are on a collision course, mechanisms of avoidance, such as relegation of each religion to intracommunal bounds, may provide the best, if not the only, means to prevent em-

---

on abortion, but such positions should only be excluded so long as they cannot be independently supported on the basis of secular arguments.

30. In this connection, opponents on religious grounds to abortion would, save in the most extraordinary circumstances, never be obligated to have an abortion. Religious proponents of abortion, on the other hand, cannot be given equivalent assurances, for if abortion were banned on secular grounds, they could not be exempted from such prohibition.

31. In this connection, it is interesting to note the contrast between the ways in which the U.S. Supreme Court and the German Constitutional Court have approached the controversy over the constitutionality of abortion. Whereas both courts have reached fairly similar results from a practical standpoint, the U.S. Supreme Court has departed from the privacy and liberty interests of the pregnant woman, see *Roe v. Wade* (1973) and *Planned Parenthood of Southeastern Pennsylvania v. Casey* (1992), and the German Constitutional Court, from protection of the life of the unborn, see *Abortion Case* (1975) and *Abortion Case 2* (1993).

barking on a course toward mutual destruction. But, on the other hand, if avoidance extends well beyond where it is necessary, it seems bound to lead to pathologies. Specifically, excessive avoidance would tend unduly to curtail intercommunal dealings and to foster retrenchment within the walls of one's own community. Moreover, with respect to the remaining intercommunal encounters, a policy of avoidance would presumably lead to an excess of caution and indifference.

Understanding and empathy, in contrast, potentially draw communities closer together, and ought therefore to be fostered wherever a policy of avoidance is no longer needed to maintain the peace. However, although this may seem less obvious than in the case of avoidance, understanding and empathy can also lead to pathologies if pushed beyond certain limits. As already noted, exclusive reliance on the reversal of perspectives is unsatisfactory because it may lead to an excess of self-denial. Moreover, overemphasis on understanding and on empathy is likely to stunt the drive toward self-expression and self-realization and to transform the polity into a bland yet repressive environment in which controversy and difference become largely muted. Indeed, if taken too far, the fear of offending the other may become completely paralyzing.

Warding off the alienation resulting from excessive avoidance and the dull conformism stemming from an understanding steeped in disproportionate self-suppression requires recourse to certain prophylactic interpretive measures. From the standpoint of the adjudicator, it is imperative to search for interpretive paths that reduce reliance on avoidance to the necessary minimum and that emphasize the desirability and potential of diversity as much as possible. From the standpoint of the state, on the other hand, it is highly advisable to forgo any pretense to neutrality and to actively promote through education, policies, and laws the virtues of diversity and tolerance, mutual respect for self and other, and the numerous attractions of the value preferences inherent in normative pluralism.

VII. CONCLUDING REMARKS

The fear that there is nothing beyond or behind interpretation gave particular urgency and poignancy to the quest for *just* interpretations. The pursuit of that quest, moreover, has taken us on a long and varied journey from the unsettling landscape of deconstruction to the more promising terrain of reconstruction. This journey has been marked by tales of unraveling followed by efforts to recombine the resulting seemingly disparate fragments into cogent narratives suggestive of ways in which law, ethics, and politics might be harmonized. Many reasons, such as misunderstandings, faulty reasoning, failures in perception, or biases linked to vantage points, to name a few, may be responsible for disagreements on the meaning of legal norms. In societies that are pluralistic in fact, however, destabilization and problematization of meanings is traceable, above all, to the conflict among competing conceptions of the good. Due to loss of metaphysical certainty and erosion of confidence in the authority of reason and in the belief in the inevitability of progress, which were driving forces behind the emergence of modernism, the postmodern polity has experienced a seemingly insurmountable split between justice according to law and justice beyond law. Accordingly, the destabilization of legal meanings goes hand in hand with law's detachment from its traditional normative moorings. Furthermore, as a consequence of this, law loses its aura of authority and legitimacy and becomes equated with raw, unmediated power. In sum, law seemingly becomes purely political when, in fact, the destabilization of meaning proves the result of the fragmentation of its ethical base.

Under these postmodern conditions, legal interpretation emerges primarily as a source of anxiety and uncertainty. Moreover, deconstruction, which eventually proves to have paved the way to the road to recovery, looms initially as the main culprit in the undermining of seemingly stable and traditionally rooted legal meanings. With meanings uprooted, plausible interpretations greatly multiply but increasingly fail to provide any comfort as they leave matters more and more unsettled. It is no surprise, therefore, that serious efforts to solve the contemporary crisis in interpretation, as we have seen, have led back to the appealing strictures of formalism and prompted various different attempts at reinstating the authority of law by putting an end to interpretation.

Neither formalism nor the end of interpretation, however, can ultimately furnish a viable and legitimate solution to the contemporary crisis in interpretation. As our inquiry has revealed, so long as one looks to overcoming pluralism and to transcending the subjective element in interpretation as the means to overcome this crisis, all efforts to reach a satisfactory solution are bound to end in frustration. Contrary to expectations, it is only by accepting pluralism and by acknowledging that it is impossible to arrive at objective interpretations, or at some neutral and objective ground lying somewhere beyond interpretation, that we can work our way out of this crisis. More precisely, it is not only by accepting the fact of pluralism but also by embracing comprehensive pluralism as a normative imperative, and by realizing that interpretation is ultimately neither purely subjective nor objective but intersubjective as the joint product of self and other, that the path to recovery from the crisis can be located.

Pluralism, understood broadly, is thus both the source of the crisis in interpretation and the key to its solution. Moreover, deconstruction, which seems at first synonymous with the destabilization of meaning, in fact plays a key role in the process of recovering meaning under postmodern conditions. Indeed, deconstruction, understood in its broader ontological and ethical sense rather than in its narrowest purely methodological sense, is not reducible to the absolute opposite of construction or reconstruction. Instead, when properly considered, deconstruction and reconstruction make up the two sides of the same coin. They complement one another in ridding the polity of obsolete entrenched meanings derived from discarded metaphysical visions, thus clearing the way for the elaboration of intersubjectively negotiated meanings aimed at narrowing the gap between self and other.

Comprehensive pluralism turns the fact of pluralism into a normative imperative, while its correlate, comprehensive justice, transforms the impossibility of justice into the launching pad for the necessary and unending quest for greater, yet imperfect, postmetaphysical justice. Awareness of the impossibility of justice is dangerous, for it can easily mislead one into believing that all possible ways of relating to the other, no matter how oppressive, are ultimately normatively equivalent. But when such awareness is coupled with commitment to the ethos of comprehensive pluralism, it is potentially reassuring and liberating. Although this is initially bound to seem paradoxical, it is the very impossibility of justice, as revealed through the conjunction of comprehensive pluralism and comprehensive justice, that leads to the realization that not all actions are normatively equivalent and not all outcomes equally unjust. Accordingly, justice may never amount to more than a hope, but that hope renders the postmetaphysical search for greater justice or lesser injustice meaningful. Moreover, consistent with this, justice according to law can neither be fully severed from nor fully reconciled with justice beyond law. Instead, as we have seen, the two are inextricably related to one another. The postmetaphysical temptation may be to make justice according to law autonomous, but the best solution turns out to depend on it remaining at once complementary and antagonistic to justice beyond law.

Finally, in the context of comprehensive pluralism and comprehensive justice oriented toward the reconciliation of self and other, and of the consequent dual relationship between justice according to law and justice beyond law, there is room for just interpretations, but not for anything beyond interpretation. In other words, within the universe delimited by comprehensive pluralism, the two senses of just interpretations converge. Because there is nothing behind or beyond interpretation, just interpretations—in the sense of the right interpretations—are ultimately no more than just interpretations—in the sense of mere interpretations. Indeed, in the absence of a metaphysical realm beyond that of our daily existence, and of an objective reality behind the plane of our intersubjective dealings with others, interaction between self and other is through interpretation, and the optimal possible reconciliation between self and other through the best possible interpretation. In sum, all intersubjective meaning is derived from interpretation, and law, ethics, and politics, through which self and other seek to make the best of their common predicament, are at bottom but interpretation. At the end, the best we can do is to aim at a justice that depends on interpretation. That may not seem to be much, but it is everything.

CASES

Roe v. Wade, 410 U.S. 113 (1973).
Schenck v. United States, 249 U.S. 47 (1919).
Texas v. Johnson, 109 U.S. 2533 (1989).
Trimble v. Gordon, 430 U.S. 762 (1980).
Webster v. Reproductive Health Services, 492 U.S. 490 (1989).
West Coast Hotel v. Parrish, 300 U.S. 379 (1937).
Whitney v. California, 274 U.S. 357 (1927).

CANADA

Regina v. Keegstra, 3 S.C.R. 697 (1990).

FEDERAL REPUBLIC OF GERMANY

Abortion Case, 39 BVerfGE 1 (1975).
Abortion Case 2, BverfG, reprinted in 1993 EuGRZ 229 (1993).

BIBLIOGRAPHY

Abel, Richard L. 1982. Torts. In *The politics of law*, ed. David Kairys. New York: Pantheon Books.

Ackerman, Bruce. 1991. *We the people*. Vol. 1. Cambridge, Mass.: Belknap Press.

Aristotle. 1980. *Nicomachean ethics*. Trans. Martin Oswald. Indianapolis: Bobbs-Merrill.

Atiyah, P. S. 1979. *The rise and fall of freedom of contract*. Oxford: Clarendon Press.

Baker, Lynn A. 1991. Just do it: Pragmatism and progressive social change. In *Pragmatism in law and society*, ed. Michael Brint and William Weaver. Boulder, Colo.: Westview Press.

Berlin, Isaiah. 1969. Two concepts of liberty. In *Four essays on liberty*. London: Oxford University Press.

Bersani, Leo. 1995. *Homos*. Cambridge, Mass.: Harvard University Press.

Bickel, Alexander M. 1962. *The least dangerous branch: The Supreme Court at the bar of politics*. Indianapolis: Bobbs-Merrill.

Black, Henry Campbell. 1990. *Black's law dictionary*. 6th ed. St. Paul: West Publishing.

Bollinger, Lee. 1986. *The tolerant society*. New York: Oxford University Press.

Bork, Robert. 1971. Neutral principles and some First Amendment problems. *Indiana Law Journal* 47:1.

Brudner, Alan. 1990. The ideality of difference: Toward objectivity in legal interpretation. *Cardozo Law Review* 11:1133.

Coase, Ronald H. 1960. The problem of social cost. *Journal of Law and Economics* 3:1.

Cohen, Felix S. 1935. Transcendental nonsense and the functional approach. *Columbia Law Review* 35:809.

Connolly, William E. 1983. *The terms of political discourse*. 2d ed. Princeton: Princeton University Press.

Constitution Watch. 1993–94. Hungary. *East European Constitutional Review* 3/4 and 4/1:10–11.

Cover, Robert. 1983. The Supreme Court, 1982 term—forward: Nomos and narrative. *Harvard Law Review* 97:4.

———. 1995. Violence and the word. In *Narrative, violence and the law: The essays of Robert Cover,* ed. Martha Minow, Michael Ryan, and Austin Sarat. Ann Arbor: University of Michigan Press.

Crenshaw, Kimberle. 1993. Beyond racism and misogyny: Black feminism and 2 Live Crew. In *Words that wound.* Ed. Mari Matsuda et al. Boulder, Colo.: Westview Press.

Curtis, Carolyn. 1995. Putting out a contract. *Christianity Today* 39:54.

Dalton, Clare. 1985. An essay in the deconstruction of contract doctrine. *Yale Law Journal* 94:997.

Derrida, Jacques. 1976. *De la grammatologie.* Paris: Éditions de Minuit.

———. 1981. *Positions.* Paris: Éditions de Minuit.

———. 1982. *Marges—de la philosophie.* Paris: Éditions de Minuit.

———. 1986. *Glas.* Paris: Galilée.

———. 1992. Force of law: The "mystical foundation of authority." In *Deconstruction and the possibility of justice,* ed. Drucilla Cornell, Michel Rosenfeld, and David Gray Carlson. New York: Routledge.

Dewey, John. 1938. *Logic: The theory of inquiry.* New York: Henry Holt.

Diggins, John Patrick. 1994. *The promise of pragmatism.* Chicago: University of Chicago Press.

Dubois, Ellen C., et al. 1985. Feminist discourse, moral values and the law: A conversation. *Buffalo Law Review* 34:11.

Dumont, Louis. 1977. *From Mandeville to Marx.* Chicago: University of Chicago Press.

Dworkin, Ronald. 1977. *Taking rights seriously.* Cambridge, Mass.: Harvard University Press.

———. 1978. Liberalism. In *Public and private morality,* ed. Stuart Hampshire. Cambridge: Cambridge University Press.

———. 1986. *Law's empire.* Cambridge, Mass.: Belknap Press.

———. 1993. *Life's dominion.* New York: Alfred A. Knopf.

Ely, John Hart. 1980. *Democracy and distrust: A theory of judicial review.*

Fallon, Richard H., Jr. 1987. A constructivist coherence theory of constitutional interpretation. *Harvard Law Review* 100:1189.

———. 1989. What is republicanism, and is it worth reviving? *Harvard Law Review* 102:1715.

Feinman, Jay M. 1983. Critical approaches to contract law. *UCLA Law Review* 30:829.

Fish, Stanley. 1994. *There's no such thing as free speech.* New York: Oxford University Press.

Fiss, Owen. 1982. Objectivity and interpretation. *Stanford Law Review* 34:739.

Freeman, Alan. 1978. Legitimizing racial discrimination through antidiscrimination law: A critical review of Supreme Court doctrine. *Minnesota Law Review* 62:1049.

Fried, Charles. 1981. *Contract as promise: A theory of contractual obligation.* Cambridge, Mass.: Harvard University Press.

Fullinwider, Robert. 1980. *The reverse discrimination controversy.* Totowa, N.J.: Rowman and Littlefield.

Galbraith, John Kenneth. 1976. *The affluent society.* 3d ed., rev. Boston: Houghton Mifflin.

Gilligan, Carol. 1982. *In a different voice: Psychological theory and women's development.* Cambridge, Mass.: Harvard University Press.

Gilmore, Grant. 1974. *The death of contract.* Columbus: Ohio State University Press.

Goldman, Alan. 1979. *Justice and reverse discrimination.* Princeton: Princeton University Press.

Grey, Thomas. 1991. What good is legal pragmatism? In *Pragmatism in law and society,* ed. Michael Brint and William Weaver. Boulder, Colo.: Westview Press.

Gunther, Gerald. 1975. Learned Hand and the origins of modern First Amendment doctrine: Some fragments of history. *Stanford Law Review* 27:719.

Habermas, Jürgen. 1971. *Knowledge and human interests.* Boston: Beacon Press.

———. 1984. *The theory of communicative action: Reason and the rationalization of society.* Trans. Thomas McCarthy. Boston: Beacon Press.

———. 1987. *The theory of communicative action: Lifeworld and system.* Trans. Thomas McCarthy. Boston: Beacon Press.

———. 1990. *Moral consciousness and communicative action.* Trans. C. Lenhardt and S. W. Nicholsen. Cambridge, Mass.: MIT Press.

———. 1996. *Between facts and norms: Contributions to a discourse theory of law and democracy.* Trans. William Rehg. Cambridge, Mass.: MIT Press.

Hart, H. L. A. 1961. *The concept of law.* New York: Oxford University Press.

Hartz, Louis. 1955. *The liberal tradition in America.* New York: Harcourt Brace Jovanovich.

Hegel, G. W. F. 1952. *Philosophy of right.* Trans. T. M. Knox. New York: Oxford University Press.

———. 1977. *Phenomenology of spirit.* Trans. A. V. Miller. Oxford: Oxford University Press.

Herrnstein Smith, Barbara. 1990. Judgment after the fall. *Cardozo Law Review* 11:1291–1311.

Hobbes, Thomas. 1962. *Leviathan.* New York: Collier-Macmillan.

———. 1972. The citizen philosophical rudiments concerning government and society. In *Man and citizen,* ed. Bernard Gert. Indianapolis: Hackett.

Holmes, Stephen. 1988. Gag rules or the politics of omission. In *Constitutionalism and democracy,* ed. Jon Elster and Rune Slagstad. Cambridge: Cambridge University Press.

Interpretation Symposium. 1985. *Southern California Law Review* 58:1.

Jacobson, Arthur. 1989a. Autopoietic law: The new science of Niklas Luhmann (book review). *Michigan Law Review* 87:1647.

———. 1989b. Hegel's legal plenum. *Cardozo Law Review* 10:877.

———. 1990. The idolatry of rules: Writing law according to Moses, with reference to other jurisprudences. *Cardozo Law Review* 11:1079.

Kant, Immanuel. 1969. *Foundations of the metaphysics of morals,* ed. Robert P. Wolff. Trans. Lewis W. Beck. Indianapolis: Bobbs-Merrill.

———. 1970. Perpetual peace: A philosophical sketch. In *Kant's political writings,* ed. Hans Reiss. Cambridge: Cambridge University Press.

Kekes, John. 1993. *The morality of pluralism.* Princeton: Princeton University Press.

Kelman, Mark. 1981. Interpretive construction in the substantive criminal law. *Stanford Law Review* 33:591.

Kelsen, Hans. 1961. *General theory of law and the state.* Trans. A. Wedberg. New York: Russell and Russell.

Kennedy, Duncan. 1979. The structure of Blackstone's commentaries. *Buffalo Law Review* 28:205.

Key, Wilson. 1973. *Subliminal seduction.* New York: Signet Books.

Kohlberg, Lawrence. 1979. Justice as reversibility. In *Philosophy, politics, and society,* 5th ser., ed. P. Laslett and J. Fishkin. New Haven: Yale University Press.

Lacan, Jacques. 1966. *Écrits.* Paris: Éditions du Seuil.

Lempert, Richard. 1987. The autonomy of law: Two visions compared. In *Autopoietic law: A new approach to law and society,* ed. Gunther Teubner. Berlin: W. de Gruyter.

Locke, John. 1960. The second treatise of government. In *Two treatises of government,* ed. P. Laslett. New York: Mentor Books.

Luhmann, Niklas. 1985. *A sociological theory of law,* ed. Martin Albrow. Trans. Elizabeth King and Martin Albrow. London: Routledge and Kegan Paul.

———. 1987a. The unity of the legal system. In *Autopoietic law: A new approach to law and society,* ed. Gunther Teubner. Berlin: W. de Gruyter.

———. 1987b. Closure and openness: On reality in the world of law. In *Autopoietic law: A new approach to law and society,* ed. Gunther Teubner. Berlin: W. de Gruyter.

———. 1990. *Essays on self-reference.* New York: Columbia University Press.

———. 1992. Operational closure and structural coupling: The differentiation of the legal system. *Cardozo Law Review* 13:1419.

McCarthy, Thomas. 1978. *The critical theory of Jürgen Habermas.* Cambridge, Mass.: MIT Press.

———. 1990. Introduction to Jürgen Habermas, *Moral consciousness and communicative action.* Cambridge, Mass.: The MIT Press.

Macneil, Ian. 1980. *The new social contract.* New Haven: Yale University Press.

Marcuse, Herbert. 1965. Repressive tolerance. In *A critique of pure tolerance,* ed. Robert Wolff, Barrington Moore, and Herbert Marcuse. Boston: Beacon Press.

Marx, Karl. 1967. On the Jewish question. In *Writings of the young Marx on philosophy and society,* ed. and trans. Lloyd D. Easton and Kurt H. Guddat. Garden City, N.Y.: Anchor Books.

Matsuda, Mari. 1989. Public response to racist speech: Considering the victim's story. *Michigan Law Review* 87:2320.

Maturana, Humberto. 1981. Autopoiesis. In *Autopoiesis: A theory of living organization,* ed. Milan Zeleny. New York: North Holland.

Meiklejohn, Alexander. 1948. *Free speech and its relation to self-government.* New York: Harper and Row.

Michelman, Frank. 1988. Law's republic. *Yale Law Journal* 97:1493.

Mill, John Stuart. 1859. *On liberty,* ed. Elizabeth Rapaport. Indianapolis: Hackett.

Minow, Martha. 1987. Justice engendered. *Harvard Law Review* 101:10.

Monaghan, Henry P. 1988. Stare decisis and constitutional adjudication. *Columbia Law Review* 88:723.

Morvai, Krisztina. 1993–94. Retroactive justice based on international law: A recent decision by the Hungarian constitutional court. *East European Constitutional Review* 3/4 and 4/1:32–34.

Münch, Richard. 1990. Differentiation, rationalization, interpretation: The emergence of modern society. In *Differentiation theory and social change,* ed. Jeffrey Alexander et al. New York: Columbia University Press.

Norris, Christopher. 1987. *Derrida.* Cambridge, Mass.: Harvard University Press.

Nozick, Robert. 1974. *Anarchy, state and utopia.* New York: Basic Books.

Pateman, Carole. 1988. *The sexual contract.* Stanford: Stanford University Press.

Peirce, Charles S. 1956. The fixation of belief. In *The philosophy of Peirce: Selected writings,* ed. Justus Buchler. New York: AMS Press.

Perelman, Chaim. 1963. *The idea of justice and the problem of argument.* Trans. John Petrie. London: Routledge and Kegan Paul.

Peters, F. E. 1990. *Judaism, Christianity and Islam.* Princeton: Princeton University Press.

Polinsky, A. Mitchell. 1983. *An introduction to law and economics.* Boston: Little, Brown.

Popkin, Richard H. 1967. Skepticism. In *Encyclopedia of philosophy,* vol. 7, ed. Paul Edwards. New York: Collier-Macmillan.

Popper, Karl. 1966. *The open society and its enemies.* 5th ed. Princeton: Princeton University Press.

Posner, Richard A. 1977. *Economic analysis of law.* 2d ed. Boston: Little, Brown.

———. 1981. *The economics of justice.* Cambridge, Mass.: Harvard University Press.

———. 1988. *Law and literature: A misunderstood relation.* Cambridge, Mass.: Harvard University Press.

———. 1990. *The problems of jurisprudence.* Cambridge, Mass.: Harvard University Press.

———. 1991. What has pragmatism to offer law? In *Pragmatism in law and society,* ed. Michael Brint and William Weaver. Boulder, Colo.: Westview Press.

———. 1992. *Sex and reason.* Cambridge, Mass.: Harvard University Press.

———. 1995. *Overcoming law.* Cambridge, Mass.: Harvard University Press.

Pound, Roscoe. 1908. Mechanical jurisprudence. *Columbia Law Review* 8:605.

Rawls, John. 1971. *A theory of justice.* Cambridge, Mass.: Belknap Press.

———. 1993. *Political liberalism.* New York: Columbia University Press.

Raz, Joseph. 1986. *The morality of freedom.* Oxford: Oxford University Press.

Redish, Martin H. 1984. *Freedom of expression: A critical analysis.* Charlottesville, Va.: Michie.

Richards, David A. J. 1974. Free speech and obscenity law: Towards a moral theory of the First Amendment. *University of Pennsylvania Law Review* 123:45.

———. 1993. Revolution and constitutionalism in America. *Cardozo Law Review* 14:577.

Ricoeur, Paul. 1990. *Soi-même comme un autre.* Paris: Éditions du Seuil.

Rorty, Richard. 1982. *Consequences of pragmatism.* Minneapolis: University of Minnesota Press.

———. 1989. *Contingency, irony and solidarity.* Cambridge: Cambridge University Press.

———. 1990a. Afterword. *Southern California Law Review* 63:1917.

———. 1990b. Feminism and pragmatism. *Michigan Quarterly Review* 30:237.

———. 1991. The banality of pragmatism and the poetry of justice. In *Pragmatism in law and society,* ed. Michael Brint and William Weaver. Boulder, Colo.: Westview Press.

Rosenfeld, Michel. 1985. Contract and justice: The relation between classical contract law and social contract theory. *Iowa Law Review* 70:769.

———. 1987. Extremist speech and the paradox of tolerance (book review). *Harvard Law Review* 100:1457.

———. 1989a. Hegel and the dialectics of contract. *Cardozo Law Review* 10:1199.

———. 1989b. Decoding *Richmond:* Affirmative action and the elusive meaning of constitutional equality. *Michigan Law Review* 87:1729.

———. 1991a. *Affirmative action and justice: A philosophical and constitutional inquiry.* New Haven: Yale University Press.

———. 1991b. *Metro-Broadcasting v. FCC:* Affirmative action at the crossroads of constitutional liberty and equality. *UCLA Law Review* 38:583.

———. 1994. Modern constitutionalism as interplay between identity and diversity. In *Constitutionalism, identity, difference and legitimacy: Theoretical perspectives,* ed. Michel Rosenfeld. Durham: Duke University Press.

———. 1995. The identity of the constitutional subject. *Cardozo Law Review* 16:1049.

———. 1996. Restitution, retribution, political justice and the rule of law. *Constellations* 2:309.

Rottleuthner, Hubert. 1987. Biological metaphors in legal thought. In *Autopoietic law: A new approach to law and society,* ed. Gunther Teubner. Berlin: W. de Gruyter.

———. 1989. A purified sociology of law: Niklas Luhmann on the autonomy of the legal system. *Law and Society Review* 23:779.

Rousseau, Dominique. 1994. The constitutional judge: Master or slave of the Constitution? In *Constitutionalism, identity, difference and legitimacy: Theoretical perspectives,* ed. Michel Rosenfeld. Durham: Duke University Press.

Rousseau, Jean-Jacques. 1947. *The social contract,* ed. C. Frankel. Riverside, N.J.: Hafner Press.

Samuelson, Paul Anthony. 1976. *Economics.* 10th ed. New York: McGraw-Hill.

Sandel, Michael. 1982. *Liberalism and the limits of justice.* Cambridge: Cambridge University Press.

Sartre, Jean-Paul. 1956. *Being and nothingness.* New York: Philosophical Library.

Schauer, Frederick. 1979. Response: Pornography and the First Amendment. *Pittsburgh Law Review* 40:605.

———. 1982. *Free speech: A philosophical inquiry.* Cambridge: Cambridge University Press.

———. 1988. Formalism. *Yale Law Journal* 97:509.

———. 1994. Free speech and the cultural contingency of constitutional categories. In *Constitutionalism, identity, difference and legitimacy: Theoretical perspectives,* ed. Michel Rosenfeld. Durham: Duke University Press.

Schlink, Bernhard. 1994. German constitutional culture in transition. In *Constitutionalism, identity, difference and legitimacy: Theoretical perspectives,* ed. Michel Rosenfeld. Durham: Duke University Press.

Schroeder, Jeanne L. 1990. Feminism historicized: Medieval misogynist stereotypes in contemporary feminist jurisprudence. *Iowa Law Review* 75:1135.

Skillen, Anthony. 1982. Freedom of speech. In *Contemporary political philosophy,* ed. Keith Graham. Cambridge: Cambridge University Press.

Smart, J. J. C., and Bernard Williams. 1985. *Utilitarianism: For and against.* Cambridge: Cambridge University Press.

Smith, Adam. 1976a. *An inquiry into the nature and causes of the wealth of nations*, ed. E. Cannan. Chicago: University of Chicago Press.

———. 1976b. *The theory of moral sentiments*. Indianapolis: Liberty Classics.

Sophocles. 1985. *Antigone*. In *Sophocles, the Theban plays*. Trans. E. F. Watling. London: Penguin Books.

Special report. 1992. Retroactivity law overturned in Hungary. *East European Constitutional Review* 1/1:7–8.

Sullivan, Andrew. 1995. *Virtually normal: An argument about homosexuality*. New York: Alfred A. Knopf.

Sunstein, Cass R. 1986. Pornography and the First Amendment. *Duke Law Journal* 1986:589.

———. 1988. Beyond the republican revival. *Yale Law Journal* 97:1539.

———. 1993. *The partial constitution*. Cambridge, Mass.: Harvard University Press.

Symposium. 1982. Law and literature. *Texas Law Review* 60:373.

Teubner, Gunther. 1987a. Introduction to *Autopoietic law: A new approach to law and society*, ed. Gunther Teubner. Berlin: W. de Gruyter.

———. 1987b. Evolution of autopoietic law. In *Autopoietic law: A new approach to law and society*, ed. Gunther Teubner. Berlin: W. de Gruyter.

Tribe, Laurence H. 1980. The puzzling persistence of process-based constitutional theories. *Yale Law Journal* 89:1063.

———. 1992. *Abortion: The clash of absolutes*. 2d ed. New York: Norton.

Unger, Roberto Mangabeira. 1976. *Law in modern society*. New York: Free Press.

———. 1983. The Critical Legal Studies movement. *Harvard Law Review* 96:561.

Weber, Max. 1968. *Economy and society*, ed. Guenther Roth and Claus Wittich. Berkeley: University of California Press.

Weinrib, Ernest J. 1988. Legal formalism: On the immanent rationality of law. *Yale Law Journal* 97:949.

West, Cornel. 1989. *The American evasion of philosophy: A genealogy of pragmatism*. Madison: University of Wisconsin Press.

Westfall, David. 1982. Beyond abortion: The potential reach of a human life amendment. *American Journal of Law and Medicine* 8:97.

Yablon, Charles. 1987. Review: Law and metaphysics. *Yale Law Journal* 96:613.

INDEX

Designer: U.C. Press Staff
Compositor: J. Jarrett Engineering, Inc.
Text: 10/12 Baskerville
Display: Baskerville
Printer & Binder: Thomson-Shore, Inc.